Made Simple

This new instructive series
has been created
primarily for self-education
but can equally well
be used as
an aid to group study
However complex the subject,
the reader is taken
step by step,
clearly and methodically
through the course. Each volume
has been prepared by
experts,
using throughout the
Made Simple technique of teaching.
Consequently the gaining
of knowledge now becomes
an experience to be enjoyed.

GERMAN Made Simple

Eugene Jackson and
Adolph Geiger, M.A.

Advisory editor
Margaret Fröhlich-Hardy, B.A.

Made Simple Books
W. H. ALLEN London

Table of Contents

v

CHAPTER 40

CHAPTER 41

CHAPTER 42

CHAPTER 43

APPENDIX

Introduction

German Made Simple is an excellent book for the beginner who wants to make rapid progress in German, both spoken and written, in the shortest possible time. The course is ideal for the student working alone, particularly if he combines it with some of the many listening-aids available today: films, radio broadcasts, television, gramophone records, and tape-recordings. The book is equally invaluable as background instruction for those taking more formal courses, either at evening institutes or in secondary schools, studying at O-level G.C.E. and beyond.

Throughout the book the International Phonetic Alphabet is used as a guide to pronunciation. This system is explained in the beginning and, once understood, can be applied to other language study too—in particular to all the language books in the 'Made Simple' series.

In *German Made Simple* all grammatical points are explained clearly and fully, before progressing to a new topic. The student is helped to consolidate his knowledge at each stage by means of the bilingual texts, dialogues, exercises and answer keys that form each lesson. While acquiring a knowledge of the German language, the student may also learn something about Germany and German customs.

Margaret Fröhlich Hardy

o

CHAPTER 1

MEET THE GERMAN LANGUAGE

1. *German and English Belong to the Same Family of Languages*

As you proceed in your study of the German language you will note many resemblances to English in vocabulary, idioms, and grammatical structure. This is not strange, for German and English belong to the great Germanic family of languages. They are in fact language cousins. The many resemblances between German and English will be a great help to you in acquiring a good German vocabulary and in other phases of your language study.

2. *Related German and English Words*

Some of the most common German words, often repeated in everyday speech, closely resemble English words of the same meaning. The pronunciation differs, of course, but this will offer few difficulties, as you will see when you make a thorough study of German pronunciation in Chapters 2, 3, 4.

(*a*) Some common nouns. Note that all nouns are capitalized in German.

Mann	**Gras**	**Ball**	**Park**	**Hand**	**Hut**
man	grass	ball	park	hand	hat
Haus	**Wind**	**Sohn**	**Garten**	**Sommer**	**Winter**
house	wind	son	garden	summer	winter
Butter	**Mutter**	**Vater**	**Onkel**	**Schule**	**Finger**
butter	mother	father	uncle	school	finger

(*b*) Some frequently used adjectives

warm	**kalt**	**alt**	**neu**	**gut**
warm	cold	old	new	good
blau	**braun**	**lang**	**voll**	**rund**
blue	brown	long	full	round

(*c*) Some frequently used verbs

The infinitive of all German verbs ends in **-en** or **-n**. Remove these endings from the following German verbs and note the remarkable resemblance to English verbs of the same meaning.

singen	**finden**	**springen**	**bringen**	**sehen**
to sing	to find	to spring	to bring	to see
helfen	**kommen**	**senden**	**fallen**	**binden**
to help	to come	to send	to fall	to bind
beginnen	**waschen**	**haben**		
to begin	to wash	to have		

1

3. *German Is not Difficult to Pronounce and Spell*

German is a phonetic language. This means that words are generally pronounced as they are spelled and spelled as they are pronounced. There are no silent letters except **e** in the combination **ie**, and **h**, which is silent when used after a vowel to indicate that it has a long sound. This is so much simpler than in English, where such words as *height, weight, cough, rough, dough, knight, could*, etc., make English spelling and pronunciation a difficult task for the foreigner.

Each German vowel has a long and a short sound. Thus: German **a** is either long, like *a* in *father*, or short, like *u* in *unlike*. German **a** is never like *a* in *hate*, *a* in *tall*, *a* in *mare*, or *a* in *back*.

Most German words are stressed (accented) on the first syllable. Thus: **Gar-***ten*, **On-***kel*. When the first syllable is not stressed, an accent mark will be used in the vocabularies to show the stressed syllable. Thus: **Papíer** (papi:r) paper.

In Chapters 2, 3, and 4 the German sounds and their spelling are explained in detail, with suitable exercises for practice in words and sentences. These should enable you to pronounce quite well. If possible you should get some German-speaking person to help you with your pronunciation, for it is important for you to hear the sounds correctly spoken and to have your own pronunciation checked.

You can improve your pronunciation and understanding of the spoken word by listening to German recordings and radio broadcasts and by attending German films wherever possible.

4. *German Printing*

German uses two styles of printing, the Roman type which is used in English and the German type. For various reasons, among them the fact that German printed matter has a world market, and the unnecessary expense of two styles of printing, the Roman type has gained ascendancy. In modern German printed matter the German type is seldom used. However, since many of the older books and periodicals have been printed only in the German type, this style of printing will be taught in Chapter 35 of this book and used in some of the reading selections to familiarize you with it. You will find no difficulty in reading German type.

German script has been almost completely superseded by a script style of writing very similar to our English script.

5. *A Preview of Some Interesting Features of German*

(a) German Grammatical Gender

In English a male person is masculine in grammatical gender, and we refer to the person as *he*; a female person is feminine in gender and we refer to the person as *she*. All things are neuter and we refer to each thing as *it*. However, we do sometimes personify things such as cars, ships, etc., and refer to each such thing as *she*. Thus: she (the car) goes beautifully. She (the ship) is a beauty.

In German the matter of grammatical gender is quite different. Gender does not depend entirely on sex. The noun for a male is generally (not always) masculine in gender, the noun for a female is generally (not always) feminine in gender. Nouns for things are not always neuter. Some are masculine, some are feminine, and some are neuter.

(*b*) 'the' and 'a (an)' in German

The German word for the definite article 'the' is very intriguing. The English word for 'the' never changes. The German word for 'the' has six forms depending on its use in the sentence. Thus: **der** is used with masculine nouns, **die** with feminine nouns, and **das** with neuter nouns in the nominative case. Here are a few samples to whet your appetite.

Der Mann ist gut.	**Die Frau** ist gut.	**Das Haus** ist alt.
The man is good.	The woman is good.	The house is old.

You will learn about the forms and uses of the definite article in subsequent chapters.

The German word for the indefinite article 'a (an)' is **ein.** It also, as you will see, has various forms according to its use in the sentence.

(*c*) The Plural of German Nouns

German nouns do not form their plurals by adding -s or -es as is the case with most nouns in English. In general, the German nouns form their plurals in one of four ways which you will learn later. **Kindergarten,** a word borrowed from the German, is made up of the German word **Kinder,** plural of **Kind** (child), plus **Garten** (garden).

(*d*) Verb Forms

German verbs have endings which correspond to the subject pronoun. English verbs also once had endings which have long since disappeared. However, you may still see a few of them in poetry and in the Bible, which you will note are similar to German verb endings of the present day. Thus:

Old English	*Modern German*	*Old English*	*Modern German*
thou hast	**du hast**	thou comest	**du kommst**
he hath	**er hat**	he cometh	**er kommt**

A striking similarity between English and German verbs is the manner in which some very common verbs form their past tense. Thus:

Infinitive				
	singen	sing	**trinken**	drink
	beginnen	begin	**sehen**	see
Past Tense	**sang**	sang	**trank**	drank
	begann	began	**sah**	saw

There are many other interesting features of German which you will discover and master as you proceed in your study of the language. Those that have been mentioned will serve as a slight introduction to the really exciting experience which lies before you.

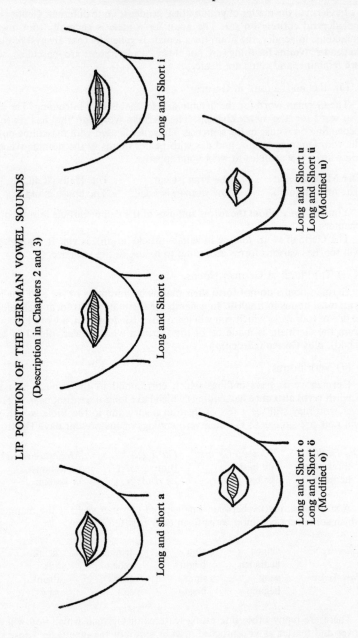

LIP POSITION OF THE GERMAN VOWEL SOUNDS
(Description in Chapters 2 and 3)

Long and Short i

Long and Short u
Long and Short ü
(Modified u)

Long and Short e

Long and short a

Long and Short o
Long and Short ö
(Modified o)

THE GERMAN CONSONANTS **L**, **R**, and **CH**
(Description in Chapters 2 and 3)

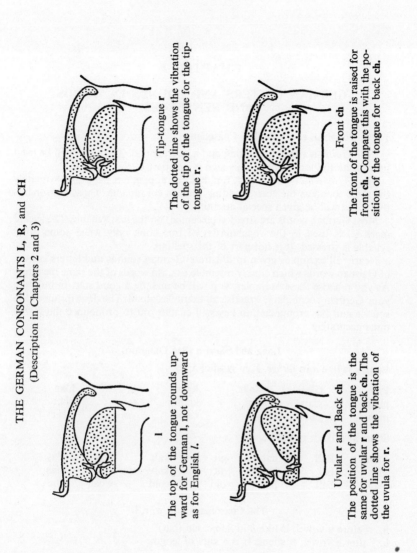

Tip-tongue **r**

The dotted line shows the vibration of the tip of the tongue for the tip-tongue **r**.

Front **ch**

The front of the tongue is raised for front **ch**. Compare this with the position of the tongue for back **ch**.

l

The top of the tongue rounds upward for German **l**, not downward as for English *l*.

Uvular **r** and Back **ch**

The position of the tongue is the same for uvular **r** and back **ch**. The dotted line shows the vibration of the uvula for **r**.

CHAPTER 2

GERMAN LETTERS AND SOUNDS IN WORDS AND SENTENCES

1 The Vowels a, e, i, o, u. The Consonants

Each German vowel has a long and a short sound. The sign : will be used to indicate the long sound. This sign is not part of the spelling.

The German consonants **b, d, f, g, h, k, m, n, p, q, t, x** have approximately the same sound as the corresponding English consonants. Those consonants that differ will be given special attention.

Most German words are stressed (accented) on the first syllable. The accent mark (′) is used in the vocabularies of this book only when some other syllable is stressed. It is not part of the spelling.

Nearly all examples given to illustrate German sounds and letters consist of German words which closely resemble English words of the same meaning. As you practise these examples, you will be making a good start in building your German vocabulary. Practise all examples aloud. The description of the sounds and the pronunciation key will enable you to pronounce the words quite accurately.

Long and Short a (See Diagram)

Long **a** is like *a* in *father*. Key symbol a:

Plan	Glas	Jahr	kam	ja	klar
pla:n	gla:s	ja:r	ka:m	ja:	kla:r
plan	glass	year	came	yes	clear

Short **a** is like u in unlike. Key a

Mann	Ball	hat	alt	kalt	was	das
man	bal	hat	alt	kalt	vas	das
man	ball	has	old	cold	what	the

The Consonants h, j, w, r, l

h, before a vowel, is like *h* in *home*. **hat** (hat)
h, after a vowel, is silent. It is a sign of length.
    Jahr (ja:r)
j is like *y* in *year*. **ja** (ja:)
w is like *v* in *van*. **was** (vas)
l is like *l* in *lip*. (For description of German **l,** see diagram.)
r is trilled as in the telephone operator's *thrrree*. The trill may be produced by the tip of the tongue (see diagram) or by the uvula (see diagram). The tip-tongue **r** and the uvular **r** are both acceptable. Use whichever is easier for you.

6

Long and Short e (See Diagram)

Long e (ee) is like *ay*[1] in *gay*. Key symbol eː

der	wer	er	geht	zehn	Tee	See
deːr	veːr	eːr	geːt	tseːn	teː	zeː
the	who	he	goes	ten	tea	sea

Short e is like *e* in *bet*. Key symbol e

Bett	Welt	wenn	es	lernt	jetzt
bet	velt	ven	es	lernt	jetst
bed	world	when	it	learns	now

In a few words long e is spelled **ee** (**Tee, See**). The silent **h** after **e** is a sign of length.

NOTE 1. Prolong English ay and note that it has two parts. The second or off-glide is the sound ee. German long e is the first part of the combination and should not glide off into ee.

Unstressed e

Unstressed **e** is like English *e* in *garden* and *father*. This sound is very common in unstressed syllables in both English and German. Key symbol *e*.

Garten	Wasser	Vater	Lehrer
gar-ten	va-ser	faː-ter	leː-rer
garden	water	father	teacher

Klasse	Jahre	lernen	haben
kla-se	jaː-re	ler-nen	haː-ben
class	years	to learn	to have

The Consonants v, z, s, ss, sch

v is like *f* in *fat*. Some German words are spelled with **v** instead of **f**. **Vater** (faː-*ter*) father

z is like *ts* in *its*. **zehn** (tseːn) ten; **Dezember** (*de*-tsem-*ber*) December

s, before a vowel, is like *z* in *zone*. **See** (zeː) sea; **seh-en** (zeːen) to see

s, at the end of a syllable is like *s* in *house*. **Glas** (glaːs); es; das; was (vas)

ss is like *ss* in *class*. **Klasse** (kla-se); **Wasser** (va-ser) water

sch is like *sh* in *shoot*. Key symbol ʃ **Schwester** (ʃves-ter) sister; *waschen* (va-ʃen) to wash

Long and Short i (See Diagram)

Long **i** (ie) is like *ee* in *meet*. Key symbol iː

wir	mir	Bier	die	sie	hier	vier
viːr	miːr	biːr	diː	ziː	hiːr	fiːr
we	me	beer	the	she	here	four

Short **i** is like *i* in *bit*. Key symbol i

Ding	Wind	Kind	Winter	ist	frisch
diŋ	vint	kint	vin-ter	ist	friʃ
thing	wind	child	winter	is	fresh

The Consonant d (Final)

At the end of a word or syllable **d** is pronounced like *t*. **Kind** (*kint*); **Wind** (*vint*)

Long and Short o (See Diagram)

Long **o** is like *o*[1] in *wrote*. Key symbol oː
Round the lips as in diagram.

Brot	**Rose**	**Sohn**	**Monat**	**rot**
broːt	roː-ze	zoːn	moː-nat	roːt
bread	rose	son	month	red

Short **o** is like *o* in *oh*. Key symbol o
Round the lips as in diagram.

Onkel	**Stock**	**kommt**	**voll**	**dort**
on-kel	ʃtok	komt	fol	dort
uncle	stick	comes	full	there

NOTE 1. Prolong English o and note that it has two parts. The second part is uː. German long o is the first part of the combination and should not glide off into uː.

The Consonants sp and st

sp is pronounced ʃp only at the beginning of a syllable. **Sport** (ʃport); **spielen** (ʃpiː-len) to play

st is pronounced ʃt only at the beginning of a syllable. **Stock** (ʃtok) stick; **stehen** (ʃteː-en) to stand

Long and Short u (See Diagram)

Long **u** is like *oo* in *root*. Key Symbol uː
Round the lips as in diagram.

Fuß	**Schule**	**Bruder**	**Hut**	**Stuhl**
fuːs	ʃuː-le	bruː-der	huːt	ʃtuːl
foot	school	brother	hat	chair

Short **u** is like *oo* in *foot*. Key symbol u.
Round the lips as in diagram.

Mutter	**Butter**	**Suppe**	**unter**	**und**
mu-ter	bu-ter	zu-pe	un-ter	unt
mother	butter	soup	under	and

Exercise No. 1. Read the following sentences aloud. Translate them. You can easily guess their meaning. The answers to all exercises are given in the Answer Section in the Appendix. Check all your answers.

1 Hier ist das Glas. Es ist voll Wasser. Das Wasser ist frisch und klar. Hier ist das Kind. Das Kind trinkt Wasser.

2 Das Kind spielt Ball. Der Ball ist rot. Der Ball rollt unter das Bett.

3 Hier ist der Tee. Dort ist der Kaffée.[1] Der Tee ist warm. Der Kaffée ist kalt. Der Vater trinkt Kaffée. Die Mutter trinkt Tee. Das Kind trinkt die Suppe.

4 Der Monat Juni[2] ist warm. Der Winter ist kalt in Kanada. Der Sommer ist warm hier.

5 Ist der Kaffée kalt? Ist der Tee warm? Ist das Bier frisch? Ist die Suppe warm? Wer trinkt Tee? Wer trinkt Kaffée? Wer trinkt die Suppe?

6 Karl[3] ist vier Jahre alt. Marie[4] ist sieben Jahre alt. Wie[5] alt ist Hans?[6] Wie alt ist der Vater? Wie alt ist die Mutter? Wie alt ist das Kind?

NOTES: 1 **Kaffée** (ka-feː) coffee. 2 **Juni** (juː-ni) June. 3 **Karl** Charles. 4 **Marie** (ma-riː) Mary. 5 **wie** (viː) how. 6 **Hans** Jack.

Grammar Notes and Practical Exercises

2 Gender of Nouns

Most (not all) nouns denoting male beings are masculine in gender and take the definite article **der**. Thus, **der Mann** the man, **der Vater** the father, **der Sohn** the son.

Most (not all) nouns denoting female beings are feminine and take the definite article **die**. Thus, **die Mutter** the mother, **die Schwester** the sister, **die Tante** the aunt.

Not all nouns denoting things are neuter. Some are masculine, some are feminine. Neuter nouns take the definite article **das**. Thus:

masculine	*feminine*	*neuter*
der Ball the ball	**die Schule** the school	**das Glas** the glass

Learn each noun with the definite article, as if the article and noun were one word. Start by memorizing the following nouns with their articles.

	masculine	*feminine*	*neuter*
der Mann	der Ball	die Mutter	das Kind
der Vater	der Hut	die Schwester	das Brot
der Sohn	der Schuh	die Tante	das Glas
der Bruder	der Tee	die Butter	das Jahr
der Onkel	der Kaffée	die Klasse	das Bier
der Lehrer	der Monat	die Schule	das Wasser

3 Definite article and noun in the nominative case.

The nominative case is the case of the subject of the sentence.

In the nominative case the definite article is **der** with masculine nouns, **die** with feminine nouns, and **das** with neuter nouns.

masculine	*feminine*	*neuter*
Der Vater ist groß.	**Die Mutter** ist jung.	**Das Kind** ist gut.
The father is tall.	The mother is young.	The child is good.
Der Ball ist rot.	**Die Schule** ist alt.	**Das Glas** ist voll.
The ball is red.	The school is old.	The glass is full.
Dies ist **der Ball.**	Das ist **die Schule.**	Das ist **das Glas.**
This is the ball.	That is the school.	That is the glass.

Note that **dies,** meaning *this*, and **das,** meaning *that*, may point out nouns of any gender.

4 Agreement of Third Person Pronouns

Third person pronouns agree in gender and number with the nouns for which they stand.

(a) Ist **der Vater** groß? Ja, **er** ist groß.	Is *the father* tall? Yes, *he* is tall.
(b) Ist **der Ball** rot? Ja, **er** ist rot.	Is *the ball* red? Yes, *it*[1] is red.
(c) Ist **die Mutter** jung? Ja, **sie** ist jung.	Is *the mother* young? Yes, *she* is young
(d) Ist **die Schule** alt? Ja, **sie** ist alt.	Is *the school* old? Yes, *it*[1] is old.
(e) Ist **das Kind** gut? Ja, **es** ist gut.	Is *the child* good? Yes, *it* is good.
(f) Ist **das Glas** voll? Ja, **es** ist voll.	Is *the glass* full? Yes, *it* is full.

	masculine	*feminine*	*neuter*
Definite Article	**der** Vater, **der** Ball	**die** Mutter, **die** Schule	**das** Kind, **das** Glas
Third Person Pron.	**er** he it	**sie** she it	**es** it it

NOTE 1. When **er** stands for a masculine thing and **sie** for a feminine thing, both are translated by *it* and not by *he* and *she*, since in English things cannot be masculine or feminine.

Exercise No. 2. Complete the answer to each question with the correct pronoun, and translate it. Check all your answers in the Answer Section.

Example 1. **Sie** ist warm. *It* is warm.

1 Ist **die Suppe** warm? —— ist warm.
2 Ist **der Lehrer** gut? —— ist gut.
3 Ist **die Schule** alt? —— ist alt.
4 Ist **der Doktor** hier? —— ist hier.
5 Ist **das Wasser** klar? —— ist klar.

6 Ist **das Bier** kalt? —— ist kalt.
7 Ist **die Butter** frisch? —— ist frisch
8 Ist **die Mutter** jung? —— ist jung.
9 Ist **der Hut** rot? —— ist rot.
10 Ist **der Ball** rot? —— ist rot.

Exercise No. 3. Complete the answer to each question by placing the correct form of the definite article (**der, die, das**) before each noun.

1 **Wer ist das?** Das ist —— Vater; —— Schwester; —— Lehrer; —— Doktor; —— Onkel; —— Mutter; —— Bruder; —— Mann; —— Kind; —— Tante.

2 **Was ist das?** Das ist —— Schule; —— Ball; —— Hut; —— Butter; —— Glas; —— Wasser; —— Tee; —— Kaffee; —— Klasse; —— Brot; —— Schuh; —— Hut.

CHAPTER 3

GERMAN LETTERS AND SOUNDS IN WORDS AND SENTENCES, CONTINUED

1. The vowel combinations *au, ei, eu*. The modified vowels *ä, ö, ü*. The *ch* sound. Final *g*.
Practise each sound aloud, first in the given words, then in the sentences below.

The Vowel Combinations au, ei, eu

au, like *ow* in *how.* Key symbol au

Auto	Haus	Frau	blau	braun	kauft
au-to:	haus	frau	blau	braun	kauft
car	house	woman	blue	brown	buys

Das Auto ist blau.
Der Mann kauft das Auto.

Die Frau kauft Kaffée und Tee.
Das Haus ist sehr (very) alt.

ei, like *ei* in *height.* Key symbol ai

Eisen	ein	eine	heiß	nein	weiß
ai-zen	ain	ai-ne	hais	nain	vais
iron	a(an)	a(an)	hot	no	white

Ist der Hut braun? Nein, er ist weiss.
Ein Mann kauft ein Auto. Es ist rot.

Eine Frau kauft Kaffée und Tee.
Das Eisen ist heiss.

eu, like *oi* in *oil.* Key symbol oy

Freund	Deutsch	heute	neu	neun
froynt	doytʃ	hoy-te	noy	noyn
friend	German	today	new	nine

Wer lernt jetzt Deutsch?
Der Freund lernt jetzt Deutsch.

Karl ist heute neun Jahre alt.
Ist die Schule hier neu?

The Modified Vowels ä, ö, ü

Long **ä,** like *ai* in *air.* The letter **ä** is another way of spelling German long **e.** Key symbol ɛ:

Bär	zählen	zählt	wählt	spät
bɛ:r	tsɛ:len	tsɛ:lt	vɛ:lt	ʃpɛ:t
bear	to count	counts	chooses	late

Das Kind zählt gut.
Ist der Bär ein Tier (animal)?
Ja, der Bär ist ein Tier.

Der Lehrer kommt heute spät.
Der Mann wählt ein Auto.

11

Short **ä**, like *e* in *bet*. The letter **ä** is just another way of spelling German short **e**. Key symbol ε.

März	Bäcker	bäckt	älter	wärmer
mɛrts	bɛ-ker	bɛkt	ɛl-ter	vɛr-mer
March	baker	bakes	older	warmer

Der Bäcker bäckt Brot.
Karl ist älter als (than) Maríe.
Florida ist wärmer als New York.

Der Monat März ist oft (often) kalt.
Hier ist es wärmer als in Kanada.

Long **ö**. Key symbol ø. No equivalent sound in English. To make long **ö**, hold lips firmly in the position for long **o** (oː) and try to say long **e** (eː). The result will be long **ö** (ø) (see diagram).

Öl	schön	hören	wir hören	er hört
øl	ʃøn	hø-ren	viːr høren	er hørt
oil	pretty	hear	we hear	he hears

Die Schwester ist sehr schön.
Das Öl ist frisch und klar.
Wir hören die Musík (mu-ziːk)

Er hört die Musík.
Die Musík ist sehr schön.
Hier ist das Öl. Es ist klar.

Short **ö**. Key symbol œ. No equivalent sound in English. Short **ö** is like long **ö**, but shorter in length (see diagram).

Köln	Löffel	zwölf	wir	öffnen
kœln	lœ-fel	tsvœlf	viːr	œf-nen
Cologne	spoon	twelve	we	open

Köln ist in Deutschland (doytʃ-lant).
Wir öffnen jetzt die Tür.
Der Löffel ist gross.

Das Kind zählt von eins bis zwölf.
(von (*fon*) from, bis to)

Long **ü**. Key symbol yː. No equivalent sound in English. It is like the French *u*. To make long **ü**, hold lips firmly in the position for uː and try to say iː. The result will be long **ü** (see diagram).

Tür	kühl	grün	fühlt	für	Schüler
tyːr	kyːl	gryːn	fyːlt	fyːr	Syːler
door	cool	green	feels	for	pupil

Eine Tür ist offen (open).
Das Wetter ist kühl.
Das Gras ist grün.
Die Rose ist für die Mutter.

Der Ball ist für das Kind.
Der Schüler lernt Deutsch.
Er fühlt das Wasser. Es ist warm.

Short **ü** (Key symbol y). No equivalent sound in English. Short **ü** is like long **ü**, but shorter in length (see diagram).

dünn	fünf	füllt	küssen	wünschen
dyn	fynf	fylt	ky-sen	vyn-ʃen
thin	five	fills	to kiss	to wish

Das Kind ist fünf Jahre alt.
Die Mutter küßt das Kind.
Wer wünscht ein Glas Wasser?

Maríe füllt das Glas voll Wasser.
Das Glas ist dünn.

Modified vowels are called **Umlaut** vowels. The dots above the letter indicate the modification (**Umlaut**).

Front ch

Front **ch**. Key symbol x. No equivalent in English. To make front **ch** press the tip of the tongue firmly against the lower teeth and try to say *ish*, *esh*. The result will be front **ch** in **ich** and **ech** (see diagram).

ich	**mich**	**nicht**	**Licht**	**reich**	**Milch**
I	me	not	light	rich	milk

Ich stehe hier.	**Ist die Frau reich?**
Er steht nicht hier.	**Nein, sie ist nicht reich.**
Ich trinke Milch.	**Ich habe das Licht.**

ich bin	**ich lerne**	**ich gehe**	**ich habe**
I am	I learn	I go	I have

sprechen	**ich spreche**	**er spricht**
ʃprexen	ich ʃprexe	eːr ʃprixt
to speak	I speak	he speaks

Ich spreche Deutsch.	**Ich habe kein (no) Auto.**
Er spricht kein Deutsch.	**Ich bin Studént.** (ʃtuː-dent)
Wir sprechen nicht Englisch.	**Er ist kein Student.**

Back ch

Back **ch**. Key symbol x. No equivalent sound in English. It is used after the vowels **a, o, u**. To make back **ch** place the tongue in position for **k**, and breathe out strongly as for **h**. This gives a sound like an outgoing snore (see diagram).

acht	**Buch**	**Kuchen**	**Tochter**	**sucht**
axt	buːx	kuːxen	tox-ter	zuːxt
eight	book	cake	daughter	looks for

Wer hat das Buch?	**Ist der Kuchen warm?**
Ich habe das Buch.	**Nein, er ist nicht warm.**
Wie alt ist die Tochter?	**Wer sucht mich?**
Sie ist acht Jahre alt.	**Die Mutter sucht dich** (you).

Final g

At the end of a word **g** is pronounced like **k**, except after **i**, where **g** is pronounced like front **ch**.

richtig right	**fertig** finished	**Tag** day	**Weg** way
(*rix-tix*)	(*fer-tix*)	(*tak*)	(*veːk*)

Grammar Notes and Practical Exercises

1 The indefinite article *ein* (a, an), *kein* (not a, no)

Compare the forms of **der** with those of **ein**.

Der Ball ist hier.	**Die Tür** ist offen.	**Das Glas** ist voll.
The ball is here.	The door is open.	The glass is full.
Ein Ball ist hier.	**Eine Tür** ist offen.	**Ein Glas** ist voll.
A ball is here.	A door is open.	A glass is full.

	masculine		*feminine*		*neuter*	
Nom.	der	ein	die	eine	das	ein

Ein has no ending in the nominative masculine and neuter. In the feminine the ending is **e**. **Kein** (not a, no) has the same case forms as **ein**.

Kein Ball ist hier.	**Keine Tür** ist offen.	**Kein Glas** ist voll.
No (not a) ball is here.	No (not a) door is open.	No (not a) glass is full.

Exercise No. 4. In each sentence substitute for the definite article the correct form of the indefinite article, and of **kein**.

Beispiel (bai-ʃpiːl): Example: **Das Kind** spielt Ball. **Ein** (**kein**) **Kind** spielt Ball.

1 **Der Plan** ist gut.	7 **Die Schwester** lernt Englisch.
2 **Das Bett** ist neu.	8 **Die Tür** ist hier.
3 **Das Auto** ist blau.	9 **Das Glas** ist dort.
4 **Die Tochter** ist hier.	10 **Die Schule** ist neu.
5 **Die Frau** kauft Tee.	11 **Das Haus** ist grün.
6 **Der Bruder** lernt Deutsch.	12 **Die Tochter** ist zwölf Jahre alt.

2 Some German verb endings

(a)	**gehen**	**kommen**	**lernen**	**kaufen**	**zählen**	**spielen**
	to go	to come	to learn	to buy	to count	to play

In the infinitive most German verbs end in **-en**. A few end in **-n**. That part of the verb to which the ending is added is called the *stem*. **geh-, komm-, lern-,** etc., are the stems of **gehen, kommen, lernen,** etc.

(b)	**ich gehe**	I go	**ich lerne**	I learn	**ich zähle**	I count
	ich komme	I come	**ich kaufe**	I buy	**ich spiele**	I play

When the subject is **ich** most German verbs end in **-e**.

(c)	**er geht**	he goes	**er lernt**	he learns	**Hans zählt**	Jack counts
	sie kommt	she comes	**wer kauft**	who buys	**Anna spielt**	Anna plays

When the subject is **er, sie** or **es**; a singular noun; **wer** or **was**—most German verbs end in **-t**.

(d)	**wir gehen**	we go	**wir lernen**	we learn	**wir zählen**	we count
	wir kommen	we come	**wir kaufen**	we buy	**wir spielen**	we play

When the subject is **wir** all German verbs end in **-en** or **-n**, like the infinitive.

NOTE: The German verb has no special emphatic or progressive forms. Thus: **ich lerne** = I learn, I do learn, I am learning; **er kauft** = he buys, he is buying, he does buy; etc.

Exercise No. 5. Complete the verb in each sentence with the correct ending.

Beispiel: 1. Der Bruder lernt Deutsch.

1 Der Bruder lern— Deutsch.   2 Wir lern— Englisch.   3 Sie kauf— ein Buch.   4 Der Stuhl steh— dort.   5 Ich spiel— nicht Tennis.   6 Das Kind ha— Brot und Butter.   7 Der Doktor komm— heute.   8 Wer trink— Kaffee? 9 Er trink— Bier.   10 Der Schüler lern— gut.   11 Wir spiel— Ball.   12 Es

steh— dort. 13 Marie sing— schön. 14 Sie sing—sehr schön. 15 Wir
hab— kein Buch. 16 Er zähl— von eins bis zehn. 17 Wer spiel— Ball?
18 Was steh— dort?

3 The negative *nicht*

Der Mann ist **nicht** reich.	The man is *not* rich.
Ich gehe **nicht** nach Hause.	I am *not* going home.
Wir spielen **nicht** Tennis.	We do *not* play tennis.

nicht corresponds to the English *not*.

4 The formation of questions

Lernt **der Schüler** Deutsch?	Is the pupil learning German?
Ja, er lernt Deutsch.	Yes, he is learning German.
Spricht **die Frau** Englisch?	Does the woman speak English?
Nein, sie spricht nicht Englisch.	No, she does not speak English.

In questions that require a **ja** (yes) or a **nein** (no) answer, the subject stands
after the verb.

Exercise No. 6. Answer these questions in the negative.

Beispiel: 1. Spielt das Kind Ball? Nein, es spielt nicht Ball.

1 Spielt das Kind Ball? 2 Geht der Schüler nach Hause? 3 Ist der Bruder
zwölf Jahre alt? 4 Ist das Wetter kühl? 5 Kauft der Mann das Auto?[1]
6 Ist er älter als die Schwester? 7 Ist das Haus sehr alt? 8 Singt Marie
schön? 9 Kommt der Doktor heute?[1] 10 Kommt Anna spät nach Hause?

NOTE 1. Put **nicht** at the end of the answer.

CHAPTER 4

Part 1. **THE GERMAN ALPHABET;**
SUMMARY OF LETTERS AND SOUNDS

Part 2. **IMPORTANT WORDS AND EXPRESSIONS**
FROM DAILY LIFE

You have learned the German letters and their sounds, and have practised them in words and sentences. In practising these letters and their sounds, you have acquired a small vocabulary of common words, and learned a few simple grammatical facts.

Part 1 of this chapter starts with the complete German alphabet in Roman print, and the names of the letters. German type will be taught later. (See Chapter 1, section 4.)

It is most important to memorize the German alphabet by practising it aloud, since the names of the letters, with one exception (**y**), illustrate their sounds.

The alphabet is followed by a summary of vowel and consonant sounds with pronunciation key.

Part 2 includes some of the most important words and expressions used in daily life.

Practise all these words and expressions aloud. It is not necessary to memorize them at this point, except where memorization is indicated, for they will appear later many times. However, in practising the words and expressions aloud you will memorize many of them without trying and greet them as old friends when you meet them later.

Der Erste Teil (ɛr-ste tail) The First Part

Das Deutsche A B C   The German A B C

A	a	(aː)	H	h	(haː)	O	o	(oː)	U	u	(uː)
B	b	(beː)	I	i	(iː)	P	p	(peː)	V	v	(fou)
C	c	(tseː)	J	j	(jot)	Q	q	(kuː)	W	w	(veː)
D	d	(deː)	K	k	(kaː)	R	r	(er)	X	x	(iks)
E	e	(eː)	L	l	(el)	S	s	(es)	Y	y	(ipsilon)
F	f	(ɛf)	M	m	(em)	T	t	(teː)	Z	z	(tset)
G	g	(geː)	N	n	(en)						
ä	(a-Umlaut)		ö	(o-Umlaut)		ü	(u-Umlaut)				

Qu appears in a few words, and is pronounced *kv*. Thus: **Quartiér** (kvar-**tiːr**) quarters.

y is found only in a few proper names. Thus: **Meyer** (also spelled **Meier** and **Mayer**) and **Bayern** (**bai**-ern) Bavaria.

THE DOUBLE LETTER ss (ß).

You will frequently meet the symbol ß in modern German printed matter. It is pronounced as ss. It is used: (*a*) after long vowels (große—big) and diphthongs (**heißen**—to be called); (*b*) before t (**er haßt**—he hates); and (*c*) at the end of a syllable or word, irrespective of whether the vowel is long or short (**er muß**—he must, **groß**—big).

Summary of Vowel Sounds
Long

Ger. Vowel	a	e	i	o	u
Pron. Key	aː	eː	iː	oː	uː

a   **Vater (faː-ter)** father
e   **zehn (tseːn)** ten
i (ie) **wir (viːr)**, we; **die (diː)**, the
o   **Brot (broːt)**, bread
u   **Schule (ʃuː-le)**, school
a   **zählen (tseː-len)**, to count
o   **hören (høø-ren)**, to hear
u   **fühlen (fyː-len)**, to feel

Short

Ger. Vowel	a	e	i	o	u
Pron. Key	a	e	i	o	u

a   **Mann (man)** man; **was (vas)** what
e   **Wetter (ve-ter)** weather
i   **Winter (vin-ter)**, winter
o   **Onkel (on-kel)**, uncle
u   **Butter (bu-ter)**, butter
a   **März (mɛrts)**, March
o   **zwölf (tsœlf)**, twelve
u   **füllen (fyl-len)**, to fill

Indefinite e   **Rose (roː-ze)**   **Garten (gar-ten)**   **Mutter (mu-ter)**

Summary of Consonant Sounds Needing Special Attention

v	f **voll (fol)**	s	(final) **Glas (glaːs)**
j	(like *y* in *young*) **jung (juŋ)**	ss	**Wasser (va-ser)**
w	**Wetter (ve-ter)**	ß	**Fuß (fuːs)**
l	**lieben (liː-ben)**	sch	**Schuh (ʃuː)**
qu	**Quartier (kvaː-tiːr)**	sp	(initial) **spielen (ʃpiː-len)**
r	**rot (roːt)**	st	(initial) **stehen (ʃteː-en)**
z	**zehn (tseːn)**	ch	(front) **ich, nicht (ix, nixt)**
s	(before a vowel) **Sohn (zoːn)**	ch	(back) **acht, Buch (axt, buːx)**

NOTE. The phonetic sign ŋ corresponds to the English sound *ng* in *ring*, but there is a slight stress on the *g*.

Final b d g
At the end of a word:

d > t	**Kind** (*kint*), child	**-ig > -ich**	**fertig (fer-tix)** finished
b > p	**Jakob (ja-kop)**, Jacob	**-ag > -ak**	**Tag (taːk)** day
g > k	except after **i**, where g becomes front **ch**	**-eg > -ek**	**Weg (veːk)** way

Exercise No. 7. Practise these words aloud.

ja Jahr	Jahre	jung	Juni	Vater	voll	vier	von
jaː jaːr	jaː-re	juɲ	juː-ni	faː-ter	fol	fiːr	fon
Wasser	**Winter**	**Wind**	**Welt**	**was**	**wenn**	**wir**	**wie**	**warm**
vas-ser	vin-ter	vint	velt	vas	ven	viːr	viː	varm
zehn	**zwölf**	**März**	**Dezember**		**zählen**	**Zigarétte**
tseːn	tsvœlf	mɛrts	deː-tsem-ber		tsɛː-len	tsi-ga-rɛ-te
Sohn	**September**	**Rose**	**Musík**	**sagen**	**singen**	**sitzen**	**sehen**
zoːn	zep-tɛmber	roː-ze	muː-ziːk	zaː-gen	ziɲ-gen	zit-sen	zeː-en
Schule	**Schwester**	**Deutsch**	**Englisch**	**wünschen**	**frisch**	**Studént**
ʃuː-le	ʃvɛs-ter	doytʃ	ɛɲ-liʃ	vyn-ʃen	friʃ	ʃtu-dent
Sport	**spielen**	**sprechen**	**er spricht**	**Stock**	**Stuhl**	**stehen**
ʃport	ʃpiː-len	ʃpre-xen	eːr ʃprixt	ʃtok	ʃtuːl	ʃteː-en

Der Zweite Teil (tsvai-te tail) The Second Part
Important Words and Expressions in Daily Life

A. **Bitte** (bi-te), Please
Herr Schmidt (her ʃmit), Mr. Smith
Frau Schmidt (frau ʃmit), Mrs. Smith
Fräulein Schmidt (froy-lain), Miss Smith
Verzeihen Sie (ver-tsai-en ziː), Pardon
Ich möchte (moex-te), I should like
Guten Tag (guː-ten taːk), Good day
Danke (dan-ke) Thanks
Vielen Dank (fiː-len), Many thanks
Bitte schön (bi-te ʃøn), You're welcome
Guten Morgen (guː-ten mor-gen), Good morning
Guten Abend (guː-ten aː-bent), Good evening
Gute Nacht (guː-te naxt), Good night

B. Read each heading aloud and complete it with the words listed under it.
Wieviel kostet . . . (viː-fiːl) How much does . . . cost?

Beispiel: Wieviel kostet der Bleistift?

der **Bleistift** (blai-ʃtift), pencil
die **Feder** (feː-der), pen
das **Buch** (buːx), book
der **Hut** (huːt), hat
das **Hemd** (hemt), shirt
die **Bluse** (bluː-ze) blouse
das **Kleid** (klait), dress
die **Kravátte** (kra-va-te), necktie

das **Auto** (au-toː), car
die **Jacke** (ja-ke), jacket
die **Uhr** (uːr), clock
die **Seife** (zai-fe), soap
das **Parfüm** (par-fym), perfume
die **Handtasche** (hant-taʃe), handbag
das **Brot**, bread
der **Anzug** (an-tsuːk), suit

Ich möchte (ix mœx-te)[1] I should like

eine **Tasse Kaffée** (ta-se ka-feː), a cup of coffee
eine **Tasse Tee** (ta-se teː), a cup of tea
ein **Glas Wasser** (glas va-ser), a glass of water
ein **Zimmer mit Bad** (tsi-mer mit baːt), a room with bath
eine **Zeitung** (tsai-tuɲ), a newspaper
eine **Speisekarte** (ʃpai-ze-kar-te), a menu

telefonieren (te-le-fo-**ni**:-ren), to telephone
essen (ɛ-sen), to eat
spazíeren gehen (ʃpa-**tsi**:-ren ge:-en), to go for a walk
ins Kino gehen (ins **ki**:-no: ge:-en), to go to the cinema
ins Theater gehen (ins te:- **a**:-ter ge:-en), to go to the theatre
ins Konzért gehen (ins kon-**tsert** ge:-en), to go to the concert
schlafen gehen (**ʃla**:-fen ge:-en), to go to sleep
nach Hause gehen (nax **hau**-ze ge:-en), to go home

NOTE 1. ch in **möchte** is soft as in **ich**.

Bitte, können Sie mir sagen, wo... ist? (*bite kœnen zi: mi:r sa:gen vo:... ist*)

Please, can you tell me where... is?

Beispiel: Bitte, können Sie mir sagen, wo die Karlstraße ist?

die Karlstraße (karl-**ʃtra**-se), Charles Street
das Hotél Adler (ho:-**tel** a:-dler), Eagle Hotel
der Bahnhof (**ba**:n-ho:f), station
das Postamt (**post**-amt), post office
die Toilette (twa:-**lɛ**-te), toilet (ladies' room)
das Muséum (mu:-**ze**:-um), museum
das Telefón (te-le-**fo**:n), telephone
die Polizeiwache (po-li-**tsai**-va-xe), police station
der Wartesaal[1] (**var**-te-za:l), waiting room
der Parkplatz (**park**-plats), parking space

NOTE 1. aa is pronounced as long a (a:). **Der Saal** (za:l), hall, room; **das Paar** (pa:r) pair; **das Haar** (ha:r) hair.

C. **Die Zahlen von eins bis einundzwanzig** (di: **tsa**:-len fon ains bis **ain**-un-tsvan-tsix). The numerals from one to twenty-one. Memorize:

1 eins	7 sieben (**zi**:-ben)	13 dreizehn	18 achtzehn
2 zwei (tsvai)	8 acht	14 vierzehn	19 neunzehn
3 drei	9 neun (noyn)	15 fünfzehn	20 zwanzig
4 vier (fi:r)	10 zehn (tse:n)	16 sechzehn	(tsvan-tsix)
5 fünf	11 elf	17 siebzehn	21 einundzwanzig
6 sechs (zeks)[1]	12 zwölf (tsvœlf)		

NOTE 1. The combination -chs is pronounced -*ks*.

D. The days of the week

(der) Sonntag (**zon**-ta:k), Sunday
(der) Montag (**mo**·n-ta:k), Monday
(der) Dienstag (**di**:n-sta:k) Tuesday
(der) Mittwoch (**mit**-vox), Wednesday
(der) Donnerstag (**don**-er-sta:k), Thursday
(der) Freitag (**Frai**-ta:k), Friday
(der) Samstag (**sam**-sta:k) Saturday
der Tag (ta:k) day

Gespräch (ge-ʃprɛːx) Conversation

Guten Tag.	(guː-ten taːk)	Good day.
Guten Tag.	(guː-ten taːk)	Good day.
Wie geht's?	(viː geːts)	How are you?
Gut, danke. Und dir?	(guːt da-nke unt diːr)	Well, thanks. And you?
Danke, sehr gut.	(dan-ke seːr guːt)	Thanks, very well.
Auf Wiedersehen!	(auf viː-der-zeː-en)	Good-bye.

CHAPTER 5

WER IST HERR CLARK?
WHO IS MR. CLARK?

You have acquired a good working knowledge of German pronunciation and are familiar with a considerable number of words and expressions. You are now ready for a closer study of the German language. Follow all directions for study, reading aloud, and speaking. Remember: the only way to learn to speak a language is by speaking it.

This chapter will introduce you to Mr. Clark, a London businessman who is as eager as you are to learn German. You will also meet his congenial teacher, Mr. Müller, a German by birth but now a British subject. As he teaches Mr. Clark, he will also teach you in a pleasant and interesting way.

So, **Viel Glück** (good luck) and **Glückliche Reise** (happy journey) as you accompany Mr. Clark on the road which leads to a practical knowledge of the German language.

How to Study Each Chapter

Read the German text silently, referring to the English when necessary to get the meaning. Cover up the English text and read the German text silently. Practise aloud the words and expressions under **Wortschatz** (vocabulary).

Then read the German text aloud, pronouncing carefully. Finally, study Grammar Notes and Practical Exercises.

Check your answers to each exercise in the Answer Section.

WER IST HERR CLARK?	WHO IS MR. CLARK?
1 Robert Clark ist Kaufmann.	1 Robert Clark is a businessman.
2 Er ist Engländer.	2 He is an Englishman.
3 Er ist kein Deutscher.	3 He is not a German.
4 Sein Büro ist in London.	4 His office is in London.
5 Er wohnt aber nicht in London.	5 However, he does not live in London.
6 Der Vorort, wo die Familie Clark wohnt, ist nicht weit von London.	6 The suburb where the Clark family lives is not far from London.
7 Herr Clark ist verheiratet.	7 Mr. Clark is married.
8 Seine Frau heißt Helene Clark.	8 His wife's name is Helen Clark.
9 Herr und Frau Clark haben vier Kinder, zwei Knaben und zwei Mädchen.	9 Mr. and Mrs. Clark have four children, two boys and two girls.
10 Die Knaben heißen Karl und Wilhelm.	10 The boys are called Charles and William.

11 **Die Mädchen heißen Marie und Anna.**

11 The girls are named Mary and Anna.

12 **Herr Clark ist vierzig Jahre alt.**

12 Mr. Clark is forty years old.

13 **Seine Frau ist sechsunddreißig Jahre alt.**

13 His wife is thirty-six years old.

14 **Karl ist zwölf Jahre alt.**

14 Charles is twelve years old.

15 **Wilhelm ist zehn Jahre alt.**

15 William is ten years old.

16 **Marie ist acht Jahre alt.**

16 Mary is eight years old.

17 **Anna ist fünf Jahre alt.**

17 Anna is five years old.

18 **Alle außer Anna gehen zur Schule.**

18 All except Anna go to school.

19 **Anna geht nicht zur Schule.**

19 Anna does not go to school.

20 **Sie ist noch zu jung für die Schule.**

20 She is still too young for school.

Wortschatz (vort-ʃats) Vocabulary

der Engländer (ɛn-lɛnder), English-man; **England,** England

das Büro (by-roː), office

der Herr, gentleman, sir, Mr.

das Kind (kint), child

der Knabe (knaː-be), boy

das Mädchen (mɛːt-xen), girl

das Jahr, year

wohnen (voː-nen), to live

jung, young; **alt,** old

verheiratet (fer-hai-raː-tet), married

weit (vait), far; **nah,** near

noch, still; **noch nicht,** not yet

zu (tsuː), too; **zu viel,** too much

für, for; **von,** from

aber, but; **und** (unt), and

sein, his (like **ein** and **kein**)

alle (al-le), all; **viele,** many

Die Familie (fa-miː-lie) The Family

der Vater	father	die Schwester	sister
der Sohn	son	die Tante	aunt
der Bruder	brother	die Großmutter	grandmother
der Onkel	uncle	die Eltern	parents
der Großvater	grandfather	der Mann	man, husband
die Mutter	mother	die Frau	woman, wife
die Tochter	daughter	die Kinder	children

Deutsche Ausdrücke (doyt-ʃe aus-dry-ke) German Expressions

heißen, to be called, to be named

Wie heißen Sie? What is your name?

Ich heiße Engel. My name is Engel.

Wie heißt er? What is his name?

Er heißt Müller. His name is Müller.

Was sind Sie von Beruf? What are you by profession? What is your occupation (trade)?

Ich bin Lehrer. I am a teacher.

Sie ist Lehrerin.[1] She is a teacher.

Herr B. ist Arzt. Mr. B. is a doctor.

Herr C. ist Kaufmann. Mr. C. is a businessman.

Frau C. ist Hausfrau. Mrs. C. is a housewife.

Herr K. ist Student. Mr. K. is a student.

zur Schule gehen to go to school.

Wir gehen zur Schule. We go to school.

NOTE 1. Masculine nouns denoting persons are often made feminine by adding **-in.**

der Lehrer *m.* **die Lehrerin** *f.*, teacher

der Schüler *m.* **die Schülerin** *f.*, pupil

der Student *m.* **die Studentin** *f.*, student

der Freund *m.* **die Freundin** *f.*, friend

Grammar Notes and Practical Exercises

1 Noun plurals

German nouns do not form their plurals by adding -s or -es, as is the case with most English nouns. Here are some familiar nouns arranged in groups according to the way they form their plurals. Most German nouns form their plurals in one of the ways indicated below.

	Singular		Plural		Type of Plural
Group I	der Lehrer	teacher	die Lehrer	teachers	–
	der Bruder	brother	die Brüder	brothers	¨
	das Mädchen	girl	die Mädchen	girls	–
	das Fräulein	Miss, young lady	die Fräulein	young ladies	–
Group II	der Hut	hat	die Hüte	hats	¨e
	der Sohn	son	die Söhne	sons	¨e
	das Jahr	year	die Jahre	years	–e
Group III	der Mann	man	die Männer	men	¨er
	das Buch	book	die Bücher	books	¨er
	das Kind	child	die Kinder	children	–er
Group IV	der Knabe	boy	die Knaben	boys	–n
	die Feder	pen	die Federn	pens	–n
	der Herr	gentleman	die Herren	gentlemen	–en

Nouns of Group I add no ending to form the plural. They generally add an **Umlaut** to **a, o,** or **u** within the word.

Nouns of Group II add **-e**. They generally add an **Umlaut** to **a, o,** or **u** within the word.

Nouns of Group III add **-er**. They always add an **Umlaut** to **a, o,** or **u** within the word.

Nouns of Group IV add **-n** or **-en**. They never add an **Umlaut**.

The best way to learn noun plurals is to repeat aloud and write both singular and plural of nouns as they occur. Later you will learn a few helpful rules. Here is one: All nouns ending in **-chen** or **-lein** are neuter and do not change in the plural. Remember as models: **das Mädchen; das Fräulein** *pl.* **die Mädchen; die Fräulein.**

The definite article in the plural is **die** for all genders. The indefinite article **ein** has no plural, and the plural of **kein** is **keine.**

Die Knaben und **die Mädchen** sind dort.   The boys and the girls are there.
Keine Knaben und **keine Mädchen** sind dort. No boys and no girls are there.

Exercise No. 8.   Read the first sentence in each pair aloud. Read the second sentence in each pair, inserting the plural of the noun in heavy type.

Beispiel: 1. Die Kinder zählen vons eins bis zehn.

1 **Das Kind** zählt von eins bis zehn.
  Die —— zählen von eins bis zehn.
2 **Der Knabe** wohnt nicht hier.
  Die —— wohnen nicht hier.
3 **Das Buch** ist nicht neu.
  Die —— sind nicht neu.
4 **Das Mädchen** singt schön.
  Die —— singen schön.
5 **Der Lehrer** lehrt Deutsch und Englisch.
  Die —— lehren Deutsch und Englisch.

6 Wo ist **die Feder** und **das Buch?**
Wo sind die —— und die ——?
7 **Das Fräulein** lernt jetzt Deutsch.
Die —— lernen jetzt Deutsch.
8 **Der Herr** spielt sehr gut Tennis.
Die —— spielen sehr gut Tennis.
9 **Der Hut** ist blau und weiß.
Die —— sind blau und weiß.

10 **Der Sohn** kommt heute nicht.
Die —— kommen heute nicht.
11 Wohnt **der Bruder** weit von hier?
Wohnen die —— weit von hier?
12 **Der Mann** hat ein Büro in London.
Die —— haben ein Büro in London.

2 The Present Tense of *gehen*, to go

Singular		Plural	
ich gehe	I go	wir gehen	we go
du gehst	you go	ihr geht	you go
er, sie, es geht	he, she, it goes	sie gehen	they go

Polite form (P.F.), singular and plural: **Sie gehen** you go.

(*a*) The endings of nearly all German verbs in the present tense are like those of **gehen.**

(*b*) **du gehst, ihr geht, Sie gehen,** are all translated *you go.*
We say **du** (familiar singular) in addressing a relative, a close friend, a child, or an animal.
We say **ihr** (familiar plural) in addressing more than one relative, close friend, child, or animal.
We say **Sie** to all others whether singular or plural. This is called the polite form (P.F.) and always takes a capital letter.

Karl, **du gehst** zu schnell.	Charles, you are going too fast.
Kinder, **ihr geht** zu langsam.	Children, you are going too slowly.
Herr Braun, **Sie gehen** zu früh.	Mr. Braun, you are going too early.
Wohin **gehen Sie,** meine Herren?	Where are you going, (my) gentlemen?

(*c*) The present tense may be translated in three ways.

ich gehe, I go, do go, am going; **du gehst,** you go, do go, are going; etc.

(*d*) To form a question, invert subject and verb.

Wohin gehen Sie? Where are you going?
Gehen die Kinder zur Schule? Are the children going to school?

(*e*) To form the negative, use **nicht** (not).

Sie geht nicht zur Schule. She does not go to school.
Gehen Sie nicht in die Stadt? Are you not going to town?

3 The Imperative (command form)

Fam. Sing. **Geh(e)** nach Hause, Kind! Go home, child.
Fam. Plur. **Geht** nach Hause, Kinder! Go home, children.
P.F. Sing. **Gehen Sie** nach Hause, Herr Schmidt! Go home, Mr. Schmidt.
P.F. Plur. **Gehen Sie** nach Hause, meine Damen und Herren! Go home, ladies and gentlemen.

The *imperative singular, familiar* (**du** understood), ends in **-e,** which is often dropped.

The *imperative plural*, *familiar* (**ihr** understood), is like the verb form with **ihr** in the present tense.

The *imperative polite form*, *singular* and *plural*, is like the polite form in the present tense with Sie following the verb.

4 Familiar Verbs like *gehen* in the Present Tense

singen	lernen	lehren	trinken	kommen	kaufen
to sing	to learn	to teach	to drink	to come	to buy
zählen	wohnen	hören	spielen	stehen	wünschen
to count	to live	to hear	to play	to stand	to wish

Exercise No. 9. Complete the verbs with the correct personal endings.

1 Was kauf— Sie, Fräulein Braun? Ich kauf— Bücher. 2 Was kauf— Herr Braun? Er kauf— Hüte. 3 Komm— die Mädchen heute? Nein, sie komm— heute nicht. 4 Sing— die Mädchen und die Knaben schön? Ja, sie sing— sehr schön. 5 Spiel—ihr heute Ball, Kinder? Nein, wir spiel— heute Tennis. 6 Lern— du Englisch, Anna? Ja, ich lern— Englisch. 7 Wo wohn— der Kaufmann? Er wohn— nicht weit von hier. 8 Ich hör— Musik. Wer spiel—? 9 Wo steh— die Stühle? Sie steh— dort. 10 Was trink— du, Fritz? Ich trink— Milch.

Exercise No. 10. Complete each sentence with the correct imperative form of the given verb.

Beispiel: 1. Lerne Deutsch, Karl!

1 (Lernen) —— Deutsch, Karl!
2 (Gehen) —— langsam, Kinder!
3 (Spielen) —— nicht Ball hier, Knaben!
4 (Trinken) —— die Milch, Anna!
5 (Singen) —— nicht so laut, Fräulein!
6 (Kommen) —— nicht spät, meine Herren!
7 (Stehen) —— hier, Karl und Anna!
8 (Kaufen) Bitte —— das Auto, Papa!
9 (Zählen) —— von eins bis zehn, mein Kind!
10 (Kaufen) —— die Bücher, Herr Braun!

Exercise No. 11. Fragen Questions

Re-read the text **Wer ist Herr Clark?** Then answer the following questions orally and in writing, referring to the text if necessary. Check your written answers in the Answer Section. Follow this procedure with all **Fragen** exercises.

1 Was ist Herr Clark von Beruf? 2 Ist er ein Deutscher? 3 Wo ist sein Büro? 4 Wohnt er in London? 5 Was ist nicht weit von London? 6 Wie alt ist der Kaufmann? 7 Wie heißt seine Frau? 8 Wie alt ist sie? 9 Wie viele Kinder haben Herr und Frau Clark? 10 Wie heißen die zwei Knaben? 11 Wie alt sind sie? 12 Wie heißen die zwei Mädchen?

Question Words

wer, who **was,** what **wie,** how **wie viele,** how many **warum,** why **wo,** where

Exercise No. 12. Übersetzen Sie ins Deutsche! (Translate into German.)

1 This is a suburb. It is not far from London.   2 Mr. C. and his (seine) family live here. 3 Mr. C. is a businessman. He is not a doctor.   4 The businessman has a wife and four children, two boys and two girls.   5 His wife's name is Helen. (His wife is called . . .)   6 The boys are older than the girls.   7 Anna is five years old. She does not go to school.   8 What is your name and where do you (Sie) live?   9 Are the children playing ball? They are not playing ball. 10 Go home, child! Go home, children! 11 Do not go, Mr. Schmidt!   12 Stand here, ladies and gentlemen!

NOTE. 1. older than, älter als.

CHAPTER 6

DAS HAUS VON HERRN CLARK
THE HOME OF MR. CLARK

1 Das Haus von Herrn Clark ist ein Einfamilienhaus mit Garten.
2 Das Haus ist nicht groß.
3 Es ist aber schön und bequem.
4 Es hat sieben Zimmer: das Wohnzimmer, das Eßzimmer, die Küche, drei Schlafzimmer und ein Arbeitszimmer für Herrn Clark.
5 Außerdem hat das Haus zwei Badezimmer.
6 Das Wohnzimmer ist groß, hell und schön möbliert.
7 Es hat zwei Fenster.
8 Durch die Fenster sieht man einen Garten.
9 Das Eßzimmer ist nicht so groß wie das Wohnzimmer.
10 Hier sieht man u. a. (unter anderem) einen Tisch, ein Büfett und sechs Stühle.
11 Der Tisch ist rund.
12 Die sechs Stühle stehen um den Tisch.
13 Ein Schlafzimmer ist ziemlich groß.
14 Das ist für die Eltern.
15 Zwei Schlafzimmer sind etwas kleiner.
16 Das sind die Kinderschlafzimmer, eins für die zwei Knaben und eins für die zwei Mädchen.
17 Beide Kinderschlafzimmer haben zwei Betten, zwei Tischlein, zwei Stühle, einen Kleiderschrank, eine Kommode, und einige Bilder.
18 Ja, das Haus von Herrn Clark ist wirklich schön und bequem.

1 The home of Mr. Clark is a one-family house with a garden.
2 The house is not large.
3 It is, however, beautiful and comfortable.
4 It has seven rooms: the living-room, the dining-room, the kitchen, three bedrooms, and a study for Mr. Clark.
5 In addition, the house has two bathrooms.
6 The living-room is large, bright, and beautifully furnished.
7 It has two windows.
8 Through the windows one sees a garden.
9 The dining-room is not as large as the living-room.
10 Here one sees, among other things, a table, a sideboard, and six chairs.
11 The table is round.
12 The six chairs stand around the table.
13 One bedroom is rather large.
14 That is for the parents.
15 Two bedrooms are somewhat smaller.

16 Those are the children's bedrooms, one for the two boys and one for the two girls.

17 Both children's bedrooms have two beds, two little tables, two chairs, a wardrobe, a chest of drawers, and some pictures.

18 Yes, the house of Mr. Clark is really beautiful and comfortable.

Wortschatz

das Bett, bed; **das Bettchen,**[1] little bed
der Tisch, table; **das Tischlein,**[1] little table
das Büfett, sideboard, buffet
die Kommóde, dresser, chest of drawers
das Fenster, window; **die Tür,** door
die Wohnung, flat, apartment, home
das Zimmer, room
bequém (bekve:m) comfortable
hell, light; **dunkel,** dark

klein, small; **kleiner,** smaller
kennen, to know, be acquainted with
möbliert (mø-bli:rt), furnished
rund (runt), round
wirklich (virk-lix), really
ziemlich (tsi:m-lix), rather
außerdem (au-ser-de:m), besides, in addition
beide, both; **einige,** several
etwas, somewhat, something
um, around; **mit,** with
so groß wie, as large as

NOTE 1. **-chen** or **-lein** added to a noun signifies 'little', or 'fondness for' the person or thing mentioned. Thus: **Brüderlein** little brother or dear brother; **Schwesterchen** little or dear sister.

Das Einfamilienhaus (ain-fa-mi:-lien-haus) The One-Family House

das Arbeitszimmer (**ar**-baits-tsi-mer), workroom, study
das Badezimmer (**ba:**-de-tsi-mer), bathroom
das Eßzimmer (**es**-tsi-mer), dining-room

das Schlafzimmer (**ʃla:f**-tsi-mer), bedroom
das Wohnzimmer (**vo:n**-tsi-mer), living-room
die Küche (ky-xe), kitchen
der Hausflur (haus-flu:r), hall

Deutsche Ausdrücke

Hier sieht man viele Häuser. Here one sees many houses.

Hier lernt man viel Deutsch. Here you learn much German.
Dort singt man oft. There people often sing.

NOTE: **man** (one, you, people) is an indefinite pronoun.

Grammar Notes and Practical Exercises

1 More noun plurals. Practise singular and plural aloud.

| GROUP I. *Singular* | der Schüler | das Zimmer | das Fenster |
| *Plural:* No ending | die Schüler | die Zimmer | die Fenster |

| GROUP II. *Singular* | der Stuhl | der Tisch | die Wand |
| *Plural:* Adds -e | die Stühle | die Tische | die Wände |

| GROUP III. *Singular* | das Haus | das Buch | das Bild |
| *Plural:* Adds -er | die Häuser | die Bücher | die Bilder |

GROUP IV. *Singular* die Tür die Frau die Schule
Plural: Adds -n or -en die Türen die Frauen die Schulen

Exercise No. 13. Change the subject nouns in these sentences to the plural. Be careful to make any necessary changes in the verbs.

Beispiel: Das Zimmer ist groß. **Die Zimmer** sind groß.

1 **Der Tisch** ist rund. 2 **Das Fenster** ist offen. 3 **Die Tür** ist nicht offen.
4 **Das Bild** ist schön. 5 **Das Fräulein** spielt nicht Tennis. 6 **Der Herr** lernt Englisch. 7 **Die Frau** singt schön. 8 **Der Schüler** spielt Ball. 9 **Der Stuhl** steht dort. 10 **Die Schule** ist nicht weit von hier.

Grammar Notes and Practical Exercises

2 Present Tense of *sehen,* to see; *haben,* to have

ich sehe	wir sehen	ich habe	wir haben
du siehst	ihr seht	du hast	ihr habt
er, sie, es sieht	sie sehen	er, sie, es hat	sie haben
P.F. Sie sehen		*P.F.* Sie haben	

Imperative: sieh! seht! sehen Sie!   habe! habt! haben Sie!

The endings of **sehen** and **haben** are like those of **gehen**. Note, however, the change from **e** to **ie** in the second and third persons singular of **sehen** and in the familiar imperative singular. You will meet other verbs like **sehen**.

Haben drops the letter **b** in the second and third person singular.

3 The Accusative Case: Nouns, Definite and Indefinite Articles; *kein, wer, was*

The accusative case is the case of the direct object. In these examples observe how the noun, the definite and indefinite articles, and the interrogative pronoun are expressed in the accusative.

Wen sehen Sie? Ich sehe

den Mann	**die** Frau	**das** Kind
einen Mann	**eine** Frau	**ein** Kind
keinen Mann	**keine** Frau	**kein** Kind
die Männer	**die** Frauen	**die** Kinder
keine Männer	**keine** Frauen	**keine** Kinder

Whom do you see? I see

the man	the woman	the child
a man	a woman	a child
no man	no woman	no child
the men	the women	the children
no men	no women	no children

Was sehen Sie? Ich sehe

den Tisch	**die** Feder	**das** Buch
einen Tisch	**eine** Feder	**ein** Buch
keinen Tisch	**keine** Feder	**kein** Buch
die Tische	**die** Federn	**die** Bücher
keine Tische	**keine** Federn	**keine** Bücher

What do you see? I see

the table	the pen	the book
a table	a pen	a book
no table	no pen	no book
the tables	the pens	the books
no tables	no pens	no books

The Definite Article
Singular

	masculine	feminine	neuter
Nom.	**der** Mann	**die** Frau	**das** Kind
Acc.	**den** Mann	**die** Frau	**das** Kind

Plural

	masc. fem. neut.
Nom.	**die** Männer (Frauen, Kinder)
Acc.	**die** Männer (Frauen, Kinder)

The Indefinite Article and *kein*

Nom.

  ein (kein)   **eine (keine)**   **ein (kein)**   (No plural of **ein**) **keine**

Acc.

  einen (keinen)   **eine (keine)**   **ein (kein)**   (No plural of **ein**) **keine**

Note the ending -en in the masculine accusative singular of **der, ein,** and **kein.**

Nouns are generally identical in the nominative and accusative singular and always identical in the nominative and accusative plural.

Interrogative Pronouns—*wer, was*

Nom.

Wer ist hier?   **Was** ist hier?   *Who* is here?   *What* is here?

Acc.

Wen sehen Sie?   **Was** sehen Sie?   *Whom* do you see?   *What* do you see?

Exercise No. 14. Practise aloud.

Ich habe einen Bruder.	Ich sehe eine Feder.
Hast du eine Schwester?	Du siehst keine Uhr.
Der Herr hat zwei Brüder.	Er sieht das Haus.
Er hat auch zwei Schwestern.	Sie sieht das Haus nicht.
Wir haben einen Garten.	Was seht ihr, Kinder?
Habt ihr einen Garten, Kinder?	Wir sehen einen Tisch.
Die Mädchen haben einen Garten.	Wen sehen die Knaben?
Haben Sie einen Garten, Herr Schmidt?	Sie sehen den Lehrer.

Exercise No. 15. Answer these questions with the accusative singular of the nouns in parenthesis.

Beispiel: A. Er sieht den Tisch, etc. **B.** Ich sehe die Frau, etc.

A. Was sieht er? Er sieht (der Tisch; das Tischlein; das Zimmer; der Stuhl; kein Ball; keine Schule; kein Schuh; kein Garten).
B. Wen sehen Sie? Ich sehe (die Frau; der Lehrer; das Mädchen; der Bruder; die Tante; die Schwester; der Kaufmann; der Sohn; eine Tochter; kein Schüler; ein Lehrer; ein Kind; keine Frau; kein Mädchen).

4 The Accusative Case, Third Person Pronoun.

Sehen Sie den Mann?	Sehen Sie die Frau?	Sehen Sie das Kind?
Ich sehe **ihn** (him).	Ich sehe **sie** (her).	Ich sehe **es** (it).

Sehen Sie die Männer, die Frauen, die Kinder?
Ich sehe **sie** (them).

Sehen Sie den Tisch?	Sehen Sie die Feder?	Sehen Sie das Buch?
Ich sehe **ihn** (it).	Ich sehe **sie** (it).	Ich sehe **es** (it).

Sehen Sie die Tische, die Türen, die Häuser?
Ich sehe **sie** (them).

	masculine	*feminine*	*pneuter*	*lural m. f. n.*
Nom,	**er,** he, it	**sie,** she, it	**es,** it	**sie,** they
Acc.	**ihn,** him, it	**sie,** her, it	**es,** it	**sie,** them

5 Prepositions with the Accusative
durch, through; **für,** for; **gegen,** against, towards; **ohne,** without; **um,** around; and a few other prepositions always take the accusative case.

durch den Garten	für die Mutter	gegen den Stuhl	um den Tisch
durch die Tür	für den Vater	gegen das Fenster	um die Schule
durch das Haus	für das Kind	gegen die Tür	um das Haus
durch die Gärten	für die Kinder	gegen die Tische	um die Häuser

Exercise No. 16. Practise aloud. Translate.

kennen—to know, to be acquainted with a person or thing

— Kennen Sie den Kaufmann, Robert Clark?
— Ich kenne ihn sehr gut.
— Kennen Sie Frau Clark?
— Ja, ich kenne sie.

— Kennen Sie die Kinder von Robert Clark?
— Nein, ich kenne sie nicht.
— Kennen Sie das Haus, wo er wohnt?
— Ich kenne es. Es ist ein Einfamilienhaus.

Exercise No. 17. Complete the answers to each question with the correct third person pronoun. The pronoun must agree in number and gender with the noun.

Beispiel: 1. Ja, ich sehe **ihn.**

1 Sehen Sie den Garten dort?	Ja, ich sehe ——.
2 Sehen Sie das Einfamilienhaus dort?	Ja, wir sehen ——.
3 Ist der Hut für den Vater?	Ja, er ist für ——.
4 Sind die Blumen hier für die Mutter?	Ja, sie sind für ——.
5 Ist das Schlafzimmer für die Kinder?	Ja, es ist für ——.
6 Zählen die Lehrer die Schüler?	Ja, sie zählen ——.
7 Suchen Sie das Museum, Fräulein?	Ja, ich suche ——.
8 Stehen die Kinder um den Lehrer?	Nein, sie stehen nicht um ——.
9 Wünschen Sie die Zeitung, mein Herr?	Nein, ich wünsche —— nicht.
10 Kauft der Herr den Tisch und die Stühle?	Nein, er kauft —— nicht.

Exercise No. 18. Fragen

Re-read the text **Das Haus von Herrn Clark.** Then answer the following questions orally and in writing.

1 Was für[1] ein Haus hat Herr Clark? 2 Ist das Haus groß? 3 Ist das Haus bequem oder unbequem?[2] 4 Wie viele Zimmer hat das Haus? 5 Für wen ist das Arbeitszimmer? 6 Wie viele Badezimmer hat das Haus? 7 Ist das Wohnzimmer hell oder dunkel?[3] 8 Was sieht man durch die Fenster? 9 Was sieht man im Eßzimmer? 10 Ist der Tisch rund oder viereckig?[4] 11 Wo stehen die Stühle? 12 Für wen ist das große[5] Schlafzimmer? 13 Was sehen wir im[6] Kinderschlafzimmer? 14 Haben die Mädchen ein Zimmer oder zwei?

NOTES: 1 **was für** what kind of. 2 (**un**-be-kveːm) uncomfortable. 3 **dunkel** dark. 4 (**fir**-ɛk-ix) four-cornered, square. 5 Adjectives have special endings when they precede the noun. You will learn more about this later. 6 **im** = in the.

Exercise No. 19. Übersetzen Sie!

1 The home of Mr. C. is not large. It (**Es**) has a garden. 2 Do you (**Sie**) see the garden? 3 We see the table. Six chairs are standing around the table. 4 One bedroom is for the boys. One table is for the girls. 5 They have a wardrobe and a dresser. 6 The rooms are not large, but they are comfortable. 7 The room has a table and a chair, but it has not a dresser. 8 Have you (**du**) a brother and a sister? I have two brothers, but I have no sisters.

CHAPTER 7

WARUM LERNT HERR CLARK DEUTSCH?
WHY IS MR. CLARK LEARNING GERMAN?

1 Wir wissen schon, Robert Clark ist Kaufmann in London.
2 Er ist nämlich Importhändler.
3 Er importiert Kunstgegenstände und andere Dinge aus Deutschland.
4 Er hat einen Vertreter in München.
5 Der Vertreter heißt Heinrich Schiller.
6 Im Sommer will Herr Clark eine Reise nach Deutschland machen.
7 Er will seinen Vertreter besuchen.
8 Er will mit ihm über Geschäftssachen reden.
9 Er will auch interessante Plätze in Deutschland besuchen.
10 Aber Herr Clark spricht kein Deutsch.
11 Sein Vertreter spricht kein Englisch.
12 Deswegen lernt Herr Clark Deutsch.
13 Herr Clark hat einen Deutschlehrer.
14 Er heißt Karl Müller.
15 Er spricht fließend Deutsch.
16 Er wohnt nicht weit von Herrn Clark.
17 Jeden Dienstag und Donnerstag hat Herr Clark eine Deutschstunde.
18 Die Deutschstunde ist fast immer bei Herrn Clark.
19 Herr Clark ist intelligent und fleißig.
20 Schnell lernt er, wie viele Dinge auf Deutsch heißen.
21 Der Lehrer, Herr Müller, fragt: Was ist dies? Was ist das?
22 Der Schüler, Herr Clark, antwortet: Dies ist ein Bleistift. Dies ist eine Feder. Das ist ein Buch, ein Heft, die Tinte, usw. (und so weiter).
23 Der Lehrer fragt: Was sehen Sie?
24 Der Schüler antwortet: Ich sehe einen Bleistift, eine Feder, ein Buch, usw.
25 Der Lehrer fragt: Wie heißen Sie? Was sind Sie von Beruf?
26 Der Schüler antwortet: Ich heiße Robert Clark. Ich bin Kaufmann.
27 Der Schüler lernt auch dieses Gespräch:
—Guten Tag. Wie geht es Ihnen?
—Danke, sehr gut. Und Ihnen?
—Danke, sehr gut. Auf Wiedersehen.

1 We already know Robert Clark is a businessman in London.
2 He is, that is to say, an importer.
3 He imports art objects and other things from Germany.
4 He has an agent in Munich.
5 The agent's name is Henry Schiller.
6 In the summer Mr. Clark wants to make a trip to Germany.
7 He wants to visit his agent.

8 He wants to talk with him about business matters.
9 He also wants to visit interesting places in Germany.
10 But Mr. Clark speaks no German.
11 His agent speaks no English.
12 Therefore Mr. Clark is learning German.
13 Mr. Clark has a German teacher.
14 His name is Karl Müller.
15 He speaks German fluently.
16 He lives not far from Mr. Clark.
17 Every Tuesday and Thursday Mr. Clark has a German lesson.
18 The German lesson is almost always at Mr. Clark's home.
19 Mr. Clark is intelligent and diligent.
20 He learns quickly what many things are called in German.
21 The teacher, Mr. Müller, asks: What is this? What is that?
22 The pupil, Mr. Clark, answers: This is a pencil. This is a pen. That is a book, a notebook, the ink, etc.
23 The teacher asks: What do you see?
24 The pupil answers: I see a pencil, a pen, a book, etc.
25 The teacher asks: What is your name? What is your occupation?
26 The pupil answers: My name is Robert Clark. I am a businessman.
27 The pupil also learns this conversation:
— Good day. How are you?
— Very well, thank you. And you?
— Very well, thank you. Good-bye.

Wortschatz

Beginning with this vocabulary, the plural of all nouns is indicated.

der Bleistift (blai-ſtift), *pl.* **-e,** pencil
die Feder, *pl.* **-n,** pen; **die Tinte,** *pl.* **-n,** ink
die Füllfeder, *pl.* **-n,** fountain pen
der Importhändler, *pl.* **-,** importer
der Vertreter (fer-tre:-ter), *pl.* **-,** agent
das Ding, *pl.* **-e,** thing
die Stunde, *pl.* **-n,** hour, lesson
die Deutschstunde, German lesson
besúchen, to visit
fragen, to ask; **antworten,** to answer
machen, to do, to make
wissen, to know (facts)

andere, others; **einige,** some, a few
fleißig, industrious
intelligent (hard g), intelligent
interessánt interesting
fast, almost
fließend, fluent, fluently
immer, always; **nimmer,** never
schnell, quick, quickly
schon, already
deswegen (des-ve:-gen), therefore
bei, at the house (home) of
nämlich, namely, that is to say

Gegenteile (ge:-gen-tai-le) Opposites

Das Gegenteil von **fleißig** ist **faul.**
   The opposite of *industrious* is *lazy.*
Das Gegenteil von **immer** ist **nimmer.**
   The opposite of *always* is *never.*

Karl ist nicht **faul,** sondern[1] **fleißig.**
   Charles is not *lazy,* but *industrious.*
Die Schule ist nicht **groß,** sondern **klein.**
   The school is not *large,* but *small.*

NOTE 1. Use **sondern** (but) in the sense of *but on the contrary*. Otherwise use **aber**. Thus:

Das Haus ist nicht groß, aber es ist bequem. The house is not large *but* it is comfortable.

Das Haus ist nicht groß, sondern klein. The house is not large, but (on the contrary) small.

Compound Nouns

German is fond of compound nouns. You have met a number of them in Chapter 6: **das Badezimmer, das Eßzimmer, das Einfamilienhaus,** etc. If you know the meaning of each part of the compound, you can usually get the meaning of the whole. The gender of the last noun in the compound is the gender of the whole word. Practise the following aloud:

die Deutschstunde *pl.* -n	**die Geschäftssache** *pl.* -n	**der Kunstgegenstand** *pl.* ᵉe
(doytʃ-ʃtun-de)	(ge-ʃɛfts-za-xe)	(kunst-geː-gen-ʃtant)
the German lesson	the business matter	the art object

Deutsche Ausdrücke

Eine Reise machen, to take (make) a trip
Wann machen Sie eine Reise nach Berlin?
Wie heißt das auf deutsch? =
Wie sagt man das auf deutsch? =
  How do you say that in German?
auf deutsch, in German; **auf englisch,** in English; **auf französisch,** in French
usw. = **und so weiter** = and so forth
jeden Dienstag, every Tuesday
jeden Donnerstag, every Thursday
bei Herrn Clark, at Mr. Clark's house
Wie geht's (dir)? How are you?
  (Used in addressing a friend, child or relative)
Wie geht es Ihnen? How are you?
  (Used in addressing anyone else.)

Grammar Notes and Practical Exercise

1 Present tense of *antworten, reden, sprechen, sein*

antworten	reden	sprechen	sein
to answer	*to talk*	*to speak*	*to be*
ich antworte	ich rede	ich spreche	ich bin
du antwortest	du redest	du sprichst	du bist
er, sie, es antwortet	er, sie, es redet	er, sie, es spricht	er, sie, es ist
wir antworten	wir reden	wir sprechen	wir sind
ihr antwortet	ihr redet	ihr sprecht	ihr seid
sie antworten	sie reden	sie sprechen	sie sind
P.F. Sie antworten	*P.F.* Sie reden	*P.F.* Sie sprechen	*P.F.* Sie sind

(*a*) When the stem of a verb ends in **-t** or **-d** (**antwort-en, red-en**) the letter **-e** is inserted before **-st** and **-t** for ease of pronunciation.

(*b*) Short **-e** in the stem of some verbs becomes **i** in the **du** and **er, sie, es** forms (**du sprichst, er spricht**), and in the imperative familiar singular (*sprich!*).

Exercise No. 20. Kurze Dialóge Brief Dialogues. Read aloud.

1 — Wer fragt?
 — Der Lehrer fragt.
 — Wer antwortet?
 — Die Schüler antworten.
2 — Sprechen Sie Deutsch?
 — Ja, ich spreche Deutsch.
 — Spricht das Fräulein Deutsch?
 — Nein, sie spricht nur[1] Englisch.
3 — Spricht man hier Deutsch?
 — Ja, hier spricht man Deutsch.
 — Spricht man hier Französisch?
 — Nein, hier spricht man kein Französisch.
4 — Ist Herr Clark Lehrer oder Arzt?[2]
 — Er ist weder[3] Lehrer noch[3] Arzt.
 — Was ist er denn?[4]
 — Er ist Kaufmann.

NOTES. 1 **nur,** only. 2 **Arzt** (artst), doctor 3. **weder** (ve:der), . . . **noch,** neither
. . . nor. 4 **denn,** then (often used for emphasis). The word for *then* (time) is
dann. Dann geht er nach Hause. *Then* he goes home.

2 Word order—normal and inverted

In normal word order the verb follows the subject. *Subject–Verb.*

> **Herr Clark lernt** schnell. **Er hat** einen Vertreter in München.

In inverted word order the subject follows the verb. *Verb–Subject.*
In German, inverted word order is very common. It is used:

(*a*) In questions.

> **Lernt Herr Clark** schnell? **Hat er** einen Vetreter in München?

(*b*) In the polite form of the imperative.

> Bitte, **antworten Sie** auf deutsch! Please answer in German.

(*c*) When a simple sentence or independent clause begins with some word
or words other than the subject.

Schnell lernt Herr Clark Deutsch. **In München** hat er einen Vertreter. **Jeden
Donnerstag** hat er eine Deutschstunde. **Hier** spricht man Deutsch.

The words: **und** (and), **aber** (but), **sondern** (but), **oder** (or), **denn** (because),
which are called co-ordinating conjunctions, do not cause inverted word
order.

**Ich lerne Deutsch, und er lernt Französisch. Herr Clark ist Kaufmann, aber
Herr Braun ist Lehrer.**

3 Word order—position of infinitives

The infinitive is placed at the end of a simple sentence or independent
clause.

> Er will seinen Vertreter **besuchen.** He wants to visit his agent.
> Er wil eine Reise **machen.** He wants to take a trip.

Exercise No. 21. Read these sentences, putting the words in heavy type first.

Beispiel: In München hat der Kaufmann einen Vertreter.

1 Der Kaufmann hat einen Vertreter **in München.** 2 Er lernt **deswegen** Deutsch. 3 Herr Clark hat **jeden Dienstag** eine Deutschstunde. 4 Der Lehrer wohnt **nicht weit von hier.** 5 Man spricht **hier** Deutsch. 6 Wir sehen einen Garten **durch die Fenster.** 7 Sechs Stühle stehen **um den Tisch.** 8 Die Kinder gehen **heute** nicht zur Schule.

Exercise No. 22 Complete each sentence by translating the English words in parenthesis.

Beispiel 1. Ich will den Lehrer fragen.

1 Ich will den Lehrer (to ask).
2 Ich will den Vater (to visit).
3 Ich will schnell (to answer).
4 Ich will fließend Deutsch (to speak).
5 Ich will nicht zu laut (to talk).
6 Er will (a hat) kaufen.
7 Er will (art objects) importieren.
8 Er will nicht (far from here) wohnen.
9 Er will (the businessman) sehen.
10 Er will (industrious) sein.

Exercise No. 23. Fragen

Re-read the text: **Warum lernt Herr Clark Deutsch?** Then answer the following questions.

1 **Wer ist Kaufmann?** 2 **Was importiert er?** 3 **Wo hat er einen Vertreter?** 4 **Ist München in Deutschland?** 5 **Wen will Herr Clark besuchen?** 6 **Worüber[1] will er mit ihm reden?** 7 **Spricht der Vertreter Englisch?** 8 **Wer hat einen Deutschlehrer?** 9 **Wie heißt sein Lehrer?** 10 **Wie alt ist der Lehrer?** 11 **Wo wohnt er?** 12 **Wann[2] hat Herr Clark eine Deutschstunde?** 13 **Wo ist fast immer die Deutschstunde?** 14 **Wer ist intelligent und fleißig?** 15 **Wie lernt er?**

NOTES: 1 **worüber** about what. 2 **Wann** when?

Exercise No. 24. Übersetzen Sie!

1 Who speaks German? Mr. M. speaks German. 2 Do you (Sie) speak German? No, I do not speak German. 3 Who asks: What is this? And what is that? 4 Does Mr. C. answer well? Is he intelligent and industrious? 5 Whom does Mr. C. want to visit? He wants to visit his representative in Munich. 6 I want to make a trip to Germany. Therefore I am learning German. 7 Mr. C. is neither (**weder**) a teacher nor (**noch**) a doctor. He is a businessman. 8 The boys are not lazy but (**sondern**) industrious.

CHAPTER 8

DINGE, DINGE, DINGE, ÜBERALL DINGE
THINGS, THINGS, THINGS, EVERYWHERE THINGS

1 Das Arbeitszimmer von Herrn Clark.

2 Das Zimmer ist nicht groß.

3 Im Zimmer sehen wir ein Pult, einen Stuhl vor dem Pult, einen Lehnstuhl, ein Sofa und viele Bücherbretter mit Büchern.

4 An der Wand sehen wir eine Landkarte von Deutschland (Westdeutschland und Ostdeutschland).

5 Heute abend ist der Lehrer wieder beim Kaufmann. Der Lehrer sitzt auf dem Sofa. Der Kaufmann sitzt im Lehnstuhl.

6 Der Lehrer, Herr Müller, redet.

7 M: Überall sind viele, viele Dinge—im Hause, im Park, auf der Straße, in der Schule.

Hier in England spricht man Englisch und nennt die Dinge auf englisch; in Frankreich nennt man die Dinge auf französisch; in Spanien nennt man die Dinge auf spanisch; in Italien nennt man die Dinge auf italienisch; und. . . .

8 C: Jawohl, und in Deutschland spricht man Deutsch, und man muß die Dinge auf deutsch nennen!

9 M: Ausgezeichnet! Sie lernen schnell. Nennen Sie mir nun einige Dinge hier im Zimmer!

10 C: Das ist ja leicht. Dies ist ein Lehnstuhl; das ist ein Sofa; das sind Bücherbretter; das ist ein Pult; und. . . .

11 M: Gut. Nun sagen Sie mir, bitte: Was liegt auf dem Pult?

12 C: Ein Bleistift, eine Füllfeder, einige Briefe und Papiere liegen dort.

13 M: Was macht man mit Bleistift und Feder?

14 C: Man schreibt damit.

15 Da reicht der Lehrer dem Kaufmann ein Buch und fragt: „Was für ein Buch ist dies?"

16 Der Kaufmann antwortet: „Das ist ein Wörterbuch."

17 Der Lehrer gibt dem Kaufmann andere Dinge und fragt immer wieder: Was ist dies? Und was ist das? Und Herr Clark antwortet immer schnell und richtig.

18 Endlich sagt der Lehrer zum Kaufmann: „Das ist für heute abend genug. Ich muß jetzt gehen. Wir haben am Donnerstag wieder eine Stunde, nicht wahr?"

19 „Stimmt," antwortet Herr Clark.

20 Beide Herren gehen aus dem Zimmer. Herr Clark geht mit Herrn Müller zur Tür, gibt ihm die Hand und sagt zu ihm: „Bis Donnerstag, auf Wiedersehen!"

1 The study of Mr. Clark.

2 The room is not big.

3 In the room we see a desk, a chair in front of the desk, an easy-chair, a sofa, and many book-shelves with books.

4 On the wall we see a map of Germany (West Germany and East Germany).

5 This evening the teacher is again at the home of the businessman. The teacher is sitting on the sofa. The businessman is sitting in the easy-chair.

6 The teacher, Mr. Müller, is speaking.

7 M: Everywhere there are many, many things—in the house, in the park, on the street, in the school.

Here in England one speaks English and gives the names of things in English; in France one gives the names of things in French; in Spain one gives the names of things in Spanish; in Italy one gives the names of things in Italian; and . . .

8 C: Yes indeed, and in Germany one speaks German and one must give the names of things in German.

9 M: Splendid. You learn quickly. Now tell me the names of some things here in the room.

10 C: That is indeed easy. This is an easy-chair; that is a sofa; those are bookshelves; that is a desk; and . . .

11 M: Good. Now tell me please: What is lying on the desk?

12 C: A pencil, a fountain pen, a few letters, and papers are lying there.

13 M: What does one do with pencil and pen?

14 C: One writes with them.

15 Then the teacher hands the businessman a book and asks: 'What kind of a book is this?'

16 The businessman answers: 'That is a dictionary.'

17 The teacher gives other things to the businessman and asks again and again: What is this? and what is that? And Mr. Clark always answers quickly and correctly.

18 Finally, the teacher says to the businessman: 'That is enough for this evening. I must go now. On Thursday we have another lesson, don't we?'

19 'That's right,' answers Mr. Clark.

20 Both gentlemen go out of the room. Mr. Clark goes with Mr. Müller to the door, shakes hands with him, and says to him: 'Till Thursday, good-bye.'

Wortschatz

der **Brief,** *pl.* **-e,** the letter
das **Papiér** *pl.* **-e** (pa-pi:r), paper
der **Lehnstuhl,** *pl.* **-̈e,** easy-chair
das **Pult,** *pl.* **-e,** desk; das **Sofa,** *pl.* **-s,**[1] sofa
die **Landkarte,** *pl.* **-n,** map
das **Bücherbrett,** *pl.* **-er,** bookshelf
geben, to give; **reichen,** to hand
nennen, to name, tell the name of
leicht, easy; **schwer,** difficult

da, there; **dann,** then
endlich (ent-lix), finally
nun, now; **jetzt,** now
überall (y:-ber-al), everywhere
wieder, again; **immer wieder,** again and again
jedesmal, everytime
mir, me, to me, for me (*dat. of* **ich**)
bis, until
damit, with it, with them

NOTE 1. A few German words borrowed from English or French have a plural in **-s. das Auto die Autos; das Büro die Büros; das Sofa die Sofas**

Einige Länder and Sprachen von Europa (oy-ro:-pa)
Some Countries and Languages of Europe

das Land	Deutschland	Frankreich	Spanien	Itálien
	doytʃ-lant	frank-raix	ʃpa:-nien	i-ta:-lien
die Sprache	Deutsch	Französisch	Spanisch	Italiénisch
	doytʃ	fran-tsø-ziʃ	ʃpa:niʃ	i-ta-lie:-niʃ

Deutsche Ausdrücke

heute abend, this evening
heute morgen, this morning
ja, indeed (*for emphasis*)
Das ist ja leicht. That is indeed easy.
Stimmt! (ʃtimt) That's correct.
Was für ein, what kind of
Was für ein Mann ist er?
What kind of a man is he?

Er gibt ihm die Hand.
He shakes hands with him.
Nicht wahr? Isn't it true?
Er kommt heute, nicht wahr?
He is coming today, isn't he?
Er spricht Deutsch, nicht wahr?
He speaks German, doesn't he?

Grammar Notes and Practical Exercises

1 Present Tense of *geben*, to give; *müssen*, to have to, must

ich gebe	wir geben	ich muß	wir müssen
du gibst	ihr gebt	du mußt	ihr müßt
er, sie es gibt	sie (Sie) geben	er, sie es muß	sie (Sie) müssen

Imperative: **gib! gebt! geben Sie!**

(*a*) Note the change from **e** to **i** in the second and third person singular of **geben,** and in the imperative singular.

(*b*) Note the irregularity of **müssen,** with no **e-** ending in the first and third persons, singular.

2 The Dative or 'to' Case: Nouns, Definite and Indefinite Articles

In the sentence: I give the man the book, the direct object is *the book* and the indirect object is *the man*, with 'to' understood. Another way of saying this sentence is: I give the book *to* the man.

In German the indirect object is in the *dative* or 'to' case. The direct object is, of course, in the *accusative* case. In the following sentences note the formation of articles and nouns in the dative cases, singular and plural.

Ich gebe **dem (einem) Mann** das Buch.   I give *the (a) man* the book.
Ich gebe **der (einer) Frau** die Feder.   I give *the (a) woman* the pen.
Ich gebe **dem (einem) Kind** den Ball.   I give *the (a) child* the ball.

Ich gebe ⎰ **den Männern** ⎱ die Bücher.   I give ⎰ *the men* ⎱ the books.
         ⎱ **den Frauen** ⎰   ⎱ *the women* ⎰
           den Kindern   *the children*

Definite Article

	Singular			Plural
	masc.	fem.	neut.	m.f.n.
Nom.	der	die	das	die
Dat	dem	der	dem	den
Acc.	den	die	das	die

Indefinite Article

	Singular			Plural
	masc.	*fem.*	*neut.*	*m.f.n.*
Nom.	ein	eine	ein	keine (no)
Dat.	einem	einer	einem	keinen
Acc.	einen	eine	ein	keine

(a) The dative case endings of the definite and indefinite articles (and **kein**) in the singular are: masculine and neuter, **-em**; feminine, **-er**; in the plural: **-en**.

(b) Nouns usually show no change in the dative singular. However, most masculine and all neuter monosyllables may add **-e**.

(c) The dative plural of nouns always ends in **-n**. If the nom. plur. ends in **-n**, of course no **-n** is added. Thus:

Plur. Nom.

die Schüler	die Kinder	die Söhne	die Mädchen	die Knaben

Plur. Dat.

den Schülern	den Kindern	den Söhnen	den Mädchen	den Knaben

(d) The indirect (dative) object must always precede the direct object noun.

3 Some common verbs that may take indirect objects

geben, to give   **bringen,** to bring   **reichen,** to hand   **schreiben,** to write
zeigen, to show   **senden,** to send   **kaufen,** to buy   **schenken,** to present

Exercise No. 25. Complete the answer to each question with the dative of the noun in parenthesis.

Beispiel: 1. Er reicht **dem Lehrer** das Buch.

1 Wem reicht er das Buch?	Er reicht —— das Buch. (der Lehrer)
2 Wem geben Sie einen Ball?	Wir geben —— einen Ball. (das Kind)'
3 Wem gibt er die Hand?	Er gibt —— die Hand. (der Freund)
4 Wem schenkt die Mutter eine Uhr?	Sie schenkt —— eine Uhr. (die Tochter)
5 Wem schreiben die Kinder einen Brief?	Sie schreiben —— einen Brief. (die Mutter)
6 Wem bringt der Vater Bilder?	Er bringt —— Bilder. (die Kinder)
7 Wem zeigt er die Landkarte?	Er zeigt —— die Landkarte. (die Schüler)
8 Wem kauft[1] die Mutter die Hüte?	Sie kauft —— die Hüte. (die Mädchen)

NOTE 1. **kaufen** to buy (something, *accusative*; for somebody, *dative*).

4 Dative: Third Person Pronouns; Interrogative *wem*? to whom?

Wem geben Sie die Bücher?	*To whom* are you giving the books?
Ich gebe **ihm (dem Mann)** die Bücher.	I am giving *him* (*the man*) the books.
Ich gebe **ihr (der Frau)** die Bücher.	I am giving *her* (*the woman*) the books.
Ich gebe **ihm (dem Kind)** die Bücher.	I am giving *him* (*the child*) the books.

Ich gebe **ihnen** { den Männern / den Frauen / den Kindern } die Bücher.

I am giving *them* $\left\{\begin{array}{l} \textit{the men} \\ \textit{the women} \\ \textit{the children} \end{array}\right\}$ the books.

The Interrogative *wer*

Nom.	wer	who
Dat.	**wem**	(to) *whom*
Acc.	wen	whom

Third Person Pronouns

	Singular			*Plural*
Nom.	er	sie	es	sie
Dat.	**ihm**	**ihr**	**ihm**	**ihnen**
Acc.	ihn	sie	es	sie

Exercise No. 26. Complete the answer to each question with the dative case of the correct third person pronoun.

Beispiel: 1. Ja, ich gebe **ihnen** den Ball.

1 Gibst du **den Kindern** den Ball?   Ja, ich gebe —— den Ball.
2 Senden Sie **den Frauen** die Blumen?   Ja, wir senden — die Blumen.
3 Kaufen Sie **der Tochter** ein Kleid?   Ja, ich kaufe — ein Kleid.
4 Schreibt er **dem Lehrer** einen Brief?   Nein, er schreibt —— keinen Brief.
5 Zeigt er **den Schülern** die Bilder?   Ja, er zeigt —— die Bilder.
6 Schenkst du **dem Vater** eine Uhr?   Ja, ich schenke —— eine Uhr.
7 Bringt sie **der Schwester** das Kleid?   Ja, sie bringt —— das Kleid.
8 Sendet er **der Mutter** den Hut?   Nein, er sendet —— den Hut nicht.

Grammar Notes and Practical Exercises

5 Prepositions with the dative

The following prepositions *always* take the dative case. Memorize them.

aus	out of	**nach**	after, to, towards
außer	except, outside of	**seit**	since, for
bei	by, at, at the house of, with	**von**	from, about, of
mit	with	**zu**	to (usually with persons)

These contractions are very common:

bei dem = beim   **von dem = vom**   **zu dem = zum**   **zu der = zur**

The prepositions **an** at, on, up against; **auf** on, upon, on top of; **in** in; and **vor** before, in front of, are used in this chapter with the dative case.

an der Wand	on the wall	**vor dem Pult**	in front of the desk
auf dem Pult	on the desk	**in dem Zimmer**	in the room
auf der Straße	on the street	**in dem Lehnstuhl**	in the armchair
auf dem Sofa	on the sofa	**in der Schule**	in the school

In Chapter 9 you will learn more about these prepositions and others like them, which *sometimes* take the dative and *sometimes* the accusative.

Exercise No. 27. Read these sentences aloud. Translate them.

1 Der Lehrer ist wieder beim Kaufmann.
2 Jeden Dienstag geht er zum Kaufmann.
3 Das Haus von Herrn C. hat sieben Zimmer.
4 Die Herren gehen aus dem Zimmer.
5 Herr C. geht mit ihm zur Tür.
6 Er sagt zum Lehrer: ,,Auf Wiedersehen!"
7 Zwei von den Kindern sind Knaben.
8 Zwei von ihnen sind Mädchen.
9 Alle außer Anna gehen zur Schule.
10 Im Sommer reist Herr C. nach München.
11 Was gebt ihr der Mutter zu Weihnachten?[1]
12 Wir geben ihr ein Halstuch.[2]
13 Warum gehen Sie nicht zum Arzt?
14 Wir kommen eben[3] vom Arzt.

NOTES: 1 **Zu Weihnachten** (vai-nax-ten) for Christmas. 2 **das Halstuch** scarf.
3 **eben** just now.

Exercise No. 28. Complete these phrases with the correct dative case endings.

1 aus d— Hause	6 mit ein— Feder	11 von d— Bilder—(*pl.*)
2 bei d— Lehrer	7 zu d— Kaufmann	12 zu d— Kinder—(*pl.*)
3 mit ein— Buch	8 von d— Mutter	13 von d— Herr—(*pl.*)
4 von d— Schule	9 bei d— Arzt	14 seit zwei Jahr—(*pl.*)
5 nach ein— Stunde	10 mit d— Schüler—(*pl.*)	15 seit zwei Monat—(*pl.*)

Exercise No. 29. Fragen

Re-read the text: **Dinge, Dinge Überall Dinge.** Then answer these questions.

1 Ist das Zimmer von Herrn Clark groß? 2 Was sehen wir an der Wand?
3 Wo steht ein Stuhl? 4 Wer ist heute abend wieder beim Kaufmann? 5 Wo sitzt
der Lehrer? 6 Wo sitzt der Kaufmann? 7 Was sieht man überall? 8 Wo spricht
man Englisch? 9 Wo muß man Deutsch sprechen? 10 Was liegt auf dem Pult?
11 Womit (with what) schreibt man? 12 Was reicht der Lehrer dem Kaufmann? 13 Wann haben die Herren wieder eine Deutschstunde? 14 Wer geht mit
Herrn Müller zur Tür? 15 Wie heißt ,,Wörterbuch" auf englisch?

Exercise No. 30. Übersetzen Sie!

1 This evening the teacher is again at the house of (**bei**) the businessman.
2 Mr. C. is sitting in the armchair. 3 The teacher hands him a pencil and
asks in German, 'What does one do (**macht man**) with a pencil?' 4 'One writes
with it,' answers Mr. C. 5 Finally, Mr. M. says to the businessman, 'That is
enough for this evening.' 6 He goes with him to the door. 7 To whom are
you sending the pictures? 8 They are coming out of the study.

CHAPTER 9

STADT UND VORSTADT
CITY AND SUBURB

1 Die Herren Clark und Müller gehen in das Arbeitszimmer. Herr Müller setzt sich auf das Sofa. Herr Clark stellt einen Tisch vor das Sofa und setzt sich dann in den Lehnstuhl. Auf dem Tisch ist ein Aschenbecher. Neben dem Aschenbecher sind Zigaretten und ein Feuerzeug.

2 Herr Müller legt seine Zigarette auf den Aschenbecher und beginnt zu reden.

3 M: Sie wohnen in der Vorstadt, aber Ihr Geschäft und Ihr Büro sind in der Stadt. Jeden Wochentag fahren Sie mit dem Zug in die Stadt, um das Geschäft zu führen. Sagen Sie doch mal: Wohnen Sie gern in der Vorstadt?

4 C: Zwar wohne ich gern in der Vorstadt, ich aber habe die Stadt auch gern.

5 M: Warum haben Sie die Stadt gern?

6 C: In der Stadt gibt es Bibliotheken, Theater, Museen, Universitäten, usw.

7 M: Es gibt auch Fabriken, Lagerhäuser, Lärm, Rauch und auf den Strassen Menschenmassen, die hin und her laufen.

8 C: Sehr richtig! Deswegen wohne ich lieber in der Vorstadt. Hier ist das Leben still und gemütlich.

9 M: Hat Frau Clark das Leben in der Vorstadt gern?

10 C: Sie hat es sehr gern. Dann und wann fährt sie in die Stadt, um Freunde zu besuchen, oder in den großen Läden Einkäufe zu machen.

11 M: Gibt es auch gute Schulen in der Vorstadt?

12 C: Die Schulen sind viel besser als in der Stadt, und die Kinder lieben ihre Lehrer und Lehrerinnen.

13 M: Das Leben in der Vorstadt scheint recht schön zu sein!

14 C: Da haben Sie recht, Herr Müller.

15 M: Ich muß Sie loben, Herr Clark. Sie machen ja große Fortschritte im Deutschen.

16 C: Es ist sehr nett von Ihnen,[1] das zu sagen.

1 Mr. Clark and Mr. Müller go into the study. Mr. Müller sits down on the sofa. Mr. Clark puts a table in front of the sofa and then sits down in an easychair. On the table is an ashtray. Next to the ashtray are cigarettes and a lighter.

2 Mr. Müller puts his cigarette on the ashtray and begins to talk.

3 M: You live in the suburbs, but your business and your office are in the city. Every weekday you ride by train into the city in order to do business. Tell me then: Do you like to live in the suburbs?

4 C: To be sure, I like to live in the suburbs, but I also like the city.

5 M: Why do you like the city?

6 C: In the city there are libraries, theatres, museums, universities, etc.

7 M: There are also factories, warehouses, noise, smoke, and on the streets crowds of people who are running to and fro.

8 C: That's right. Therefore I prefer to live in the suburbs. Here life is quiet and comfortable.

9 M: Does Mrs. Clark like life in the suburbs?

10 C: She likes it very much. Now and then she goes into the city in order to visit friends or to shop in the big stores.

11 M: Are there also good schools in the suburbs?

12 C: The schools are much better than in the city, and the children love their masters and mistresses.

13 M: Life in the suburbs seems to be very pleasant.

14 C: You are right there, Mr. Müller.

15 M: I must praise you, Mr. Clark. You are indeed making good progress in German.

16 C: It's very nice of you to say that.

NOTE 1. **Ihnen** dative case of **Sie**. It is like the dative of **sie** (they), but always with a capital letter.

Wortschatz

der Aschenbecher, *pl.* -, ashtray
das Feuerzeug, *pl.* -e, lighter
die Stadt, *pl.* ⁻e, city
die Zigarette, *pl.* -n, cigarette
die Fabrík, *pl.* -en, factory
das Lagerhaus, *pl.* ⁻er, warehouse
das Geschäft, *pl.* -e, business
der Laden, *pl.* ⁻. store, shop
der Mensch, *pl.* -en, human being, man
die Menschenmasse, *pl.* -n, crowd of people
das Leben, *pl.*, -, life; die Zeit, *pl.* -en, time
der Lärm, noise; der Rauch, smoke
das Museum, *pl.* Muséen, museum
die Universität (u-ni-vɛr-zi-tɛːt), *pl.* -en, university
die Bibliothék (bi-bli-o-teːk), *pl.* -en, library
das Theáter (teː-aː-ter), *pl.* -, theatre
  ins Theater gehen, to go to the theatre
der Zug, *pl.* ⁻e, train
beginnen, to begin; scheinen, to seem
führen, to lead; das Geschäft führen, to carry on (do) business
legen, to put; loben, to praise
besser, better; besser als, better than
gemütlich, pleasant, comfortable
nett, nice; nett von Ihnen, nice of you
hin und her, to and fro
dann und wann, now and then

gern, gladly   **lieber,** more gladly, preferably

A verb + **gern** indicates *liking* for a particular thing or action.
A verb + **lieber** indicates *preference* for a particular thing or action.

Ich habe die Stadt gern, aber ich habe die Vorstadt lieber.	I like the city, but I prefer the suburbs.
Er geht gern ins Kino, aber er geht lieber ins Theater oder ins Konzert.	He likes to go to the cinema but he prefers to go to the theatre or to a concert.

Es gibt, there is, there are

Es gibt (*lit.* it gives) + an object means *there is* or *there are.*

Es gibt viel Lärm in der Straße.	There is a lot of noise in the street.
Es gibt viele Theater in der Stadt.	There are many theatres in the city.
Was gibt's Neues? Es gibt nichts Neues.	What's your news? There's nothing to report.

In the sense of *to be present* (or *absent*) use es ist or es sind.

Es ist kein Arzt da.	There is no doctor there.
Es sind heute fünf Schüler abwesend.	There are five pupils absent today.

Deutsche Ausdrücke

zwar = es ist wahr = it is true
Sie haben recht. You are right.
Sie haben unrecht. You are wrong.
Er macht Fortschritte. He makes progress.
Sie macht Einkäufe. She shops, goes shopping (makes purchases).

um . . . zu, in order to
Sie geht in die Stadt, um Einkäufe zu machen. She goes to the city to shop.
Ich arbeite, um Geld zu verdienen. I work in order to earn money.

Grammar Notes and Practical Exercises

1 Present Tense of *laufen*, to run; *fahren*, to ride

ich laufe	wir laufen	ich fahre	wir fahren
du läufst	ihr lauft	du fährst	ihr fahrt
er, sie, es läuft	sie (Sie) laufen	er sie, es fährt	sie (Sie) fahren
Imperative: laufe! lauft! laufen Sie!		fahre! fahrt! fahren Sie!	

Some verbs add an *Umlaut* to the vowel a in the second and third person singular. This *Umlaut* does not appear in the imperative.

2 Prepositions with the Dative or Accusative

You have already learned:

The prepositions **durch, für, gegen, ohne, um** always take the accusative case.

The prepositions **aus, außer, bei, mit, nach, seit, von, zu** always take the dative case.

You will now learn nine prepositions, which sometimes take the dative and sometimes the accusative case. They are usually called the 'doubtful prepositions'. Memorize them.

an	on, at, up against	über	over, above
auf	on, upon, on top of	unter	under, among
hinter	behind	vor	before, in front of
in	in, into	zwischen	between
neben	next to, near		

Some common contractions are:

an dem = am   an das = ans   auf das = aufs   in dem = im   in das = ins

Study the following sentences and you will easily discover the rule which will tell you when to use the dative and when the accusative after the doubtful prepositions.

Wo? Where (place where)
Dative

1 Das Bild ist **an der Wand.**
The picture is on the wall.

2 Herr M. sitzt **auf dem Stuhl.**
Mr. M. is sitting on the chair.

3 Der Garten ist **hinter dem Haus.**
The garden is behind the house.

4 Das Büro ist **in der Stadt.**
The office is in the city.

5 Der Tisch ist **neben dem Sofa.**
The table is next to the sofa.

6 Das Porträt hängt **über dem Klavier.**
The portrait hangs over the piano.

7 Der Ball liegt **unter dem Bett.**
The ball is lying under the bed.

8 Das Kind steht **vor der Tür.**
The child stands before the door.

9 Der Stuhl steht **zwischen den Fenstern.**
The chair stands between the windows.

Wohin? Where (place to which)
Accusative

1 Er hängt das Bild **an die Wand.**
He hangs the picture on the wall.

2 Herr C. setzt sich **auf den Stuhl.**
Mr. C. sits down on the chair.

3 Hans läuft **hinter das Haus.**
Jack runs behind the house.

4 Jeden Tag fährt er **in die Stadt.**
Every day he rides into the city.

5 Er stellt den Tisch **neben das Sofa.**
He puts the table next to the sofa.

6 Er hängt es **über das Klavier.**
He hangs it over the piano.

7 Der Ball rollt **unter das Bett.**
The ball rolls under the bed.

8 Das Kind läuft **vor die Tür.**
The child runs in front of the door.

9 Er stellt ihn **zwischen die Fenster.**
He puts it between the windows.

The doubtful prepositions take the dative case when they indicate *place where*. They answer the question **wo? Wo** steht der Stuhl? Where is the chair standing?

They take the accusative when they indicate *place to which*. They answer the question **wohin. Wohin** stellt er den Stuhl? Where is he putting the chair?

Exercise No. 31. Practise aloud.

Wo ist der Kaufmann? Er ist im (in dem) Arbeitzimmer (im Büro; im Theater; im Konzert; in der Fabrik; in der Vorstadt; im Garten).

Wohin geht der Kaufmann? Er geht ins (in das) Arbeitszimmer (ins Büro; ins Theater; ins Konzert; in die Fabrik; in die Vorstadt; in den Garten).

Wo ist der Knabe? Er ist im (in dem) Hause (im Park; im Garten; im Wasser; in der Schule; auf dem Gras).

Wohin läuft der Knabe? Er läuft ins (in das) Haus (in den Park; in den Garten; ins Wasser; in die Schule; auf das Gras).

Wo liegt der Ball? Er liegt unter dem Bett (neben dem Klavier; hinter der Tür; zwischen den Fenstern; vor dem Mädchen; auf der Straße).

Wohin rollt der Ball? Er rollt unter das Bett (neben das Klavier; hinter die Tür; zwischen die Fenster; vor das Mädchen; auf die Straße).

Exercise No. 32. Fill in the missing dative or accusative endings.

Beispiel: 1 Das Auto fährt vor **die** Schule.

1 Das Auto fährt vor d— Schule. **2** Die Herren sitzen oben in d— Arbeitszimmer. **3** Hängen Sie das Bild dort an d— Wand! **4** In d— Stadt gibt es viele Bibliotheken. **5** Er muß jeden Wochentag in d— Stadt fahren. **6** Der Kaufmann setzt sich neben d— Lehrer. **7** Die Kinder spielen nicht auf d— Straße. **8** Die Papiere liegen hier unter d— Bücher—. **9** Er stellt den Aschenbecher auf d— Tisch. **10** Was steht dort hinter d— Tür? **11** Er hängt den Hut hinter d— Tür. **12** Das Bild hängt zwischen d— Fenster— (*pl.*).

3 *da*(r) and *wo*(r) combined with prepositions

Liegt das Buch auf dem Tisch?	Is the book lying on the table?
Ja, es liegt **darauf.**	Yes, it is lying *on it*.
Schreiben sie **mit den Federn?**	Are they writing with the pens?
Ja, sie schreiben **damit.**	Yes, they are writing *with them*.
Worauf liegt das Buch?	*On what* is the book lying?
Es liegt auf dem Tisch.	It is lying on the table.

4 Some common combinations of *da*(r) and *wo*(r) + a preposition

damit	with it, with them	**womit**	with what
darauf	on it, on them	**wovon**	from, of, about what
dafür	for it, for them	**worauf**	on what
darin	in it, in them	**wofür**	for what
davon	from, of, about it (them)	**worin**	in what

Compare the above forms with the old English words *therewith, wherewith, therein, wherein,* etc.

da(r) and **wo**(r) + *a preposition* refer only to things, never to persons. When prepositions are used with persons, personal pronouns must be used. Thus:

mit wem	with whom	**womit**	with what
mit ihm (ihr, etc.)	with him (her, etc.)	**damit**	with it or them (things)
von wem	from whom	**wovon**	from what
von ihm (ihr, etc.)	from him (her, etc.)	**davon**	from it or them (things)

Exercise No. 33. Fragen

Re-read the text: **Stadt und Vorstadt.** Then answer these questions.

1 Wohin gehen Herr Clark und Herr Müller? **2** Wohin setzt sich Herr Müller? **3** Wohin setzt sich Herr Clark? **4** Wohin stellt Herr Clark den Tisch? **5** Was steht darauf? **6** Was steht neben dem Aschenbecher? **7** Wohin legt der Lehrer seine Zigarette? **8** Wo wohnt der Kaufmann? **9** Wohin fährt er jeden Wochentag? **10** Wo ist sein Büro? **11** Wohnt er lieber in der Vorstadt als in der Stadt? **12** Wer geht dann und wann in die Stadt? **13** Wie ist das Leben in der Vorstadt? **14** Wo sind die Schulen besser, in der Stadt oder in der Vorstadt? **15** Wer macht grosse Fortschritte im Deutschen?

Exercise No. 34. Übersetzen Sie!

1 We go into the study.   2 A sofa and an easy-chair are in the study.   3 In front of the sofa is a table. 4 On (an) the wall are pictures. 5 You are right, a map is hanging between the two windows. 6 Mr. M. is sitting in the easy-chair. 7 Mr. C. sits down on the sofa. 8 Put your cigarette on the ashtray. 9 We do not live in the city. 10 I travel into the city every weekday.

CHAPTER 10

DAS WOHNZIMMER DES KAUFMANNS
THE LIVING-ROOM OF THE BUSINESSMAN

1 Wir wissen schon, das Haus des Kaufmanns ist nicht groß. Es ist doch nett und bequem. Die Zimmer des Hauses sind alle schön möbliert. Wir kennen schon das Arbeitszimmer. Sehen wir uns nun das Wohnzimmer näher an!

2 Das Wohnzimmer hat zwei große Fenster.

3 In einer Ecke des Zimmers, neben einem Fenster, steht ein Klavier. Eine Photographie der vier Kinder von Herrn Clark steht auf dem Klavier. Außer dem Klavier sind im Zimmer ein Sofa, mehrere Stühle, zwei Tische, drei Lampen, ein Radio, ein Fernsehapparat, und einige Bilder. An der Wand hinter dem Klavier hängt das Porträt einer Frau.

4 Heute abend sitzen die Herren Clark und Müller während des Deutschunterrichts im Wohnzimmer. Sie plaudern. Hier ist ein Teil des Gesprächs.

5 M: Wessen Porträt hängt dort an der Wand hinter dem Klavier?

6 Das ist das Porträt meiner Frau.

7 M: Spielt Frau Clark Klavier?

8 C: Ja, sie spielt Klavier und zwar sehr gut.

9 M: Spielen Sie auch Klavier?

10 C: Leider nicht. Ich schwärme für Musik, spiele aber kein Musikinstrument. Während des Winters gehen wir oft ins Konzert.

11 M: Sie sind sicher Kunstliebhaber.

12 C: Das versteht sich. Ich bin ja der Chef einer Firma, die[1] Kunstgegenstände importiert, nicht wahr?

13 M: Und Sie finden das Geschäft interessant?

14 C: Außerordentlich interessant.

15 M: Nun, ich möchte mit Ihnen über das Geschäft weitersprechen, aber ich muß gehen, denn es ist schon spät.

16 Sie geben sich die Hand und sagen: „Auf Wiedersehen!"

NOTE 1. *die* (*which*) is used here as a relative pronoun and agrees with its antecedent **Firma** in number and gender. It is in the nominative case, subject of the relative clause. Observe that in subordinate clauses the verb stands last.

1 We already know the home of the businessman is not large. It is, however, nice and comfortable. The rooms of the house are all beautifully furnished. We are already acquainted with the study. Let us now have a closer look at the living-room.

2 The living-room has two large windows.

3 In a corner of the room, near a window, stands a piano. A photograph of Mr. Clark's four children stands on the piano. Beside the piano, there are a

sofa, several chairs, two tables, three lamps, a radio, a television, and some pictures in the room. On the wall behind the piano hangs the portrait of a woman.

4 This evening Mr. Clark and Mr. Müller are sitting in the living-room during the German lesson. They are chatting. Here is part of the conversation.

5 M: Whose portrait hangs over there on the wall behind the piano?
6 C: That is the portrait of my wife.
7 M: Does Mrs. Clark play the piano?
8 C: Yes, she plays the piano very well indeed.
9 M: Do you also play the piano?
10 C: Unfortunately not. I'm enthusiastic about music, but I don't play any musical instrument. During the winter we often go to concerts.
11 M: You are, I am sure, an art lover.
12 C: That goes without saying. I am as you know the head of a firm which imports art objects.
13 M: And do you find the business interesting?
14 C: Extremely interesting.
15 M: Well, I should like to talk further with you about the business, but I must go, for it is already late.
16 They shake hands and say: 'Good-bye.'

Wortschatz

der **Chef**, *pl.* **-s**, head, manager, boss
die **Firma**, *pl.* **-en**, firm
das **Musíkinstrument**,[1] *pl.* **-e**, musical instrument
das **Klavier** (kla-**vi:**r), *pl.* **-e**, piano
das **Radio**, *pl.* **-s**, radio
der **Fernsehapparát**, *pl.* **-e**,[2] television set
die **Kunst**, *pl.* **⁻e**, art
der **Kunstliebhaber**, *pl.* **-**, art lover
das **Porträt**, *pl.* **-s**, portrait
die **Photographie**, *pl.* **-n**,[3] photograph
die **Ecke**, *pl.* **-n**, corner
die **Lampe**, *pl.* **-n**, lamp
der **Deutschunterricht**, German instruction
finden, to find
hängen, to hang

schwärmen für, to be enthusiastic about
verstéhen, to understand
mehrere (*me:/rere*), several
nah, near; **näher**, nearer
nun, now
spät, late; **früh**, early
außerordentlich,[4] extremely
doch, nevertheless, however
sicher, sure, surely, I am sure
uns, us, to us, for us (dat. and acc. of **wir**)
mein, my (like **ein**, **kein**)
denn, for, because
Ich muß gehen, denn es ist schon spät.
über, over, about (in the sense of about, **über**, always takes the *acc.*)

NOTES. 1 mu:-**zik**-in-stru-ment. 2 **fern**-ze:-a-pa-ra:t. 3 fo:-to-gra-**fi:** 4 au-ser-or-**dent**-lix.

Deutsche Ausdrücke

das versteht sich, that goes without saying (that is understood)

Wir möchten ein neues Auto kaufen.
We would like to buy a new car.

möchte, should like, would like
Ich möchte darüber weiter sprechen.
I should like to talk further
about it.

leider, unfortunately
Ich kann leider nicht gehen.
Unfortunately I cannot go.

Grammar Notes and Practical Exercises

1 Present Tense of *kennen*, to know, to be acquainted with a person or a thing; *wissen*, to know (facts)

ich kenne	wir kennen	ich weiß	wir wissen
du kennst	ihr kennt	du weißt	ihr wißt
er, sie, es kennt	sie (Sie) kennen	er, sie, es weiß	sie (Sie) wissen

The present of **kennen** is regular. Note carefully the irregular singular of **wissen.**

kennen means *to know* in the sense of to be acquainted with, to be familiar with.

wissen means to know facts.

Ich kenne den Mann.	I know (am acquainted with) the man.
Wir kennen das Haus.	We know (are acquainted with) the house.
Ich weiß, wo er wohnt.	I know where he lives.
Er weiß, wie sie heißt	He knows her name.

Exercise No. 35. Practise aloud.

1 — Kennst du den Mann?
— Ich kenne ihn gut.
— Weißt du, wo er wohnt?
— Das weiß ich nicht.
2 — Kennst du dieses Haus?
— Ja, es ist die Wohnung eines Kaufmanns.
— Weißt du vielleicht, wie er heißt?
— Ja, ich weiß es; er heißt Robert Clark.

3 — Wissen Sie, was er verkauft?
— Er verkauft Kunstgegenstände.
— Wo ist sein Geschäft?
— Ich weiß es nicht.
4 — Kennen Sie dieses Fräulein?
— Natürlich kenne ich sie.[1]
— Wissen Sie, wie alt sie ist?
— Das weiß ich nicht.

NOTE 1. The pronoun **sie** is commonly used for **das Fräulein** and **das Mädchen.**

2 The Genitive Case

The genitive case is another name for the possessive case.

In English possession is expressed by '*s* and *s*', and by the preposition *of.*

> The man's house (the house of the man) is new.
> The pupils' books (the books of the pupils) are old.

In the following sentences note the formation of the article and noun in the genitive case.

| Das Haus **des Mannes** ist neu. | The house *of the man* (the man's house) is new. |
| Das Kleid **der Frau** ist weiss. | The dress *of the woman* (the woman's dress) is white. |

Der Ball **des Kindes** ist rot.

The ball *of the child* (the child's ball) is red.

Die Hüte **der Männer, der Frauen und der Kinder** sind schön.

The hats *of the men, women,* and *children* are pretty. (The men's, women's, and children's hats are pretty.)

	Definite Article					**Indefinite Article**			
	Singular			*Plural*		*Singular*			*Plural*
	masc.	fem.	neut.	m.f.n.		masc.	fem.	neut.	m.f.n.
Nom.	der	die	das	die	Nom.	ein	eine	ein	keine
Gen.	des	der	des	der	Gen.	eines	einer	eines	keiner
Dat.	dem	der	dem	den	Dat.	einem	einer	einem	keinen
Acc.	den	die	das	die	Acc.	einen	eine	ein	keine

(*a*) The genitive case endings of the definite and indefinite articles (and **kein**) in the singular are: masculine and neuter **-es**; feminine **-er**; in the plural **-er**.

(*b*) Most masculine and neuter nouns add **-s** or **-es** in the genitive singular.[1] One-syllable nouns often add **-es**.[1]

N.	der Lehrer	das Mädchen	der Hut
G.	des Lehrers	des Mädchens	des Hutes
N.	der Mann	das Kind	
G.	des Mannes	des Kindes	

(*c*) Feminine nouns add no endings in the singular.

N.	die Mutter	die Schwester	die Tochter
G.	der Mutter	der Schwester	der Tochter
N.	die Tür	die Wand	
G.	der Tür	der Wand	

(*d*) The nominative plural of the noun remains unchanged in the genitive plural.

Nom. Plur.	die Lehrer	die Hüte	die Männer
Gen. Plur.	der Lehrer	der Hüte	der Männer
Nom. Plur.	die Schwestern	die Mädchen	
Gen. Plur.	der Schwestern	der Mädchen	

(*e*) The noun in the genitive case usually follows the noun by which it is possessed.

ein Teil des Gesprächs   die Zimmer des Hauses   Das Portrait einer Frau

(*f*) A phrase with **von** is often used instead of a genitive. Thus:

die Wohnung von Herrn[1] Clark = die Wohnung des Herrn[1] Clark

NOTE 1. A few masculine and neuter nouns add **-n** or **-en** in the genitive case. Such nouns add **-n** or **-en** in all other cases, singular and plural. Nouns of this type you have met already are: **der Knabe**, gen. **des Knaben**, *pl.* **die Knaben; der Herr**, *gen.* **des Herrn**, *pl.* **die Herren; der Student**, gen. **des Studenten**, *pl.* **die Studenten.**

3 The Interrogative Pronoun *wer* in the Genitive Case

Wessen Hut ist grau?	Whose hat is grey?
Der Hut des Lehrers ist grau.	The teacher's hat is grey.
Wessen Hüte sind schön?	Whose hats are pretty?
Die Hüte der Frauen sind schön.	The women's hats are pretty.

Nom. **wer,** who   *Gen.* **wessen,** whose   *Dat.* **wem,** to whom
Acc. **wen,** whom

4 Genitive Prepositions

Very few prepositions take the genitive case. The most common are: **während** during; **wegen** on account of; **anstatt (statt)** instead of; **trotz** in spite of. Thus: **während der Nacht** during the night.

Exercise No. 36. Practise aloud.

1 Wessen Wohnung ist nicht groß? Die Wohnung des Kaufmanns (des Lehrers, der Lehrerin, das Arztes, des Schülers, der Schülerin, des Freundes, der Freundin, der Frauen, der Herren) ist nicht groß.
2 Wessen Porträt hängt an der Wand? Das Porträt des Vaters (der Mutter, des Kindes, des Onkels, der Tante, des Bruders, der Schwester, der Kinder) hängt an der Wand.
3 Wessen Hüte liegen auf dem Sofa? Die Hüte der Knaben (der Mädchen, der Kinder, der Schüler, der Schülerinnen, der Lehrer, der Lehrerinnen) liegen auf dem Sofa.

Exercise No. 37. Complete the sentences with the missing genitive case endings.
1 Wo ist die Wohnung d— Kaufmann—?   2 Die Farbe d— Klavier— ist schwarz. 3 Die Farbe d— Automobil— (*sing.*) ist blau. 4 Die Farbe d— Kleid— (*pl.*) ist grün. 5 Die Farbe d— Tinte ist schwarz. 6 Die Farbe d— Bleistift— (*pl.*) ist rot. 7 Dort hängt das Porträt ein— Frau. 8 Hier hängt das Porträt ein— Mann—. Die Farben d— Landkarte sind grün, grau und braun. 10 Wo ist die Wohnung d— Arzt—? 11 Ich arbeite während d— Tag—, aber er arbeitet während d— Nacht. 12 Wegen d— Lärm— kann ich nicht arbeiten.

Exercise No. 38. Fragen

Re-read the text: **Das Wohnzimmer des Kaufmanns.** Then answer these questions.
1 Was wissen wir schon? 2 Was kennen wir schon? 3 Wo steht ein Klavier? 4 Steht eine Photographie darauf? 5 Wessen Photographie steht auf dem Klavier? 6 Wessen Porträt hängt über dem Klavier? 7 Wo sitzen die Herren während der Deutschstunde? 8 Wessen Frau spielt sehr gut Klavier? 9 Wohin gehen Herr und Frau Clark oft im Winter? 10 Ist das Geschäft des Kaufmanns interessant? 11 Ist Herr Clark der Chef der Firma?

Exercise No. 39. Übersetzen Sie!
1 Are you acquainted with the businessman's firm?   2 Mr. C. is the head of the firm. 3 We know where the businessman lives. 4 His house is in the

suburbs. 5 The rooms of the house are not large. 6 A piano is in a corner of the living-room. 7 A photograph of the children is on the piano. 8 The colour of the piano is black. 9 On (**an**) the wall hangs the portrait of (**von**) Mrs. C. 10 The boys' room (the room of the boys) is larger than the girls' room (room of the girls).

CHAPTER 11

REVISION OF CHAPTERS 1–10

Summary of Some Common Nouns (Singular and Plural)

Practise these nouns aloud, in the singular and plural.

GROUP I No Ending Added (Umlaut where possible)

der Vater	die Väter	der Onkel	die Onkel
der Bruder	die Brüder	der Garten	die Gärten
der Lehrer	die Lehrer	das Mädchen	die Mädchen
der Schüler	die Schüler	das Fräulein	die Fräulein
	das Zimmer	die Zimmer	
	das Theater	die Theater	
	die Mutter	die Mütter	
	die Tochter	die Töchter	

GROUP II Adds -e

der Sohn	die Söhne	der Bleistift	die Bleistifte
der Hut	die Hüte	der Tisch	die Tische
der Stuhl	die Stühle	die Hand	die Hände
der Tag	die Tage	die Wand	die Wände
	die Stadt	die Städte	
	das Ding	die Dinge	
	das Jahr	die Jahre	
	das Papier	die Papiere	

GROUP III Adds -er (Umlaut where possible)

der Mann	die Männer	das Haus	die Häuser
das Kind	die Kinder	das Bild	die Bilder
	das Buch	die Bücher	
	das Land	die Länder	

GROUP IV Adds -n or -en

der Herr	die Herren	die Schule	die Schulen
der Mensch	die Menschen	die Tante	die Tanten
der Knabe	die Knaben	die Strasse	die Strassen
	die Stunde	die Stunden	
	die Schwester	die Schwestern	
	die Lehrerin	die Lehrerinnen	

56

Verbs

1 gehen	16 hören	31 er spricht
2 kommen	17 spielen	32 geben
3 machen	18 schreiben	33 er gibt
4 stehen	19 sagen	34 fahren
5 sitzen	20 fragen	35 er fährt
6 liegen	21 antworten	36 laufen
7 legen	22 er antwortet	37 er läuft
8 reichen	23 kennen	38 haben
9 wohnen	24 reden	39 er hat
10 senden	25 er redet	40 sein
11 hängen	26 zählen	41 er ist
12 besuchen	27 bringen	42 wissen
13 plaudern	28 sehen	43 er weiß
14 lernen	29 er sieht	44 müssen
15 lehren	30 sprechen	45 er muß

1 to go	16 to hear	31 he speaks
2 to come	17 to play	32 to give
3 to make	18 to write	33 he gives
4 to stand	19 to say	34 to ride
5 to sit	20 to ask	35 he rides
6 to lie	21 to answer	36 to run
7 to put	22 he answers	37 he runs
8 to hand	23 to know (persons)	38 to have
9 to live (dwell)	24 to talk	39 he has
10 to send	25 he talks	40 to be
11 to hang	26 to count	41 he is
12 to visit	27 to bring	42 to know (facts)
13 to chat	28 to see	43 he knows
14 to learn	29 he sees	44 to have to
15 to teach	30 to speak	45 he must

Prepositions—*Memorize in the Numbered Order*

With Dative Only

1 aus	4 mit	7 von
2 außer	5 nach	8 zu
3 bei	6 seit	

1 out of	4 with	7 from, of
2 besides, except	5 after, to	8 to
3 at the house of	6 since	

With Accusative Only

1 durch	3 gegen	5 um
2 für	4 ohne	

1 through	3 against, towards	5 round, around
2 for	4 without	

With Dative (place where)   With Accusative (place to which)

1 an	4 in	7 unter
2 auf	5 neben	8 vor
3 hinter	6 über	9 zwischen

1 at, on (up against)	4 in, into	7 under
2 on, on top of	5 near, next to	8 before
3 behind	6 over, above	9 between

With Genitive Only

| 1 während | 3 anstatt (statt) | 1 during | 3 instead of |
| 2 wegen | 4 trotz | 2 on account of | 4 in spite of |

Expressions

1 Hier spricht man Deutsch.
2 Wie heißen Sie?
3 Ich heiße Schmidt.
4 Er macht eine Reise.
5 mal = einmal
6 Sagen Sie mal . . . !
7 Sehen wir uns mal das Haus an!
8 Ich wohne gern hier.
9 auf deutsch (auf englisch)
10 Er wohnt lieber in der Stadt.
11 Sie macht Einkäufe.
12 also
13 Stimmt!
14 Er macht Fortschritte.
15 Jawohl!
16 Er gibt ihm die Hand.
17 Sie ist zu Hause.
18 Ich gehe nach Hause.

1 Here one speaks (they, people speak) German.
2 What is your name?
3 My name is Schmidt.
4 He is taking a trip.
5 once, just
6 Just tell me. . . .
7 Just let us have a look at the house.
8 I like living here.
9 in German (in English)
10 He prefers to live in the city.
11 She goes shopping.
12 so, and so, thus
13 That's correct.
14 He makes progress.
15 Yes, indeed.
16 He shakes hands with him.
17 She is at home.
18 I am going home.

Exercise No. 40. Select the words from Column II which best complete the sentences begun in Column I.

Beispiel: (1d) Ich bin ein Importeur von Kunstgegenständen aus Deutschland.

I	II
1 Ich bin ein Importeur von	(*a*) sind dort auf dem Aschenbecher.
2 Jeden Dienstag sitzt Herr Müller	(*b*) dort auf den Aschenbecher.
3 Nennt man in Deutschland die Dinge	(*c*) denn da ist es still und gemütlich.
4 Legen Sie, bitte, Ihre Zigarette	(*d*) Kunstgegenständen aus Deutschland.
5 Während des Deutschunterrichts	(*e*) leider spiele ich kein Musikinstrument.
6 Ich wohne lieber in der Vorstadt,	(*f*) auf deutsch oder auf englisch?
7 Die Zigaretten und das Feuerzeug	(*g*) im Arbeitszimmer beim Kaufmann.
8 Ich schwärme für die Musik, aber	(*h*) eine Reise nach Deutschland machen.
9 Im Sommer möchte ich	(*i*) und das Haus des Kaufmanns an!
10 Sehen wir uns nun den Garten	(*j*) rauchen die Herren Zigaretten.

Exercise No. 41. Make compound nouns of the following pairs of nouns.

Translate them. Remember: The gender of the compound noun is that of the last noun in the compound. Thus: **die Hand + der Schuh = der Handschuh** glove (*lit.* handshoe)

1 **das Haus + die Tür**	6 **das Deutsch + der Lehrer**
2 **die Wand + die Uhr**	7 **die Wörter + das Buch**
3 **der Schlaf + das Zimmer**	8 **das Geschäft(s) + die Reise**
4 **die Bilder + das Buch**	9 **die Musik + das Instrument**
5 **der Garten + das Haus**	10 **der Vater + das Land**

Grammar Revision and Practical Exercises

1. Noun Declensions

You have learned the forms and uses of four cases of nouns with the definite and indefinite article and **kein**.

To decline a noun with its article means to give all four cases in the singular and plural. This is called a declension, and is a handy method for summarizing and remembering the case forms. Here are the declensions of some familiar nouns.

	Singular	*Plural*
Nom.	**der (ein) Vater**	**die (keine) Väter**
Gen.	**des (eines) Vaters**	**der (keiner) Väter**
Dat.	**dem (einem) Vater**	**den (keinen) Vätern**
Acc.	**den (einen) Vater**	**die (keine) Väter**

	Singular	*Plural*
Nom.	**das (ein) Kind**	**die (keine) Kinder**
Gen.	**des (eines) Kindes**	**der (keiner) Kinder**
Dat.	**dem (einem) Kind(e)**	**den (keinen) Kindern**
Acc.	**das (ein) Kind**	**die (keine) Kinder**

	Singular	*Plural*
Nom.	**der (ein) Sohn**	**die (keine) Söhne**
Gen.	**des (eines) Sohnes**	**der (keiner) Söhne**
Dat.	**dem (einem) Sohn(e)**	**den (keinen) Söhnen**
Acc.	**den (einen) Sohn**	**die (keine) Söhne**

	Singular	*Plural*
Nom.	**die (eine) Frau**	**die (keine) Frauen**
Gen.	**der (einer) Frau**	**der (keiner) Frauen**
Dat.	**der (einer) Frau**	**den (keinen) Frauen**
Acc.	**die (eine) Frau**	**die (keine) Frauen**

2. Rules of Noun Declension

In the Singular

(*a*) Feminine nouns take no endings in the singular.

(*b*) Most masculine and all neuter nouns add **-s** or **-es** in the genitive singular; usually **-s** with nouns of more than one syllable and **-es** with one-syllable nouns.

(*c*) Masculine and neuter nouns of one syllable may add **-e** in the dative singular.

(*d*) The nominative and accusative singular are usually alike.

In the Plural

(*a*) The nominative plural of nouns must be memorized.

(*b*) The genitive and accusative plural are like the nominative.

(c) The dative plural must add -n unless the nominative plural already ends in -n (den Vätern, den Söhnen, den Kindern, den Frauen).

Exercise No. 42. Practise aloud.

Wer ist hier?   *Who* is here?

Nom. Sing.   Der Vater (der Sohn, das Kind, die Frau) ist hier.
Nom. Plur.   Die Väter (die Söhne, die Kinder, die Frauen) sind hier.

Wessen Bücher liegen dort? *Whose* books are lying there?

Gen. Sing.   Die Bücher **des Vaters** (des Sohnes, des Kindes, der Frau) liegen dort.
Gen. Plur.   Die Bücher **der Väter** (der Söhne, der Kinder, der Frauen) liegen dort.

Wem geben Sie die Bücher? To *whom* are you giving the books?

Dat. Sing.   Ich gebe **dem Vater** (dem Sohn, dem Kind[e], der Frau) die Bücher.
Dat. Plur.   Ich gebe **den Vätern** (den Söhnen, den Kindern, den Frauen) die Bücher.

Wen sehen Sie dort? *Whom* do you see there?

Acc. Sing.   Ich sehe **den Vater** (den Sohn, das Kind, die Frau) dort.
Acc. Plur.   Ich sehe **die Väter** (die Söhne, die Kinder, die Frauen) dort.

3. Masculine nouns with -n or -en endings

Masculine nouns ending in -e, -t or -r add -n (or -en) to the nominative to form all other cases, singular and plural. Thus:

	Singular	*Plural*	*Singular*	*Plural*
Nom.	der Knabe	die Knaben	der Student	die Studenten
Gen.	des Knaben	der Knaben	des Studenten	der Studenten
Dat.	dem Knaben	den Knaben	dem Studenten	den Studenten
Acc.	den Knaben	die Knaben	den Studenten	die Studenten

	Singular	*Plural*
Nom.	der Herr	die Herren
Gen.	des Herrn	der Herren
Dat.	dem Herrn	den Herren
Acc.	den Herrn	die Herren

Exercise No. 43. Complete these sentences with the correct case endings.

Beispiel: 1. Die Wohnung des Kaufmanns ist nicht groß.

1 D— Wohnung d— Kaufmann— ist nicht groß.   2 Herr Clark hat ein— Wohnung in d— Vorstadt. 3 D— Zimmer d— Wohnung sind schön möbliert. 4 D— Freund— d— Kinder kommen heute. 5 Sehen wir nun d— Wände d— Zimmer— (*sing.*) an. 6 Einige Bild— hängen an d— Wänden. 7 In d— Eßzimmer sehen wir ein— Tisch. 8 D— Tisch ist rund. 9 Um d— Tisch stehen sechs Stühle. 10 D— Lehrer sitzt auf ein— Stuhl. 11 D— Kaufmann setzt sich auf d— Sofa. 12 Über d— Klavier hängt das Porträt ein— Frau. 13 Herr Clark hat ein— Vertreter in München. 14 Er will d— Vertreter besuchen. 15 München ist ein—Stadt in Westdeutschland.

Exercise No. 44. Answer each question using the proper case of the noun in parenthesis. Use plural of noun where indicated.

Beispiel: 1. Der Lehrer hat eine Wohnung in der Stadt.

1 Wer hat eine Wohnung in der Stadt? (der Lehrer)   2 Wessen Kinder spielen im Garten? (der Kaufmann)   3 Wem bringst du den Hut? (die Schwester) 4 Wen lieben die Kinder? (die Lehrerin, *pl.*)   5 Was suchen die Knaben? (der Ball) 6 Zu wem spricht der Lehrer? (der Schüler, *pl.*)   7 Wessen Porträt hängt im Wohnzimmer? (die Frau)   8 Womit schreibt der Knabe? (der Bleistift) 9 Womit schreibt das Mädchen? (die Feder)   10 Wen fragt der Vater? (das Kind, *pl.*)   11 Wem geben Sie die Briefe? (die Mutter)

Zwei Dialoge

Read each dialogue silently several times, using the English translation to make certain of the meaning. Then practise the German text aloud many times. Follow this procedure with all dialogues.

WO IST DIE THOMASSTRAßE?

1 Verzeihen Sie, mein Herr, können Sie mir sagen, wo die Thomasstraße ist?
2 Gehen Sie immer gerade aus, Fräulein.
3 Ist es weit?
4 Nein, Fräulein, es ist nur eine kurze Strecke.
5 Danke vielmals.
6 Bitte schön, Fräulein.

1 Pardon me, Sir, can you tell me where Thomas Street is?
2 Continue straight ahead, Miss.
3 Is it far?
4 No, Miss, it's only a short distance.
5 Thank you very much.
6 Don't mention it, Miss.

WO HÄLT DER BUS?

1 Bitte, mein Herr, wo hält der Bus?
2 Er hält dort an der Ecke, Fräulein.
3 Ich danke Ihnen sehr, mein Herr.
4 Bitte sehr.

1 Please, Sir, where does the bus stop?
2 It stops on the corner over there, Miss.
3 Thank you very much, Sir.
4 You're very welcome.

Exercise No. 45. Das erste Lesestück (The first reading passage)

How to read the Lesestück

Read the passage silently from beginning to end to get the meaning as a whole. Re-read the passage. Most of the new words are given in the footnotes. Look up the meaning of any other words you may not know in the German–English vocabulary at the end of this book.

Read the passage silently a third time. Then translate it and check your translation with that given in the Answer Section.

Follow this procedure in all other reading passages.

HERR CLARK LERNT DEUTSCH

Herr Clark ist ein Kaufmann. Er importiert Kunstgegenstände aus Deutschland. Sein Büro ist in einem Hochhaus in der Stadt London. Seine Wohnung aber ist nicht in der Stadt, sondern[1] in einem Vorort nicht weit davon entfernt.[2] Jeden Wochentag fährt Herr Clark mit dem Zug in die Stadt und führt dort sein Geschäft.

Die Firma des Herrn Clark hat einen Vertreter in Deutschland. Er heißt Heinrich Schiller und wohnt in der Stadt München. Im Frühling dieses[3] Jahres macht Herr Clark eine Reise nach Deutschland, um Herrn Schiller zu besuchen.[4] Er will mit seinem Vertreter über wichtige[5] Geschäftssachen reden. Leider[6] spricht Herr Schiller kein Englisch, und Herr Clark spricht kein Deutsch. Deswegen beginnt Herr Clark, Deutsch zu lernen.

Herr Clark hat einen guten Lehrer. Dieser ist ein Deutscher von Geburt[7] und heißt Karl Müller. Jeden Dienstag und Donnerstag kommt der Lehrer in die Wohnung seines Schülers, um ihm eine Deutschstunde zu geben.[8] Herr Clark ist fleißig und intelligent und lernt schnell. Während der ersten Stunde lernt er diese deutschen Ausdrücke auswendig[9]: Guten Tag; Wie geht es Ihnen? Vielen Dank; Bitte schön; Auf Wiedersehen; u.s.w. (und so weiter). Er kennt schon die deutschen Namen für viele Dinge in seinem Wohnzimmer und kann auf diese Fragen richtig antworten: Was ist dies? Was ist das? Wo ist das? Warum ist das? usw.

Herr Müller ist mit dem Fortschritt[10] seines Schülers sehr zufrieden,[11] und er sagt: „Sehr gut. Das ist genug für heute. Ich komme Donnerstag wieder. Auf Wiedersehen."

NOTES: 1 but rather. 2 **davon entfernt** from it. 3 of this. 4 **um . . . zu besuchen** in order to visit. 5 important. 6 unfortunately. 7 by birth. 8 **um . . . geben** in order to give. 9 by heart. 10 progress. 11 satisfied.

Exercise No. 46. **Das zweite Lesestück** (The second reading passage)

DEUTSCHLAND

Deutschland liegt in Mitteleuropa.[1] Seit dem Ende des Zweiten Weltkriegs[2] ist Deutschland in zwei Teile geteilt,[3] Westdeutschland[4] und Ostdeutschland.[5] Die Elbe trennt[6] die zwei Teile Deutschlands.

Westdeutschland ist die Bundesrepublik Deutschland.[7] Ostdeutschland ist die Deutsche Demokratische Republik.[8]

Die Hauptstadt[9] von Westdeutschland ist Bonn. Die Hauptstadt von Ostdeutschland ist Ost-Berlin.

Unter[10] den grossen Städten in Westdeutschland sind Köln, München, Stuttgart, Frankfurt, Düsseldorf und die grossen Hafenstädte,[11] Hamburg und Bremen. Unter den grossen Städten in Ostdeutschland sind Leipzig, Dresden, Chemnitz.

NOTES: 1 Central Europe. 2 **der Zweite Weltkrieg** the Second World War. 3 divided. 4 West Germany. 5 East Germany. 6 separates. 7 the Federal Republic of Germany. 8 the German Democratic Republic. 9 capital. 10 among. 11 seaport cities.

CHAPTER 12

EIN FREUND BESUCHT HERRN CLARK IN SEINEM BÜRO
A FRIEND VISITS MR. CLARK IN HIS OFFICE

Wilhelm Engel ist ein Freund von Herrn Clark. Sein Büro ist im selben Gebäude wie das Büro des Herrn Clark.

Herr Engel spricht fließend Deutsch. Er weiß, sein Freund studiert seit einigen Monaten Deutsch, und er will erfahren, was für Fortschritte er macht.

Eines Tages sitzt Herr Clark an seinem Schreibtisch und liest Briefe. Plötzlich öffnet jemand die Tür und tritt ins Büro.

Es ist sein Freund Wilhelm Engel.

Herr Engel beginnt sofort Deutsch zu sprechen, und Herr Clark antwortet ihm[1] auf deutsch.

E: Wie geht's, mein Freund?

C: Sehr gut, danke. Und dir?[3]

E: Sehr gut. Ich höre, du[2] lernst seit einigen Monaten Deutsch.

C: Das ist wahr. Ich beabsichtige nämlich, im Sommer eine Reise nach Deutschland zu machen.

E: Geschäftsreise oder Vergnügungsreise?

C: Beides. Ich will den Vertreter unserer Firma in München besuchen und mit ihm unsere Geschäftsangelegenheiten besprechen. Dann hoffe ich, andere Städte und interessante Plätze in Deutschland, Österreich und in der Schweiz zu besuchen.

E: Spricht euer[4] Vertreter kein Englisch?

C: Ich glaube, nein. Ich hoffe, mit ihm Deutsch zu sprechen.

E: Fährst du mit dem Dampfer, oder fliegst du?

C: Ich fliege.

E: Hast du schon die Flugfahrkarte gekauft und einen Platz reserviert?

C: Noch nicht. Aber morgen gehe ich ins Auskunftsbüro der Fluglinie, um einen Platz zu reservieren, und Einzelheiten über den Fahrplan zu erfahren.

E: Donnerwetter! Du sprichst ja wunderbar Deutsch!

C: Es ist sehr nett von dir,[3] das zu sagen. Ich hoffe, noch besser zu sprechen.

E: Nun, glückliche Reise!

Sie geben sich die Hand. Herr Engel verlässt das Büro.

NOTES: 1 **Antworten** and a number of other verbs take a dative object. 2 As Mr. Clark and Mr. Engel are very good friends, they use the familiar **du**. **Sie duzen sich.** They say **du** to each other. 3 **dir** is the dative case of **du**. 4 **euer** poss. adjective, familiar form plural, your.

William Engel is a friend of Mr. Clark. His office is in the same building as the office of Mr. Clark.

Mr. Engel speaks German fluently. He knows his friend has been studying German for some months and he wants to find out what progress he is making.

One day Mr. Clark is sitting at his desk and reading letters. Suddenly someone opens the door and steps into the office.

It is his friend William Engel.

Mr. Engel begins immediately to speak German, and Mr. Clark answers him in German.

E: How are you, my friend?

C: Very well, thanks. And you?

E: Very well. I hear you have been studying German for several months.

C: That is true. I intend, you know, to make a trip to Germany in the summer.

E: A business trip or a pleasure trip?

C: Both. I want to visit the representative of our firm in Munich and discuss our business matters with him. Then I hope to visit other cities and interesting places in Germany, in Austria, and in Switzerland.

E: Doesn't your agent speak any English?

C: I think not. I hope to speak German with him.

E: Will you travel by steamship or will you fly?

C: I shall fly.

E: Have you already bought the flight ticket and reserved a place?

C: Not yet. But tomorrow I am going to the information bureau of the airline to reserve a seat and find out details about the timetable

E: The dickens! You speak German splendidly.

C: It is very nice of you to say that. I hope to speak even better.

E: Well, happy voyage!

They shake hands. Mr. Engel leaves the office.

Wortschatz

der Fahrplan, *pl.* ⁝e, timetable
das Gebäude, *pl.* -, building
die Einzelheit, *pl.* -en, detail
beábsichtigen, to intend
bespréchen, to discuss
erfáhren, to find out; fliegen, to fly
glauben, to believe; hoffen, to hope
lesen, to read; studíeren, to study
treten, to step; er tritt ins Zimmer
reserviéren, to reserve

verlássen, to leave, to go away from
noch, still, yet; noch nicht, not yet
wunderbar, wonderful
plötzlich, suddenly
sofort, immediately, at once
selb, same; im selben Gebäude, in the same building
jemand, somebody; niemand, nobody
dir, you, to you (*dative of du*)
mir, me, to me (*dative of ich*)

Practise aloud.

das Auskunftsbüro	die Fluglinie	die Geschäftsreise
aus-kunfts-by-ro:	fluːk-liː-nie	ge-ʃɛfts-rai-ze
information office	airline	business trip
die Flugfahrkarte	die Vergnügungsreise	die Geschäftsangelegenheit
fluːk-faːr-kar-te	fer-gnyː-guṇs-rai-ze	ge-ʃɛfts-an-ge-leː-gen-hait
flight ticket	pleasure trip	business matter

Deutsche Ausdrücke

eines Tages, eines Morgens, eines Nachmittags, eines Abends one day, one morning, one afternoon, one evening.

Glückliche Reise! Happy journey!

Karl antwortet ihm (ihr, mir, dir, Ihnen) auf deutsch. Charles answers him (her, me, you *fam.*, you *pol.*) in German.

The verb **antworten** takes a dative object.

Donnerwetter! The dickens! Thunder and lightning!

seit wann? since when? **wie lange?** how long? **Seit wann (wie lange) studiert er Deutsch? Er studiert Deutsch seit einem Jahr.** Since when has he been studying German? He has been studying German for a year.

An action begun in the past and continuing in the present is expressed in German by the present tense, in English by the present perfect.

Grammar Notes and Practical Exercises

1. Present Tense of *lesen*, to read; *treten*, to step; *wollen*, to want

ich lese	wir lesen	ich trete	wir treten	ich will	wir wollen
du liest	ihr lest	du trittst	ihr tretet	du willst	ihr wollt
er liest	sie (Sie) lesen	er tritt	sie (Sie) treten	er will	sie (Sie) wollen
Imperative: lies! lest! lesen Sie!		tritt! tretet! treten Sie!			

(*a*) **lesen** is like **sehen** (**ich sehe, du siehst**, etc.), and **treten** is like **sprechen** (**ich spreche, du sprichst**, etc.).

(*b*) The singular of **wollen** is irregular. The **ich** and **er, sie, es** forms have no endings. Compare with **müssen** (Chapter 8, Grammer Note 1, p. 40) and **wissen** (Chapter 10, Grammer Note 1 p. 52).

Exercise No. 47. Practise aloud.

Ich will Deutsch lernen.	**Wir wollen ins Theater gehen.**
Willst du eine Reise machen?	**Wollt ihr das Buch lesen?**
Er will seinen Freund besuchen.	**Die Kinder wollen ins Kino gehen.**
Sie will ein Kleid kaufen.	**Sie wollen jetzt nicht spielen.**
Was wollen Sie tun?	**Wollen Sie mit uns gehen?**

2. Possessive adjectives (*ein*-words)

For every personal pronoun there is a corresponding possessive adjective.

Pers. Pron.		*Possessive Adjective*				*Pers. Pron.*		*Possessive Adjective*			
		masc.	*fem.*	*neut.*				*masc.*	*fem.*	*neut.*	
ich	I	mein	meine	mein	my	wir	we	unser	uns(e)re	unser	our
du	you	dein	deine	dein	your	ihr	you	euer	eu(e)re	euer	your
er	he	sein	seine	sein	his	sie	they	ihr	ihre	ihr	their
sie	she	ihr	ihre	ihr	her	Sie	you	Ihr	Ihre	Ihr	your
es	it	sein	seine	sein	its						

The possessive adjectives agree in number, gender, and case with the nouns they refer to. In these sentences compare the endings of the possessive adjective with those of **ein** and **kein**.

1 **Ein** Bleistift liegt auf dem Pult.
  Mein Bleistift liegt auf dem Pult.
2 **Eine** Feder liegt auf dem Tisch.
  Deine Feder liegt auf dem Tisch.

3 **Ein** Buch liegt auf dem Stuhl.
   Sein Buch liegt auf dem Stuhl.
4 **Keine** Bilder sind an der Wand.
   Uns(e)re Bilder sind an der Wand.
5 Seht ihr **einen** Lehrer, Kinder?
   Seht ihr **eu(e)ren** Lehrer, Kinder?
6 Die Farbe **eines** Bleistifts ist schwarz.
   Die Farbe **meines** Bleistifts ist schwarz.
7 Die Farbe **einer** Feder ist rot.
   Die Farbe **ihrer** Feder ist rot.
8 Karl spielt mit **keinen** Kindern.
   Karl spielt mit **uns(e)ren** Kindern.
9 Haben Sie **einen** Hut, Herr Schmidt?
   Haben Sie **Ihren** Hut, Herr Schmidt?
10 **Keine** Mädchen lernen Französisch.
   Uns(e)re Mädchen lernen Französisch.

(*a*) The endings of the possessive adjectives are exactly like those of **ein** and **kein.** Possessive adjectives and **kein** are called **ein**-words.

| | **ein, kein** | | | | **ein**-word **unser** | | |
| | *Singular* | | | *Plural* | *Singular* | | | *Plural* |
	masc.	*fem.*	*neut.*	*m.f.n.*	*masc.*	*fem.*	*neut.*	*m.f.n.*
N.	ein	eine	ein	keine	*N.* uaser	uns(e)re[1]	unser	uns(e)re
G.	eines	einer	eines	keiner	*G.* uns(e)res	uns(e)rer	uns(e)res	uns(e)rer
D.	einem	einer	einem	keinen	*D.* uns(e)rem	uns(e)rer	uns(e)rem	uns(e)ren
A.	einen	eine	ein	keine	*A.* uns(e)ren	uns(e)re	unser	uns(e)re

NOTE 1. (e) means that the letter **e** may be omitted.

(*b*) Note carefully that **ein, kein,** and all **ein**-words have no endings in the nominative masculine singular, and in the nominative and accusative neuter singular. The other endings are like those of **der.**

(*c*) Just as there are three words for you (**du, ihr, Sie**), so there are three words for your (**dein, euer, Ihr**).

Use a form of **dein** (your) in speaking to a person whom you would address with **du** (you).

Use a form of **euer** (your) in speaking to persons whom you would address with **ihr** (you).

Use a form of **Ihr** (your), always capitalized, in speaking to one or more persons whom you would address with **Sie** (you).

Hast du deine Bücher, Karl?	Have you your books, Charles?
Habt ihr eure Bücher, Kinder?	Have you your books, children?
Haben Sie Ihre Bücher, meine Damen und Herren?	Have you your books, ladies and gentlemen?

Exercise No. 48. Practise aloud. Translate.

1 — Wo wohnt der Vertreter Ihrer Firma?
   — Der Vertreter unsrer Firma wohnt in München.
   — Seit wann wohnt er dort?
   — Er wohnt seit einem Jahr dort.

2 — Wessen Porträt ist das?
— Es ist das Porträt meiner Frau.
— Ist dies die Photographie Ihrer Kinder?
— Ja, dies ist die Photographie unsrer vier Kinder.
3 — Ist deine Wohnung in der Stadt?
— Nein, meine Wohnung ist in der Vorstadt.
— Und wo ist dein Büro?
— Mein Büro ist in der Stadt.
4 — Wo ist eure Schule, Kinder?
— Unsre Schule ist in der Karlstraße.
— Geht ihr dahin[1] zu Fuß?[2]
— Nein, wir fahren mit dem Autobus.

NOTES: 1 **dahin** there (to that place).   2 **zu Fuß gehen** to go on foot, to walk.

Exercise No. 49. Complete these sentences by translating the words in parenthesis.

1 Wo ist die Wohnung (of your) Freundes, Karl? 2 Wo sind (your) Eltern, Kinder? 3 Wo ist (your) Büro, Herr Clark? 4 Die Farbe (of her) Kleider ist blau. 5 Die Farbe (of his) Hutes ist grau. 6 Die Farbe (of their) Hauses ist weiß. 7 Wir gehen mit (our) Eltern ins Kino. 8 Das Bild (of your) Kinder ist sehr schön, Frau Clark. 9 Er will (my) Automobil kaufen. 10 Sie will (her) Freundinnen besuchen. 11 Wir wollen mit (our) Lehrer sprechen. 12 Wollen Sie mir (your) Hut geben?

Exercise No. 50. Fragen

Re-read the text: **Ein Freund besucht Herrn Clark.** Then answer these questions.

1 Wer ist Herr Engel? 2 Wo ist sein Büro? 3 Spricht er Deutsch? 4 Was will er erfahren? 5 Wo sitzt Herr Clark eines Tages? 6 Was liest er? 7 Wer tritt plötzlich in sein Büro? 8 Beginnt Herr Engel sofort, auf deutsch zu sprechen? 9 Antwortet Herr Clark seinem Freund auf englisch? 10 Wie lange studiert Herr Clark schon Deutsch? 11 Wann beabsichtigt Herr Clark, eine Reise nach Deutschland zu machen? 12 Fährt er nach Deutschland mit dem Dampfer oder fliegt er? 13 Wohin geht er morgen? 14 Was tun[1] die Herren am Ende[2] des Gesprächs?

NOTES: 1 **tun** to do — ich tue, du tust, er tut, wir tun, ihr tut, sie tun. 2 **das Ende** the end; **am Ende** at the end.

Exercise No. 51. Übersetzen Sie!

1 Mr. Engel, a friend of (**von**) Mr. Clark, steps into his office. 2 He asks in German, 'How long have you (**du**) been studying German?' 3 I want to make a trip to Germany. 4 Why do you want to go to Germany? 5 Our firm has an agent in Munich. 6 Doesn't the agent of your firm speak English? 7 The agent of our firm does not speak English. 8 Mr. Clark, do you (**Sie**) live in the city? No, my house is in the suburbs.

CHAPTER 13

ZAHLEN, ZAHLEN, UND WIEDER ZAHLEN
NUMBERS, NUMBERS, AND AGAIN NUMBERS

1 Sie wissen, Herr Clark, daß die Namen von Dingen und Personen sehr wichtig sind.[1] Sie wissen auch, daß es unmöglich ist,[1] einen Satz ohne Verben zu bilden.

2 Das ist wahr, Herr Müller.

3 Nun, es gibt Wörter, die ebenso wichtig sind wie Hauptwörter und Zeitwörter. Ja, es ist nicht möglich, ohne diese Wörter an unsere moderne Zivilisation zu denken. Raten Sie einmal, welche Wörter ich meine.

4 Ich glaube, Sie meinen Zahlen.

5 Sie haben recht. Nun, vielleicht nennen Sie mir einige Fälle im modernen Leben, wo man Zahlen braucht.

6 Gewiß. Nichts ist leichter. Wir brauchen Zahlen zum Kaufen und Verkaufen.

7 Ha, ha, ha! Jeder Geschäftsmann denkt immer an Kaufen und Verkaufen. Aber ohne Geld sind die Zahlen nicht viel wert, nicht wahr?

8 Richtig. Wir brauchen auch die Zahlen, um das Datum, die Stunden des Tages, die Temperatur, Quantitäten, usw. anzugeben. Wir brauchen sie zum Telephonieren; für das Radio; für alle Wissenschaften und für tausend andere Dinge mehr.

9 Zahlen, Zahlen und wieder Zahlen. Ja, Herr Clark, man kann ohne Zahlen nicht auskommen. Aber es ist eine Sache, die Zahlen auf deutsch zu kennen; es ist eine andere Sache, sie rasch und richtig im täglichen Leben zu gebrauchen.

10 Sie haben recht. Ich will alles tun, was möglich ist, die Zahlen zu verstehen und richtig zu gebrauchen.

11 Indessen will ich Ihnen sagen, daß Sie im Studium des Deutschen rasche Fortschritte machen.[1]

12 Sie sind sehr gütig, Herr Müller.

13 Ach nein. Es ist die Wahrheit. Nun genug für heute. Auf Wiedersehen!

14 Bis zum nächsten Donnerstag, Herr Müller.

NOTE 1. Observe the position of the verb at the end of the subordinate clause introduced by daß. This type of word order will be explained in Chapter 14.

1 You know, Mr. Clark, that the names of things and persons are very important. You also know that it is impossible to form a sentence without a verb.

2 That is true, Mr. Müller.

3 Well, there are words which are just as important as nouns and verbs. Indeed, it is not possible to think of our modern civilization without these words. Just guess which words I mean.

4 I believe you mean numbers.

5 You are right. Now you will perhaps mention to me some cases in modern life where one needs numbers.

6 Certainly. Nothing is easier. We need numbers for buying and selling.

7 Ha, ha, ha! Every businessman always thinks of buying and selling. But without money, numbers are not worth much, are they?

8 That's right. We also need numbers to indicate the date, the hours of the day, the temperature, quantities, etc. We need them for telephoning; for the radio; for all the sciences and for a thousand other things.

9 Numbers, numbers, and again numbers. Yes, Mr. Clark, one cannot get along without numbers. But it is one thing to be familiar with numbers in German; it is another thing to be able to use them quickly and correctly in daily life.

10 You are right. I will do everything that is possible to understand numbers and use them correctly.

11 In the meantime I want to tell you that you are making rapid progress in the study of German.

12 You are very kind, Mr. Müller.

13 Oh no. It is the truth. Well, enough for today. Good-bye.

14 Until next Thursday, Mr. Müller.

Wortschatz

die **Zahl**, *pl.* -en, number
das **Datum**, *pl.* die, **Daten**, date
die **Quantität**, *pl.* -en, quantity
die **Temperatúr**, temperature
der **Fall**, *pl.* ·e, case
das **Hauptwort**, *pl.* ·er, noun (das Substantiv)
das **Zeitwort**, *pl.* ·er, verb (das Verb)
die **Persón**, *pl.* -en, person
die **Zivilisatión**,[1] *pl.* -en, civilization
angeben, to mention, state
brauchen, to need
gebrauchen, to use
denken (an) + *acc.*, to think (of)
meinen, to mean

raten, to guess
gut, good; **gütig**, kind
gewiß = **sicher**, sure, surely
möglich, possible; **unmöglich**, impossible
modérn, modern; **únmodern**, not modern
rasch = **schnell**, quick, quickly
viel, much; **nichts**, nothing
wichtig, important; **unwichtig**, unimportant
ebenso (e:-ben-zo:), just as
indessen, in the meantime
ohne (*prep.* + *acc.*), without
also, so, thus, therefore, well, then

NOTE 1. The ending -tion in German is pronounced -tsio:n. Nouns in **-tion** are always feminine: die **Nation** (na-tsio:n); die **Zivilisatión** (tsi-vi-li-za-**tsio:n**); die **Statión** (ʃta-tsio:n); die **Lektión** (*lek-tsyon*); die **Portión** (por-tsio:n).

Infinitives Used as Nouns

Infinitives may be used as nouns. Such nouns are always neuter.

kaufen, to buy
das **Kaufen**, the buying
zum **Kaufen**, for buying
Zum Kaufen braucht man Geld.
  For buying one needs money.
verkaufen, to sell

das **Verkaufen**, the selling
zum **Verkaufen**, for selling
telephonieren, to telephone
das **Telephonieren**, the telephoning
zum **Telephonieren**, for telephoning

Deutsche Ausdrücke

viel wert, worth a great deal
nicht viel wert, not worth much
Bis zum nächsten Dienstag, Donnerstag, usw. Until next Tuesday, Thursday, etc.

ohne etwas auszukommen, to get along without something
Es ist unmöglich, ohne Geld auszukommen. It is impossible to get along without money.

Grammar Notes and Practical Exercise

1 Die Zahlen von 1 bis 100. The Numerals from 1 to 100

1 eins	11 elf	21 einundzwanzig	53 dreiundfünfzig
2 zwei	12 zwölf	22 zweiundzwanzig	60 sechzig
3 drei	13 dreizehn	23 dreiundzwanzig	64 vierundsechzig
4 vier	14 vierzehn	24 vierundzwanzig	70 siebzig
5 fünf	15 fünfzehn	25 fünfundzwanzig	75 fünfundsiebzig
6 sechs	16 sechzehn	30 dreißig (drai-six)	80 achtzig
7 sieben	17 siebzehn	31 einunddreißig	85 fünfundachtzig
8 acht	18 achtzehn	40 vierzig (fir-tsix)	90 neunzig
9 neun	19 neunzehn	42 zweiundvierzig	95 fünfundneunzig
10 zehn	20 zwanzig (tswan-tsix)	50 fünfzig (fynf-tsix)	100 hundert

For the pronunciation of numbers 1 to 21, see Chapter 4, the Second Part, section C.

Exercise No. 52. Read each expression aloud. Then write out the numbers in German.

(*a*) 30 Stühle	(*h*) 19 Knaben	(*o*) 100 Menschen
(*b*) 10 Bücher	(*i*) 14 Mädchen	(*p*) 39 Briefe
(*c*) 50 Studenten	(*j*) 31 Bilder	(*q*) 28 Lehrer
(*d*) 12 Häuser	(*k*) 25 Freunde	(*r*) 36 Lehrerinnen
(*e*) 7 Städte	(*l*) 43 Freundinnen	(*s*) 15 Straßen
(*f*) 60 Schüler	(*m*) 89 Männer	(*t*) 12 Wörter
(*g*) 70 Schülerinnen	(*n*) 90 Kinder	

Exercise No. 53. Read each sentence aloud. Then answer in a complete sentence, giving the number in German.

Beispiel: 1. Die Woche hat sieben Tage.

1 Wie viele[1] Tage hat die Woche? 2 Wie viele Monate hat das Jahr? 3 Wie viele Stunden hat der Tag? 4 Wie viele Minuten hat die Stunde? 5 Wie viele Sekunden hat die Minute? 6 Wieviel Tage hat der Monat September? 7 Wieviel Tage hat der Monat Juli? 8 Wie viele Staaten[2] sind in den Vereinigten Staaten? 9 Wie alt ist der Vater? (40 Jahre) 10 Wie alt ist die Mutter? (36 Jahre) 11 Wieviel ist ein Dutzend?[3] 12 Wie viele Finger hat die Hand?

NOTES: 1 **wie viele** how much or how many. In colloquial speech you will also find **wieviel** without the final **e**. 2 **der Staat** (ʃtaːt) *pl.* **die Staaten** state; **die Vereinigten Staaten** the United States. 3 **das Dutzend** dozen.

2 Present Tense of *können*, **to be able, can;** *tun*, **to do**

ich kann	wir können	ich tue	wir tun
du kannst	ihr könnt	du tust	ihr tut
er, sie, es kann	sie (Sie) können	er, sie, es tut	sie (Sie) tun

Note the irregular singular of **können**. Compare with the singular of **müssen** (Chapter 8, Grammar Note 1, p. 40); **wissen** (Chapter 10, Grammar Note 1, p. 52); **wollen** (Chapter 12, Grammar Note 1, p. 65).

Exercise No. 54. Practise aloud.

Ich kann das nicht schreiben.	Wir können das nicht glauben.
Du kannst das nicht lernen.	Ihr könnt das nicht bringen.
Er kann das nicht kaufen.	Können die Eltern heute kommen?
Sie kann das nicht finden.	Können Sie morgen kommen?

Exercise No. 55. Practise aloud.

— Was tun Sie?	— Was tust du, mein Kind?
— Ich schreibe einen Brief.	— Ich höre Radio.
— Was tut Hans?	— Was tut Marie?
— Er spielt Klavier.	— Sie spielt mit ihrer Puppe (doll).

3 The *der*-words, *dieser, jener, jeder, welcher, aller*

A number of words take almost the same endings as **der** and are called **der**-words. Five of these are: **dieser** this (*pl.* these); **jener** that (*pl.* those); **jeder** each, every; **welcher** which, what; and **aller** all. In the following sentences compare the endings of **dieser** with those of **der**.

Der Bleistift ist rot.	Ich gebe dem Lehrer das Papier.
Dieser Bleistift ist rot.	Ich gebe diesem Lehrer das Papier.
Die Feder ist schwarz.	Die Farbe des Bleistifts ist rot.
Diese Feder ist schwarz.	Die Farbe dieses Bleistifts ist rot.
Das Buch ist neu.	Die Lehrer sind meine Freunde.
Dieses Buch ist neu.	Diese Lehrer sind meine Freunde.
Sehen Sie das Buch?	Karl spielt mit den Knaben.
Sehen Sie dieses Buch?	Karl spielt mit diesen Knaben.

The Definite Article — *der*					The *der*-word — *dieser*			
	Singular			Plural		Singular			Plural
	masc.	*fem.*	*neut.*	*m.f.n.*		*masc.*	*fem.*	*neut.*	*m.f.n.*
N.	der	die	das	die	N.	dieser	diese	dieses	diese
G.	des	der	des	der	G.	dieses	dieser	dieses	dieser
D.	dem	der	dem	den	D.	diesem	dieser	diesem	diesen
A.	den	die	das	die	A.	diesen	diese	dieses	diese

The endings of **dieser** are like those of **der** except in the neuter nominative and accusative, where **-es** take the place of **-as**.

The endings of other **der**-words (**jener, jeder, welcher, aller**) are exactly like those of **dieser**.

Like **der**, the **der**-words agree in number, gender, and case with their nouns: **dieses Buch, jenes Buch, jeder Knabe, welche Frau, alle Menschen.**

Exercise No. 56. Substitute the correct form of **dieser** and **jener** for the definite article in heavy type.

Beispiel: 1. Dieser (jener) Kaufmann wohnt in der Vorstadt.

1 **Der** Kaufmann wohnt in der Vorstadt.   2 Die Wohnung **des** Kaufmanns ist nicht groß. 3 Sein Büro ist in **dem** Hochhaus. 4 Sehen Sie **die** Landkarte von Deutschland? 5 Hinter **dem** Hause ist ein Garten. 6 Wir müssen **die** Wörter schreiben. 7 Geben Sie **den** Mädchen die Hüte! 8 Ich verstehe **das** Wort nicht. 9 Die Eltern **der** Kinder sind heute in der Schule. 10 Der Vater **der** Frau ist Arzt.

Exercise No. 57. Make a question of each statement using the correct form of **welcher** in place of the form of **dieser**.

Beispiel: 1 Welches Haus hat keinen Garten?

1 **Dieses** Haus hat keinen Garten. 2 **Dieser** Mann hat die Vorstadt nicht gern. 3 **Dieser** Lehrer hat zwanzig Schüler in seiner Klasse. 4 **Dieses** Schlafzimmer ist für die Mädchen. 5 Er muß mit **diesem** Bleistift schreiben. 6 Alle Schüler können **diese** Bücher lesen. 7 Der Schüler kennt **diese** Wörter. 8 Wir kennen **diese** Herren nicht. 9 Sie muß **diese** Wörter schreiben. 10 Sie will mit **diesen** Kindern sprechen.

Exercise No. 58. Fragen

Re-read the text: **Zahlen, Zahlen und wieder Zahlen.** Then answer these questions.

1 Wie heißt dieses Kapitel? 2 Was für Wörter sind ebenso wichtig wie die Zeitwörter und Hauptwörter? 3 Kann man im modernen Leben ohne Zahlen auskommen? 4 Gibt es viele Fälle, wo man Zahlen gebraucht? 5 An was denkt der Kaufmann zuerst? 6 Kann man ohne Geld kaufen und verkaufen? 7 Geben Sie zwei andere Fälle an, wo man im täglichen Leben Zahlen gebraucht!

Exercise No. 59. Übersetzen Sie!

1 How much does this hat cost? (25 marks). 2 How many students has this class? (15 students). 3 How old is that house? (100 years). 4 A week has seven days and a year has twelve months. 5 The month of July has thirty-one days. 6 Can you count from 1 to 100? 7 Which car are you buying? I am buying that car. 8 I cannot read these words.

CHAPTER 14

DAS GELDSYSTEM IN DEUTSCHLAND
THE MONETARY SYSTEM IN GERMANY

1 Voriges Mal, Herr Clark, sagten wir, daß es sehr schwer ist, ohne Zahlen, das heißt, ohne Rechnen (Mathematik) an die moderne Zivilisation zu denken. Es ist ebenso schwer, ohne Mathematik an eine Reise zu denken. Man braucht Mathematik sehr oft auf einer Reise, nicht wahr?

2 Das weiß jeder Reisende. Man braucht Mathematik, um Geld zu wechseln, um Fahrkarten zu kaufen, um für Mahlzeiten und Hotelrechnungen zu zahlen, um Gepäck zu wiegen, um Entfernungen zu schätzen, um in den großen Warenhäusern, in den Läden und auf dem Markt einzukaufen.

3 Kennen Sie das Geldsystem Deutschlands. Herr Clark?

4 Das versteht sich! Ich kenne es gründlich. Ich bin doch Importeur von deutschen Kunstgegenständen, nicht wahr? Die Geldeinheit in Deutschland ist die Mark. Das englische Pfund is ungefähr zehn Mark wert.

5 Wenn Sie zehn Pfund gegen Mark wechseln, wieviel Mark bekommen Sie?

6 Ich bekomme ungefähr hundert Mark.

7 Wenn Sie hundert Pfund gegen Mark wechseln, wieviel Mark bekommen Sie dann?

8 Ich bekomme ungefähr eintausend Mark.

9 Richtig! Und nun weiter: Sie gehen zum Bahnhof. Sie wollen zwei Fahrkarten kaufen. Jede Karte kostet sechzehn Mark, und Sie geben dem Beamten am Kartenschalter einen Fünfzigmarkschein. Wieviel Mark gibt er Ihnen zurück?

10 Zweimal sechzehn macht zweiunddreißig. Fünfzig weniger zweiunddreißig macht achtzehn. Er gibt mir achtzehn Mark zurück.

11 Sehr gut. Nächstes Mal sprechen wir über diese wichtige Sache weiter. Sie kennen ja das Sprichwort: Übung macht den Meister.

12 Jawohl. Dieses Sprichwort kenne ich.

1 Last time, Mr. Clark, we said that it is very difficult to think of modern civilization without numbers, that is to say without mathematics. It is just as difficult to think of a trip without mathematics. One uses mathematics very often on a trip, doesn't one?

2 Every traveller knows that. One uses mathematics in order to change money, to buy travel tickets, to pay for meals and hotel bills, in order to weigh luggage, to estimate distances, to do shopping in the big department stores, in the shops, and in the markets.

3 Do you know the monetary system of Germany, Mr. Clark?

4 That goes without saying! I know it thoroughly. I am an importer of German art objects, am I not? The monetary unit in Germany is the mark. The English pound is worth about 10 marks.

5 If you change ten pounds for marks, how many marks do you get?

6 I get about 100 marks.

7 If you change one hundred pounds into marks, how many marks do you get then?

8 I get about 1,100 marks.

9 Right. And now to continue: You go to the railway station. You want to buy two tickets. Each ticket costs sixteen marks, and you give the clerk at the booking office a fifty-mark note. How many marks does he give you back?

10 Two times sixteen makes thirty-two. Fifty minus thirty-two makes eighteen. He gives me back eighteen marks.

11 Very good. Next time we will go on speaking about this important matter. You know, of course, the proverb: Practice makes perfect. (*Lit.* practice makes the master.)

12 Yes, indeed. I know this proverb.

Wortschatz

der Bahnhof, *pl.* ⸚e, railway station
der Kartenschalter, *pl.* -, booking office
der Beámte, *pl.* -n, employee (clerk)
die Fahrkarte, *pl.* -n, ticket
der Reisende, *pl.* -n, traveller
das Gepäck, baggage
die Rechnung, *pl.* -en, bill, account
die Entférnung, *pl.* -en, distance
der Zehnmarkschein, *pl.* -e ten-mark bill
die Mathematík, mathematics

die Mahlzeit, *pl.* -en, meal
die Sache, *pl.* -n, thing
der Markt, *pl.* ⸚e, market
bekommen, to receive, to get
schätzen, to gauge, to estimate, to value
wiegen, to weigh (something)
wechseln (vek-seln), to change
gründlich, thoroughly
ungefähr, about, approximately
weit, far; weiter, further

Ein Sprichwort

Übung macht den Meister.   Practice makes perfect.

Das deutsche Geldsystem   The German Monetary System

The monetary unit in Germany is the German mark. The **Deutsche Mark, DM = 100 Pfennig.**
The English £ equals about 10.00 DM.

NOTE: This rate of exchange is approximately correct on 1 January 1968, and is, of course, subject to constant variation.

Deutsche Ausdrücke

nächstes Mal, next time
voriges Mal, last time
diesmal, this time
auf dem Markt, in the market

Geld wechseln, to change money
Ich will hundert Pfund gegen Mark wechseln. I want to change one hundred pounds into marks.

Grammar Notes and Practical Exercises

1 Die Zahlen über hundert. Read all numbers aloud.

100 hundert	1000 tausend	eine Millión
200 zweihundert	2000 zweitausend	zwei Millionen
300 dreihundert	3000 dreitausend	drei Millionen
900 neunhundert	100000 hunderttausend	hundert Millionen
156 hundertsechsundfünfzig	1265 tausendzweihundertfünfundsechzig	
529 fünfhundertneunundzwanzig	1929 tausendneunhundertneunundzwanzig	
875 achthundertfünfundsiebzig	5697 fünftausendsechshundertsiebenund-neunzig	

Im Jahre In the Year

1492 vierzehnhundertzweiundneunzig   1776 siebzehnhundertsechsundsiebzig
1809 achtzehnhundertneun   1964 neunzehnhundertvierundsechzig

Exercise No. 60. Write out these numbers in German.

(*a*) 500   (*c*) 746   (*e*) 136   (*g*) 1,640   (*i*) im Jahre 1620
(*b*) 625   (*d*) 247   (*f*) 999   (*h*) 5,320   (*j*) im Jahre 1970

2 Subordinate Word Order—the Subordinating Conjunctions *daß*, *wenn*

You are familiar with normal and inverted word order. (See Chapter 7, Grammar Note 2, p. 36).

Normal: Subject–Verb. **Frau Clark fährt heute** in die Stadt.
Inverted: Verb–Subject. Heute **fährt Frau Clark** in die Stadt.

Normal and inverted word order are found in simple sentences and main clauses.

Subordinate word order, as the name indicates, is found only in subordinate clauses.

Compare the position of the verb in the simple sentences, paragraph A, with the position of the verb when these sentences are changed to subordinate clauses, paragraph B.

A. 1 Die Wohnung des Kaufmanns **ist** nicht groß.
   2 Ein Porträt **hängt** über dem Klavier.
   3 Sie **fährt** mit dem Auto in die Stadt.
   4 Wir **machen** eine Reise.
   5 Wir **brauchen** viel Geld.

B. 1 Ich weiß, daß die Wohnung des Kaufmanns nicht groß **ist**.
   2 Wir wissen, daß ein Porträt über dem Klavier **hängt**.
   3 Frau Clark besucht ihre Freundinnen, wenn sie mit dem Auto in die Stadt **fährt**.
   4 Wir brauchen Geld, wenn wir eine Reise **machen**.
   5 Wenn wir eine Reise **machen, brauchen wir** viel Geld.

In subordinate clauses the verb must stand last. This is called subordinate or transposed word order.

The conjunctions **daß** (that) and **wenn** (when, if) are called subordinating conjunctions. They introduce subordinate clauses.

The subordinate clause may precede the main clause. In that case the main clause has inverted word order (Sentence 5).

3 The Co-ordinating Conjunctions und, aber, sondern, oder, denn

The conjunctions und *and*; aber *but, however*; sondern *but, on the contrary*; oder *or*; and denn *for, because*; have no effect on word order. They are called co-ordinating conjunctions.

Karl lernt Englisch, und Wilhelm lernt Französisch.
Das Haus des Herrn Clark ist nicht groß, aber es ist sehr bequem.
Er hat die Vorstadt sehr gern, denn es ist still und gemütlich dort.

Exercise No. 61. Read each sentence to yourself. Read it aloud several times. By such repetition you will get a 'feeling' for the correct word order.

1 Jeder Schüler weiß, daß die Verben und Hauptwörter wichtig sind. 2 Wir wissen, daß Herr Clark ein Importeur von Kunstgegenständen ist. 3 Wenn er nach Hause kommt, spielt er mit seinen Kindern. 4 Herr Müller sagt, daß sein Schüler grosse Fortschritte macht. 5 Man kann nicht reisen, wenn man kein Geld hat. 6 Wenn die Kinder in der Schule sind, ist es im Hause sehr still. 7 Sie gehen zu Fuß zur Schule, wenn das Wetter schön ist. 8 Wenn das Wetter schön ist, gehen sie zu Fuß zur Schule. 9 Ich glaube, daß dieser Hut zehn Mark kostet. 10 Sie wissen ja, daß unsre Firma einen Vertreter in München hat. 11 Jeder Reisende weiß, daß wir auf einer Reise Mathematik gebrauchen. 12 Wenn man hundert Pfund gegen Mark wechselt, bekommt man ungefähr 1000 Mark. 13 Wir wissen, daß das Pfund ungefähr zehn Mark wert ist. 14 Anna geht in den Kindergarten, denn sie ist zu jung für die Schule. 15 Ich möchte eine Reise nach Europa machen, aber ich habe nicht genug Geld.

Exercise No. 62. Combine each of the sentences using the conjunction indicated. Make any necessary changes in word order. Subordinate clauses are always set off by commas.

Beispiel: 1. Die Schüler sitzen sehr still, wenn der Lehrer ins Zimmer **kommt.**

1 Die Schüler sitzen sehr still. (wenn) Der Lehrer kommt ins Zimmer.
2 Die Kinder gehen zu Fuß zur Schule. (wenn) Das Wetter ist schön.
3 Wir wissen es.[1] (daß) Dieser Kaufmann hat einen Vertreter in München.
4 Mein Freund lernt schnell. (denn) Er ist intelligent und fleißig.
5 (Wenn)[2] Ich bin in München. Ich will[2] mit diesem Mann reden.
6 Ich weiß es.[1] (daß) Sie machen im Sommer eine Reise nach Deutschland.
7 Wir möchten dieses Auto kaufen. (aber) Es ist viel zu teuer.
8 Man muß die Dinge auf deutsch nennen. (wenn) Man ist in Deutschland.
9 Ich kann heute nicht gehen. (denn) Ich habe viel zu tun.
10 Unsere Freunde gehen ins Kino. (und) Wir müssen zu Hause bleiben.[3]

NOTES: 1 Omit es in the combined sentence. 2 See Grammar Note 2B. 3 bleiben, to remain.

Exercise No. 63. Fragen

Review the numbers 1–1,000. Then answer these questions in complete sentences.

1 Wieviel Pfennig hat eine Mark? 2 Wieviel Mark ist das Pfund wert? 3 Etwas kostet 150 DM. Wenn Sie dem Verkäufer einen 500 Markschein (Fünfhundertmarkschein) geben, wieviel Geld bekommen Sie zurück? 4 Ein Automobil kostet 5790 DM. Wenn Sie dem Autohändler[1] einen Scheck für sechstausend Mark

geben, wieviel Geld gibt er Ihnen zurück? 5 Sie haben in Ihrem Geldbeutel[2] zwei Tausendmarkscheine; einen 500 Markschein (Fünfhundertmarkschein); drei Hundertmarkscheine; 3.50 DM (drei Mark fünfzig Pfennig). Wieviel Geld haben Sie im ganzen?[3] 6 Ein Anzug kostet 210 (zweihundertzehn) DM. Wenn Sie dem Verkäufer dreihundert Mark geben, wieviel bekommen Sie zurück? 7 Wieviel ist eine Million geteilt durch zehn?

NOTES: 1 der Autohändler car dealer. 2 der Geldbeutel purse. 3 Im ganzen in all.

Exercise No. 64. Übersetzen Sie!

1 Every traveller needs money. 2 He must use mathematics when he changes money. 3 Can you change this 500-mark bill? No, I have only 450 marks. 4 One pound is worth about ten marks, and one mark has 100 pennies (Pfennig). 5 I need some (etwas) money. Can you (du) lend me 1,000 marks? 6 The monetary system of Germany is easy to learn. 7 This car costs 6,763 marks. 8 I know that the monetary system of Germany is easy.

CHAPTER 15

ARITHMETISCHE PROBLEME IM RESTAURANT, AUF DEM BAHNHOF, IM LADEN

PROBLEMS IN ARITHMETIC IN THE RESTAURANT, AT THE STATION, IN THE SHOP

1 Reden wir heute abend etwas mehr über den Gebrauch von Mathematik auf der Reise, Herr Clark. Wir speisen im Restaurant; wir sind vier. Die Mahlzeiten kosten wie folgt: 12 Mark, 9 Mark, 11 Mark und 8 Mark. Wir lassen dem Kellner 10% als Trinkgeld.[1] Was ist die Rechung für alle zusammen? Und wieviel das Trinkgeld?

2 Die Summe für alle beträgt vierzig Mark. Das Trinkgeld ist vier Mark.

3 Sehr gut. Nun bin ich auf dem Bahnhof und trage einen schweren Handkoffer. Er wiegt dreißig Kilo. Wieviel ist das Gewicht des schweren Handkoffers in Pfund?

4 Das ist nicht schwer. Ein Kilo ist ungefähr 2.2 (zwei Punkt zwei) Pfund. Man multipliziert 30 (dreißig) mit 2.2 (zwei und zwei Zehntel). Der Handkoffer wiegt 66 (sechsundsechzig) Pfund.

5 Richtig. In Deutschland und in den anderen Ländern auf dem europäischen Kontinent rechnet man die Entfernung nicht in Meilen sondern in Kilometern. Wissen Sie, wie man Kilometer in Meilen umrechnet?

6 Gewiß. Ich dividiere durch acht und multipliziere dann mit fünf. 80 (achtzig) Kilometer also gleichen 50 (fünfzig) Meilen. Das ist doch leicht, nicht wahr?

7 Sie rechnen schnell und gut, Herr Clark. Nun noch ein Problem, das letzte. Sie gehen in einen großen Laden. Sie kaufen ein Paar Handschuhe für sich selbst zu zwölf Mark, zwei Paar Handschuhe für Ihre Frau zu sechzehn Mark das Paar, zwei Ledergürtel für die Knaben zu sechs Mark das Stück, und zwei seidene Taschentücher für die Mädchen zu vier Mark. Was ist der Betrag von allen Ihren Einkäufen?

8 64 (vierundsechzig) Mark. Wenn ich der Verkäuferin einen Hundertmarkschein gebe, dann bekomme ich 36 (sechsunddreißig) Mark zurück.

9 Ausgezeichnet! Nun genug Mathematik für heute. Am Donnerstag müssen wir über die Tageszeit sprechen. Das ist ein sehr wichtiges Thema.

10 Schön. Ich erwarte ein interessantes Gespräch.

11 Also, bis Donnerstag, Herr Clark.

NOTE 1. In Germany the tip is usually included in the bill as a charge for service (Bedienungszuschlag).

1 Let us talk a little more this evening about the use of mathematics on a trip, Mr. Clark. We are eating in a restaurant; there are four of us. The meals cost as follows: 12 marks, 9 marks, 11 marks, and 8 marks. We leave the waiter 10% as a tip. What is the bill altogether? And how much is the tip?

2 The amount for all is forty marks. The tip is four marks.

3 Very good. Now I am at the station and I am carrying a heavy suitcase. It weighs thirty kilos. What is the weight of the heavy suitcase in pounds?

4 That is not difficult. One kilo is about 2·2 pounds. One multiplies 30 by 2·2 (2 and $\frac{2}{10}$). The suitcase weighs 66 pounds.

5 Correct. In Germany and in other countries on the European continent, one measures distance not in miles but in kilometres. Do you know how one converts kilometres into miles.

6 Certainly. I divide by eight and then multiply by five. Thus, 80 kilometres equals 50 miles. That is really easy, isn't it?

7 You are doing sums quickly and well, Mr. Clark. Now one more problem, the last one. You go into a large store. You buy a pair of gloves for yourself for twelve marks, two pairs of gloves for your wife at sixteen marks a pair, two leather belts for the boys at six marks each, and two silk handkerchiefs for the girls at four marks. What is the total of all your purchases?

8 Sixty-four marks. If I give the saleswoman a hundred-mark note, then I receive 36 marks back.

9 Excellent. Well, enough mathematics for today. On Thursday we must speak about the time of day. That is a very important topic.

10 Good. I expect an interesting conversation.

11 Until Thursday then, Mr. Clark.

Wortschatz

das **Problém** (pro-bleːm), *pl.* -e, problem

der **Betrág**, *pl.* ⁖e, amount, sum, total

das **Gewícht**, *pl.* -e, weight

das **Restauraйt** (res-tau-rant) *pl.* -s, restaurant

der **Kellner**, *pl.* -, waiter

das **Trinkgeld**, *pl.* -er, tip

der **Ledergürtel**, *pl.* -, leather belt

der **Handschuh**, *pl.* -e, glove

das **Taschentuch**, *pl.* ⁖er, handkerchief

das **Stück**, *pl.* -e, piece; das **Pfund** *pl.* -e, pound

die **Meile**, *pl.* -n, mile

der **Gebrauch**, *pl.* ⁖e, use, custom

die **Tageszeit**, *pl.* -en, time of day

wiegen, to weigh (**es wiegt**, it weighs)

betrágen, to amount to

dividíeren durch, to divide by

multiplizíeren mit, to multiply by

erwárten, to expect, to await

rechnen, to reckon, calculate

um-rechnen, to convert, to change

speisen, to eat, dine

letzt, last; **erst**, *first*

seiden, silk, silken

schwer, heavy, hard; **leicht**, light, easy

zusámmen, together

selbst, self; **ich selbst**, I myself

The Doer

The word for the *doer* in German is often formed by adding **-er** to the verb stem. Sometimes an **Umlaut** is also added.

arbeiten	to work	**lehren**	to teach	**lesen**	to read
Arbeiter	worker	**Lehrer**	teacher	**Leser**	reader
		verkaufen	to sell		
		Verkäufer	seller		

Deutsche Ausdrücke

ein Paar (*noun*) a pair; **Ich kaufe ein Paar Schuhe, ein Paar Handschuhe, ein Paar Strümpfe, ein Paar Socken.** I am buying a pair of shoes, a pair of gloves, a pair of stockings, a pair of socks.

ein paar (*adj.*) a few (like **einige** a few). **Ich habe ein paar (einige) alte Anzüge.** I have a couple of (a few) old suits.

Sechzehn Mark das Stück. Sixteen marks each. German says *the* piece.

Grammar Notes and Practical Exercises

1 Present Tense of *tragen*, **to carry;** *lassen*, **to leave, to let, to allow.**

ich trage	wir tragen	ich lasse	wir lassen
du trägst	ihr tragt	du läßt	ihr laßt
er, sie, es trägt	sie (Sie) tragen	er, sie, es läßt	sie (Sie) lassen
Imperative: trage! tragt! tragen Sie!		lasse! laßt! lassen Sie!	

Note the vowel change of **a** to **ä** in second and third person singular.

2 About Adjective Endings

Predicate adjectives have no endings. Thus: Der Mann ist **groß.** Die Frau ist **jung.** Das Kind ist **klein.**

When adjectives *precede* nouns they always have endings. The pattern of endings depends upon:

A. Whether the adjective is preceded by a **der**-word (**der, dieser, jener, welcher, aller**).

B. Whether the adjective is preceded by an **ein**-word (**ein, kein, mein, dein, sein, unser, euer, ihr, Ihr**).

C. Whether no **der**-word or **ein**-word precedes the adjective.

A. Adjectives preceded by a **der**-word (**dieser, jener, jeder, welcher, aller**)

Der (Dieser) junge Mann ist mein Bruder.
Die (Diese) junge Frau ist meine Schwester.
Das (Dieses) gute Kind ist acht Jahre alt.
Ich kenne den (diesen) jungen Mann.
Ich kenne die (diese) junge Frau.
Ich kenne das (dieses) gute Kind.

N.B. When any **der**-word precedes an adjective, the adjective ends in **-e** in the nominative (*m.f.n.*) and in the accusative (*f.n.*). In all other cases singular and plural the ending is **-en.** Thus:

Singular

N.	der (dieser)	gute Mann	die (jene)	junge Frau
G.	des (dieses)	guten Mannes	der (jener)	jungen Frau
D.	dem (diesem)	guten Mann(e)	der (jener)	jungen Frau
A.	den (diesen)	guten Mann	die (jene)	junge Frau

N.	das (jenes)	gute Kind
G.	des (jenes)	guten Kindes
D.	dem (jenem)	guten Kind(e)
A.	das (jenes)	gute Kind

Plural

N.	die (diese)	guten Männer	die (jene)	jungen Frauen
G.	der (dieser)	guten Männer	der (jener)	jungen Frauen
D.	den (diesen)	guten Männern	den (jenen)	jungen Frauen
A.	die (diese)	guten Männer	die (jene)	jungen Frauen

N.	die (jene)	guten Kinder
G.	der (jener)	guten Kinder
D.	den (jenen)	guten Kindern
A.	die (jene)	guten Kinder

Exercise No. 65. Complete these sentences with the correct adjective endings.

Beispiel: 1. Der kleine Mann trägt den schweren Koffer.

1 Der klein— Mann trägt den schwer— Koffer. 2 Das Gewicht des schwer— Koffers ist 66 Pfund. 3 Was ist in diesem schwer— Koffer? 4 Die schwer— Koffer stehen im groß— Wartesaal des Bahnhofs. 5 Der rund— Tisch steht in dem Eßzimmer. 6 Um diesen rund— Tisch stehen sechs Stühle. 7 Ich schreibe mit dem rot— Bleistift. 8 Haben Sie die neu— Hefte? 9 Jene deutsch— Bücher sind sehr interessant. 10 Nennen Sie die Farben dieser deutsch— Landkarte! 11 Welche englisch— Bücher lesen Sie?

B. Adjectives preceded by ein-words (ein, kein, mein, dein, sein, unser, euer, ihr, Ihr).

Singular

N.	ein (kein)	guter Sohn	eine (unsere)	gute Tochter
G.	eines (keines)	guten Sohnes	einer (unserer)	guten Tochter
D.	einem (keinem)	guten Sohn(e)	einer (unserer)	guten Tochter
A.	einen (keinen)	guten Sohn	eine (unsere)	gute Tochter

N.	ein (Ihr)	gutes Buch
G.	eines (Ihres)	guten Buches
D.	einem (Ihrem)	guten Buch(e)
A.	ein (Ihr)	gutes Buch

Plural

N.	keine	guten Söhne	unsere	guten Töchter
G.	keiner	guten Söhne	unserer	guten Töchter
D.	keinen	guten Söhnen	unseren	guten Töchtern
A.	keine	guten Söhne	unsere	guten Töchter

N.	Ihre	guten Bücher
G.	Ihrer	guten Bücher
D.	Ihren	guten Büchern
A.	Ihre	guten Bücher

N.B. In the dative plural: **der**-words, **ein**-words, adjectives and nouns all end in the letter **-n.**

After any **ein**-word the endings of the adjective are exactly like the adjective endings after a **der**-word, except in the *singular nominative masculine,* and in the *singular nominative and accusative neuter.* In these cases the adjective must have the endings which the **ein**-word lacks.

dieser gute Mann	dieses gute Kind
ein guter Mann	ein gutes Kind

Exercise No. 66. Complete these sentences with the correct adjective endings.

1 Herr Clark ist ein englisch— Kaufmann.   2 Sein Büro ist in der Stadt, aber sein Haus ist in einem klein— Vorort.¹ 3 Er wohnt in einem schön— Einfamilienhaus. 4 Hinter dem Haus ist ein klein— Garten. 5 Die Kinder des Kaufmanns spielen gern in ihrem klein—Garten. 6 Herr Clark hat in der groß— Stadt München einen tüchtig—² Vertreter. 7 Im Sommer will der Kaufmann eine kurz— Reise nach Deutschland machen. 8 Er will seinen deutsch— Vertreter in München besuchen.   9 Jeden Monat sendet dieser Vertreter eine groß— Bestellung³ an die Firma von Herrn Clark. 10 Ein schwer— Koffer steht im Wartesaal.

Notes: 1 der Vorort, suburb. 2 tüchtig, able, diligent. 3 die Bestellung, order.

C. Adjectives not preceded by ein-words or der-words.

In these sentences compare the endings of the adjectives with those of dieser.

Dieser Kaffee ist teuer.	Diese Milch ist gut.
Guter Kaffee ist teuer.	Frische Milch ist gut.

Dieses Wasser ist klar.
Frisches Wasser ist klar.

Ich habe diesen Kaffee gern.	Ich trinke diese Milch.
Ich habe guten Kaffee gern.	Ich trinke frische Milch.

Trinken Sie dieses Wasser?
Trinken Sie frisches Wasser?

When an adjective is not preceded by an ein-word or der-word it has the same endings as dieser, except in the genitive singular, masculine and neuter, where -en takes the place of -es.

die Farbe dieses Weines (dieses Bieres)   the colour of this wine (of this beer)
die Farbe guten Weines (guten Bieres)   the colour of good wine (of good beer)

Exercise No. 67. Fragen

Re-read the text: **Arithmetische Probleme im Restaurant, auf dem Bahnhof, im Laden.** Then answer these questions.

1 Worüber (about what) wollen die Herren heute reden?   2 Wie viele Personen speisen im Restaurant? 3 Wieviel beträgt die Rechnung für alle? 4 Wieviel lassen Sie dem Kellner als Trinkgeld? 5 Was für einen Handkoffer trägt der Herr? 6 Wieviel wiegt dieser schwere Handkoffer? 7 Rechnet man auf dem europäischen Kontinent die Entfernung in Meilen oder in Kilometern? 8 Wohin geht Herr Clark, um Einkäufe zu machen? 9 Was ist der Betrag von allen Einkäufen im Laden? 10 Was ist das Thema für Donnerstag? 11 Ist das ein wichtiges oder unwichtiges Thema? 12 Was für ein Gespräch erwartet Herr Clark?

Exercise No. 68. Übersetzen Sie!

1 This suitcase is heavy. It is a heavy suitcase. He is carrying a heavy suitcase. 2 This store is large. They always buy in this large store. 3 This

conversation is interesting. I am expecting an interesting conversation. 4 These gloves are very beautiful. I am buying these beautiful gloves. 5 She is buying a silk handkerchief. 6 This problem is difficult. This is a difficult problem. 7 There are (**Es gibt**) large stores in this city. 8 That hat is new. She is buying a new hat.

CHAPTER 16

WIEVIEL UHR IST ES?
WHAT TIME IS IT?

1 Herr Müller redet.

2 Die Tageszeit! Jedermann will wissen: Wieviel Uhr ist es? Um wievel Uhr kommt das Flugzeug an? Um wieviel Uhr fährt der Zug ab? Um wieviel Uhr beginnt die Prüfung? Um wieviel Uhr fängt die Vorstellung an? Um wieviel Uhr stehen Sie auf?

3 Also, Herr Clark, ich spiele die Rolle des Beamten am Kartenschalter auf dem Bahnhof zu Frankfurt. Sie spielen, als Übung, die Rolle des Reisenden. Sie wollen eine Fahrkarte kaufen. Sie wünschen Auskunft. Bitte, wollen Sie anfangen?

4 Der Reisende, Hr. C. Der Beamte, Hr. M.

— Eine Fahrkarte zweiter Klasse nach Köln, bitte.

— Einfach oder Rückfahrkarte?

— Geben Sie mir eine Rückfahrkarte, bitte. Wieviel kostet das?

— Achtunddreißig Mark.

(Der Beamte gibt dem Reisenden die Fahrkarte. Dieser[1] zahlt.)

— Um wieviel Uhr fährt der Zug von Frankfurt ab, und wann kommt er in Köln an?

— Es gibt täglich einige Züge nach Köln. Ein guter Zug fährt um 14 (vierzehn) Uhr ab und kommt um 16.50 Uhr (sechzehn Uhr fünfzig) in Köln an.

— Ich danke Ihnen[2] sehr.

— Bitte schön.

5 Herr Müller: Großartig, Herr Clark! Sie spielen Ihre Rolle wunderbar.

Jetzt spiele ich die Rolle des Angestellten an der Kasse im Kino. Sie spielen die Rolle des Touristen. Sie wünschen Auskunft über die Vorstellung. Bitte fangen Sie an!

6 Der Tourist, Hr. C. Der Angestellte, Hr. M.

— Bitte, sagen Sie mir: Um wieviel Uhr fängt die Vorstellung an.

— Wir haben drei Vorstellungen. Die erste beginnt um 1.20 (ein Uhr zwanzig) nachmittags; die zweite beginnt um 4.20 (vier Uhr zwanzig); und die dritte um 7.10 (sieben Uhr zehn) abends.

— Gibt es auch einen Film mit den letzten Neuigkeiten?

— Sie meinen die Wochenschau. Natürlich. Zwanzig Minuten vor dem Hauptfilm.

— Was ist der Preis für eine Karte?

— Die Karte kostet zwei Mark.

— Bitte, geben Sie mir zwei Karten für die dritte Vorstellung.

(Der Angestellte gibt dem Touristen die Karten. Dieser[1] zahlt.)

7 Herr M: Ausgezeichnet! Ich muß es wieder sagen. Sie spielen Ihre Rolle wunderbar.

8 Herr C: Danke bestens. Es war für mich eine interessante und wertvolle Übung.

NOTES: 1. **Dieser** (the latter) refers to the last one mentioned, i.e. **der Tourist.** The first one mentioned, **der Angestellte,** would be referred to as **jener** (the former). 2 **Ihnen,** dative of **Sie.** The verb **danken** takes a dative object. You will meet other verbs that take a dative object.

1 Mr. Müller is speaking.

2 The time of day! Everybody wants to know: What time is it? At what time does the plane arrive? At what time does the train leave? At what time does the examination begin? At what time does the performance begin? At what time do you get up?

3 Well, Mr. Clark, I'll play the role of the employee in the ticket office at the railway station in Frankfurt. You will play, for practice, the role of the traveller. You want to buy a ticket. You wish for information. Please, will you begin?

4 The traveller, Mr. C. The clerk, Mr. M.

— A second class ticket for Cologne, please.

— Single or return?

— Give me a return ticket, please. How much does that cost?

— Thirty-eight marks.

(The employee gives the traveller the ticket. The latter pays.)

— At what time does the train leave Frankfurt, and at what time does it arrive in Cologne?

— There are several trains daily for Cologne. A good train leaves at 14.00 hours and arrives in Cologne at 16.50 hours.

— I thank you very much.

— Don't mention it.

5 Mr. Müller: Splendid, Mr. Clark! You play your role wonderfully.

Now I shall play the role of the clerk in the box-office in the cinema. You will play the role of the tourist. You want information about the performance. Please, begin.

6 The tourist, Mr. C. The employee, Mr. M.

— Please tell me what time the performance begins.

— We have three performances. The first begins at 1.20 p.m.; the second at 4.20; and the third at 7.10 in the evening.

— Is there also a film with the latest news?

— You mean the newsreel (*lit.* weekly review). Of course. Twenty minutes before the main film.

— What is the price of a ticket?

— A ticket costs two marks.

— Please give me two tickets for the third performance.

(The employee gives the tourist the tickets. The latter pays.)

7 Mr. M: Splendid! I must say it again, you play your role wonderfully.

8 Mr. C: Thanks a lot. It was an interesting and valuable exercise for me.

Wortschatz

der Reisende *pl.* **-n,** traveller	**die Prüfung** *pl.* **-en,** test, examination
der Beámte *pl.* **-n,** employee, clerk	**ab-fahren,** to leave, depart
der Angestellte *pl.* **-n,** employee	**an-fangen,** to begin
die Karte *pl.* **-n** ticket	**an-kommen,** to arrive

der Preis *pl.* -e, price, cost
der Film *pl.* -e, film
die Wochenschau, newsreel (weekly review)
die Neuigkeiten, news
die Rolle *pl.* -n, role
die Übung *pl.* -en, practice, exercise

ab-gehen, to leave, to go off, depart
auf-stehen, to get up
wünschen, to wish; zahlen, to pay
als as; als Übung, as (for) practice
wertvoll, valuable
jedermann, everyman, everybody

Words Dealing with Travel

der Bahnhof *pl.* ⁻e, railway station
auf dem Bahnhof, at the railway station
der Flughafen *pl.* ⁻, airport
das Flugzeug *pl.* -e, aeroplane
der Dampfer *pl.* -, steamer
der Zug *pl.* ⁻e, train
der Wartesaal *pl.* -säle, waiting room
Ich reise mit dem Dampfer (dem Zug, dem Autobus, dem Flugzeug). I travel by steamer (train, autobus, plane).
Ich fliege morgen nach Frankfurt. I fly to Frankfurt tomorrow.
eine Fahrkarte erster (zweiter, dritter) Klasse, a first (second, third) class ticket
eine einfache Fahrkarte, eine Rückfahrkarte, a single ticket, a return ticket
Wann kommt der Zug von Köln an? When does the train from Cologne arrive?
Wann fährt der Zug von Köln ab? When does the train leave Cologne?
Der Zug von Hamburg hat fünf Minuten Verspätung. The train from Hamburg is five minutes late (*lit.* has five minutes delay).

Deutsche Ausdrücke

Bitte please; ich bitte, I ask, I request; bitten um, to ask for, to request; Ich bitte um eine Antwort. I ask for an answer.
Bitte schön. Don't mention it.
Ich wünsche Auskunft. I want information.
Ausgezeichnet! Excellent!
Großartig! Splendid!
Wunderbar! Wonderful!

Grammar Notes and Practical Exercises

1 Time of day

Wieviel Uhr ist es? or Wie spät ist es?	What time is it?
1.00 Es ist ein Uhr or Es ist eins.	It is one o'clock.
2.00 Es ist zwei Uhr or Es ist zwei.	It is two o'clock.
3.00 drei Uhr; 4.00 vier Uhr; usw.	three o'clock; four o'clock; etc.
3.10 zehn Minuten nach drei	ten minutes past three
3.15 ein Viertel nach drei	quarter past three
3.30 halb vier	half past three
3.45 ein Viertel vor vier	quarter to four
3.50 zehn Mimuten vor vier	ten minutes to four
Um wieviel Uhr? Um eins; um ein Viertel nach zehn; usw.	At what time? At one; at quarter past ten; etc.

In general, the method of expressing time is the same in English and German. **vor** = to and **nach** = after, past. But watch for the half hours. They are expressed with reference to the next hour. Thus: 9.30 = **halb zehn** (half an hour towards ten); 12.30 = **halb eins;**[1] etc.

NOTE 1. The quarter hours may also be expressed in the same way. Thus 3.15 = **(ein) Viertel** (towards) **vier;** 3.45 = **drei Viertel vier;** etc.

In train and plane timetables, also in theatre announcements, time is usually indicated by the 24-hour clock beginning with midnight (24.00). This eliminates the need for a.m. and p.m. and for the German expressions: **morgens,** in the morning, **nachmittags,** in the afternoon, and **abends,** in the evening. Thus:

6.30 (sechs Uhr dreißig) = 6.30 a.m.
10.15 (zehn Uhr fünfzehn) = 10.15 a.m.
12.00 (zwölf Uhr) = 12.00 noon
14.00 (vierzehn Uhr) = 2.00 p.m.
17.20 (siebzehn Uhr zwanzig) = 5.20 p.m.
23.10 (dreiundzwanzig Uhr zehn) = 11.10 p.m.

Exercise No. 69. Say and write the German for these time expressions, using the 12-hour clock.

Beispiel: 10.15 = ein Viertel nach zehn; 4.55 = fünf Minuten vor fünf.

(a) **1.15**	(c) **8.15**	(e) **3.20**	(g) **11.00**	(i) **12.30**	(k) **9.45**
(b) **5.10**	(d) **2.45**	(f) **3.55**	(h) **4.20**	(j) **7.30**	(l) **10.23**

Exercise No. 70. Read these sentences giving the time according to the 24-hour clock.

Beispiel: 1. Ein guter Zug geht um einundzwanzig Uhr 10 ab.

1 Ein guter Zug geht um 21.10 ab. 2 Dieser Zug kommt um 17.25 in Köln an. 3 Der Schnellzug nach Bremen fährt um 15.14 ab. 4 Der Zug von Hamburg hat zehn Minuten Verspätung. Er kommt gegen 8.25 an. 5 Es gibt Züge nach Bonn um 6.25 und 18.50. 6 Das Flugzeug verläßt den Flughafen in London um 19.00 Uhr. Es kommt um 20.10 am Flughafen in München an. 7 Die Opernvorstellung beginnt heute abend um 19.30. 8 Die erste Vorstellung im Kino beginnt um 14.30. 9 Die letzte Vorstellung endet um 22.30.

2. Separable verbs. Present tense of **aufstehen** to stand up, to get up

I get up early every day. You get up early every day, etc.

Ich **stehe** jeden Tag früh **auf.**	Wir **stehen** jeden Tag früh **auf.**
Du **stehst** jeden Tag früh **auf.**	Ihr **steht** jeden Tag früh **auf.**
Er **steht** jeden Tag früh **auf.**	Sie **stehen** jeden Tag früh **auf.**

Imperative: **Stehe** jeden Tag früh **auf! Steht** jeden Tag früh **auf! Stehen Sie** jeden Tag früh **auf!**

(a) Verbs often have prefixes which may separate from the verb itself. Such prefixes are called *separable prefixes,* and the verbs to which they are attached are called *separable verbs.*

The stress in separable verbs is always on the prefix. The meaning of a separable verb is usually the meaning of the simple verb plus the meaning of the prefix. Thus: **auf-stehen,** to stand up, to get up; **ab-gehen,** to go away, to leave; **ab-fahren,** to go away, to leave; **zurück-geben,** to give back; **zurück-kommen,** to come back; **an-fangen,** to begin. A hyphen is used in the vocabularies to indicate separable prefixes.

(*b*) The separable prefix goes to the end of a simple sentence or main clause in the present tense and in the imperative.

Sie gibt uns fünf Mark **zurück.**	She gives us back five marks.
Wann geht der Schnellzug **ab?**	When does the express train leave?
Steht um sieben Uhr **auf, Kinder!**	Get up at seven o'clock, children.

Exercise No. 71. Complete these sentences with the present tense of the verbs in parentheses or with the imperative (impv.) if so indicated.

Beispiel: 1. Um 8 Uhr **fangen wir** die Prüfung **an.**

1 (anfangen) Um 8 Uhr —— wir die Prüfung ——.
2 (zurückgeben) Er —— uns fünf Mark ——.
3 (abfahren) Wer —— morgen früh um 6 Uhr ——?
4 (aufstehen) Warum —— Sie so früh ——?
5 (zurückkommen) Wann —— du vom Kino ——?
6 (anfangen) Wir —— die Arbeit um 9 Uhr ——.
7 (ankommen) Wie spät —— der Zug von Köln ——?
8 (anfangen, *impv.*) —— Sie die Arbeit jetzt ——!
9 (aufstehen, *impv.*) —— sofort ——, Kinder!
10 (zurückkommen, *impv.*) —— bald ——, Marie!

3 First and second person pronouns (nominative, dative and accusative)

	Singular			*Plural*			*Polite: Sin. and Plur.*	
N.	ich I	**du** you		**wir** we	**ihr** you		**Sie** you	
D.	mir (to) me	**dir** (to) you		**uns** (to) us	**euch** (to) you		**Ihnen** (to) you	
A.	mich me	**dich** you		**uns** us	**euch** you		**Sie** you	

NOTE: The polite form is like the third person plural: *N.* **sie,** *D.* **ihnen,** *A.* **sie;** but each case of the polite form must be given a capital letter.

Exercise No. 72. Complete the sentences by translating the pronouns in parentheses.

1 Diese Karte ist für (me). 2 Bitte, bringen Sie (me) den Handkoffer. 3 Ist dieser Brief für (you), Herr Braun? 4 Bitte, sagen Sie (us), was Sie wollen! 5 Ich möchte (you) diese neuen Bilder zeigen, Herr Braun. 6 Wir können (you) nicht alles sagen, Kinder. 7 Wir sprechen eben von (you), Karl. 8 Die Mutter sucht (you), Wilhelm. 9 Verstehen Sie (me)? 10 Wir verstehen (you, *pol.*) nicht. 11 Geben Sie (me) die Fahrkarte zurück!

Exercise No. 73. Fragen

Re-read the text: Wieviel Uhr ist es? Then answer these questions.

1 Wer will wissen, wieviel Uhr es ist? 2 Wer spielt die Rolle des Reisenden auf dem Bahnhof zu Frankfurt? 3 Was will der Reisende kaufen? 4 Wieviel kostet die Fahrkarte nach Köln? 5 Kauft er eine Fahrkarte erster oder zweiter

Klasse? 6 Gibt es nur einen Zug nach Köln? 7 Welche Rolle spielt Herr Clark im Kino? 8 Was wünscht der Tourist? 9 Wie viele Vorstellungen gibt es? 10 Wann fängt die letzte Vorstellung an? 11 Wie heißt der Film mit den letzten Neuigkeiten? 12 Wieviele Karten kauft der Tourist?

Exercise No. 74. Übersetzen Sie!

1 What time is it? It is quarter past nine. 2 Thank you. Don't mention it. 3 At what time does the last performance begin? 4 The last performance begins at half past seven. 5 What is the price of a ticket? 6 The tourist pays for two tickets. 7 Are you travelling by plane or by train? 8 I am travelling neither (**weder**) by train nor (**noch**) by plane. I am travelling by car. 9 At what time does the plane leave for Hamburg? It leaves at 18.20. 10 The bus from Düsseldorf arrives at 14.10.

CHAPTER 17

REVISION OF CHAPTERS 12-16

SUMMARY OF NOUNS (SINGULAR AND PLURAL)

Practise these nouns aloud, singular and plural. Thus: **der Kellner, die Kellner; der Preis, die Preise.**

der Kellner	*pl.* -	das Stück	*pl.* -e
der Verkäufer	*pl.* -	der Markt	*pl.* ⁇e
der Schalter	*pl.* -	das Flugzeug	*pl.* -e
der Preis	*pl.* -e	das Problem	*pl.* -e
der Zug	*pl.* ⁇e	der Bahnhof	*pl.* ⁇e
der Film	*pl.* -e	das Wort	*pl.* ⁇er
das Paar	*pl.* -e	das Ei	*pl.* -er
das Trinkgeld	*pl.* -er	die Wahrheit	*pl.* -en
das Taschentuch	*pl.* ⁇er	die Prüfung	*pl.* -en
die Sache	*pl.* -n	die Rechnung	*pl.* -en
die Meile	*pl.* -n	die Übung	*pl.* -en
die Summe	*pl.* -n	die Vorstellung	*pl.* -en
die Fahrkarte	*pl.* -n	die Verkäuferin	*pl.* -nen
die Person	*pl.* -en	die Mahlzeit	*pl.* -en
die Nummer	*pl.* -n	die Gelegenheit	*pl.* -en

Some Rules for Gender:

All nouns ending in **-chen** or **-lein** are neuter (**das Mädchen, das Fräulein**).

All nouns ending in **-heit, -ung, -in** are feminine (**die Wahrheit, die Übung, die Lehrerin**).

Nearly all nouns ending in **-e**, denoting things, are feminine (**die Schule, die Sache, die Meile**).

Some rules for plurals:

Nouns in **-chen** and **-lein** do not change in the plural (**das Mädchen** *pl.* -; **das Fräulein** *pl.* -).

Feminine nouns of more than one syllable add **-n** or **-en** (**die Schwester** *pl.* -n, **die Übung** *pl.* -en). Exceptions—only two (**die Mutter** *pl.* ⁇; **die Tochter** *pl.* ⁇). Nouns with **-in** double the **-n** in the plural (**die Lehrerin, die Lehrerinnen**), before adding **-en**.

Verbs

1 fliegen	8 reservieren	15 bekommen
2 glauben	9 studieren	16 verstehen
3 hoffen	10 speisen	17 erwarten
4 brauchen	11 rechnen	18 wollen
5 zahlen	12 denken (an) + *acc.*	19 er will
6 wünschen	13 verlassen	20 können
7 bleiben	14 gebrauchen	21 er kann

1 to fly	8 to reserve	15 to receive
2 to believe	9 to study	16 to understand
3 to hope	10 to dine	17 to await
4 to need	11 to reckon	18 to want
5 to pay	12 to think (of)	19 he wants
6 to wish	13 to leave	20 to be able
7 to remain	14 to use	21 he can

Verbs with stem change (e> ie, e > i, and a > ä) in second and third person singular.

sehen	lesen	sprechen	treten	geben	zurückgeben
to see	to read	to speak	to step	to give	to give back
ich sehe	**lese**	**spreche**	**trete**	**gebe**	**gebe zurück**
du siehst	**liest**	**sprichst**	**trittst**	**gibst**	**gibst zurück**
er sieht	**liest**	**spricht**	**tritt**	**gibt**	**gibt zurück**

fahren	tragen	lassen¹	verlassen²	laufen	anfangen
to ride	to carry	to leave	to leave	to run	to begin
ich fahre	**trage**	**lasse**	**verlasse**	**laufe**	**fange an**
du fährst	**trägst**	**lässt**	**verlässt**	**läufst**	**fängst an**
er fährt	**trägt**	**lässt**	**verlässt**	**läuft**	**fängt an**

NOTES: 1 **Er lässt ein Trinkgeld.** He leaves a tip.   2 **Er verlässt die Stadt.** He leaves (goes away from) the city.

Expressions

1 **Glückliche Reise!**	Happy journey!
2 **Donnerwetter!**	The dickens!
3 **eines Tages**	one day
4 **eines Morgens**	one morning
5 **eines Abends**	one evening
6 **Es freut mich**	I am glad
7 **Es freut uns**	We are glad
8 **denken (an)** + *acc.*	to think (of)
9 **zu Fuß gehen**	to go on foot (walk)
10 **Wir gehen zu Fuß**	We go on foot (walk)
11 **Fangen wir an!**	Let's begin!
12 **Pfund gegen Mark wechseln**	to change pounds for marks
13 **Sie geben sich die Hand**	They shake hands
14 **alles, was möglich ist**	everything possible
15 **Seit wann sind Sie hier?**	Since when have you been here?
16 **Es ist nicht viel wert.**	It is not worth much.

Exercise No. 75. Complete these sentences by translating the words in parentheses.

1 **Ich möchte** (to change marks for pounds).   2 **Sein alter Freund wünscht ihm eine** (happy journey). 3 **Herr Clark** (is making great progress), **denn er ist fleißig und intelligent.** 4 **Was wünschen Sie? Ich wünsche** (information) **über die Vorstellungen.** 5 **Wir gehen zur Station** (on foot), **wenn das Wetter schön ist.** 6 **An wen denken Sie?** (I am thinking of) **meinen alten Schulfreund.** 7 (One evening) **sitzen wir im Arbeitszimmer und sprechen über die Tageszeit.** 8 (Since when) **studieren Sie Deutsch?** 9 (I have been studying) **seit zwei Jahren Deutsch.** 10 (I shake hands with him) **und sage: Auf Wiedersehen.** 11 (I am glad), **dich zu sehen.** 12 (Let's begin). **Es ist schon spät.**

Exercise No. 76. Kurze Gespräche

Practise these short conversations aloud. Translate them.

1 — Was lesen Sie? — Ich lese die deutsche Zeitung.[1] — Was liest er? — Er liest eine englische Zeitung.

2 — Was gibst du der Mutter zum Geburtstag?[2] — Ich gebe ihr ein seidenes[3] Taschentuch. — Was gibt ihr Karl? — Er gibt ihr ein schönes Halstuch.[4]

3 — Spricht Herr Kurz Englisch und Französisch? — Er spricht weder Englisch noch Französisch. Er spricht nur Deutsch.

4 — Welchen Anzug trägt[5] er heute? — Er trägt seinen neuen, braunen Anzug.

5 — Um wieviel Uhr verläßt er jeden Tag das Haus? — Er verlässt Punkt sieben Uhr das Haus.

6 — Wie lange bleiben Sie hier in dieser Stadt? — Ich bleibe ein ganzes[6] Jahr hier.

7 — Haben Sie einen grossen Handkoffer? — Ich habe einen großen und einen kleinen. — Leihen[7] Sie mir, bitte, den großen. — Gerne.[8]

8 — Was für ein[9] hübsches Kleid! — Was für ein schöner Garten! — Was für eine schöne Frau!

NOTES: 1 **die Zeitung** the newspaper. 2 **der Geburtstag** birthday; **zum Geburtstag** for (her) birthday. 3 **seiden** silk. 4 **das Halstuch** scarf. 5 **tragen** to carry or to wear. 6 **ganz** whole. 7 **leihen** to lend. 8 **gerne** gladly. 9 **Was für ein ... !** What a ... !

Exercise No. 77. Select the words from Column II which best complete the sentences in Column I.

I	**II**
1 Frau Clark geht in den großen Laden	(*a*) Geschäftsreise nach Europa zu machen.
2 In Deutschland rechnet man das	(*b*) um Punkt halb sieben auf.
3 Ich beabsichtige, im Sommer eine	(*c*) und jetzt will ich einen grauen kaufen.
4 Jedermann weiß, daß man ohne	(*d*) wenn sie immer fleißig sind.
5 Ich stehe jeden Tag außer Sonntag	(*e*) und kauft neue Kleider für die Kinder.
6 Wenn Sie im Juni nach Europa reisen,	(*f*) Gewicht nicht in Pfund sondern in Kilos.
7 Wissen Sie, um wieviel Uhr	(*g*) daß Sie eine ganze Woche hier bleiben.
8 Ich habe einen blauen Anzug,	(*h*) Geld nicht auskommen kann.
9 Es freut uns zu erfahren,	(*i*) der Zug von Hamburg ankommt?
10 Alle Schüler können Deutsch lernen,	(*j*) müssen Sie sofort einen Platz reservieren.

Grammar Review and Practical Exercises

1 Review Adjective Endings (See Chapter 15, Grammar Notes 2 (*a*), (*b*), (*c*), pp. 80 and 81.)

Exercise No. 78. Complete these sentences with the correct case of the adjective expression in parentheses.

Beispiel: **1.** Wir kaufen der Mutter **ein seidenes Halstuch.**

1 Wir kaufen der Mutter (ein seidenes Halstuch). 2 Ich schreibe mit (der rote Bleistift). 3 Er trägt (ein schwerer Handkoffer). 4 Er trägt (der schwere Handkoffer in den Wartesaal). 5 Das Porträt (eine schöne Frau) hängt über dem Klavier. 6 Herr Müller ist der Vertreter (dieser englische Kaufmann). 7 Die Zigaretten liegen auf (jener kleine Tisch). 8 Die Stühle stehen um (der runde Tisch). 9 Was für (ein schönes Mädchen)! 10 Deutschland ist auf (der europäische Kontinent). 11 Der Vertreter (diese große Firma) heißt Müller. 12 Die Herren sitzen in (das gemütliche Zimmer) des Kaufmanns. 13 Ich will (kein altes Auto) kaufen. 14 Das Gewicht (unser schwerer Koffer) ist 66 Pfund. 15 Er will (sein deutscher Vertreter) in München besuchen.

Exercise No. 79. Change the adjective expressions in heavy type to the plural. Change the verb whenever necessary.

Beispiel: **1. Die jungen Männer** sitzen in dem Arbeitszimmer.

1 **Der junge Mann** sitzt in dem Arbeitszimmer. 2 **Dieses schöne Bild** kostet 100 DM. 3 Wir sprachen eben von **unsrem deutschen Lehrer.** 4 Kennen Sie **dieses kleine Mädchen?** 5 Wo ist die Wohnung **deiner neuen Freundin?** 6 **Die deutsche Übung** ist nicht schwer. 7 Wo ist **das neue Heft?** 8 Ich habe **kein deutsches Buch.** 9 Wo wohnen die Eltern **jenes hübschen Kindes?** 10 Das können Sie in **der deutschen Zeitung** lesen. 11 **Lieber** (dear) **Freund.** 12 **Liebe Freundin.**

2 Summary of First, Second, and Third Person Pronouns—Nominative, Dative, Accusative

	Singular				*Plural*			*Sing. and Plur.*
	1*st*	2*nd*	3*rd*		1*st*	2*nd*	3*rd*	*Polite*
N.	ich	du	er	sie es	*N.*	wir	ihr	sie	Sie
D.	mir	dir	ihm	ihr ihm	*D.*	uns	euch	ihnen	Ihnen
A.	mich	dich	ihn	sie es	*A.*	uns	euch	sie	Sie

Exercise No. 80. Read each question. Complete each answer by translating the pronouns in parentheses.

Beispiel: **1 Herr Müller lehrt uns Deutsch.**

1 **Wer lehrt euch Deutsch?**

1 **Herr Müller lehrt** (us) **Deutsch.**

2 **Kennen Sie Herrn Braun?**

2 **Wir kennen** (him) **sehr gut.**

3 **Wo erwartet mich der Professor?**

3 **Er erwartet** (you *pol.*) **im Arbeitszimmer.**

4 **Ist Doktor Schulz bei Ihnen?**

4 **Ja, er ist bei** (us).

5 **Schreibst Du dem Onkel einen Brief?**

5 **Ja, ich schreibe** (him) **einen langen Brief.**

6 **Was gebt ihr der Mutter zum Geburtstag?**

6 **Wir geben** (her) **eine goldene Uhr.**

7 **Für wen ist dieser neue Anzug?**

7 **Er ist für** (you), **Herr Engel.**

8 **Kannst du mir zehn Mark leihen?**

8 **Ich kann** (you *fam.*) **nur fünf Mark leihen.**

9 **Haben Sie meine deutsche Zeitung?**

9 **Nein, ich habe** (it) **nicht.**

10 Wo ist der Aschenbecher?	10 (It) ist auf dem kleinen Tisch.
11 Wo ist die Füllfeder?	11 (It) ist dem großen Pult.
12 Wo ist mein deutsches Heft?	12 (It) ist in diesem Schlafzimmer.

Zwei Dialoge.

Re-read instructions on p. 61 about 'Dialoge'.

Der erste Dialog
IHRE UHR GEHT NACH

— Sie kommen ja zu spät. Die Vorstellung fängt schon an.

— Entschuldigen Sie, daß ich spät komme. Wegen des Verkehrs mußte mein Taxi sehr langsam fahren.

— Wie spät ist es nach Ihrer Uhr?

— Halb neun.

— Ihre Uhr geht nach. Es ist schon zwanzig Minuten vor neun.

— Ich glaube, Ihre geht ein bißchen vor. Auf der Uhr da drüben ist es erst fünfundzwanzig Minuten vor neun.

The First Dialogue
YOUR WATCH IS SLOW

— Why, you're late. The performance has just begun.

— Excuse me for being late. On account of the traffic my taxi had to go very slowly.

— What time is it by your watch?

— Half past eight.

— Your watch is slow. It is already twenty minutes to nine.

— I believe your watch is a little fast. On the clock over there it is only twenty-five minutes to nine.

Der zweite Dialog
IM AUTOBUS—WO MUSS MAN AUSSTEIGEN?

— Entschuldigen Sie, bitte. Wo muß ich aussteigen, um nach dem Hauptpostamt zu kommen? (nach dem Bahnhof, nach der Frauenkirche, nach der britischen Gesandtschaft, usw.)

— Sie müssen am Odeonsplatz aussteigen. usw.

— Ist es weit von hier?

— Nein, nicht sehr weit. Ich werde die Haltestelle ausrufen.

The Second Dialogue
IN THE BUS—WHERE MUST ONE GET OFF?

— Excuse me, please. Where must I get off for the main post office? (the railway station, the Church of Our Lady, the British Embassy, etc.)

— You must get off at Odeon Square, etc.

— Is it far from here?

— No, not very far. I will call out the stop.

Exercise No. 81. Lesestück (Re-read instructions on p. 61).

KARL STUDIERT NICHT GERN MATHEMATIK

Karl kommt eines Tages aus der Schule und sagt zu seiner Mutter: „Ich lerne Mathematik nicht gern. Sie ist zu schwer. Warum müssen wir so viele Übungen und Aufgaben[1] machen? Wir haben doch Rechenmaschinen,[2] nicht wahr?

Die Mutter sieht ihren Sohn an und sagt: „Du hast unrecht, mein Kind. Man kann nichts ohne Mathematik tun. Man braucht Mathematik nicht nur[3] im täglichen Leben sondern auch[4] auf allen Gebieten[5] der Wissenschaft." Die Mutter hört auf[6] zu sprechen, denn sie sieht, ihr Sohn gibt nicht auf das acht,[7] was sie sagt.

„Sage einmal, lieber Junge, interessiert dich das Fußballspiel nicht?"

„Ach was, Mutter! Du machst Spaß."[8]

„Nun also, wenn die Hotspurs acht Spiele gewinnen[9] und drei verlieren,[10] weißt du welchen Prozentsatz[11] der Spiele sie gewinnen?"

Karl antwortet: „Für den Prozentsatz der Spiele brauche ich keine Mathe-, matik. Ich finde doch alles in der Zeitung ausgerechnet.[12] Du hast aber recht Mutter. Ich muß mehr lernen. Ich hoffe eines Tages auf eine Universität zu gehen,[13] und deswegen muß ich die Schulprüfungen gut bestehen,[14] nicht nur in Mathematik, sondern auch in den anderen Fächern."[15]

NOTES: 1 die Aufgabe task, exercise. 2 calculating machines. 3 and 4 nicht nur . . . sondern auch not only . . . but also. 5 auf . . . Wissenschaft in all fields of science. 6 auf-hören to stop. 7 achtgeben auf to pay attention to. 8 You're joking. 9 win. 10 lose. 11 percentage. 12 worked out. 13 auf . . . gehen to go to a university. 14 eine Prüfung bestehen to pass an examination. 15 das Fach subject.

CHAPTER 18

DER WERKTAG DES HERRN CLARK
MR. CLARK'S WORKING DAY

1 Herr Clark, darf ich Sie fragen, wie Sie einen Werktag verbringen?

2 Gewiß. Wenn ich in mein Büro gehe, muß ich um sechs Uhr aufstehen. Ich wasche mich, rasiere mich und ziehe mich an. Das dauert ungefähr eine halbe Stunde. Gegen sieben setze ich mich zum Frühstück an den Tisch im Eßzimmer.

3 Und Ihre Frau steht auch so früh auf?

4 Ja, meine Frau steht früh auf, und wir frühstücken zusammen. Ich habe das natürlich sehr gern. Wir haben eine gute Gelegenheit, uns über die Kinder, sowie auch über andere Dinge zu unterhalten.

5 Was essen Sie zum Frühstück?

6 Gewöhnlich habe ich Orangensaft, Speck mit Ei, Toast oder Semmeln und Kaffee.

7 Wie ich sehe, essen Sie ein nahrhaftes Frühstück. Und dann nach dem Frühstück?

8 Um halb acht bin ich bereit im Auto nach der Station zu fahren, wo ich den Zug nehme. Manchmal stehen die Kinder früh genug auf, um mich zu sehen, ehe ich weggehe.

9 Um wieviel Uhr erreichen Sie Ihr Büro?

10 Ich erreiche das Büro um neun Uhr. Im Büro lese ich zuerst die Post, dann diktiere ich meiner Sekretärin einige Briefe und führe Telephongespräche mit verschiedenen Kunden. Ich tue im allgemeinen alles, was ein Geschäftsmann zu tun hat.

11 Wann essen Sie zu Mittag?

12 Fast immer um ein Uhr. Ich brauche nur ungefähr zwanzig Minuten zum Essen.

13 Das ist sehr wenig! In Deutschland macht man es anders mit dem Essen. Die Deutschen verbringen viel Zeit bei den Mahlzeiten, besonders beim Mittagessen. Das ist für sie die Hauptmahlzeit. Aber davon sprechen wir ein anderes Mal. Was tun Sie nach dem Mittagessen?

14 Oft besuchen mich Kunden. Von Zeit zu Zeit gehe ich zu den Kunden.

15 Um wieviel Uhr beenden Sie Ihre Arbeit?

16 Ich verlasse Punkt fünf mein Büro. Ich komme um ein Viertel nach sechs nach Hause. Ich spiele ein wenig mit den Kindern, bevor wir uns zum Abendessen an den Tisch setzen.

17 Nach einem solchen Tag sind Sie wohl etwas müde.

18 Jawohl, Herr Müller. Und ich freue mich sehr, zu Hause zu sein.

1 Mr. Clark, may I ask you how you spend a working day?

2 Certainly. When I go to my office I must get up at six o'clock. I wash, shave, and dress. That takes about half an hour. Towards seven o'clock I sit down at the table in the dining-room for breakfast.

3 And does your wife also get up so early?

4 Yes. My wife gets up early and we have breakfast together. Naturally I like that very much. We have a good opportunity to talk about the children and also about other things.

5 What do you eat for breakfast?

6 Usually I have orange juice, bacon and egg, toast or rolls, and coffee.

7 As I see, you eat a nutritious breakfast. And then after breakfast?

8 At half past seven I am ready to go by car to the station, where I take the train. Sometimes the children get up early enough to see me before I go.

9 At what time do you arrive at your office?

10 I reach the office at nine o'clock. In the office I read the mail first of all, then I dictate some letters to my secretary and carry on telephone conversations with various customers. In general I do everything that a businessman has to do.

11 When do you have lunch?

12 Almost always at one o'clock. I take only about twenty minutes for lunch.

13 That is very little! In Germany they do it differently with regard to eating. The Germans spend much time at meals, especially at the midday meal (lunch). That is for them the main meal. But we'll speak about that another time. What do you do after lunch?

14 Often customers come to visit me. From time to time I go to the customers.

15 At what time do you finish your day's work?

16 I leave my office at five o'clock sharp. I get home at quarter past six. I play with the children a little, before we sit down at the table to dinner.

17 After such a day you must be rather tired.

18 Yes indeed, Mr. Müller. And I am very happy to be at home.

Wortschatz

die **Hauptmahlzeit**, *pl.* -en, chief meal
das **Frühstück**, *pl.* -e, breakfast
das **Mittagessen**, *pl.* -, dinner, noon meal
das **Abendessen**, *pl.* -supper, evening meal
die **Post** mail; der **Kunde**, *pl.* -n, customer
die **Sekretärin** *pl.* -nen, secretary
die **Zeit**, *pl.* -en, time; das **Mal**, time (*See* „Deutsche Ausdrücke" below.)
beénden, to finish, to complete
dauern, to last, to take (time)
diktíeren, to dictate
erréichen, to reach
essen (ich esse, du ißt, er ißt) to eat

telephoníeren, to telephone
verbríngen, to spend (time)
weg-gehen, to go away; **er geht heute weg**
beréit, ready; **müde**, tired
halb, half; **eine halbe Stunde**
verschíeden, various; **nur**, only
natürlich, naturally, of course
besónders, especially; **anders**, otherwise
sowie, and also, as well as
solch, such
bevór = (*subordinate conj.*) before; **Er küßt die Kinder, bevor (ehe) er morgens weggeht.**

Einige Lebensmittel   Some Foods

das **Brot**, bread
das **Brötchen** *pl.* -, roll
die **Sahne**, cream
das **Ei**, *pl.* -er, egg
das **Gemüse**, vegetable
das **Obst**, fruit

die **Semmel** *pl.* -n, roll   der **Kuchen** *pl.* -, cake   der **Fisch** *pl.* -e, fish
die **Butter,** butter   der **Speck,** bacon   der **Orangensaft** (o-ran-
die **Milch,** milk   das **Fleisch,** meat   ʒen-zaft) orange juice

NOTE 1. ʒ is pronounced like Eng. *s* in *measure*.

Deutsche Ausdrücke

das **Mal,** time; **das erste Mal, das zweite Mal,** the first time, the second time.
-**mal** is used in many compounds to express 'number of times' or 'definite
point of time'. Thus: **einmal,** one time, once; **zweimal,** two times, twice;
dreimal, three times; **manchmal,** sometimes; **keinmal,** no time; **diesmal,** this
time; **letztesmal,** last time.
zum Frühstück, for breakfast
zum Abendessen, for supper
zum Mittagessen, for dinner
wohl, indeed, surely, is used for emphasis. **Sie sind wohl müde nach einem
solchen Tag.** You are surely tired after such a day.
dauern, to last, to take (time)
Die Prüfung dauerte zwei Stunden. The examination lasted two hours.

Grammar Notes and Practical Exercise

1 Present tense of *nehmen* to take; *dürfen* to be permitted, may

ich nehme	wir nehmen	ich darf	wir dürfen
du nimmst	ihr nehmt	du darfst	ihr dürft
er, sie, es nimmt	sie (Sie) nehmen	er, sie, es darf	sie (Sie) dürfen

Imperative: **nimm! nehmt! nehmen Sie!**

Exercise No. 82. Read aloud. Translate.

1 **Darf ich Sie fragen, wie alt Sie sind?** 2 **Darf ich Sie um Ihren Namen
bitten?** 3 **Darf ich das Zimmer verlassen?** 4 **Darf ich Ihnen das Brot reichen?**
5 **Darf ich Sie um Feuer**[1] **bitten?** 6 **Darf ich Ihnen meine Freundin vorstellen?**[2]
7 **Dürfen wir hereinkommen?**[3] 8 **Um halb drei dürfen sie die Schule verlassen.**
9 **Die Kinder dürfen nicht auf der Straße spielen.** 10 **Es darf niemand**[4] **in dieses
Zimmer eintreten.**[5] 11 **Darf ich Ihnen eine Zigarette anbieten?**[6] 12 **Keiner**[7] **darf
hereinkommen.**

NOTES: 1 **das Feuer,** fire, a light for smoking. 2 **vor-stellen,** to introduce.
3 **herein-kommen,** to come in. 4 **niemand,** nobody. 5 **ein-treten,** to step into.
6 **an-bieten,** to offer. 7 **keiner** = **niemand.**

2 Reflexive verbs. Present tense of *sich setzen* to seat oneself, to sit down

ich setze **mich**	I sit down	wir setzen **uns**	we sit down
du setzt **dich**	you sit down	ihr setzt **euch**	you sit down
er setzt **sich**	he sits down	sie setzen **sich**	they sit down
sie setzt **sich**	she sits down	Sie setzen **sich**	{ you sit down
es setzt **sich**	it sits down		{ you sit down

Imperative: Setze **dich,** Hans! Setzt **euch,** Kinder! Setzen **Sie sich,** meine
Herren!

The reflexive pronouns in the first and second person singular and plural are like the accusative of the personal pronouns (**mich, dich, uns, euch**).

For the third person and the polite form, the reflexive pronoun is **sich** in both the singular and plural. Thus **sich** may mean *oneself, himself, herself, itself, themselves, yourself* (*pol.*), *yourselves* (*pol.*). The polite **sich** does not take a capital letter.

3 Some common reflexive verbs

Note that German reflexive verbs are not always translated by English reflexive verbs.

sich waschen	to wash oneself	ich wasche mich	du wäschst dich
sich rasiéren	to shave oneself	ich rasiere mich	er rasiert sich
sich anziehen	to dress oneself	ich ziehe mich an	sie zieht sich an
sich freuen	to be glad (happy)	ich freue mich	wir freuen uns
sich unterhálten	to converse	ich unterhalte mich	sie unterhalten sich
sich amüsiéren	to amuse (enjoy) oneself, to have a good time	ich amüsiere mich	Sie amüsieren sich

Exercise No. 83. Read the following questions and answers aloud. Translate them.

1 **Um wieviel Uhr stehst du auf?**
  Ich stehe um sieben Uhr auf.
2 **Ziehst du dich schnell an?**
  Ja, ich ziehe mich schnell an.
3 **Amüsieren sich die Kinder im Park?**
  Sie amüsieren sich sehr.
4 **Worüber unterhalten sich die Eltern beim Frühstück?**
  Sie unterhalten sich über die Kinder.

5 **Um wieviel Uhr setzen Sie sich zum Frühstück?**
  Wir setzen uns um halb acht zum Frühstück.
6 **Rasieren Sie sich jeden Morgen?**
  Ja, ich rasiere mich fast jeden Morgen.

Exercise No. 84. Complete each German sentence with the correct reflexive pronoun.

Beispiel: 1. Ziehe dich an, Karl! Zieht euch an, Kinder!

1 Get dressed, Charles. Get dressed, children.
2 How are you enjoying yourselves this evening?
3 I don't feel well today.
4 The boy is already shaving himself.
5 They are conversing about the weather.
6 Is he feeling tired after work?
7 We must dress quickly.
8 At ten o'clock we sit down at the table.
9 Why don't you sit down?
10 William, wash and dress yourself.
11 Please sit down in the dining-room.
12 We are glad when papa arrives.

1 **Ziehe —— an, Karl! Zieht —— an, Kinder!**
2 **Wie amüsieren Sie —— heute abend?**
3 **Ich fühle —— heute nicht wohl.**

4 Der Junge rasiert —— schon.
5 Sie unterhalten —— über das Wetter.
6 Fühlt er —— müde nach der Arbeit?
7 Wir müssen —— schnell anziehen.
8 Um zehn Uhr setzen wir —— an den Tisch.
9 Warum setzen Sie —— nicht?
10 Wilhelm wasch —— und zieh —— an!
11 Bitte, setzen Sie —— in das Eßzimmer!
12 Wir freuen ——, wenn Papa ankommt.

4 Separable verbs in subordinate clauses

In subordinate clauses separable verbs, like simple verbs, must stand last. However, note that the prefix does *not* separate from the verb in subordinate word order.

Normal word order: **Der Zug fährt um 7.45 ab. Herr Clark geht morgens weg.**

Subordinate word order: **Ich weiß, daß der Zug um 7.45 abfährt. Herr Clark küßt die Kinder, bevor er morgens weggeht.**

Exercise No. 85. Read aloud and translate.

1 Herr Clark steht jeden Werktag früh auf. 2 Er wäscht sich und rasiert sich sehr schnell. 3 Er zieht sich schnell an. 4 Herr Clark und seine Frau frühstücken zusammen. 5 Er fährt mit dem Auto nach der Station. 6 Der Zug kommt bald[1] an. 7 Herr Clark steigt mit vielen anderen Leuten in den Zug ein. 8 Der Zug fährt in einigen Minuten ab. 9 Der Zug kommt in einer halben[2] Stunde in London an. 10 Alle Passagiere steigen aus. 11 Herr Clark geht zu Fuß in sein Büro. 12 Er arbeitet tüchtig[3] den ganzen Tag.[4]

NOTES: 1 **bald** (balt) soon. 2 **halb** (halp) half. 3 **tüchtig** (tyxtix) diligently. 4 Duration of time and definite time are expressed by the accusative: **den ganzen Tag** all day, **jeden Tag** every day.

Exercise No. 86. Make a subordinate clause out of each sentence in Exercise No. 85 by beginning with **Wir wissen, daß . . .**

Beispiel: Wir wissen, (1) daß Herr Clark jeden Werktag früh aufsteht; (2) daß er sich sehr schnell wäscht und rasiert; usw.

Exercise No. 87. Fragen

Re-read the text: **Der Werktag des Herrn Clark.** Then answer these questions.

1 Um wieviel Uhr muß Herr Clark aufstehen, wenn er in sein Büro geht? 2 Wieviel Zeit braucht er, um sich zu waschen, sich zu rasieren und sich anzuziehen? 3 Um wieviel Uhr setzt er sich zum Frühstück? 4 Frühstückt er allein oder mit seiner Frau? 5 Unterhalten sie sich während des Frühstücks über die Kinder? 6 Was hat Herr Clark gewöhnlich zum Frühstück? 7 Stehen die Kinder immer auf, bevor er weggeht? 8 Fährt er im Auto nach der Station oder geht er zu Fuß? 9 Was liest er, sobald[1] er im Büro ankommt? 10 Mit wem telephoniert er? 11 Wieviel Zeit braucht er zum Mittagessen? 12 Um wieviel Uhr verläßt er sein Büro? 13 Um wieviel Uhr kommt er nach Hause? 14 Fühlt er sich müde am Ende des Tages? 15 Freut er sich, zu Hause zu sein?

NOTE 1. **sobald** (*subordinate conjunction*) as soon as. Note the subordinate word order.

Exercise No. 88. Übersetzen Sie!

1 The children get up early and dress themselves quickly.   2 They are not permitted to play before breakfast. 3 We sit down to breakfast at seven o'clock in the morning. 4 They sit down for supper at six o'clock in the evening. 5 When do you sit down to dinner? 6 I work very hard and feel tired at the end (**am Ende**) of the day. 7 After supper they talk about the children. 8 We are glad to see you (**Sie**),

CHAPTER 19

DIE KLEINE ANNA WAR KRANK
LITTLE ANNA WAS ILL

1 Es war im Monat Februar. Es schneite, und das Wetter war sehr kalt, als Herr Müller zum Haus des Herrn Clark kam und klingelte. Karl, der ältere Sohn des Kaufmanns, kam zur Tür und öffnete sie.

2 Er sagte: „Guten Abend, Herr Müller, Kommen Sie herein! Geben Sie mir, bitte, Ihren Hut und Überzieher! Papa wartet auf Sie im Arbeitszimmer."

3 Herr Müller erwiderte: „Danke schön"; gab ihm Hut und Überzieher und ging ins Arbeitszimmer, wo Herr Clark ihn erwartete.

4 Sie begannen sofort zu plaudern.

5 Wie geht es Ihnen heute, Herr Müller?

6 Sehr gut, danke. Und Ihnen? Und was macht Ihre Familie?

7 Mir geht's gut, danke. Aber unsere kleine Anna ist krank.

8 Das tut mir sehr leid. Was fehlt ihr?

9 Sie hat Halsschmerzen und Fieber. Der Doktor sagt, Anna hat die Grippe. Sie soll so viel wie möglich ruhen und viel Fruchtsaft trinken. Er verschrieb ihr auch eine Medizin. Heute abend geht es ihr ein wenig besser. Sie schläft jetzt ruhig.

10 Es freut mich, das zu hören. Sagen Sie mir, bitte, geht Anna zur Schule?

11 Sie geht in den Kindergarten, denn sie ist noch zu jung für die Schule. Sie ist erst fünf Jahre alt.

12 Die Herren redeten noch eine Weile über Herrn Clarks Familie, über die Schulen in der Vorstadt und über andere Dinge.

13 Endlich sagte Herr Müller: „Es ist Zeit, daß ich gehe. Hoffentlich fühlt sich die kleine Anna bald wohlauf und munter."

14 Herr Clark dankte ihm, ging mit ihm zur Tür und half ihm mit dem Überzieher.

15 Sie gaben sich die Hand und sagten: „Auf Wiedersehen!"

1 It was in the month of February. It was snowing and the weather was very cold when Mr. Müller came to the home of Mr. Clark and rang the doorbell. Charles, the older son of the businessman, came to the door and opened it.

2 He said: 'Good evening, Mr. Müller. Come in! Please give me your hat and overcoat. Daddy is waiting for you in the study.'

3 Mr. Müller answered: 'Thank you very much,' gave him his hat and overcoat and went into the study, where Mr. Clark was waiting for him.

4 They began to chat immediately.

5 How are you today, Mr. Müller?

6 Very well, thank you. And you? And how is your family?

7 I'm fine, thank you. But our little Anna is ill.

8 I'm very sorry. What is the matter with her?

9 She has a sore throat and a temperature. The doctor says Anna has the 'flu. She is to rest as much as possible and drink a lot of fruit juice. He also prescribed a medicine for her. This evening she feels a little better. She is now sleeping quietly.

10 I am glad to hear that. Tell me, please, does Anna go to school?

11 She goes to kindergarten, because she is still too young for school. She is only five years old.

12 The men talked a while longer about Mr. Clark's family, about the schools in the suburbs and other things.

13 Finally Mr. Müller said: 'It is time for me to go. I hope little Anna will soon feel well and lively.'

14 Mr. Clark thanked him, went with him to the door, and helped him with his overcoat.

15 They shook hands and said 'Good-bye'.

Wortschatz

der Überzieher *pl.* -, overcoat
die Medizín *pl.* -en, medicine
eine Weile, a while
danken + *dat. object*, to thank
erwarten, to await, expect
helfen + *dat. object*, to help
warten auf + *acc.*, to wait for
heréin-kommen, to come in
klingeln, to ring
ruhen, to rest
verschréiben (*past* verschrieb), to prescribe
alt, old; älter, older

krank, ill; die Krankheit *pl.* -en, illness
gesúnd, well; die Gesúndheit, health
ruhig, still, quiet, quietly
munter, cheerful; traurig, sad
hoffentlich, I hope, let us hope
(Hoffentlich kommt er bald. I hope he will soon be coming)
als, when (*subordinate conj.*, used with past tense). Als er ins Haus hereinkam, grüßte ihn Karl. When he came into the house, Charles greeted him.

Sprichwort

Es geht nichts über die Gesundheit   Nothing is better than good health.

Deutsche Ausdrücke

Was fehlt ihm?—Er hat Zahnweh (Kopfweh). What is the matter with him?—He has a toothache (a headache).

Was fehlt ihr?—Sie hat die Grippe. What is the matter with her?—She has 'flu.

Was fehlt Ihnen?—Ich habe Schnupfen. What is the matter with you?— I have a cold (head cold).

Das tut mir leid. I am sorry.

Das tut uns leid. We are sorry.

Er war krank. Jetzt geht es ihm besser. He was ill. Now he is feeling better.

Ich war krank. Jetzt geht es mir besser. I was ill. Now I am feeling better.

Wir rufen den Arzt. We call the doctor.

Er verschrieb eine Medizin. He prescribed a medicine.

Grammar Notes and Practical Exercises

1 Present Tense of *schlafen,* to sleep; *sollen,* shall, to be supposed to, to be said to.

ich schlafe	wir schlafen	ich soll	wir sollen
du schläfst	ihr schlaft	du sollst	ihr sollt
er, sie, es schläft	sie (Sie) schlafen	er, sie, es soll	sie (Sie) sollen

Imperative: schlafe! schlaft! schlafen Sie! Note the irregular singular of **sollen.**

Exercise No. 89. Repeat each German sentence aloud several times.

1 Ännchen soll viel Fruchtsaft trinken.
2 Wir sollen auf den Arzt warten.
3 Sollen wir diese Aufgabe machen?
4 Sie sollen sehr reich sein.
5 Sollen wir fahren oder zu Fuß gehen?
6 Was soll ich damit machen?
7 Du darfst gehen, aber um vier Uhr mußt du zurück sein.
8 „Du sollst nicht stehlen!"[1]

1 Annie is to drink much fruit juice.
2 We are to wait for the doctor.
3 Shall we do this exercise?
4 They are said to be very rich.
5 Shall we ride or go on foot?
6 What shall I do with it?
7 You may go, but you must be back at four o'clock.
8 'Thou shalt not steal.'

NOTE 1. **sollen** may be used in place of the imperative, as in the Ten Commandments.

2 Regular and Irregular Verbs in English

Regular verbs form their past tense by adding **-ed** to the verb stem. Irregular verbs form their past tense by changing the stem vowel. Thus:

	Regular		
Infinitive	to learn	to work	to talk
Past	I learned	I worked	I talked

	Irregular		
Infinitive	to come	to give	to see
Past	I came	I gave	I saw

In German there are likewise regular verbs called **weak verbs,** and irregular verbs called **strong verbs.**

3 The Past Tense of Weak Regular Verbs in German

	lernen, to learn		antworten, to answer
	I learned, you learned, etc.		I answered, you answered, etc.
ich lernte	wir lernten	ich antwortete	wir antworteten
du lerntest	ihr lerntet	du antwortetest	ihr antwortetet
er, sie, es lernte	sie (Sie) lernten	er, sie, es antwortete	sie (Sie) antworteten

A weak verb forms its past tense by adding **-te** or **-ete** to the infinitive stem, without any vowel change in the stem. The ending **-ete** is necessary for reasons of pronunciation when the stem ends in **-d, -t,** or **-fn.** Thus:

antworten   antwortete   reden   redete   öffnen   öffnete

The personal endings of the past tense of weak verbs are like those of the present, except that the third person singular, like the first person, ends in **-e.**

The past tense may be translated in three ways. Thus: **ich lernte:** I learned, I was learning, I did learn; you learned, etc.

4 Some Familiar Weak Verbs, Present and Past

Infinitive	*Present*	*Past*
sagen	ich sage	ich sagte
fragen	ich frage	ich fragte
machen	ich mache	ich machte
danken	ich danke	ich dankte
wohnen	ich wohne	ich wohnte
warten	ich warte	ich wartete
arbeiten	ich arbeite	ich arbeitete
reden	ich rede	ich redete
öffnen	ich öffne	ich öffnete
kaufen	ich kaufe	ich kaufte
sich setzen	ich setze mich	ich setzte mich
haben	ich habe	ich hatte[1]

NOTE 1. The past tense of **haben** drops **-b** from the stem and doubles the **-t.** Thus: **ich hatte, du hattest; er hatte, wir hatten; ihr hattet, sie hatten.**

Exercise No. 90. Change these sentences to the past tense.

Beispiel: 1. Der ältere Sohn des Kaufmanns öffnete die Tür.

1 Der ältere Sohn des Kaufmanns öffnet die Tür. 2 Was sagt der Junge? 3 Was antwortet Herr Müller? 4 Sein Vater wartet auf Herrn Müller im Arbeitszimmer. 5 Sie reden über das Wetter. 6 Ich mache große Fortschritte. 7 Ich lerne Deutsch. 8 Wir setzen uns um acht Uhr an den Tisch im Eßzimmer. 9 Sie kauft ein paar Handschuhe. 10 Wohnst du in der Vorstadt? 11 Ich wohne in der Stadt. 12 Habt ihr einen guten Lehrer? 13 Wir haben eine gute Lehrerin. 14 Was fragt der Tourist? 15 Diese Leute arbeiten in der Fabrik.

5. The Past Tense of Strong Irregular Verbs

kommen, to come		**gehen,** to go	
I came, was coming, did come, etc.		I went, was going, did go, etc.	
ich kam	wir kamen	ich ging	wir gingen
du kamst	ihr kamt	du gingst	ihr gingt
er sie, es kam	sie (Sie) kamen	er, sie, es ging	sie (Sie) gingen

A strong verb forms its past tense by changing the stem vowel, sometimes along with consonant changes. You must learn **kommen—kam—, gehen—ging, stehen—stand,** just as little school children must learn *come—came, go—went, stand—stood,* etc.

The personal endings of the past tense of a strong verb are like those of the present, except that the first and third persons singular have no endings.

6 Some Familiar Strong Verbs, Present and Past

Infinitive	*Present*	*Past*
schreiben	er schreibt	er schrieb
beginnen	er beginnt	er begann
stehen	er steht	er stand
sitzen	er sitzt	er saß
sehen	er sieht[1]	er sah
lesen	er liest	er las
helfen	er hilft[1]	er half
sprechen	er spricht[1]	er sprach
geben	er gibt	er gab
nehmen	er nimmt	er nahm
fahren	er fährt[1]	er fuhr
tragen	er trägt	er trug
laufen	er läuft	er lief
sein	er ist	er war[2]

NOTES: 1 Only strong verbs have the vowel changes **e > ie, e > i** and **a > ä** in the present tense, second and third person singular. 2 The complete past of **sein**, to be: **ich war, du warst, er war; wir waren, ihr wart, sie waren.**

7 Expressions Referring to Past Time

> **gestern,** yesterday
> **gestern abend,** last night
> **gestern früh,** yesterday morning
> **vorgestern,** the day before yesterday
> **vor einer Woche,** a week ago
> **vor einem Monat,** a month ago
> **vor zwei Jahren,** two years ago
> **vor** + *the dative* of a noun of time = ago

Exercise No. 91.   Change these sentences to the past tense.

Beispiel: 1. Ich stand um sieben Uhr auf.

1 Ich stehe um sieben Uhr auf. 2 Die Kinder stehen manchmal früh auf. 3 Wann essen Sie zu Mittag? 4 Wir fahren mit dem Auto nach der Stadt. 5 Es gibt jeden Tag drei Vorstellungen. 6 Um wieviel Uhr kommt der Zug in Bonn an? 7 Um wieviel Uhr geht der Zug von Hamburg ab? 8 Er trägt den Koffer in den Wartesaal. 9 Viele Leute stehen auf dem Bahnsteig. 10 Die Herren sitzen den ganzen Tag im Arbeitszimmer. 11 In der deutschen Klasse sprechen wir immer Deutsch. 12 Schreibst du einen Brief an Frau Braun?

Exercise No. 92.   Re-read the text: **Die kleine Anna war krank.** Then answer these questions.

1 Was ist der Titel[1] dieses Kapitels?[2] 2 In welchem Monat war es? 3 Wie war das Wetter? 4 Wer kam zur Wohnung des Herrn Clark? 5 Wer öffnete ihm die Tür? 6 Was gab der Lehrer dem Jungen? 7 Wo wartete Herr Clark auf den

Lehrer? 8 Wer war krank? 9 Was fehlte ihr? 10 Hatte sie die Grippe? 11 Was sollte (should) Anna trinken? 12 Ging es ihr am Abend besser? 13 Worüber redeten die Herren eine Weile? 14 Wer ging mit Herrn Müller zur Tür? 15 Was sagten sie, als sie sich die Hand gaben?

NOTES: 1 **der Titel,** *pl.* -, title, heading. 2 **das Kapitel,** *pl.* -, chapter.

Exercise No. 93. Übersetzen Sie!

1 It was the month of March. 2 I came to the house of Mr. C. and his older son opened the door. 3 He said, 'Good evening, come in.' 4 I gave him my hat and raincoat. 5 Mr. C. was waiting for me in his study. 6 We sat down and began to talk. 7 Little Anna was sick. 8 What was the matter with her? (**Was fehlte . . .?**) 9 Anna had 'flu. 10 She had a temperature and a headache.

CHAPTER 20

WELCH SCHRECKLICHES WETTER!
WHAT TERRIBLE WEATHER!

1 Es war im Monat März. Es goß in Strömen, als Herr Müller das Haus des Herrn Clark erreichte. Er klingelte und Wilhelm, der jüngere Sohn, öffnete die Tür. Herr Müller trat ein.

2 Wilhelm sagte zu ihm: ,,Guten Abend, Herr Müller. Welch schreckliches Wetter! Kommen Sie herein, kommen Sie ins Haus. Sie sind durch und durch naß. Bitte, geben Sie mir Ihren Regenmantel und Ihren Hut. Stellen Sie Ihren Regenschirm in den Schirmständer. Ihre Gummischuhe können Sie im Hausflur lassen.''

3 Herr Müller gab ihm seinen Hut und seinen Regenmantel und antwortete: ,,Danke schön. Es regnet sehr stark, aber kalt ist es nicht. Ich erkälte mich sicher nicht. Ist dein Papa zu Hause?''

4 Jawohl. Er wartet auf Sie im Wohnzimmer. Da ist er schon.

5 Guten Abend, Herr Müller. Es freut mich, Sie zu sehen, aber es ist nicht gut, bei solch schrecklichem Wetter auszugehen. Kommen Sie doch ins Eßzimmer und trinken Sie eine Tasse Tee und etwas Whisky, um sich ein wenig zu wärmen.

6 Danke, danke vielmals, Herr Clark. Ich bin ganz naß. Trinken wir eine Tasse Tee! Und während wir den Tee trinken, können wir über das Wetter sprechen. Das ist ein vielbesprochenes Thema und ist besonders passend für diesen Abend.

7 Die Herren gingen ins Eßzimmer und sprachen mit lebhaften Stimmen. Sie setzten sich, und Frau Clark brachte ihnen auf einem Servierbrett zwei Tassen mit Untertassen, eine Teekanne, eine Zuckerdose, einige Teelöffel und eine Torte. Sie stellte alles auf den Tisch. Sie nahm eine Flasche Whisky vom Büfett herunter und stellte sie neben die Teekanne. Dann verließ sie das Eßzimmer.

8 ,,Bitte, Herr Müller, ich schenke Ihnen ein,'' sagte Herr Clark. Er goß den Tee in die Tassen ein und dazu für jeden ein Gläschen Whisky.

9 Während sie den Tee tranken, sprachen sie lebhaft weiter.

10 Draußen regnete es noch immer.

1 It was the month of March. It was raining in torrents when Mr. Müller reached Mr. Clark's house. He rang the doorbell, and William, the younger son, opened the door. Mr. Müller entered.

2 William said to him: 'Good evening, Mr. Müller. What terrible weather! Come in, come into the house. You are wet through and through. Please give me your raincoat and your hat. Put your umbrella into the umbrella stand. You can leave your rubber boots in the hall.'

3 Mr. Müller gave him his hat and raincoat, and answered: 'Thank you. It is raining very hard, but it is not cold. I'll surely not catch a cold. Is your father at home?'

4 Yes indeed. He is waiting for you in the living room. Here he is now.

5 Good evening, Mr. Müller. I am glad to see you, but it is not nice to go out in such terrible weather. Do come into the dining-room and have a cup of tea and some whisky in order to warm yourself a bit.

6 Thanks, many thanks, Mr. Clark. I am soaked through (*lit.* I am quite wet). Let's drink a cup of tea. And while we drink tea we can speak about the weather. That is a much discussed topic and it is especially fitting for this evening.

7 The men went into the dining-room talking in lively voices. They sat down and Mrs. Clark brought them a tray, two cups and saucers, a teapot, a sugar bowl, some teaspoons, and a cake. She put everything on the table. She took down a bottle of whisky from the sideboard and put it next to the teapot. Then she left the dining-room.

8 'Please, Mr. Müller, let me serve you,' said Mr. Clark. He poured the tea into the cups and along with it a glass of whisky for each.

9 While they were drinking the tea they continued to speak in a lively manner.

10 Outside it continued to rain.

Wortschatz

die Flasche *pl.* -n, bottle
der Gummischuh *pl.* -e, rubber boot
der Regenmantel *pl.* ¨, raincoat
der Regenschirm *pl.* -e, umbrella
der Schirmständer *pl.* -, umbrella stand
die Torte *pl.* -n, cake
das Servierbrett *pl.* -er, tray
aus-gehen, to go out
ein-schenken, to serve, pour
sich erkälten, to catch cold
stellen, to put
sich wärmen, to warm oneself

bringen (*past* brachte), to bring
jung, young; jünger, younger
kräftig, strong; schwach, weak
lebhaft, lively
naß, wet; trocken, dry
stark, strong; es regnet stark, it is raining heavily
passend, suitable, fitting
schrecklich, terrible
vielbesprochen (viːlbeʃproxen), much talked of
dazu, in addition, along with it
während (*sub. conj.*), while

Das Tischgeschirr Tableware

das Messer *pl.* -, knife
die Gabel *pl.* -n, fork; der Löffel *pl.* -, spoon
der Teelöffel *pl.* -, teaspoon
der Eßlöffel *pl.* -, tablespoon
die Tasse *pl.* -n, cup.

die Untertasse *pl.* -n, saucer
die Zuckerdose *pl.* -n, sugar-bowl
die Teekanne *pl.* -n, teapot
der Krug *pl.* ¨e, jug
der Teller *pl.* -, dish, plate

Das Wetter

Wie ist das Wetter? How is the weather?

Das Wetter ist schön; warm; kalt; kühl; windig; stürmisch. The weather is nice; warm; cold; cool; windy; stormy.

Es regnet heute. Es regnete gestern. It is raining today. It rained yesterday.

Es schneit. Es schneite gestern. It is snowing. It snowed yesterday.

Es regnet in Strömen. It is raining very hard (in streams).

Es regnete immer weiter. It continued to rain.
Ist dir (Ihnen) kalt? Mir ist kalt. Are you cold? I am cold.
Ist ihm warm? Ihm ist warm. Is he warm? He is warm.
Ist ihr kalt? Ihr ist nicht kalt. Is she cold? She is not cold.

Note carefully. In German we do not say: I am cold (warm); you are cold (warm), etc.; but *literally:* To me (to you, to him, to her, etc.) it is cold (warm).

Grammar Notes and Practical Exercises

1 Some familiar separable verbs, infinitive, present and past

Infinitive		*Present* (er)	*Past* (er)
auf-stehen	to get up, stand up	er steht . . . auf	er stand . . . auf
an-kommen	to arrive	er kommt . . . an	er kam . . . an
ab-gehen	to go off, leave	er geht . . . ab	er ging . . . ab
ab-fahren	to depart, leave	er fährt . . . ab	er fuhr . . . ab
an-fangen	to begin	er fängt . . . an	er fing . . . an
ein-treten	to step in, enter	er tritt . . . ein	er trat . . . ein
ein-steigen	to get on (train)	er steigt . . . ein	er stieg . . . ein
aus-steigen	to get off (train)	er steigt . . . aus	er stieg . . . aus
sich an-ziehen	to dress oneself	er zieht sich . . . an	er zog sich . . . an
weiter-sprechen	to go on speaking	er spricht . . . weiter	er sprach . . . weiter
zurück-gehen	to go back	er geht . . . zurück	er ging . . . zurück
zurück-geben	to give back	er gibt . . . zurück	er gab . . . zurück
ein-giessen	to pour (in)	er gießt . . . ein	er goß . . . ein
herab-nehmen	to take down	er nimmt . . . herab	er nahm . . . herab

a. The separable prefix of a verb stands at the end of a simple sentence or main clause in the present and past tenses.

Ich ziehe mich schnell an. I dress   **Ich zog mich schnell an.** I dressed
(myself) quickly.   (myself) quickly.

b. In subordinate clauses the separable verb stands last in the present and past tenses; but the prefix does not separate from the verb.

Wir steigen aus, sobald der Zug   We get off as soon as the train arrives.
ankommt.

Wir stiegen aus, sobald der Zug   We got off as soon as the train arrived.
ankam.

2 *hin* and *her*

hin- and **her-** are often attached to separable prefixes.

hin shows that the action is *away* from the observer or *away* from some given point.

her shows that the action is *towards* the observer or *towards* some given point. Thus:

Someone outside the house says:

Der Doktor geht ins Haus hinein. (away from the observer)
Der Doktor kommt aus dem Haus heraus. (towards the observer)

Someone inside the house says:

Kommen Sie herein! Come in! (towards the speaker)
Gehen Sie hinaus! Go out! (away from the speaker)

Exercise No. 94. Change these sentences from the present to the past tense.

Beispiel: 1. Sie sprachen lebhaft weiter.

1 Sie sprechen lebhaft weiter. 2 Stehen Sie früh auf? 3 Um wieviel Uhr kommt der Zug aus Bonn an? 4 Um wieviel Uhr fährt der Zug nach Frankfurt ab? 5 Die dritte Vorstellung fängt um neun Uhr an. 6 Viele Passagiere steigen aus. 7 Andere Passagiere steigen ein. 8 Wir ziehen uns die neuen Anzüge an. 9 Ich gebe Ihnen zehn Mark zurück. 10 Ich nehme die Flasche vom Büfett herab. 11 Er tritt eben ein. 12 Wir gehen ins Museum hinein.

3 More Subordinating Conjunctions

bevor, ehe, before; **während,** while; **sobald,** as soon as; **ob,** whether; **weil,** because; **bis,** until

Practise the German sentences aloud.

Herr Clark küßte die Kinder, bevor er wegging.	Mr. Clark kissed the children before he left.
Während wir den Tee trinken, können wir über das Wetter sprechen.	While we are drinking tea we can talk about the weather.
Er liest die Post, sobald er im Büro ankommt.	He reads the mail as soon as he arrives at the office.
Weißt du, ob er meine Füllfeder hat?	Do you know whether he has my fountain pen?
Er lernt Deutsch, weil er Deutschland besuchen will.	He is learning German because he wants to visit Germany.
Alle warteten, bis er nach Hause kam.	All waited until he came home.

4 wann, als, wenn

wann (when) is used in direct and indirect questions.

Wann kommt er? Weißt du, wann er kommt? When is he coming? Do you know when he is coming?

Als (when) is used with verbs in any past tense.

Als er das Haus erreichte, regnete es. When he reached the house it was raining.

Wenn (when) is used with verbs in the present or future.

Wenn Sie kommen, dann gehe ich. When you come, then I'll go.

wenn (whenever, if) is used with any tense of the verb.

Wenn ich ihn sah, war er immer müde. Whenever I saw him, he was always tired.

Wenn man Geld hat, kann man reisen. If one has money, one can travel.

Exercise No. 95. Combine each pair of sentences using the conjunction in parenthesis.

Warning: In subordinate clauses the verb stands last.

Beispiel: 1. Sie kauften die Karten, während wir draußen warteten.

1 Sie kauften die Karten. (während) Wir warteten draußen. 2 Die Familie setzte sich zum Abendessen. (sobald) Herr Clark kam nach Hause. 3 Am Abend ist er sehr müde. (weil) Er arbeitet fleißig den ganzen Tag. 4 Wissen Sie? (ob) Der Zug kommt pünktlich an. 5 Ein Freund trat ins Zimmer. (als) Herr Clark

diktierte seiner Stenographin Briefe. 6 (Als) Herr Müller erreichte Herrn Clarks Wohnung. Es regnete[1] in Strömen. 7 Wir können dieses Auto nicht kaufen. (weil) Es kostet zu viel. 8 Alle Passagiere steigen aus. (wenn) Der Zug kommt in Hamburg an. 9 (Wenn) Papa kommt nach Hause. Die Kinder freuen sich.[1] 10 (Während) Du spielst. Ich muß[1] arbeiten.

NOTE 1. Remember: when the subordinate clause comes first, the main clause must have inverted word order.

Exercise No. 96. Fragen

Re-read the text: **Welch schreckliches Wetter!** Then answer these questions.

1 Was ist der Titel dieses Kapitels? 2 Wie war das Wetter, als Herr Müller die Wohnung des Kaufmanns erreichte? 3 Wer öffnete ihm die Tür? 4 Was gab der Lehrer dem Jungen? 5 Wer erschien,[1] als Wilhelm mit dem Lehrer sprach? 6 Was sollte[2] Herr Müller trinken, um sich zu wärmen? 7 Welches Thema war besonders passend für diesen Abend? 8 In welches Zimmer gingen die zwei Herren? 9 Wer brachte ihnen zwei Tassen mit Untertassen, eine Teekanne, usw.? 10 Was nahm sie vom Büfett herunter? 11 Wohin stellte sie die Flasche Whisky? 12 Blieb[3] Frau Clark im Eßzimmer? 13 Worüber sprachen die Herren, als sie den Tee tranken?

NOTES: 1 **erscheinen,** to appear (*past* **erschien**). 2 should, ought. 3 **bleiben,** to remain (*past* **blieb**).

Exercise No. 97. Übersetzen Sie!

1 It was raining, but Mr. M. went out anyway (**doch**). 2 When he reached the house he was wet through and through. 3 The younger son of Mr. C. opened the door and said, 'Come in quickly.' 4 Mr. M. stepped in quickly. 5 Now Mr. C. came into the hall (**die Hausflur**). 6 He said to his teacher, 'Come into the dining-room and drink a cup of tea. We can talk about the weather while we are drinking tea.' 8 The two stepped into the dining-room.

CHAPTER 21

DAS KLIMA DEUTSCHLANDS
THE CLIMATE OF GERMANY

1 Die beiden Herren saßen immer noch im Eßzimmer. Sie redeten weiter, während sie Tee tranken. Draußen regnete es noch. Herr Müller fühlte sich wohl. Es war ihm nicht mehr kalt.

2 Er sagte zu seinem Schüler: ,,Hier in London geht das Klima von einem Extrém zum anderen."

3 Das stimmt, Herr Müller. Im Sommer ist es heiß. Im Winter ist es kalt. Es wird manchmal sogar sehr kalt. Von Zeit zu Zeit bekommen wir auch Schnee.

4 Aber der Frühling ist schön, nicht wahr, Herr Clark?

5 Gewiß. Im Frühling wird das Wetter recht schön. Der Monat März ist zwar oft stürmisch, so wie heute abend, aber im April fällt ein warmer Regen. Im Mai werden die Wiesen und Felder grün. Im Juni ist der Himmel blau, und die Sonne scheint hell und klar.

Welche Jahreszeit gefällt Ihnen am besten, Herr Müller?

6 Mir gefällt der Herbst am besten. Ich mag die kühle, frische Luft. Ich mag den klaren Himmel. Auf dem Lande nehmen die Bäume viele Farben an. Und Sie, Herr Clark, welche Jahreszeit haben Sie am liebsten?

7 Ich habe den Frühling am liebsten, wo alles grünt. Aber reden wir ein wenig von dem Klima Deutschlands. Gibt es in Deutschland einen großen Unterschied zwischen den Jahreszeiten?

8 Sie sind ganz verschieden, aber es gibt nicht solche plötzlichen Veränderungen, wie es hier der Fall ist.

9 Das muß doch schön sein. Aber der Winter ist kalt, nicht wahr?

10 Der Winter ist wohl kalt, besonders im nördlichen Teil, aber im allgemeinen mildert der atlantische Golfstrom die Kälte. Im Sommer ist es beinahe überall in Deutschland sehr angenehm. Aber am schönsten ist gewöhnlich der Frühling. Dann gehen die Deutschen am liebsten spazieren. Wenn die Kinder den Kuckuck im Walde hören, freuen sie sich und singen:

> Kuckuck! Kuckuck! ruft's aus dem Wald;
> Lasset[1] uns singen, tanzen und springen,
> Frühling, Frühling, wird[2] es nun bald.

11 Das ist ein schönes Lied, Herr Müller.

12 Ja, und der Frühling ist eine schöne Jahreszeit, Herr Clark.

NOTES: 1 **lasset**, poetic form of **laßt**. 2 *Lit.* es wird = it is becoming.

1 The two gentlemen were still sitting in the dining-room. They continued to speak while they were drinking tea. Outside it was still raining. Mr. Müller was feeling fine. He did not feel cold any more.

2 He said to his pupil: 'Here in London the climate goes from one extreme to another.'

113

3 That's right, Mr. Müller. In summer it is hot. In winter it is cold. Sometimes it even becomes very cold. From time to time we also get snow.

4 But spring is beautiful, isn't it, Mr. Clark?

5 Certainly, in spring the weather becomes really beautiful. The month of March is often stormy to be sure, just as this evening; but in April a warm rain falls. In May the meadows and fields become green. In June the sky is blue and the sun shines bright and clear. What season do you like best, Mr. Müller?

6 I like the autumn best. I like the cool fresh air. I like the clear sky. In the country the trees take on many colours. And you, Mr. Clark, what season do you like best?

7 I like spring best when everything becomes green. But let us talk a little about the climate of Germany. Is there in Germany a great difference between the seasons?

8 They are quite different, but there are no such sudden changes as you have here (*lit.* is the case).

9 That must be nice indeed. But the winter is cold, isn't it?

10 The winter is cold to be sure, especially in the northern part, but in general the Atlantic Gulf Stream lessens the cold. In summer it is very comfortable nearly everywhere in Germany. But spring is usually most beautiful. Then the Germans like best of all to go walking. When the children hear the cuckoo in the woods they are happy and they sing:

> Cuckoo! Cuckoo! it echoes through the woods.
> Let us sing, dance and jump;
> Spring, spring is coming soon.

11 That is a beautiful song, Mr. Müller.

12 Yes, and spring is a beautiful season, Mr. Clark.

Wortschatz

die Kälte, cold; die Hitze, heat
der Schnee, snow; der Regen, rain
die Luft, air; der Himmel, sky
das Feld *pl.* -er, field
der Wald *pl.* ¨er, forest
die Wiese *pl.* -n, meadow
die Veränderung *pl.* -en, change
der Unterschied *pl.* -e, difference
an-nehmen (*past* nahm ... an), to take on
gefällen + *dat. object* (*past* gefiel), to please

singen (*past* sang), to sing
tanzen, to dance
spaziéren gehen, to go for a walk
angenehm, pleasant
beináhe = fast, almost
sogár, even
am schönsten, most beautiful
am besten, best
weder ... noch, neither ... nor

Die Jahreszeiten The Seasons

der Frühling	der Sommer	der Herbst	der Winter
im Frühling	im Sommer	im Herbst	im Winter

Die Monate des Jahres

Januar (ja-nu-aːr)	Mai (mai)	September (sεp-tem-ber)
Februar (feː-bru-aːr)	Juni (juː-ni)	Oktober (ok-toː-ber)
März (mεrts)	Juli (juː-li)	November (noː-vem-ber)
April (a-pril)	Augúst (au-gust)	Dezember (deː-tsem-ber)

All months take the masculine article **der**.

Deutsche Ausdrücke

You have learned that a verb plus **gern** means to like a thing or action; a verb plus **lieber** means to prefer a thing or action. Note now that a verb plus **am liebsten** means to like a thing or action best of all.

Ich habe den Herbst gern. Er hat den Sommer lieber. Sie hat den Frühling am liebsten. I like autumn. He prefers summer. She likes spring best of all.

spazieren-gehen, to go for a walk

Sie geht gern spazieren. Ich spiele lieber Tennis. Er spielt am liebsten Fußball. She likes to go walking. I prefer to play tennis. He likes best of all to play football.

Grammar Notes and Practical Exercises

1 Present tense of *werden* to become, to get; *mögen* to like, to care to, may.

I become, you become, etc.

		I like, you like, etc.	
ich werde	wir werden	ich mag	wir mögen
du wirst	ihr werdet	du magst	ihr mögt
er, sie, es wird	sie (Sie) werden	er, sie, es mag	sie (Sie) mögen

Exercise No. 98. Practise the German sentences aloud.

A. 1 Ich werde hungrig. 2 Wirst du hungrig? 3 Er wird müde. 4 Werden Sie müde? 5 Wir werden ungeduldig.[1] 6 Werden Sie ungeduldig? 7 Ihr werdet zu laut, Jungen. 8 Der Lehrer wird böse.[2] 9 Es wird kalt. 10 Es wird dunkel.

A. 1 I am getting hungry. 2 Are you getting hungry? 3 He is getting tired. 4 Are you getting tired? 5 We are getting impatient. 6 Are you getting impatient? 7 You are getting too noisy, boys. 8 The teacher is getting angry. 9 It is becoming cold. 10 It is becoming dark.

NOTES: 1 **geduldig**, patient; **ungeduldig**, impatient. 2 **böse**, angry.

B. 1 Ich mag den klaren Himmel. 2 Magst du nicht die gesunde, frische Luft? 3 Sie mag mich nicht. 4 Wir mögen nicht spielen. 5 Es mag sein, daß er kein Geld hat. 6 Er mag sagen, was er will, wir glauben ihm nicht.

B. 1 I like the clear sky. 2 Don't you like the healthy, fresh air? 3 She doesn't like me. 4 We don't care to play. 5 It may be that he has no money. 6 He may say what he wants, we don't believe him.

Note that **mögen** (to like) is equivalent to the expressions of *verbs* + **gern(e).** **Gern(e)** can also be used with **mögen.**

Ich mag diesen Lehrer = Ich mag diesen Lehrer gern = I like this teacher.
Ich mag nicht (gern) spielen = Ich spiele nicht gern. = I don't like to play.

2 Inseparable verbs. Present tense of *bekommen* to receive and *erfahren* to find out

I receive, you receive, etc.

		I find out, you find out, etc.	
ich bekomme	wir bekommen	ich erfahre	wir erfahren
du bekommst	ihr bekommt	du erfährst	ihr erfahrt
er, sie, es bekommt	sie (Sie) bekommen	er, sie, es erfährt	sie (Sie) erfahren

Simple verbs may add prefixes which *do not* separate from the verb as do the separable prefixes. Such prefixes are called *inseparable prefixes*, and the verbs to which they are attached are called *inseparable verbs*. The prefixes **be-, emp-, ent-, er-, ge-, ver-, zer-** are always inseparable. Here are examples of inseparable verbs, most of which you already know. The stress is always on the verb, never on the inseparable prefix.

Simple Verbs	Inseparable Verbs
suchen, to seek	**besúchen,** to visit
kommen, to come	**bekómmen,** to receive
sprechen, to speak	**bespréchen,** to discuss
tragen, to carry	**betrágen,** to amount to
stehen, to stand	**entstéhen,** to arise
fahren, to ride, travel	**erfáhren,** to find out
lassen, to leave (something),	**verlássen,** to leave
to let, to relinquish	(to go away from)
warten, to wait	**erwárten,** to await
zählen, to count	**erzählen,** to relate
fallen, to fall	**gefállen,** to please
kaufen, to buy	**verkáufen,** to sell
schreiben, to write	**verschréiben,** to prescribe
stehen, to stand	**verstéhen,** to understand
brechen, to break	**zerbréchen,** to break to pieces

The meaning of the inseparable prefix is generally not obvious as is the case with the separable prefixes. However, **zer-** clearly indicates 'to pieces'.

The past tense of inseparable verbs is formed in the same way as that of the simple verbs. Thus:

Infin.	besuchen	bekommen	besprechen	betragen		entstehen	erfahren
Past	besuchte	bekam	besprach	betrug		entstand	erfuhr

Infin.	erwarten	gefallen	verkaufen	verschreiben	verstehen	zerbrechen
Past	erwartete	gefiel	verkaufte	verschrieb	verstand	zerbrach

Exercise No. 99. Change these sentences to the past tense.

Beispiel: 1. Ich besuchte Herrn Clark in seinem Büro

1 Ich besuche Herrn Clark in seinem Büro. 2 Er erwartet mich dort um elf Uhr. 3 Wir beginnen sofort Deutsch zu sprechen. 4 Er versteht mich, und ich verstehe ihn. 5 Wir besprechen wichtige Geschäftssachen. 6 Ich erfahre, daß er große Fortschritte im Deutschen macht. 7 Um zwölf Uhr gehen wir in ein Restaurant zum Mittagessen. 8 Die Rechnung für die zwei Mahlzeiten beträgt £1 10s. (ein Pfund zehn). 9 Während wir die Rechnung bezahlen,[1] entsteht ein grosser Lärm auf der Straße. 10 Wir gehen auf die Straße hinaus, um zu sehen, was los ist.[2]

NOTES: 1 **bezahlen** to pay (*past.* **bezahlte**). 2 **Was ist los?** What's the matter?

3 Verbs that take a dative object

Certain German verbs take a dative object.

antworten:	**Er antwortete *mir* nicht.**	He did not answer *me*.
danken:	**Ich danke *Ihnen* für die Bücher.**	I thank *you* for the books.
helfen:	**Wir halfen *ihr* mit der Aufgabe.**	We helped *her* with the exercise.

glauben:	Ich kann *ihm* nicht glauben.	I cannot believe *him*.
verzeihen:	Verzeihen Sie (*mir*).	Pardon (*me*).
gehören:	Dieses Buch gehört *dem Lehrer*.	This book belongs *to the teacher*.
fehlen:	Was fehlte *dem Kind*?	What was the matter with *the child*? (*Lit*. What was lacking *to the child*?)
gefallen:	Das gefällt *dir* nicht.	That doesn't please *you*.

The verb **gefallen** + *a dat.* to please, is another way of expressing 'liking'.

Das gefällt uns am besten. = That pleases *us* best. = *We* like that best.

Exercise No. 100. Complete these sentences by translating the English words.

1 **Warum antworten Sie** (her) **nicht?** 2 **Was fehlt** (your *fam.* father)? 3 **Diese schöne Wohnung** (belongs to) **dem Kaufmann.** 4 **Helfen Sie** (them) **bitte mit ihren Aufgaben!** 5 (Pardon me), **daß ich spät komme!** 6 **Ich danke** (you *pol.*) **vielmals.** 7 **Er sagt, daß es wahr ist, aber wir** (don't believe him). 8 (To whom) **gehört dieses neue Auto?** 9 **Es gehört** (us). 10 **Der neue Mantel gefällt** (my sister) **nicht.** 11 (We like) **unser neues Zimmer.** Translate: Our new room pleases us. 12 **Gefallen** (them) **diese Kleider?**

Exercise No. 101. Fragen

Re-read the text: **Das Klima Deutschlands.** Then answer these questions.

1 **Was taten die Herren, während sie Tee und Whisky tranken?** 2 **Wie fühlte sich Herr Müller?** 3 **War es ihm noch kalt?** 4 **Wie ist der Winter in London?** 5 **Bekommt man oft Schnee?** 6 **Wie wird das Wetter im Frühling?** 7 **Was für ein Regen fällt?** 8 **Welche Jahreszeit gefällt Herrn Müller am besten?** 9 **Was mag er im Herbst?** 10 **Welche Jahreszeit hat Herr Clark am liebsten?** 11 **Welche Jahreszeit ist am schönsten in Deutschland?** 12 **Was tun die Deutschen am liebsten im Frühling?** 13 **Was tun die Kinder, wenn sie den Kuckuck hören?** 14 **Nennen Sie die vier Jahreszeiten!**

Exercise No. 102. Übersetzen Sie!

1 The four seasons are spring, summer, autumn, and winter. 2 I like spring. She prefers summer. He likes autumn best of all. 3 In spring I like to go walking. 4 In summer he likes to play tennis. 5 In autumn they like to play football. 6 In winter they like to go ski-ing (**Schilaufen**). 7 It is now spring and the days are getting longer (**länger**). 8 They are discussing the climate of Germany.

CHAPTER 22

EINE ANGENEHME ÜBERRASCHUNG!
A PLEASANT SURPRISE

Der Kaufmann erzählt seinem Lehrer von einer angenehmen Überraschung.

— Herr Müller, ich hatte heute eine höchst angenehme Überraschung, von der ich Ihnen erzählen will.

— Bitte, erzählen Sie davon, Herr Clark.

— Um halb zwölf war ich im Begriff, meiner Sekretärin einen Brief zu diktieren, als meine Frau und Kinder plötzlich in mein Büro traten. Ich stand auf und sagte: ,,Was für eine Überraschung!"

Es war das erste Mal, daß meine Familie in mein Büro kam, und die Kinder bewunderten alle die Dinge, die sie im Büro sahen: die Schreibmaschinen, allerlei deutsche Gegenstände und Muster deutscher Keramik; die illustrierten Zeitschriften, die auf dem Tische lagen; und besonders die vielen bunten Plakate an den Wänden.

Die kleine Anna, die erst fünf Jahre alt ist, war besonders neugierig und fragte allerlei über ,,Papas Büro."

Das Büro, in dem ich seit zwei Jahren arbeite, ist im zehnten Stock eines Hochhauses. Die Kinder schauten zum Fenster hinaus und sahen den blauen Himmel, der heute wolkenlos war, und die Sonne, die so hell schien. Sie sahen die Automobile, die auf der Straße vorbeifuhren. Von dem zehnten Stock schienen diese ganz klein zu sein.

Als der Besuch zu Ende war, gingen wir alle in ein Restaurant, das sich nicht weit von meinem Büro befindet. Alle aßen mit gutem Appetit, besonders Karl, mein älterer Junge, der immer riesigen Appetit hat.

— Herr Clark, das war wohl eine schöne Überraschung, die Sie heute hatten.

— Jawohl, sie machte mir große Freude.

The businessman tells his teacher about a pleasant surprise.

— Mr. Müller, today I had a most pleasant surprise which I want to tell you about.

— Please tell me about it, Mr. Clark.

— At half past eleven I was just dictating a letter to my secretary, when my wife and children suddenly came into my office. I got up and said: 'What a surprise!'

It was the first time that my family had come to my office, and the children admired everything that they saw in the office: the typewriters, all sorts of German objects, and samples of German ceramics; the illustrated magazines which were lying on the table; and especially the many coloured posters on the walls.

Little Anna, who is only five years old. was especially curious and asked many questions about 'Papa's office'.

The office in which I have been working for two years is on the tenth floor of an office block. The children looked out of the window and saw the blue sky, which was cloudless today, and the sun, which was shining so brightly. They saw the cars which were going by in the street. From the tenth floor these seemed to be quite small.

When the visit was over we all went to a restaurant which is not far from my office. All ate with a good appetite, especially Charles, my elder son, who always has a huge appetite.

— Mr. Clark, that was indeed a nice surprise which you had today.

— Yes indeed, it gave me great pleasure.

Wortschatz

die Überráschung, *pl.* -en, surprise
der Stock, floor (storey of building); stick
die Schreibmaschine, *pl.* -n, typewriter
das Plakát, *pl.* -e, poster
das Muster, *pl.* -, sample
die Kerámik, ceramics, pottery
liegen (*past* lag), to lie
essen (*past* aß), to eat
vorbéi-fahren (*past* fuhr ... vorbei), to go past

bewóhnen, to occupy
bewúndern, to admire
erzählen, to relate, tell
hináus-schauen, to look out
illustríert, illustrated
bunt, coloured, many coloured
neugierig, curious
riesig, huge, gigantic
höchst, highly
wolkenlos, cloudless

Deutsche Ausdrücke

im Begriff sein, to be about to, to be in the process of.
Ich war im Begriff, einen Brief zu schreiben. I was about to write a letter.
Ich habe Appetít. I have an appetite.
Ich habe Hunger (Ich bin hungrig). I am hungry.
Ich habe Durst (Ich bin durstig). I am thirsty.
Das macht mir Freude. That gives me pleasure.
sich befinden, to be located
Wo befindet sich das Büro? Where is the office? Es befindet sich in einem Hochhaus. It is in an office block.

Sprichwörter

Der Appetit kommt mit dem Essen. Appetite comes with eating.
Der Mensch ist, was er ißt. Man is what he eats.

1 Present and past of *essen* to eat

Present		Past	
ich esse	wir essen	ich aß	wir aßen
du ißt	ihr eßt	du aßest	ihr aßt
er, sie, es ißt	sie (Sie) essen	er, sie, es aß	sie (Sie) aßen

Imperative: iß! eßt! essen Sie!

2 The relative pronouns *der*, *welcher*

Der Mann, *der* dort steht, ist mein Bruder.

The man *who* stands there is my brother.

Die Frau, *die* dort steht, ist meine Schwester.	The woman *who* stands there is my sister.
Das Bild, *das* dort hängt, ist sehr alt.	The picture *which* hangs there is very old.
Der Mann, *den* Sie dort sehen, ist ein Arzt.	The man *whom* you see there is a doctor.
Die Frau, *die* Sie dort sehen, ist Lehrerin.	The woman *whom* you see there is a teacher.
Das Bild, *das* Sie dort sehen, ist teuer.	The picture *that* you see there is expensive.
Die Feder, mit *der* ich schrieb, war nicht gut.	The pen with *which* I wrote was not good.

The relative pronouns in English are: *who* (*whom*) *that, which.*

The relative pronouns in German are **der** and **welcher**. The forms of **der** are preferable.

The antecedent of a relative pronoun is the noun (or pronoun) to which it refers.

The relative pronoun agrees in number and gender with its antecedent, but it gets its case from its use in the relative clause; if it is the subject of the clause it is nominative; if it is the object it is accusative; if it is the indirect object it is dative; if it shows possession it is genitive; if it is after a preposition it has the case the preposition requires.

All relative clauses are subordinate clauses, and therefore they must have subordinate word order, i.e. the verb stands at the end of the clause. A relative pronoun may never be omitted in German. A relative clause must be set off by commas.

Forms of the Relative Pronoun *der*

	Singular				**Plural**
	masc.	fem.	neut.	m.f.n.	Meaning
Nom.	der	die	das	die	who, which
Gen.	dessen	deren	dessen	deren	whose, of which
Dat.	dem	der	dem	denen	(to) whom, which
Acc.	den	die	das	die	whom, that, which

The Relative Pronoun *welcher*

	Singular				**Plural**
	masc.	fem.	neut.	m.f.n.	Meaning
Nom.	welcher	welche	welches	welche	who, that, which
Dat.	welchem	welcher	welchem	welchen	(to) whom, which
Acc.	welchen	welche	welches	welche	whom, that, which

The relative pronoun **der** is like the definite article **der**, except in the genitive case singular and plural, and in the dative plural—these cases add a syllable.

The relative pronoun **welcher** (who, that, which) is like the **der**-word **welcher**, except that it is never used in the genitive case.

Exercise No. 103. Read each sentence aloud. Translate it. Note particularly the relative pronouns.

The **welcher** form (in parentheses) is allowable, but the **der** form is preferable.

1 Die Kinder bewunderten alle Dinge, **die** (**welche**) sie im Büro sahen. 2 Das

Büro, **das (welches)** Herr Clark seit zwei Jahren bewohnt, befindet sich in einem großen Hochhaus. 3 Die Autos, **die (welche)** unten auf der Straße vorbeifuhren, schienen sehr klein zu sein. 4 Herr Clark hatte heute eine angenehme Überraschung, von **der (welcher)** er seinem Lehrer erzählen will. 5 Kennen Sie den Herrn, **der (welcher)** gestern ins Büro hereinkam? 6 Ja, er ist der deutsche Freund, von **dem (welchem)** Herr Clark uns erzählte. 7 Dieser Freund wohnt in einem Vorort, **dessen** Einwohner meistens[1] in der Stadt arbeiten. 8 Die Bilder, von **denen (welchen)** wir gestern sprachen, sind sehr teuer. 9 Gefällt dir der Mantel, **den (welchen)** ich gestern kaufte? 10 Frau Clark, **deren** Tochter krank ist, läßt den Doktor kommen.[2] 11 Die Schüler, **deren** Bücher und Hefte hier liegen, sollen sie sofort wegnehmen. 12 Die kleine Anna, **die (welche)** erst fünf Jahre alt ist, hatte die Grippe.

NOTES: 1 for the most part. 2 sends for the doctor.

Exercise No. 104. Complete these sentences with the correct form of the relative pronoun (**der, die, das**).

Beispiel: 1 Wo ist der Student, **dessen** Bücher und Hefte hier liegen?

1 Wo ist der Student, (whose) **Bücher und Hefte hier liegen?** 2 **Die kleine Anna,** (who) **erst fünf Jahre alt ist, bewunderte alles.** 3 **Hier ist der Bleistift,** (which) **Sie suchten.** 4 **Wo sind die Leute, mit** (whom) **Sie sprachen?** 5 **Die Kinder sahen den blauen Himmel,** (that) **wolkenlos war.** 6 **Das Restaurant,** (which) **sie besuchten, war nicht weit vom Büro.** 7 **Das war wirklich eine angenehme Überraschung,** (which) **wir heute hatten.** 8 **Die Kinder,** (who) **sehr hungrig waren, aßen mit gutem Appetit.** 9 **Wo wohnt der Junge,** (to whom) **du die Bilder sendest?** 10 **Der Herr, für** (whom) **er arbeitete, heißt Schmidt.**

3 wo(r) + a preposition used in place of a relative pronoun with a preposition

Relative pronouns preceded by a preposition may be replaced by (wo)r plus a preposition if the antecedent is a thing or things. These combinations cannot be used if the antecedents are persons. Thus:

Die Feder, **womit** (= **mit der**) ich schrieb, ist nicht gut.
The pen with which I was writing is not good.
Es war ein kleiner Tisch, **worauf** (= **auf dem**) die Zeitungen lagen.
It was a small table on which the newspapers were lying.

but: Der Herr, **mit dem** ich sprach, ist mein Deutschlehrer.
The man with whom I was speaking is my German teacher.

Exercise No. 105. In each sentence substitute for the relative pronoun preceded by a preposition one of the following: **womit, worauf, woran, worin, wodurch, wovon.**

Beispiel: 1. Die Stühle, **worauf** wir saßen, waren sehr unbequem.

1 Die Stühle, **auf denen** wir saßen, waren sehr unbequem. 2 Das Restaurant, **von dem** ich Ihnen erzählte, befindet sich fünf Straßen von hier. 3 Die Tische, **an denen** wir zu Mittag aßen, waren im Garten. 4 Der Autobus, **mit dem** wir nach der Stadt fuhren, war groß und bequem. 5 Der Zug, **auf welchen** wir warteten, hatte eine Stunde Verspätung. 6 Kennen Sie alle die Bücher, **von denen** er sprach? 7 Das Hochhaus, **in dem** sich sein Büro befindet, hat fünfzehn Stock. 8 Der Vorot, **durch den** wir schnell fuhren, hatte schöne, alte Häuser.

4 *Wer* and *was* as **relative pronouns**

(*a*) **wer** is used as a relative pronoun in the sense of *he who* or *whoever*.

Wer viele Freunde hat, ist glücklich.	*He who* has many friends is happy.
Wer jetzt gehen will, kann gehen.	*Whoever* wants to go now may go.

(*b*) **was** is used as a relative pronoun in the sense of *what, that which, whatever*. It is also used after such antecedents as **alles** all, **nichts** nothing, **etwas** something, **viel** or **vieles** much.

Alles, was sie sahen, war ihnen neu.	*All that* they saw was new to them.
Was er sagt, ich glaube ihm nicht.	*Whatever* he says, I don't believe him.

Memorize these proverbs (**Sprichwörter**).

Nicht alles, was glänzt, ist Gold.	All that glitters is not gold.
Wer A sagt, muß auch B sagen.	He who says A must also say B.
Wer zuletzt lacht, lacht am besten.	He who laughs last, laughs best.

Exercise No. 106. Re-read the text: **Eine angenehme Überraschung!** Then answer these questions.

1 Wovon erzählte der Kaufmann seinem Lehrer? 2 Was war er im Begriff zu tun, als seine Frau und Kinder ins Büro eintraten? 3 Was tat er, als er die Familie eintreten sah? 4 Was lag auf einem Tisch in seinem Büro? 5 Was bewunderten die Kinder besonders? 6 Wer war besonders neugierig? 7 Wie lange arbeitet Herr Clark schon in diesem Büro? 8 In welchem Stock des Hochhauses befindet sich das Büro? 9 Was sahen die Kinder auf der Straße, als sie zum Fenster hinausschauten? 10 Wohin gingen alle, als der Besuch zu Ende war? 11 Wo befindet sich dieses Restaurant? 12 Wie aßen alle? 13 Wer hat immer riesigen Appetit? 14 Freute sich Herr Clark über den Besuch seiner Familie? 15 Was bedeutet[1] das Sprichwort: „Der Appetit kommt mit dem Essen.'' auf englisch?

NOTE 1. **bedeuten** to mean. **Was bedeutet . . .?** What is the meaning of . . .?

Exercise No. 107. Übersetzen Sie!

1 One day the family of Mr. C. visited him in his office. It was a surprise. 2 The children admired all the things that they saw in his office. 3 They admired the coloured posters which were on the walls and the magazines which were lying on the table. 4 It was almost one o'clock and the children were hungry. 5 Mr. C. said, 'I know a good restaurant which is not far from here.' 6 Charles, who always has a huge appetite, said 'Let's go!'

CHAPTER 23

REVISION OF CHAPTERS 18-22

Weak (Regular) Verbs. No Vowel Change

Infinitive		Past Tense
1 **dauern**	to last	**es dauerte**
2 **machen**	to make	**ich (er) machte**
3 **spielen**	to play	**ich (er) spielte**
4 **brauchen**	to need	**ich (er) brauchte**
5 **stellen**	to put	**ich (er) stellte**
6 **fragen**	to ask	**ich (er) fragte**
7 **sagen**	to say	**ich (er) sagte**
8 **wohnen**	to live	**ich (er) wohnte**
9 **danken**	to thank	**ich (er) dankte**
10 **lernen**	to learn	**ich (er) lernte**
11 **lehren**	to teach	**ich (er) lehrte**
12 **ruhen**	to rest	**ich (er) ruhte**
13 **regnen**	to rain	**es regnete**
14 **schneien**	to snow	**es schneite**
15 **kaufen**	to buy	**ich (er) kaufte**
16 **öffnen**	to open	**ich (er) öffnete**
17 **reden**	to talk	**ich (er) redete**
18 **antworten**	to answer	**ich (er) antwortete**
19 **besuchen**	to visit	**ich (er) besuchte**
20 **erzählen**	to relate	**ich (er) erzählte**
21 **arbeiten**	to work	**ich (er) arbeitete**
22 **plaudern**	to chat	**ich (er) plauderte**
23 **verkaufen**	to sell	**ich (er) verkaufte**
24 **bewohnen**	to occupy	**ich (er) bewohnte**
25 **verdienen**	to earn	**ich (er) verdiente**
26 **erwarten**	to await	**ich (er) erwartete**

Strong (Irregular) Verbs. Vowel Changes

Infinitive		Present	Past
1 **gehen**	to go	**er geht**	**er ging**
2 **kommen**	to come	**er kommt**	**er kam**
3 **stehen**	to stand	**er steht**	**er stand**
4 **sehen**	to see	**er sieht**	**er sah**
5 **lesen**	to read	**er liest**	**er las**
6 **nehmen**	to take	**er nimmt**	**er nahm**
7 **geben**	to give	**er gibt**	**er gab**
8 **sitzen**	to sit	**er sitzt**	**er saß**
9 **sprechen**	to speak	**er spricht**	**er sprach**
10 **treten**	to step	**er tritt**	**er trat**
11 **essen**	to eat	**er ißt**	**er aß**

123

12 liegen	to lie	er liegt	er lag
13 trinken	to drink	er trinkt	er trank
14 beginnen	to begin	er beginnt	er begann
15 finden	to find	er findet	er fand
16 scheinen	to shine	er scheint	er schien
17 schreiben	to write	er schreibt	er schrieb
18 tragen	to carry	er trägt	er trug
19 fahren	to ride	er fährt	er fuhr
20 waschen	to wash	er wäscht	er wusch
21 laufen	to run	er läuft	er lief
22 tun	to do	er tut	er tat

Past Tense of *sein* and *haben*

ich war	wir waren	ich hatte	wir hatten
du warst	ihr wart	du hattest	ihr hattet
er, sie, es war	sie (Sie) waren	er, sie, es hatte	sie (Sie) hatten

Expressions

1 **im allgemeinen** in general
2 **vor einem Monat (einem Jahr, einer Woche, sechs Jahren)** a month (a year, a week, six years) ago
3 **Er war im Begriff zu gehen.** He was about to go.
4 **Was macht Ihre (deine) Familie?** How is your family?
5 **Es freut mich, das zu hören.** I am glad to hear that.
6 **Das macht mir viel Freude.** That gives me much pleasure. That makes me very happy.
7 **Sie war krank. Jetzt geht es ihr besser.** She was ill. Now she is feeling better.
8 **Was fehlt dir (ihm, ihr, Ihnen)?** What is the matter with you (him, her, you *pol.*)?
9 **Ich habe Kopfschmerzen.** I have a headache.
10 **Das tut mir leid.** I am sorry.
11 **Wo befindet sich das Büro?** Where is the office?
12 **Ich habe den Sommer gern.** I like summer.
13 **Er hat den Herbst lieber.** He prefers autumn.
14 **Sie hat den Frühling am liebsten.** She likes spring best.
15 **den Doktor kommen lassen** to send for the doctor. **Ich lasse den Doktor kommen.**
16 **zum Frühstück (Mittagessen, Abendessen)** for breakfast (dinner, supper)
17 **Was ist los?** What's the matter? What's up?

Exercise No. 108. Complete these sentences by translating the words in parentheses.

1 (I am sorry to hear), **daß Ihr Bruder krank ist.** 2 **Sagen Sie mir:** (What is the matter with him?) 3 **Er hat** (a headache and a temperature). 4 **Sie war krank,** (but now she is feeling better). 5 (Five years ago) **wohnten wir in einem kleinen Vorort.** 6 **Ich habe Tee gern, aber** (I prefer coffee). 7 **Mein Büro** (is) **in einem großen Hochhaus.** 8 (It gave me great pleasure) **zu erfahren, daß Sie Deutsch lernen.** 9 **Wir mußten** (to send for the doctor). 10 **Was essen Sie gewöhnlich** (for supper)? 11 (We are sorry), **daß Sie nicht kommen können.**

Exercise No. 109. From Group II select the opposite of each word in Group I.

GROUP I

1 Gesundheit	7 es tut mir leid
2 weggehen	8 nichts
3 hinausgehen	9 hin
4 immer	10 etwas
5 jemand	11 das gefällt mir nicht
6 sich setzen	12 mir ist warm

GROUP II

(*a*) hereinkommen	(*g*) nimmer, nie, niemals
(*b*) nichts	(*h*) mir ist kalt
(*c*) zurückkommen	(*i*) Krankheit
(*d*) alles	(*j*) es macht mir Freude
(*e*) her	(*k*) Ich habe das gern
(*f*) niemand, keiner	(*l*) aufstehen

Exercise No. 110. Select the group of words in Column II which best complete each of the sentences begun in Column I.

Beispiel: (1*c*) Das Wetter ist gar nicht kalt, aber mir ist kalt.

I	II
1 Das Wetter ist gar nicht[1] kalt,	(*a*) stand Herr Clark auf und begrüßte
2 Nehmen Sie meinen Regenschirm,	ihn.
3 Während sie über das Wetter	(*b*) daß Herr Clark vier Kinder hat.
sprachen,	(*c*) aber mir ist kalt.
4 Wir mußten den ganzen Sommer	(*d*) der Zug von Hamburg pünktlich
arbeiten,	ankommt?
5 Tee ist ein Getränk,[2]	(*e*) denn es regnet in Strömen.
6 Als der Freund ins Büro trat,	(*f*) um genug Reisegeld zu verdienen.
7 Die Mutter ließ den Doktor	(*g*) das Sie sicherlich erwärmt.
kommen,	(*h*) brachte ihnen Frau Clark Tee
8 Können Sir mir sagen, ob	und Whisky.
9 Bevor Herr Clark den Zug nahm,	(*i*) weil Anna Kopfschmerzen hatte.
10 Die Leser dieses Buches wissen,	(*j*) als der Vater früh heimkam.[3]
11 Die Kinder freuten sich sehr,	(*k*) kaufte er den Kindern Süßigkeiten.[4]

NOTES: 1 **gar nicht** not at all. 2 **das Getränk** beverage. 3 **heim-kommen** = **nach Hause kommen**. 4 sweets.

Grammar Revision and Exercises

1 The modal auxiliaries—present tense

You are familiar with the following six verbs, which are called 'modal auxiliaries'.

dürfen	to be permitted, may	**müssen**	to have to, must
können	to be able, can	**wollen**	to want, to desire
mögen	to like, care to, may	**sollen**	to be supposed to, to be said to, shall

Present Tense of the Modal Auxiliaries

ich darf	kann	mag	muß	soll	will
du darfst	kannst	magst	mußt	sollst	willst

er, sie, es darf	kann	mag	muß	soll	will
wir dürfen	können	mögen	müssen	sollen	wollen
ihr dürft	könnt	mögt	müßt	sollt	wollt
sie, Sie dürfen	können	mögen	müssen	sollen	wollen

All six modal auxiliaries are irregular in the singular of the present tense.

Exercise No. 111. Fill in the correct present-tense form of the verb in parentheses.

Beispiel: 1 Herr Clark muß eine Reise machen.

1 Herr Clark (müssen) eine Reise machen. 2 Ich (wollen) meinen Vertreter besuchen. 3 (Können) er Deutsch sprechen? 4 Wir (müssen) früh aufstehen. 5 Der Zug (sollen) pünktlich um neun Uhr ankommen. 6 Ich (mögen) nicht spielen, denn ich bin müde. 7 (Dürfen) ich hereinkommen? 8 Er (wollen) sich ein Paar Schuhe kaufen. 9 (Können) Sir mir zehn Mark leihen? 10 Wann (sollen) ich da sein? 11 (Dürfen) er das Zimmer verlassen? 12 Ich (müssen) einen Brief schreiben. 13 Wir (wollen) ins Kino gehen. 14 (Können) du mitkommen? 15 Wieviel Trinkgeld (sollen) ich geben? 16 (Wollen) du einen Regenmantel kaufen? 17 Was (können) ich für Sie tun? 18 Er (mögen) die kühle, frische Luft.

2 The modal auxiliaries—past tense

ich durfte	konnte	mochte	musste	sollte	wollte
du durftest	konntest	mochtest	musstest	solltest	wolltest
er, sie, es durfte	konnte	mochte	musste	sollte	wollte
wir durften	konnten	mochten	mussten	solten	wollten
ihr durftet	konntet	mochtet	musstet	solltet	wolltet
sie, Sie durften	konnten	mochten	mussten	sollten	wollten

The model auxiliaries form their past tense like weak (regular) verbs by adding **-te** to the stem. Note, however, that the four verbs that have an **Umlaut** in the infinitive drop it in the past tense; also that **mögen** becomes **mochte**.

The meanings of the past tense of the modals are:

ich (er) durfte	I (he) was allowed
ich (er) konnte	I (he) was able, could
ich (er) mochte	I (he) liked, cared to
ich (er) musste	I (he) had to, was compelled to
ich (er) sollte	I (he) was to, was supposed to, ought to, should
ich (er) wollte	I (he) wanted, desired

Note that **ich mochte** = I liked. **Ich möchte** (I should like) is an expression which you have met many times.

Grammar Revision and Exercises

Exercise No. 112. Translate the verb in parentheses.

Beispiel: 1 Ich wollte nach München fahren

1 (I wanted) **nach München fahren.** 2 (We were to) **bis Seite[1] 50 (fünfzig) lesen.** 3 (I was able) **ihm nur ein Pfund leihen.** 4 (We did not care to) **ins Kino gehen.** 5 (We could not) **ohne das Wörterbuch auskommen.[2]** 6 Niemand (was permitted) **im Theater rauchen.** 7 Die Jungen (were not allowed) **auf der Straße Fußball**

spielen. 8 (I liked) **die frische, klare Luft des Vororts.** 9 **Alle** (wanted) **das deutsche Museum besuchen.** 10 (We were to) **zu Fuß gehen.**

NOTES: 1 **die Seite,** *pl.* **-n,** page. 2 **aus-kommen,** to get along.

3 Subordinate word order (Revision Chapter 14, Grammar Note 2, p. 75; Chapter 20, Grammar Note 4, p. 111)

Subordinate conjunctions: **daß** that; **weil** because; **ehe, bevor** before; **sobald** as soon as; **während** while; **bis** until; **wenn** if, or when (*with present tense*); **als** when (*with past tense*); **ob** whether. In surbordinate clauses the verb must stand last.

Exercise No. 113. Combine each pair of sentences with the conjunctions indicated.

Beispiel: 1 Ich muß Ihnen sagen, daß ich nicht gehen kann.

1 **Ich muß es Ihnen sagen.** (daß) **Ich kann nicht gehen.** 2 **Wir können unsere Aufgaben nicht machen.**[1] (wenn) **Die Kinder machen so viel Lärm.** 3 **Niemand durfte reden.** (als) **Wir machten das Examen.**[2] 4 **Er will nicht warten.** (bis) **Der Doktor kommt nach Hause.** 5 **Wir konnten nicht spazieren gehen.** (weil) **Es regnete in Strömen.** 6 **Sie mag nicht Tennis spielen.** (weil) **Sie ist müde.** 7 **Du darfst nach Hause gehen.** (sobald) **Du bist mit der Arbeit fertig.** 8 **Die Kinder sollen sich die Hände waschen.**[3] (bevor) **Sie setzen sich an den Tisch.** 9 **Ich mußte arbeiten.** (während) **Alle amüsierten sich.** 10 **Alle Schüler mußten aufstehen.** (als) **Der Lehrer trat ins Zimmer herein.** 11 **Ich weiß nicht,** (ob) **Der Autobus fährt um sieben Uhr ab.** 12 **Weißt du?** (ob) **Wir haben für morgen eine Aufgabe.**

NOTES: 1 **eine Aufgabe machen,** to do an exercise (to do homework). 2 **ein Examen machen,** to take an examination. 3 The children are to wash their hands. (*Lit.* to wash to themselves the hands.)

Grammar Revision and Exercises

4 Past tense of weak and strong verbs (Chapter 19, Grammar Notes 4, 6, pp. 105, 106; Chapter 20, Grammar Note 1, p. 110)

Exercise No. 114. Change this passage to the past tense.

Beispiel: 1 Ich stand jeden Werktag früh auf.

1 **Ich stehe jeden Werktag früh auf.** 2 **Ich wasche und rasiere mich.** 3 **Ich ziehe mich schnell an.** 4 **Meine Frau und ich frühstücken zusammen.** 5 **Nach dem Frühstück fahre ich mit dem Auto zum Bahnhof.** 6 **Viele Leute warten schon auf dem Bahnsteig.**[1] 7 **Der Zug kommt bald an.** 8 **Ich steige mit vielen anderen Passagieren in den Zug ein.** 9 **Der Zug fährt in einigen Minuten ab.** 10 **Auf dem Zug versuchen**[2] **einige Passagiere ein bißchen**[3] **zu schlafen.** 11 **Andere lesen Zeitungen, Bücher oder Zeitschriften.** 12 **In einer halben Stunde kommt der Zug in London an, und alle Passagiere steigen aus.**

NOTES: 1 **der Bahnsteig,** *pl.* **-e,** platform. 2 **versuchen,** to try. 3 **ein bißchen,** a little, a little bit.

5 Expressions of definite time and duration of time

Nouns used in expressions of definite time or duration of time (*without prepositions*) are in the accusative case.

| Jeden Werktag arbeitet er acht Stunden. | He works eight hours every workday. |
| Er arbeitete nur einen Monat hier. | He worked here only a month. |

jeden Tag	every day	einen Tag	for one day	den ganzen Tag	the whole day
jede Woche	every week	eine Woche	for one week	die ganze Woche	the whole week
jedes Jahr	every year	ein Jahr	for one year	das ganze Jahr	the whole year

ZWEI DIALOGE

| Der erste Dialog | The First Dialogue |
| ZWEI FREUNDE BEGEGNEN SICH AUF DER STRASSE | TWO FRIENDS MEET IN THE STREET |

— Wie geht's, mein Freund?	— How are you, my friend?
— Ich fühle mich nicht wohl.	— I don't feel well.
— Was fehlt dir?	— What's the matter with you?
— Ich habe Kopfschmerzen.	— I have a headache.
— Das tut mir leid. Warum nimmst du denn nicht etwas Aspirin?	— I'm sorry to hear that. Well, why don't you take some aspirin?
— Das tue ich, sobald ich nach Hause komme.	— I'll do that as soon as I get home.

| Der zweite Dialog | The Second Dialogue |

ICH HABE HUNGER

— Wollen wir etwas essen?	— Shall we eat something?
— Mit Vergnügen. Ich habe Hunger. Kennen Sie ein gutes Restaurant?	— With pleasure. I'm hungry. Do you know a good restaurant?
— Fahren Sie eine kurze Strecke gerade aus; dort ist ein Restaurant mit guter deutscher Küche.	— A short distance straight ahead there is a restaurant serving good German cooking.
— Gut. Gehen wir dahin.	— Fine. Let's go there.

Exercise No. 115. Lesestück

HERR CLARK WAR KRANK

Am Donnerstag, den zwanzigsten April, um acht Uhr abends erreichte Herr Müller das Haus seines Schülers. Der ältere Sohn, ein Junge von zwölf Jahren, öffnete die Tür und grüßte[1] den Lehrer höflich.[2] Sie gingen in das Wohnzimmer, wo Herr Clark gewöhnlich seinen Lehrer erwartete.

Aber heute abend war er nicht da. Frau Clark war auch nicht da. Herr Müller wunderte sich[3] sehr und fragte den Jungen: ,,Wo ist denn dein Papa?'' Der Sohn antwortete traurig:[4] ,,Der Papa ist krank. Er ist im Bett, denn er hat eine Erkältung[5] mit Fieber. Mutter versuchte Sie anzurufen, um Ihnen zu sagen, Sie sollten heute abend nicht kommen. Das Telephonfräulein[6] sagte aber, Ihr Telephon ist gestört.''[7]

Der Lehrer sagte: ,,Es tut mir leid, daß Herr Clark krank ist. Ich wünsche ihm gute Besserung.[8] Wenn er nächste Woche wieder gesund und munter[9] ist, können wir zwei Stunden nacheinander[10] studieren. Also bis auf den nächsten Dienstag. Adieu, Junge." Der Knabe erwiderte: „Adieu, Herr Müller."

NOTES: 1 **grüssen,** to greet. 2 politely. 3 **sich wundern,** to wonder, be surprised. 4 sadly. 5 a cold. 6 telephone operator. 7 out of order. 8 recovery. 9 cheerful. 10 one after the other, in succession.

CHAPTER 24

MÖGEN SIE DAS KINO?
DO YOU LIKE THE CINEMA?

1 Eines Abends[1] war Herr Clark allein zu Hause, als Herr Müller bei ihm eintrat. Frau Clark war im Kino mit den Kindern. Daher war ein Gespräch über das Kino und das Theater sehr passend. Das Gespräch folgt.

2 Herr Clark, Sie wissen nun, wie man um Auskunft über die Vorstellungen im Kino bittet. Sagen Sie mir aber: Mögen Sie das Kino?

3 Dann und wann sehe ich gern einen guten Film, aber im allgemeinen habe ich kein Interesse für das Kino. Es ist eigentlich nicht nach meinem Geschmack.

4 Dann gehen Sie lieber ins Theater?

5 Ohne Zweifel haben meine Frau und ich es viel lieber. Wir besuchen das Theater von Zeit zu Zeit und genießen ein gutes Lustspiel, ein Drama oder eine Operette.

6 Wenn Sie das Theater besuchen, sitzen Sie lieber in einer Loge, im Parkett, oder im zweiten Rang (Balkon)?

7 Wir sitzen lieber im Parkett, aber das ist meistens zu teuer für uns. Deswegen sitzen wir gewöhnlich im ersten Rang, erste, zweite, dritte Reihe, oder sogar weiter hinten.

8 Und Ihre Kinder? Gehen sie auch lieber ins Theater?

9 Ach nein! Die ziehen es nicht vor. Sie lieben Schauspiele und Musikfilme in Naturfarben, die für uns sehr langweilig sind.

10 Die Kinder kennen die „Filmstars", nicht wahr?

11 Natürlich. Sie kennen sie alle sehr wohl. Sie kennen auch die berühmten Schauspieler und Schauspielerinnen vom Fernsehen.

12 Gibt es ein Kino in der Nähe Ihrer Wohnung?

13 Jawohl. Wir haben ein Kino ganz in der Nähe. Wir können in zehn Minuten zu Fuß dahingehen.

14 Welche Plätze haben die Kinder lieber im Kino, die Plätze in den ersten Reihen oder die Plätze weiter hinten?

15 Sie sitzen gerne in der zwölften, dreizehnten, vierzehnten oder fünfzehnten Reihe. Von da kann man gut sehen und hören.

16 Und was tun Sie, wenn die meisten Plätze besetzt sind?

17 Dann nehmen wir eben irgendwelche freien Plätze, entweder vorne oder hinten oder an der Seite. Aber wir mögen solche Plätze nicht. Daher kommen wir immer zeitig.

18 Herrlich, Herr Clark! Ihr Fortschritt ist erstaunlich.

19 Dafür kann ich Ihnen danken, Herr Müller.

NOTE 1. The genitive case may be used to express indefinite time: **eines Tages** one day; **eines Abends,** one evening.

1 One evening Mr. Clark was at home alone when Mr. Müller came into

his house. Mrs. Clark was at the cinema with the children. Therefore a conversation about the cinema and the theatre was quite appropriate. The conversation follows.

2 Mr. Clark, you already know how to ask for information about performances at the cinema. But tell me: do you like the cinema?

3 Now and then I like to see a good film, but in general I have no interest in the cinema. It does not really appeal to me.

4 Then you prefer to go to the theatre?

5 Without doubt. My wife and I like it much better. We go to the theatre from time to time and enjoy a good comedy, a drama, or a musical comedy.

6 When you go to the theatre, do you prefer to sit in a box, in the stalls, or in the upper circle?

7 We prefer to sit in the stalls, but that is usually too expensive for us. Therefore we usually sit in the circle, first, second, third row, or even farther back.

8 And your children. Do they, too, prefer to go to the theatre?

9 Oh no! They do not prefer it. They love plays and musical films in colour, which are very boring for us.

10 The children know the stars of the films, don't they?

11 Of course. They know them all very well. They also know the famous actors and actresses of television.

12 Is there a cinema near your home?

13 Yes indeed. We have a cinema very near us. We can walk there in ten minutes.

14 Which seats do the children prefer at the cinema, the seats in the front rows or the seats farther back?

15 They like to sit in the twelfth, thirteenth, fourteenth, or fifteenth row From there one can see and hear well.

16 And what do you do if most of the seats are occupied?

17 Then we take any vacant seats whatever, whether in front or rear or at the side. But we don't like such seats. Therefore we always come early.

18 Splendid, Mr. Clark! Your progress is amazing.

19 For this I can thank you, Mr. Müller.

Wortschatz

der **Balkón**, der **Rang**, balcony, upper circle

das **Drama**, *pl*. **-en**, drama

die **Eintrittskarte**, *pl*. **-n**, admission ticket

das **Interésse**, *pl*. **-n**, interest

die **Loge**, *pl*. **-n**, box (in theatre)

das **Lustspiel**, *pl*. **-e**, comedy

die **Operétte**, *pl*. **-n**, light opera, musical comedy

das **Parkétt**, *pl*. **-e**, orchestra (part of theatre), stalls

der **Platz**, *pl*. **-e**, seat, place

die **Reihe**, *pl*. **-en**, row

der **Schauspieler**, *pl*. **-**, actor

dahin-gehen, to go there (*past* **er ging . . . dahin**)

geníessen, to enjoy (*past* **er genoss**)

vor-ziehen, to prefer (*past* **er zog . . . vor**)

berühmt, famous

besétzt, occupied; **frei**, vacant, free

erstáunlich, astonishing

eigentlich, really

hinten, at the back; **vorne**, in front

irgenwelche, any . . . whatsoever

Deutsche Ausdrücke

ohne Zweifel, without doubt
nach meinem Geschmack, to my taste
Sind noch Plätze für heute abend zu haben? Are there any seats left (to be had)
for this evening?
Nur noch im ersten Balkon. Only in the first balcony.
Ich möchte zwei Plätze im Parkett. I should like two seats in the orchestra
(stalls).
Das Parkett ist ausverkauft. The orchestra is sold out.
Die Plätze sind alle besetzt. All the seats are taken.
Es sind keine Plätze frei. No seats are vacant.

Grammar Notes and Practical Exercises

1 The ordinal numerals

The cardinal numerals are 1, 2, 3, 4, etc. The ordinal numerals are the first,
second, third, fourth, etc. Learn the ordinals in German.

der erste	1st	der neunte	9th	der vierzigste	40th
der zweite	2nd	der zehnte	10th	der fünfzigste	50th
der dritte	3rd	der elfte	11th	der sechzigste	60th
der vierte	4th	der zwölfte	12th	der siebzigste	70th
der fünfte	5th	der dreizehnte	13th	der achtzigste	80th
der sechste	6th	der neunzehnte	19th	der neunzigste	90th
der siebente	7th	der zwanzigste	20th	der hundertste	100th
(siebte)		der dreißigste	30th	der letzte	last
der achte	8th				

Ordinal numerals are formed by adding **-te** to the cardinal numerals up to
19, and **-ste** to those above 19. **der erste** and **der dritte** are irregular.
Ordinal numerals are adjectives and take case endings like other adjectives.
Thus:

N.	der erste Tag	die zweite Woche	das dritte Jahr
G.	des ersten Tages	der zweiten Woche	des dritten Jahres
D.	dem ersten Tag	der zweiten Woche	dem dritten Jahr
A.	den ersten Tag	die zweite Woche	das dritte Jahr

Exercise No. 116. Read aloud.

1 Die Woche hat sieben Tage. In Deutschland ist der Montag der erste Tag
der Woche und der Sonntag der siebente. In England ist der Sonntag der erste
Tag der Woche und der Samstag der siebente.

2 Das Jahr hat vier Jahreszeiten. Die erste Jahreszeit ist der Frühling; die
zweite ist der Sommer; die dritte ist der Herbst; die vierte ist der Winter.

3 Das Jahr hat zwölf Monate. Der erste Monat ist der Januar; der zwölfte ist
der Dezember. Der letzte Monat des Jahres ist der Dezember.

4 Wo sitzen Sie am liebsten? Ich sitze am liebsten in der vierten Reihe des
Parketts. Wo sitzt Heinrich am liebsten? Er sitzt am liebsten in der ersten Reihe
des ersten Ranges.

2 *Das Datum.* The date

Der wievielte (vi:-fit:l-te) ist heute?   What date is today?

Den wievielten haben wir heute?	What date have we today?
Heute ist der 1. Mai (der erste Mai).	Today is 1 May.
Gestern war der 30. April (der dreißigste April).	Yesterday was 30 April.
Vorgestern war der 29. April (der neunund- zwanzigste April).	The day before yesterday was April 29.
Mein Geburtstag ist am 12. Februar (am zwölften Februar).	My birthday is on 12 February.

A full stop (.) after a numeral is an abbreviation of the ordinal. Thus: **der 1. Mai = der erste Mai; der 8. Juni = der achte Juni.**

On a certain date = **am** + ordinal + month. Thus: **am 1. Mai (am ersten Mai)** = 1 May; **am 31. Dezember (am einunddreißigsten Dezember)** = December 31; **am 12. Februar (am zwölften Februar)** = 12 February.

Exercise No. 117. Read each sentence aloud. Write out in full each date.

Beispiel: 1. am zweiundzwanzigsten Februar.

1 Karls[1] Geburtstag ist am 22. Februar. 2 Herrn Clarks Geburtstag ist am 27. August. 3 Karls Geburtstag ist am 19. Juni. 4 Wilhelms Geburtstag ist am 20. Januar. 5 Annas Geburtstag ist am 9. Juli. 6 Maries Geburtstag ist am 10. Mai. 7 Frau Clarks Geburtstag ist am 22. März. 8 Der Frühling beginnt am 21. März. 9 Der 1. Januar ist Neujahrstag. 10 Heute lernen wir das 24. Kapitel.

NOTE 1. In the case of names the genitive of possession is commonly used *before* the noun. The ending s corresponds here to the English *'s* and is used with both masculine and feminine names. Thus: **Karls (Annas, Frau Clarks, Herrn Clarks) Geburtstag.**

Exercise No. 118. Fragen

Lesen Sie noch einmal den Text: **Mögen Sie das Kino?** und beantworten Sie dann diese Fragen!

1 Wer war eines Abends allein zu Hause? 2 Wer trat bei ihm ein? 3 Warum war ein Gespräch über das Kino und das Theater an diesem Abend sehr passend? 4 Was sieht Herr Clark dann und wann gern? 5 Was ist eigentlich nicht nach seinem Geschmack? 6 Geht er lieber ins Theater oder ins Kino? 7 Was genießen Herr und Frau Clark? 8 Warum sitzen sie gewöhnlich nicht im Parkett? 9 In welcher Reihe des ersten Ranges sitzen sie gewöhnlich? 10 Was ziehen die Kinder vor, das Theater oder das Kino? 11 Wo befindet sich das Kino, in der Nähe oder weit vom Hause der Familie Clark? 12 Gehen sie zu Fuß dahin, oder fahren sie? 13 In welcher Reihe sitzen sie gerne? 14 Wessen Fortschritt im Studium der deutschen Sprache ist erstaunlich?

CHAPTER 25

WICHTIGE DATEN IN DER GESCHICHTE DEUTSCHLANDS
IMPORTANT DATES IN THE HISTORY OF GERMANY

1 Herr Clark, Sie haben die deutschen Zahlen gut gelernt. Sie wissen schon, wie man richtig und rasch rechnet. Heute üben wir Zahlen in Form von historischen Daten. Ich zitiere wichtige Daten in der deutschen Geschichte. Sie müssen für jedes Datum ein wichtiges Ereignis angeben.

2 Schön. Also fangen wir an. Ich bin bereit.

3 Also, was geschah im Jahre 9 A.D. (neun nach Christi Geburt)?

4 Das ist altdeutsche Geschichte. Die Antwort ist: die Hermanns-Schlacht. In dieser Schlacht hat der deutsche Held Hermann ein römisches Heer geschlagen.

5 Gut. Und jetzt kommen einige moderne Daten: der 18. (achtzehnte) Januar 1871.

6 Wie nett von Ihnen. Das ist kinderleicht. Der 18. Januar 1871 (achzehnhunderteinundsiebzig) ist das Datum der Vereinigung Deutschlands. Aus vielen Staaten hat man ein neues deutsches Reich gebildet.

7 Richtig. Wer war der erste Kanzler des neuen deutschen Reiches?

8 Das war Otto von Bismarck, ,,der eiserne Kanzler'' und ,,der Mann von Blut und Eisen.''

9 Sehr gut. Was geschah am 11. (elften) November 1918 (neunzehnhundertachtzehn)?

10 An jenem Tage fand der Waffenstillstand des ersten Weltkrieges statt.

11 Richtig. Nun, der 18. (achtzehnte) März 1933 (neunzehnhundertdreiunddreißig).

12 Es bezeichnet den Anfang der Diktatur Hitlers.

13 Richtig. Lassen Sie uns nun mit den Fragen fertig werden. Noch ein Datum: der 30. (dreißigste) April 1945.

14 Es bezeichnet den Niedergang und den Tod Adolf Hitlers.

15 Sehr gut. Es ist klar, Sie kennen die Geschichte Deutschlands ebenso gut wie das Geldsystem. Wir haben eine interessante Stunde gehabt. Sie haben alle meine Fragen richtig beantwortet.

16 Vielen Dank. Ich habe deutsche Geschichte in der Schule gelernt, und wie Sie sehen, habe ich nicht alles vergessen.

1 Mr. Clark, you have learned German numerals well. You already know how one calculates quickly and correctly. Today we shall practise numerals in the form of historical dates. I shall cite some important dates in German history. You must mention an important event for each date.

2 Good. Let's begin. I am ready.

3 Well, what happened in the year A.D. 9 (nine years after the birth of Christ)?

4 That's ancient German history. The answer is: the Hermann Battle. In this battle the German hero Hermann defeated a Roman army.

5 Good. And now come some modern dates: 18 January, 1871.

6 How nice of you. That is too easy. 18 January, 1871 is the date of the unification of Germany. From many states they formed a new German empire.

7 Right. Who was the first chancellor of the new German empire?

8 That was Otto von Bismarck, 'the Iron Chancellor' and 'the man of blood and iron'.

9 Very good. What happened on 11 November, 1918?

10 On that day the Armistice of the First World War took place.

11 Right. Now 18 March, 1933.

12 That denotes the beginning of the dictatorship of Hitler.

13 Correct. Let us now finish with the questions. One more date: 30 April, 1945.

14 That denotes the fall and death of Adolf Hitler.

15 Very good. It is evident that you know the history of Germany as well as its monetary system. We have had an interesting lesson. You have answered all my questions correctly.

16 Many thanks. I learned German history in school, and as you see, I have not forgotten everything.

Wortschatz

der **Anfang,** *pl.* ¨e, beginning
das **Ende,** *pl.* -en, end
das **Blut,** blood; das **Eisen,** iron
das **Heer** (he:r), *pl.* -e, army
der **Krieg,** *pl.* -e, war; der **Frieden,** peace
der **Staat** (sta:t), *pl.* -en, state
die **Stadt** (stat), *pl.* ¨e, city
an-geben, to mention, indicate
bezeichnen, to denote, indicate

schlagen, to hit, beat, defeat
statt-finden, to take place
vergéssen, to forget
zitíeren, to cite
altdeutsch, old (ancient) German
eisern, iron (*adj.*)
histórisch, historical
römisch, Roman (*adj.*)

Deutsche Ausdrücke

mit Vergnügen, with pleasure
es ist mir klar, it is evident (clear) to me
es ist ihm (ihr, Ihnen, etc.**) klar,** it is evident to him (to her, to you, etc.)

A.D. = **nach Christi Gebúrt,** after the birth of Christ (also *n. Chr.*)
A.Ch. = **vor Christi Gebúrt,** before the birth of Christ (also *v. Chr.*)

Grammar Notes and Practical Exercises

1 The present perfect tense

The present perfect tense in English is formed by the auxiliary verb *have* + the past participle of a verb. *I have learned*; *you have worked*; *he has seen*; *they have spoken*. Observe the present perfect tense in German:

lernen, to learn
I have learned the numerals well.
You have learned the numerals well; etc.

Ich habe die Zahlen gut **gelernt.**
Du hast die Zahlen gut **gelernt.**

sehen, to see
I have not seen the new film.
You have not seen the new film; etc.

Ich habe den neuen Film nicht **gesehen.**
Du hast den neuen Film nicht **gesehen.**

Er hat die Zahlen gut **gelernt.**	**Er hat** den neuen Film nicht **gesehen.**
Wir haben die Zahlen gut **gelernt.**	**Wir haben** den neuen Film nicht **gesehen.**
Ihr habt die Zahlen gut **gelernt.**	**Ihr habt** den neuen Film nicht **gesehen.**
Sie haben die Zahlen gut **gelernt.**	**Sie haben** den neuen Film nicht **gesehen.**

(*a*) The present perfect tense of most verbs in German is formed by the auxiliary **haben** + the past participle of the main verb.

(*b*) The past participle stands at the end of a simple sentence or main clause.

2 Formation of the Past Participle

Weak (Regular) Verbs

ich habe **gelernt**	I have *learned*
du hast **gearbeitet**	you have *worked*
er hat **gerechnet**	he has *reckoned*
wir haben **gekauft**	we have *bought*
ihr habt **gemacht**	you have *made*
sie haben **aufgemacht**	they have *opened*
Sie haben **verkauft**	you have *sold*

Strong (Irregular) Verbs

habe ich **geschrieben?**	have I *written*?
hast du **gelesen?**	have you *read*?
hat sie **gesprochen?**	has she *spoken*?
haben wir **gestanden?**	have we *stood*?
habt ihr **gesehen?**	have you *seen*?
haben sie **angesehen?**	have they *looked at*?
haben Sie **verstanden?**	have you *understood*?

(*a*) The past participle of weak verbs is formed by adding **-t** or **-et** to the infinitive stem and prefixing **ge-**. The ending **-et** is used when the stem ends in **-t** or **-d**, and after certain consonant groups, for ease in pronunciation (**ge-arbeit-et, ge-red-et, ge-rechn-et, ge-öffn-et**).

(*b*) The past participle of strong verbs ends in **-en** and has the prefix **ge-**. The stem vowel has to be learnt separately.

(*c*) Verbs with separable prefixes form their past participles like the simple verbs, and the prefix **ge-** stands between the separable prefix and the verb (**aufgemacht, angesehen**).

(*d*) Verbs with inseparable prefixes (**be-, emp-, ent-, er-, ge-, ver-, zer-**) do not add the prefix **ge-** to the past participle (**verkauft, verstanden**).

Exercise No. 119. Complete these sentences with the past participle of the verb in parenthesis.

Beispiel: 1 Er hat die neuen Wörter gelernt.

1 Er hat die neuen Wörter (lernen).	7 Der Tisch hat hier (stehen).
2 Ich habe ihn heute nicht (sehen).	8 Die Schüler haben gut (rechnen).
3 Sie haben gut (antworten).	9 Die Knaben haben zu viel (reden).
4 Hat Heinrich schwer (arbeiten)?	10 Niemand hat Deutsch (sprechen).
5 Er hat gestern einen Brief (schreiben).	11 Was haben Sie ihnen (verkaufen)?
6 Hast du das Porträt (ansehen)?	12 Sie hat einen neuen Hut (kaufen).

3 The Principal Parts of Verbs

Weak Verbs (Regular). No Vowel Change in Stem Vowel

Infinitive	*Present* (er, sie, es)	*Past* (ich, er, sie, es)	*Present Perfect* (er, sie, es)
lernen	er lernt	lernte	hat gelernt
fragen	er fragt	fragte	hat gefragt
reden	er redet	redete	hat geredet
antworten	er antwortet	antwortete	hat geantwortet
verkaufen	er verkauft	verkaufte	hat verkauft
haben	er hat	hatte	hat gehabt

Strong Verbs (Irregular). The Stem Vowel Changes

schreiben to write	er schreibt	schrieb	hat geschrieben
geben to give	er gibt	gab	hat gegeben
an-geben to mention	er gibt . . . an	gab . . . an	hat angegeben
lesen to read	er liest	las	hat gelesen
sehen to see	er sieht	sah	hat gesehen
an-sehen to look at	er sieht . . . an	sah . . . an	hat angesehen
sprechen to speak	er spricht	sprach	hat gesprochen
vergessen to forget	er vergißt	vergaß	hat vergessen
nehmen to take	er nimmt	nahm	hat genommen
sitzen to sit	er sitzt	saß	hat gesessen
liegen to lie	er liegt	lag	hat gelegen
stehen to stand	er steht	stand	hat gestanden
verstehen to understand	er versteht	verstand	hat verstanden
finden to find	er findet	fand	hat gefunden
statt-finden to take place	er findet . . . statt	fand . . . statt	hat stattgefunden
trinken to drink	er trinkt	trank	hat getrunken
schlagen to hit, defeat	er schlägt	schlug	hat geschlagen

All weak verbs have a like pattern, so that it is not necessary to memorize the principal parts of each verb separately.

The principal parts of strong verbs have vowel changes and must be memorized. A foreigner learning English has a similar problem. He must learn the irregular verb forms such as: *speak, spoke, spoken; give, gave, given; write, wrote, written;* etc.

4 Use of the Past and Present Perfect Tenses

In German both the past and present perfect are used to express past time.

Er kaufte sich gestern einen Hut.
Er hat sich gestern einen Hut gekauft. } He bought himself a hat yesterday.

In conversation the present perfect is generally used.

> **Haben Sie dem Heinrich geschrieben?**   Have you written to Henry?
> **Ja, ich habe ihm gestern geschrieben.**   Yes, I wrote to him yesterday.

However, to narrate a sequence of events, the past tense is preferable.

> **Ich stand um sieben Uhr auf.**   I got up at seven o'clock.
> **Ich zog mich schnell an.**   I dressed quickly.
> **Ich frühstückte, usw.**   I had breakfast, etc.

Exercise No. 120. Change these sentences to the present perfect tense.

Beispiel: 1. Herr Clark hat einen Brief an seinen Vertreter geschrieben.

1 Herr Clark schreibt einen Brief an seinen Vertreter. 2 Wir geben dem Vater eine Füllfeder zum Geburtstag. 3 Ich trinke ein Glas Bier beim Mittagessen. 4 Ich lese die Geschichte Deutschlands. 5 Die Kinder sitzen vor dem Fernsehapparat. 6 Sie antwortet richtig auf alle Fragen. 7 Was fragt der Lehrer? 8 Arbeiten Sie den ganzen Tag? 9 Jeden Abend hören wir ein Musikprogramm. 10 Was sehen die Kinder im Büro des Vaters? 11 Ich beantworte alle Fragen.

Exercise No. 121. Practise these short dialogues aloud.

1 — Hat der Lehrer schwere Fragen an Herrn Clark gestellt? — Jawohl. Er hat einige sehr schwere Fragen an ihn gestellt. — Hat Herr Clark richtig geantwortet? — Ja, er hat auf alle Fragen richtig geantwortet.

1 — Did the teacher ask Mr. Clark difficult questions? — Yes, indeed. He asked him several very difficult questions. — Did Mr. Clark answer correctly? — Yes, he answered all the questions correctly.

2 — Haben Sie einen Brief an Ihren Freund geschrieben? — Ich habe ihm vor zwei Wochen geschrieben. — Haben Sie schon eine Antwort bekommen? — Eben heute habe ich eine lange Antwort bekommen, aber ich habe sie noch nicht gelesen.

2 — Have you written a letter to your friend? — I wrote to him two weeks ago. — Have you already received an answer? — Only today I received a long answer, but I haven't read it yet.

Exercise No. 122. Lesen Sie noch einmal den Text: **Wichtige Daten in der Geschichte Deutschlands,** und dann beantworten Sie diese Fragen!

1 Wer hat die deutschen Zahlen gut gelernt? 2 Was üben die Herren heute? 3 Was zitiert der Lehrer? 4 Was muß Herr Clark tun? 5 Wer hat im Jahre 9 A.D. ein römisches Heer geschlagen? 6 Was haben die Deutschen im Jahre 1871 aus vielen Staaten gebildet? 7 Wie hieß der erste Kanzler des neuen deutschen Reiches? 8 Wer hat die Deutschen im ersten Weltkrieg besiegt? 9 In welchem Jahre hat die Diktatur von Hitler angefangen? 10 Welches Jahr bezeichnet den Niedergang Adolf Hitlers? 11 Wie hat Herr Clark alle Fragen beantwortet?

CHAPTER 26

WIE HERR CLARK GEWÖHNLICH DEN SONNTAG VERBRINGT
HOW MR. CLARK USUALLY SPENDS SUNDAY

— Herr Clark, Sie haben mir schon erzählt, wie Sie einen typischen Werktag verbringen. Seien Sie[1] so gut und erzählen Sie mir jetzt, wie Sie den vorigen Sonntag verbracht haben.

— Mit Vergnügen, Herr Müller.

Vorgestern war Sonntag. Ich bin erst um halb zehn aufgestanden. An Werktagen stehe ich, wie Sie wissen, um sechs Uhr auf. Ich habe mich gewaschen, rasiert und angezogen. Meine Frau und Kinder waren vor mir aufgestanden; aber sie hatten noch nicht gefrühstückt. Um zehn Uhr haben wir uns alle zum Frühstück gesetzt. Am Sonntag freuen wir uns natürlich, die Mahlzeiten zusammen zu nehmen.

— Und nach dem Frühstück?

— Nach dem Frühstück habe ich die Zeitung gelesen. In der Sonntagszeitung interessieren mich besonders die Artikel über auswärtige Neuigkeiten, und auch die Zeitungsbeilage. Ich interessiere mich auch für die Geschäftsbeilage, wie Sie sich wohl vorstellen können.

Die Sportnachrichten habe ich gar nicht angeschaut. Ich interessiere mich nicht für Sport. Meine zwei Jungen interessieren sich riesig dafür, besonders für Fußball und Cricket.

— Was taten die Kinder, während Sie die Zeitung lasen?

— Die jüngeren spielten und die älteren besuchten Freunde in der Nachbarschaft.

Um ein Uhr haben wir uns zum Mittagessen gesetzt. Meine Frau hatte eine schmackhafte Mahlzeit bereitet, und alle ließen es sich gut schmecken.

— Und nach dem Mittagessen?

— Nach dem Mittagessen haben die Kinder uns geplagt. Sie wollten ins Kino gehen. Wir mußten also mit ihnen ins Kino! Da haben meine Frau und ich uns furchtbar gelangweilt, aber die Kinder haben sich gut amüsiert.

Vom Kino sind wir nach Hause gegangen. Nach dem Abendbrot habe ich an einen Freund geschrieben, der neulich eine Reise nach Deutschland gemacht hat. Dann habe ich einige Kurzgeschichten in meinem deutschen Lesebuch gelesen.

Um elf Uhr bin ich zu Bett gegangen.

— Ausgezeichnet, Herr Clark. Sie haben ja alles schön erzählt. Ihre Aussprache war besonders gut.

— Dafür muß ich Ihnen danken, Herr Müller.

— Danke, Sie sind sehr liebenswürdig.

NOTE 1. The imperative of sein: Sei gut! Seid gut! Seien Sie gut! Be good.

— Mr. Clark, you have already told me how you spend a typical weekday. Be so kind as to tell me now, how you spent last Sunday.

— With pleasure, Mr. Müller.

The day before yesterday was Sunday. I did not get up until half past nine. On weekdays, as you know, I get up at six o'clock. I washed, shaved, and dressed. My wife and children had got up before me; but they had not yet had breakfast. At ten o'clock all of us sat down to breakfast. On Sunday we are naturally happy to have our meals together.

— And after breakfast?

— After breakfast I read the newspaper. In the Sunday newspaper the foreign news section interests me especially and also the supplement. I am also interested in the business section, as you can well imagine.

I did not look at the sports news at all. I am not interested in sports. My two boys are mightily interested in these, especially in football and cricket.

— What were the children doing while you were reading the newspaper?

— The younger ones were playing, and the older ones were visiting friends in the neighbourhood.

At one o'clock we sat down to dinner. My wife had prepared an excellent meal (*lit.* tasty) and everybody enjoyed eating it.

— And after dinner?

— After dinner the children pestered us. They wanted to go to the cinema. So we had to go with them to the cinema! There my wife and I were terribly bored, but the children enjoyed themselves very much.

From the cinema we went home. After supper I wrote a letter to a friend who has recently taken a trip to Germany. Then I read a few short stories in my German reader.

At eleven o'clock I went to bed.

— Excellent, Mr. Clark. You have related everything very nicely. Your pronunciation was especially good.

— For this I must thank you, Mr. Müller.

— Thank you, you are very kind.

Wortschatz

die Aussprache, *pl.* -n, pronunciation
die Beilage, *pl.* -n, section, supplement
der Fernsehapparát, *pl.* -e, television set
die Kurzgeschichte, *pl.* -n, short story
das Lesebuch, *pl.* ¨er, reader, reading book
die Nachbarschaft, *pl.* -en, neighbourhood
die Zeitschrift, *pl.* -en, magazine
bereiten, to prepare

sich langweilen, to be bored
sich interessíeren für, to be interested in
plagen, to bother, to pester
verbríngen, to spend (time)
sich vorstellen, to imagine
auswärtig, foreign
furchtbar, terrible, terribly
schmackhaft, tasty

Strong Verbs. Principal Parts

lassen, to let, to leave	er läßt	ließ	hat gelassen
sich waschen, to wash oneself	er wäscht sich	wusch sich	hat sich gewaschen
sich an-ziehen, to dress oneself	er zieht sich an	zog sich an	hat sich angezogen

Deutsche Ausdrücke

zu Bett gehen, to go to bed
sich interessieren für, to be interested in
  Wir interessieren uns nicht für Sport. We are not interested in sports.
schmecken, to taste (*takes no object*)
versuchen, to try, to taste (*takes an object*)
Das Fleisch schmeckt gut. The meat tastes good.
  Sie liessen es sich gut schmecken. They enjoyed eating (*lit.* They let it taste
    good to themselves).
  Haben Sie diese Suppe versucht? Have you tasted this soup?

Grammar Notes and Practical Exercises

1 The Past Perfect

I had learned, you had learned, etc.	I had not seen him, you had not seen him, etc.
Ich hatte Deutsch **gelernt.**	**Ich hatte** ihn nicht **gesehen.**
Du hattest Deutsch **gelernt.**	**Du hattest** ihn nicht **gesehen.**
Er, sie, es hatte Deutsch **gelernt.**	**Er, sie, es hatte** ihn nicht **gesehen.**
Wir hatten Deutsch **gelernt.**	**Wir hatten** ihn nicht **gesehen.**
Ihr hattet Deutsch **gelernt.**	**Ihr hattet** ihn nicht **gesehen.**
Sie hatten Deutsch **gelernt.**	**Sie hatten** ihn nicht **gesehen.**

The past perfect of most German verbs is formed by the past tense of the
auxiliary **haben (hatte)** + the past participle of the verb.

The past perfect is used for events which happened in the past before other
events happened.

Ich hatte Deutsch gelernt, bevor ich die Reise nach Deutschland machte.
I had learned German before I took the trip to Germany.
Er war sehr müde, denn er hatte eine lange Reise gemacht.
He was very tired, for he had taken a long trip.

2 The past participles of verbs ending in -*ieren*

Ich hatte vier Jahre auf der Universität Jena studiert.
I had studied four years at the university of Jena.
Die Kinder haben sich gut amüsiert.
The children have enjoyed themselves greatly.

The past participle of verbs in **-ieren** does not have the prefix **ge-**.

Some **-ieren** verbs you have met are: **studieren,** to study; **reservieren,** to
reserve; **sich rasieren,** to shave oneself; **interessieren,** to interest; **sich interessieren für,** to be interested in; **sich amüsieren,** to enjoy oneself, to have a good
time.

Exercise No. 123. Change these sentences from the present perfect to the past
perfect.

Beispiel: 1 Sie hatten mir von einem typischen deutschen Werktag erzählt.

1 Sie haben mir von einem typischen deutschen Werktag erzählt. 2 Er hat sich
schnell gewaschen und angezogen. 3 Unsere Familie hat schon gefrühstückt.
4 Der Vater hat die Sonntagszeitung gelesen. 5 Um sieben Uhr haben wir uns

zum Abendessen gesetzt. 6 Die Mutter hat eine schmackhafte Mahlzeit bereitet. 7 Der Kaufmann hat die Geschäftsbeilage gelesen. 8 Die Kinder haben sich im Kino gut amüsiert. 9 Wir aber haben uns furchtbar gelangweilt. 10 Was haben die Kinder getan?[1]

NOTE 1. Principal parts of **tun** to do: **er tut, tat, hat getan.**

3 Verbs with auxiliary *sein*

In older English (Shakespeare, the Bible, etc.) the use of the auxiliary *to be* instead of *to have* with the perfect tenses of certain verbs was quite common. You still meet some remnants of this usage in such expressions as:

The time is come, meaning   The time has come.

The people are gone away, meaning   The people have gone away.

This usage of the auxiliary *to be* instead of *to have* is found in quite a large number of German verbs. The verbs **kommen** (to come) and **gehen** (to go) are typical.

Present Perfect		**Past Perfect**	
I have come, you have come, etc.		I had come, you had come, etc.	
ich bin gekommen	wir sind gekommen	ich war gekommen	wir waren gekommen
du bist gekommen	ihr seid gekommen	du warst gekommen	ihr wart gekommen
er ist gekommen	sie sind gekommen	er war gekommen	sie waren gekommen
I have gone, you have gone, etc.		I had gone, you had gone, etc.	
ich bin gegangen	wir sind gegangen	ich war gegangen	wir waren gegangen
du bist gegangen	ihr seid gegangen	du warst gegangen	ihr wart gegangen
er ist gegangen	sie sind gegangen	er war gegangen	sie waren gegangen

All intransitive verbs indicating a *change of place or a change of condition* take the present of the auxiliary **sein** (**ich bin,** etc.) in the present perfect, and the past of the auxiliary **sein** (**ich war,** etc.) in the past perfect. An intransitive verb is a verb that does not take an object.

4 The principal parts of a number of sein-verbs you have already met.

Infinitive		*Present 3rd Sing.*	*Past*	*Present Perfect*
gehen	to go	er geht	ging	ist gegangen
weg-gehen	to go away	er geht . . . weg	ging . . . weg	ist weggegangen
kommen	to come	er kommt	kam	ist gekommen
an-kommen	to arrive	er kommt . . . an	kam . . . an	ist angekommen
fahren	to travel	er fährt	fuhr	ist gefahren
ab-fahren	to leave	er fährt . . . ab	fuhr . . . ab	ist abgefahren
laufen	to run	er läuft	lief	ist gelaufen
fallen	to fall	er fällt	fiel	ist gefallen
fliegen	to fly	er fliegt	flog	ist geflogen
auf-stehen	to get up	er steht . . . auf	stand . . . auf	ist aufgestanden

Note that the above are intransitive verbs indicating a change of place.

Two important intransitive verbs showing a *change of condition* are:

sterben	to die	er stirbt	starb	ist gestorben
wachsen (vak-*sen*)	to grow	er wächst (*vɛkst*)	wuchs (*vuks*)	ist gewachsen
				(*ge*-vak-*sen*)

Der Patiént ist gestern gestorben.   The patient died yesterday.
Diese Pflanzen sind schnell gewachsen.   These plants have grown quickly.

Exercise No. 124. Kurze Gespräche (Short Conversations). Practise aloud.

1 — Wo kommen Sie her? — Ich komme aus Hamburg. — Sind Sie mit dem Flugzeug gekommen? — Nein, ich bin mit dem Schnellzug gekommen.

1 — Where are you coming from? — I have come from Hamburg. — Did you come by plane? — No, I came on the express train.

2 — Wo ist Wilhelm? — Er ist zur Station gegangen, um den Vater zu erwarten. — Ist sein Bruder Karl mitgegangen? — Ja, und seine Schwester Marie ist auch mitgegangen,

2 — Where is William? — He has gone to the station to wait for his father. — Did his brother, Charles, go with him? — Yes, and his sister Marie also went with him.

3 — Wo ist Frau Müller? — Sie ist in die Stadt gefahren, um Einkäufe zu machen. — Ist sie noch nicht zurückgekommen? — Nein, noch nicht.

3 — Where is Mrs. Müller? — She has gone to town to do her shopping. — Hasn't she come back yet? — No, not yet.

Exercise No. 125. Complete the following sentences in the perfect tense with the correct form of the auxiliary **sein** or **haben** as required.

Beispiele: 1 Wir sind früh aufgestanden. 2 Wir haben um acht Uhr gefrühstückt.

1 Wir —— früh aufgestanden. 2 Wir —— um acht Uhr gefrühstückt. 3 Die Kinder —— alle ins Kino gegangen. 4 —— Sie schon die Fahrkarten gekauft? 5 Welche Geschichte —— Sie gelesen? 6 Um wieviel Uhr —— der Vater nach Hause gekommen? 7 —— der Zug schon angekommen? 8 Die Familie —— sich zum Frühstück gesetzt. 9 Alle —— im Auto in die Stadt gefahren. 10 —— sich die Kinder gut amüsiert?

Exercise No. 126. Complete the sentences of Exercise No. 125 in the past perfect tense with the correct form of the auxiliaries **sein** or **haben** as required.

Beispiele: 1 Wir waren früh aufgestanden. 2 Wir hatten um acht Uhr gefrühstückt.

Exercise No. 127. Fragen

Lesen Sie noch einmal den Text: **Wie Herr Clark gewöhnlich den Sonntag verbringt,** und dann beantworten Sie folgende Fragen!

1 Um wieviel Uhr ist Herr Clark am Sonntag aufgestanden? 2 Waren seine Frau und Kinder vor ihm aufgestanden? 3 Hatten sie schon gefrühstückt? 4 Um wieviel Uhr haben alle sich zum Frühstück gesetzt? 5 Was hat Herr Clark nach dem Frühstück getan? 6 Was taten die jüngeren Kinder, als er die Zeitung las? 7 Was taten die älteren? 8 Wer hatte eine schmackhafte Mahlzeit bereitet? 9 Wohin wollten die Kinder nach dem Mittagessen gehen? 10 Was mußten also die Eltern tun? 11 Haben die Eltern sich im Kino gelangweilt oder amüsiert? 12 Wohin sind sie vom Kino gegangen? 13 An wen hat Herr Clark nach dem Abendessen geschrieben? 14 Was hat er gelesen? 15 Um wieviel Uhr ist er zu Bett gegangen?

CHAPTER 27

HERR MÜLLER ERZÄHLT VON SICH SELBST
MR. MÜLLER TELLS ABOUT HIMSELF

1 Herr Clark, vor einigen Tagen haben Sie mir erzählt, wie Sie den Sonntag verbringen und auch anderes mehr über sich selbst und Ihre Familie. Heute möchte ich Ihnen etwas von mir selbst sagen. Mit anderen Worten, ich selbst bin das Thema des Gesprächs.

2 Das sollte sicherlich sehr interessant sein. Darf ich Sie ausfragen?

3 Jawohl, es freut mich immer, Ihre Fragen zu beantworten. Wie Sie schon wissen, bin ich in Deutschland geboren und bin jetzt Bürger von Großbritannien. Ich bin verheiratet und habe zwei Kinder.

4 Was ist Ihr Beruf?

5 Ich bin Lehrer und unterrichte an einer Sekundarschule, die ungefähr zehn Meilen von hier entfernt ist. Ich lehre Deutsch und Französisch.

6 Ach! Sie können Französisch!

7 Jawohl, ich spreche, lese und schreibe Französisch. Ich habe auf dem Gymnasium Französisch und Englisch studiert, dasselbe auch auf der Universität, und später habe ich vier Jahre lang in Paris gelebt.

8 Wann sind Sie denn in Paris gewesen?

9 Ich bin vom Jahre 1934 bis zum Jahre 1938 da gewesen. Ich war damals ein junger Mann.

10 Darf ich fragen, was Sie in Paris getan haben?

11 Ich habe als Zeitungskorrespondent in der Redaktion einer französischen Zeitung gearbeitet.

12 Und wann sind Sie nach England gekommen?

13 Ich bin im Jahre 1938 hergekommen. Glücklicherweise ist es mir gelungen, in dieses Land einzuwandern. Da ich sowohl Englisch als auch Deutsch und Französisch konnte, ist es mir bald gelungen, eine Stellung als Lehrer für Deutsch und für Französisch zu bekommen, und zwar an der Mittelschule, an der ich eben jetzt unterrichte.

14 Sie haben sich wohl hier verheiratet?

15 Ganz richtig. Ich habe ein englisches Mädchen geheiratet, und wir haben, wie Sie wissen, zwei Kinder.

16 Ich danke Ihnen, Herr Müller. Hoffentlich habe ich Sie mit meinen Fragen nicht zu sehr belästigt.

17 Im Gegenteil. Es is mir ein Vergnügen gewesen.

1 Mr. Clark, a few days ago you told me how you spend Sunday and also other things about yourself and your family. Today I should like to tell you something about myself. In other words, I myself am the topic of conversation.

2 That ought surely to be very interesting. May I ask you questions?

3 Of course, I am always glad to answer your questions. As you already know, I was born in Germany and am now a citizen of Great Britain. I am married and have two children.

4 What is your profession?

5 I am a teacher and teach in a secondary school which is about ten miles away from here. I teach German and French.

6 Oh! You know French!

7 Yes, I speak, read and write French. I studied French and also English at grammar school and the same also at university; and later I lived in Paris for four years.

8 When were you in Paris?

9 I was there from the year 1934 to the year 1938. I was then a young man.

10 May I ask what you did in Paris?

11 I worked as a newspaper correspondent in the editorial office of a French newspaper.

12 And when did you come to England?

13 I came here in 1938. Luckily, I succeeded in immigrating to this country. Since I knew English as well as German and French, I soon succeeded in obtaining a position as teacher of German and French, and, as a matter of fact, that is in the secondary school in which I am now teaching.

14 No doubt you got married here.

15 Quite right. I married an English girl and as you know we have two children.

16 I thank you, Mr. Müller. I hope I haven't annoyed you too much with my questions.

17 On the contrary; it was a pleasure for me.

Wortschatz

der Bürger, *pl.* -, citizen
das Gymnasium (gym-na:-zium),[1] *pl.* -ien, German grammar school
die Stellung, *pl.* -en, position, job
das Wort, *pl.* -e or ¨er,[2] word
Großbritannien (gro:s-bri-ta:nien), Great Britain)
belästigen, to annoy
aus-wandern, emigrate

ein-wandern, to immigrate
heiraten, to marry (someone)
sich verheiraten, to get married
leben, to live
unterrichten, to teach
entférnt, distant
sicherlich, surely
sowóhl als, as well as
selber, selbst, self

NOTES: 1 The g in **Gymnasium** is hard. 2 The plural **Worte** is used for words joined to make sense in phrases, expressions, sentences. **Wörter** are words unconnected in sense, as in vocabularies and dictionaries (**Wörterbücher**).

Deutsche Ausdrücke

Fragen stellen an + *acc.* to ask (put) questions. **Der Lehrer stellt Fragen an die Schüler.** The teacher asks the pupils questions (*lit.* puts questions to the pupils).

Ich kann Deutsch (Französisch, Englisch, usw.). I know German (French, English, etc.). This is short for **Ich kann Deutsch, usw., sprechen, lesen, schreiben.**

Ich bin am 31. Juni 1945 geboren. I was born 31 June, 1945.

selber, selbst, self. **Ich selber (selbst),** I myself; **der Lehrer selber,** the teacher himself; **Sie erzählt von sich selber.** She tells about herself. **Erzählen Sie von sich selber!** Tell about yourself.

Grammar Notes and Practical Exercises

1 Some very special verbs with the auxiliary *sein*

sein	to be	er ist	war	ist gewesen
werden	to become, to get	er wird	wurde	ist geworden
bleiben	to remain, to stay	er bleibt	blieb	ist geblieben
gelingen	to succeed	es gelingt	gelang	ist gelungen
geschehen	to happen	es geschieht	geschah	ist geschehen

(a) **Ich bin vor zwei Jahren in Paris gewesen.**

I was in Paris two years ago.

(b) **Heute ist es sehr kalt geworden.**

Today it has become very cold.

(c) **Wegen des schlechten Wetters sind wir alle zu Hause geblieben.**

Because of the bad weather, we all stayed at home.

(d) **Es ist mir gelungen, nach England auszuwandern.**

I succeeded in emigrating to England. (*Lit.* It succeeded to me to emigrate.)

Note that **gelingen** is used impersonally and is followed by a dative object. **Es gelingt mir** = I succeed; **es gelingt Ihnen** = you succeed; **es gelingt uns** = we succeed; **es gelingt meinem Freund** = my friend succeeds, etc.

(e) **Was ist geschehen? Ein Unglück ist geschehen.**

What has happened? A misfortune has happened.

Exercise No. 128. Kurze Gespräche. Practise aloud.

— **Was ist geschehen? — Der kleine Hans ist gefallen und hat sich den Arm verletzt. — Haben Sie den Doktor gerufen? — Ja, natürlich. Er ist schon hier gewesen. Er sagt, es ist nichts Schlimmes.**

— What has happened? — Little Hans fell and injured his arm. — Have you called the doctor? — Of course. He has already been here. He says, it is nothing serious.

— **Wo bist du den ganzen Nachmittag gewesen? — Ich war im Park. — Was machtest du dort? — Ich spielte Tennis.**

— Where have you been all afternoon? — I was in the park. — What were you doing there? — I was playing tennis.

— **Sie sehen müde aus. Wann sind Sie zu Bett gegangen? — Um halb zwei. —Warum sind Sie so lange aufgeblieben? — Ich mußte mich auf eine Prüfung vorbereiten.**

— You look tired. When did you go to bed? — At half past one. — Why did you stay up so long? — I had to prepare for an examination.

2 Indirect questions with *wie, wo, wann, wer, was, warum*

Direct Question	*Indirect Question*
Wie verbringen Sie gewöhnlich den Sonntag?	**Sagen Sie mir, bitte, wie Sie den Sonntag *verbringen*.**
Warum wohnen Sie in diesem kleinen Vorort?	**Darf ich fragen, warum Sie in diesem kleinen Vorort *wohnen*?**

Wann kommt der Zug von Hamburg an?	Wissen Sie, wann der Zug von Hamburg *ankommt*?
Wo unterrichten Sie jetzt?	Ich möchte fragen, wo Sie jetzt *unterrichten*.
Wer war heute morgen hier?	Weißt du, wer heute morgen *hier war*?
Was taten sie den ganzen Tag?	Er fragt, was sie den ganzen Tag *taten*?

Interrogative words (**wie, wo, was,** etc.) may introduce direct or indirect questions. Indirect questions are subordinate clauses, and, as in all subordinate clauses, the verb stands last.

3 The present and past perfect tenses in subordinate clauses

In a subordinate clause the verb, as you know, must stand last. If the verb is in the present perfect or past perfect, the *auxiliary part of the verb* (preceded by the past participle) must stand last.

Simple Sentence	*Subordinate Clause*
Herr Müller hat vier Jahre in Paris gelebt.	Wir wissen schon, daß Herr Müller vier Jahre in Paris *gelebt hat*.
Er ist im Jahre 1938 nach England gekommen.	Er sagt, daß er im Jahre 1938 nach England *gekommen ist*.
Haben Sie ein englisches Mädchen geheiratet?	Darf ich fragen, ob (whether) Sie ein englisches Mädchen *geheiratet haben*.
Hitler ist im Jahre 1933 zur Macht gekommen.	Herr M. konnte Frankreich verlassen, ehe Hitler zur Macht *gekommen ist*.

Exercise No. 129. Join each pair of sentences by means of the subordinate conjunction indicated. Remember: In subordinate clauses the verb stands last. If the tense of the verb has two parts the auxiliary must stand last.

Beispiel: 1 Herr Müller konnte eine Stellung als Lehrer bekommen, weil er Englisch gelernt hatte.

1 Herr Müller konnte eine Stellung als Lehrer bekommen. (weil) Er hatte Englisch gelernt. **2** Darf ich fragen? (warum) Sie haben Frankreich verlassen. **3** Ist es wahr? (daß) Sie sind vier Jahre in Paris gewesen. **4** Ich möchte gern wissen. (wie) Sie verbringen den Sonntag. **5** Es freut mich. (daß) Sie machen große Fortschritte im Studium der deutschen Sprache. **6** Wir mußten ins Kino gehen. (weil) Die Kinder wollten gehen. **7** Wir haben uns gelangweilt. (weil) Der Film hatte für uns kein Interesse. **8** Was taten die Kinder? (während) Die Mutter bereitete die Mahlzeit? **9** Was tat Herr Clark? (nachdem)[1] Er hatte die Zeitung gelesen. **10** Ich kann Ihnen dafür danken. (daß) Ich habe große Fortschritte im Deutschen gemacht.

NOTE 1. **nachdem** (*subordinate conjunction*) after

Exercise No. 130. Fragen

Lesen Sie noch einmal den deutschen Text: Herr Müller erzählt von sich selbst, und dann beantworten Sie diese Fragen!

1 Wer hat erzählt, wie er den Sonntag verbringt? **2** Wer möchte heute etwas von sich selbst sagen? 3 Wo ist Herr Müller geboren? 4 Ist er verheiratet oder ledig (single)? 5 In was für einer Schule unterrichtet er? 6 Was lehrt er? 7 Wo hat Herr Müller Französisch und Englisch studiert? 8 Wie lange hat er in Frankreich gelebt? 9 Wo hat er als Zeitungskorrespondent gearbeitet? 10 In welchem Jahre wanderte er in dieses Land ein? 11 Hat er hier eine Stellung an einer Sekundarschule oder an einer Universität bekommen? 12 Hat er ein englisches oder ein französisches Mädchen geheiratet?

CHAPTER 28

HERR CLARK SCHREIBT EINEN BRIEF AN SEINEN VERTRETER IN MÜNCHEN
MR. CLARK WRITES A LETTER TO HIS REPRESENTATIVE IN MUNICH

1 Herr Clark und Herr Müller sitzen im Arbeitszimmer des Herrn Clark. Der Kaufmann hat einen Brief an seinen Vertreter in München geschrieben. Er hält eine Kopie dieses Briefes in der Hand.

2 — Herr Müller, ich werde Ihnen vorlesen, was ich meinem Vetreter, Herrn Schiller, geschrieben habe.

3 — Das wird mir sehr lieb sein, Herr Clark.

4 Herr Clark liest den Brief vor, der hiermit folgt.

London, den 4. Mai 1967

Sehr geehrter Herr Schiller!

Ich freue mich, Sie zu benachrichtigen, daß ich eine Reise nach Deutschland zu machen beabsichtige. Ich werde London um 7 Uhr morgens am 31. Mai per Flugzeug verlassen und werde um 10.10 morgens am Münchener Flughafen ankommen.

Ich beabsichtige, zwei Monate in Deutschland zu verbringen. Das wird eine Vergnügungsreise und zugleich eine Geschäftsreise sein. Ich werde zwei oder drei Wochen in München bleiben und von dort aus will ich einige Ausflüge machen, um die interessantesten Plätze in der Umgebung von München zu besichtigen.

Ich werde auch andere Teile Deutschlands besuchen, vielleicht auch Oesterreich und die Schweiz.

Während meines Aufenthaltes in München werde ich mich freuen, Sie persönlich kennenzulernen. Ich habe mich stets für die großen Dienste, die Sie uns geleistet haben, und die so viel zu unserem Erfolg beigetragen haben, dankbar gefühlt. Ich weiß, daß Sie sehr beschäftigt sind, und daß Sie viel umherreisen. Deshalb schreibe ich Ihnen im voraus in der Hoffnung, daß eine Begegnung mit Ihnen möglich sein wird. Bitte mich zu benachrichtigen, ob ich das Vergnügen haben werde, Ihnen in München zu begegnen.

Seit sechs Monaten studiere ich Deutsch. Das wird Sie vielleicht überraschen. Ich hoffe, daß es mir möglich sein wird, mich mit Ihnen in Ihrer schönen Sprache zu unterhalten.

In Erwartung Ihrer umgehenden Antwort verbleibe ich mit bestem Gruß,

Ihr ergebener
Robert Clark

5 — Ausgezeichnet, Herr Clark. Sie haben in Ihrem Briefe keinen einzigen Fehler gemacht.

6 — Herr Müller, ich muß Ihnen etwas gestehen. Es gibt nämlich ein deutsches Buch mit dem Titel „Geschäftskorrespondenz." Dieses Buch ist mir sehr

149

behilflich gewesen. Dabei muß ich aber erklären, daß ich besonders Ihnen den größten Dank schulde.

7 — Das ist sehr nett von Ihnen.

8 — Die Antwort auf meinen Brief erwarte ich täglich. Sobald ich sie erhalte, werde ich sie Ihnen vorlesen.

9 — Ich freue mich schon darauf. Hoffentlich werden Sie die Antwort vor unsrer nächsten Lektion erhalten.

1 Mr. Clark and Mr. Müller are sitting in the study at Mr. Clark's house. The businessman has written a letter to his agent in Munich. He holds in his hand a copy of this letter.

2 — Mr. Müller, I shall read to you what I have written to my agent, Mr. Schiller.

3 — I shall like that, Mr. Clark.

4 Mr. Clark reads the letter, which follows herewith:

London, 4th May, 1967

Dear Mr. Schiller,

I am glad to inform you that I intend to travel to Germany. I shall leave London by plane at 7 a.m. on the 31st of May, and shall arrive at the Munich airport at 10.10 a.m.

I intend to spend two months in Germany. This will be a pleasure trip as well as a business trip. I shall stay two or three weeks in Munich, and from there I will make various excursions to see the most interesting places in the vicinity of Munich.

I shall also visit other parts of Germany, and perhaps Austria and Switzerland.

During my stay in Munich I shall be pleased to get to know you personally. I have always felt thankful to you for the great services that you have rendered us and which have contributed so much to our success. I know that you are very busy and that you travel much. Therefore I am writing you in advance in the hope that a meeting with you will be possible. Please let me know whether I shall have the pleasure of meeting you in Munich.

I have been studying German for six months. This will perhaps surprise you. I hope that it will be possible for me to converse with you in your beautiful language.

Awaiting your answer by return, I am, with kind regards,

Yours sincerely,
Robert Clark

5 — Excellent, Mr. Clark. You haven't made a single mistake in your letter.

6 — Mr. Müller, I must confess something to you. There is, you know, a German book with the title 'Commercial Correspondence'. This book has been very helpful to me. At the same time, however, I must state that I owe you especially the greatest thanks.

7 — That is very nice of you.

8 — I am daily awaiting the answer to my letter. As soon as I receive it, I shall read it to you.

9 — I am already looking forward to this. I hope you will receive the answer before our next lesson.

Wortschatz

der Aufenthalt, stay, sojourn	**besíchtigen,** to view, to see
die Begégnung, *pl.* **-en,** meeting	**erklären,** to state, to explain
der Erfólg, *pl.* **-e,** success	**umher-reisen,** to travel about
der Fehler, *pl.* **-,** mistake, error	**dankbar,** thankful
die Hoffnung, *pl.* **-en,** hope	**beschäftigt,** busy
begégnen (+ *dat. object*), to meet	**behílflich,** helpful
benáchrichtigen, to inform	**einzig,** single

Strong Verbs

bei-tragen	to contribute	**er trägt ... bei**	**trug ... bei**	**hat beigetragen**
halten	to hold	**er hält**	**hielt**	**hat gehalten**
erhalten	to receive	**er erhält**	**erhielt**	**hat erhalten**
gestehen	to confess	**er gesteht**	**gestand**	**hat gestanden**
vor-lesen	to read to, read aloud	**er liest ... vor**	**las ... vor**	**hat vorgelesen**

Deutsche Ausdrücke

einen Ausflug machen, to make an excursion
    Ich werde Ausflüge ins Gebirge machen. I'll make excursions into the mountains.
Es wird mir lieb sein. I shall enjoy it (*lit.* It will be pleasing to me).
Dienste leisten, to perform services
kennenlernen, to become acquainted with, to get to know
    Es freut mich, Sie kennenzulernen. I'm pleased to meet you.
sich auf etwas freuen, to look forward to something
    Ich freue mich auf meine kommende Reise. I am looking forward to my coming trip.

Formal Letters

Date: The date of all letters (formal and informal) is written in the accusative case.

    London, den 25. Mai 1964   **München, den 11, Juni 1964**
Formal letters usually begin:
    Sehr geehrter Herr Schiller! Sehr geehrter Herr Professor! (geehrt =
    Sehr geehrte Frau Schiller! Sehr geehrte Frau Professor! honoured)
Formal letters end:
    Ihr sehr ergebener Karl Engel } Yours sincerely (ergeben = devoted,
    Ihre sehr ergebene Maria Engel ⌡   faithful)

Grammar Notes and Practical Exercises

1 The future tense

I shall go, you will go, he, she, it will go, etc.

Ich werde morgen gehen.	**Wir werden** morgen gehen.
Du wirst morgen gehen.	**Ihr werdet** morgen gehen.
Er, sie, es wird morgen gehen.	**Sie (Sie) werden** morgen gehen.

The future tense of a verb is formed by the auxiliary **werden** (shall, will)

+ the infinitive of the verb. The infinitive must stand at the end of a simple sentence or main clause.

As you have seen (Chapter 21, Grammar Note 1, p. 115), **werden** may be used as a verb by itself, meaning *to become, to get*.

2 The present tense with future meaning

Ich gehe morgen ins Theater.	I am going to the theatre tomorrow.
Er kommt übermorgen.	He will come the day after tomorrow.
Nächsten Frühling macht er eine Reise nach Deutschland.	Next spring he will travel to Germany.

The present tense is often used in German with future meaning particularly when the verb is modified by some expression of future time such as: **morgen,** tomorrow; **übermorgen,** the day after tomorrow; **morgen früh,** tomorrow morning; **heute abend,** this evening; **morgen abend,** tomorrow evening; **heute nachmittag,** this afternoon; **bald,** soon; **später,** later; **nächstes Jahr,** next year; **nächste Woche,** next week; **nächsten Monat,** next month, etc.

Exercise No. 131. Complete these sentences with the correct form of the auxiliary **werden.**

Beispiel: 1 Herr Clark **wird** einen Brief vorlesen.

1 Herr Clark —— einen Brief vorlesen. 2 Ich —— eine Reise nach Deutschland machen. 3 Wann —— Sie London verlassen? 4 Wir —— am 1. Juni in München ankommen. 5 —— Sie viel Zeit in Deutschland verbringen? 6 Wie lange —— er in München bleiben? 7 Ein Freund fragt Herrn Clark ,,—— du einige Ausflüge von München machen?" 8 Ich —— meinem Vertreter im voraus schreiben. 9 Wer —— uns in München begegnen? 10 Hoffentlich —— diese Begegnung möglich sein.

Exercise No. 132. Change these sentences to the future.

Beispiel: 1 Die Jungen werden heute einen Ausflug machen.

1 Die Jungen machen heute einen Ausflug. 2 Ich bleibe vier Wochen in München. 3 Er besucht andere Teile von Deutschland. 4 Du gehst nicht mit. 5 Wir sind sehr beschäftigt. 6 Ich bin sehr dankbar. 7 Schreiben Sie jeden Tag einen Brief? 8 Ich komme am 1. Juni in München an. 9 Sie ist sehr behilflich. 10 Er heiratet ein englisches Mädchen.

3 The future tense in subordinate clauses

Future in Simple Sentences	*Future in Subordinate Clauses*
Er **wird** einen Brief **vorlesen.**	Ich weiß, daß er einen Brief **vorlesen wird.**
Die Kinder **werden** heute abend nicht ins Kino **gehen.**	Der Vater sagt, daß die Kinder heute abend nicht ins Kino **gehen werden.**

In a subordinate clause the auxiliary verb of the future tense must stand last, after the infinitive.

Exercise No. 133. Change each simple sentence in parentheses into a subordinate clause after the given conjunction.

Beispiel: 1 Der Kaufmann schreibt, **daß** er nach München kommen wird.

1 Der Kaufmann schreibt, **daß** (er wird nach München kommen). 2 Der Lehrer fragt mich, **ob** (ich werde den Brief vorlesen). 3 Die Kinder sagen, **daß** (sie werden ihre Freunde besuchen). 4 Ich weiß nicht, **ob** (das Wetter wird morgen schön sein). 5 Ich glaube nicht, **daß** (unsere Freunde werden heute abend kommen). 6 Ich möchte fragen, **wo** (Sie werden unterrichten). 7 Ich glaube, **daß** (niemand wird heute kommen). 8 Wir wissen, **daß** (du wirst eine schmackhafte Mahlzeit bereiten).

Exercise No. 134. Fragen

Lesen Sie noch einmal den Text: **Herr Clark schreibt einen Brief an seinen Vertreter,** und dann beantworten Sie die Fragen!

1 An wen hat Herr Müller einen Brief geschrieben? 2 Wem wird er eine Kopie dieses Briefes vorlesen? 3 Wer beabsichtigt, eine Reise nach Deutschland zu machen? 4 Wann wird er London verlassen? 5 Wird er fliegen, oder mit dem Dampfer nach Deutschland fahren? 6 Wann wird er am Münchner Flugplatz ankommen? 7 Wie lange wird er in München bleiben? 8 Welche anderen Länder wird er vielleicht besuchen? 9 Wen wird er persönlich kennenlernen? 10 Wer reist viel umher? 11 Weiß Herr Clark, daß sein Vertreter viel umherreist? 12 In welcher Stadt wird er seinem Vertreter begegnen?

CHAPTER 29

REVISION OF CHAPTERS 24-28

Weak (Regular) Verbs. No Vowel Changes

Pattern of Principal Parts:	Infinitive	Present	Past	Present Perfect
	lernen	er lernt	lernte	hat gelernt
	arbeiten	er arbeitet	arbeitete	hat gearbeitet

1 frühstücken	5 bereiten²	9 langweilen
2 heiraten¹	6 belästigen	10 interessieren⁴
3 leben	7 benachrichtigen	11 umher-reisen
4 plagen	8 begegnen³	12 ein-wandern

1 to breakfast	5 to prepare	9 to bore
2 to marry	6 to annoy	10 to interest
3 to live	7 to inform	11 to travel around
4 to plague	8 to meet	12 to immigrate

NOTES: 1. **sich verheiraten** to get married: **Er hat sich verheiratet.** 2. Verbs with inseparable prefixes (**be-, emp-, ent-, er-, ge-, ver-, zer-**) do not add **ge-** in the past participle: **Sie hat bereitet.** 3. **begegnen** takes a dative object: **Er begegnete seinem Freund.** 4. **sich interessieren für** to be interested in: **Ich habe mich für den Sport interessiert.** Verbs in **-ieren** do not add the prefix **ge-** in the past participle.

Strong (Irregular) Verbs. Vowel Changes

Infinitive		Present	Past	Present Perfect
1 an-fangen	to begin	er fängt an	fing an	hat angefangen
2 an-geben	to give, state	er gibt an	gab an	hat angegeben
3 vor-lesen	to read to, to read aloud	er liest vor	las vor	hat vorgelesen
4 vor-ziehen	to prefer	er zieht vor	zog vor	hat vorgezogen
5 statt-finden	to take place	es findet statt	fand statt	hat stattgefunden
6 gestehen	to confess	er gesteht	gestand	hat gestanden
7 erhalten	to receive	er erhält	erhielt	hat erhalten
8 verstehen	to understand	er versteht	verstand	hat verstanden
9 vergessen	to forget	er vergißt	vergaß	hat vergessen

Expressions

1 **ohne Zweifel** without doubt
2 **im Gegenteil** on the contrary
3 **mit Vergnügen** with pleasure
4 **fertig** finished, done, ready
5 **mit den Fragen fertig werden** to get finished with the questions
6 **Fragen beantworten** or **auf Fragen antworten** to answer questions
7 **einen Ausflug machen** to make an excursion
8 **Deutsch können** to know German. **Ich kann Deutsch (sprechen, lesen, schreiben). I** know German.
9 **jemanden kennenlernen** to get to know (become acquainted with) somebody. **Ich habe ihn kennengelernt.** I have made his acquaintance.

Exercise No. 135. Complete the German translation of each English sentence

1 I want to get to know my representative.	1 Ich will meinen Vertreter ——.
2 I shall ask you questions.	2 Ich werde Fragen an Sie ——.
3 You will answer the questions.	3 Sie werden auf die Fragen ——.
4 He has answered all the questions.	4 Er hat alle Fragen ——.
5 She knows German and French.	5 Sie —— Deutsch und Französisch.
6 Who will make an excursion to the lake?	6 Wer wird —— zum See machen?
7 Did your questions annoy him?	7 Haben Ihre Fragen ihn ——?
8 On the contrary. They pleased him.	8 —— Sie haben ihm——.
9 The examination is over. You have made no mistakes.	9 Das Examen ist ——. Sie haben —— gemacht,
10 We have read the letter with pleasure.	10 Wir haben den Brief —— gelesen.

Grammar Review and Exercises

1 Five tenses: present, past, present perfect, past perfect, future

	haben-verb *lernen*	*sein*-verb *gehen*
Present	ich lerne Deutsch.	Er geht schnell nach Hause.
Past	Ich lernte Deutsch.	Er ging schnell nach Hause.
Pres. Perfect	Ich habe Deutsch gelernt.	Er ist schnell nach Hause gegangen.
Past Perfect	Ich hatte Deutsch gelernt.	Er war schnell nach Hause gegangen.
Future	Ich werde Deutsch lernen.	Er wird schnell nach Hause gehen.

Intransitive verbs showing a change of place or condition take the auxiliary **sein** instead of **haben** in the compound tenses. For frequently used **sein**-verbs, see Chapter 26, Grammar Note 4, p. 142.

Exercise No. 136. Change these sentences from the past tense to the present perfect.

Beispiel: 1 Frau Clark ist zum Markt gegangen.

1 Frau Clark ging zum Markt. 2 Dort machte sie viele Einkäufe. 3 Sie bezahlte für die Einkäufe an der Kasse. 4 Sie brachte alles in ihr Auto. 5 Da vermißte[1] sie ihren Geldbeutel. 6 Sie lief zu der Kasse zurück. 7 Gott sei Dank,[2] fand sie ihren Geldbeutel an der Kasse. 8 Der Kassierer reichte ihr den Geldbeutel. 9 Frau Clark dankte dem Kassierer. 10 Sie stieg ins Auto ein.

NOTES: 1 **vermissen**, to miss. 2 Thank heavens!

2 Subordinate word order of verbs in the present perfect, past perfect and future

In subordinate word order the auxiliary must stand last, directly after the past participle or the infinitive.

Ich weiß, daß er einen neuen, braunen Anzug gekauft hat.
Ich weiß, daß er um drei Uhr nach Hause gegangen ist.
Ich weiß, daß er morgen dieses Auto kaufen wird.

3 Summary of subordinating conjunctions.

A subordinate clause is introduced by a relative pronoun or by a subordinating conjunction. Here are the most common subordinating conjunctions, most of which you already know:

daß that; **weil,** because; **da,** since (because); **wenn,** when, if; **als,** when (with past tenses); **bevor, ehe,** before; **bis,** until; **während, indem,** while; **nachdem,** after; **sobald,** as soon as; **ob,** whether; **obwohl,** although; and also interrogative words used as subordinate conjunctions in indirect questions: **wer, was, wie, wo, wann warum.**

Exercise No. 137. Translate these sentences.

1 Während die Herren über das Wetter sprachen, regnete es in Strömen. 2 Nachdem er den Tee und ein Gläschen Whisky getrunken hatte, fühlte sich Herr Müller sehr wohl. 3 Als seine Frau und Kinder ins Büro eintraten, diktierte der Kaufmann seiner Stenographin einen Brief. 4 Wenn wir das Theater besuchen, sitzen wir lieber im Parkett als im Rang. 5 Seitdem ich in England bin, unterrichte ich an dieser Schule. 6 Wir werden auf dem Bahnsteig warten, bis der Zug aus Bremen ankommt. 7 Wir wissen, daß Sie unserer Firma große Dienste geleistet haben. 8 Herr Müller kann Englisch, da er diese Sprache auf dem Gymnasium studiert hat. 9 Obwohl die Eltern das Kino nicht gern hatten, gingen sie doch mit den Kindern, um den neuen Film zu sehen. 10 Es wird Ihnen gelingen, eine gute Stellung zu bekommen, sobald Sie nach London kommen.

VIER DIALOGE

1 — Wo warst du gestern abend? — Ich war im Kino. — Was hast du dir angesehen? — Ich sah einen deutschen Film. — Hat der Film dir gefallen? — Sehr. Er war wirklich ausgezeichnet. — War es ein Film mit englischen Untertiteln? — Ja, aber ich habe beinahe alles verstanden, ohne die englischen Untertitel zu lesen.

1 — Where were you last night? — I was at the cinema. — What did you see? — I saw a German film. — Did you like the film? — Very much. It was really splendid. — Was it a film with English subtitles? — Yes, but I understood nearly everything without reading the English subtitles.

2 — Herr Braun ist krank. — Das tut mir sehr leid. Wer hat es Ihnen gesagt? — Seine Frau hat mich telephonisch angerufen. — Wann hat sie angerufen? — Heute früh.

2 — Mr. Braun is ill. — I am very sorry. Who told you about it? — His wife telephoned me. — When did she phone? — This morning.

3 — Wann sind Sie gestern abend zu Bett gegangen? — Ich bin erst um 2 Uhr morgens zu Bett gegangen. — Warum denn? — Ich mache heute ein Examen in Mathematik und mußte mich darauf vorbereiten.

3 — When did you go to bed last night? — I did not go to bed until two o'clock in the morning. — But why? — I'm taking an examination in mathematics today and had to prepare for it.

4 — Ich habe heute einen Brief erhalten. — Woher? — Von wem? — Von meinem Bruder in Afrika. — Was macht er dort? — Er ist nämlich Anthropológe (an-troː-poː-loː-ge). Setzen Sie sich zu mir. Ich werde Ihnen den Brief vorlesen.

4 — I have received a letter today. — From where? From whom? — From my brother in Africa. — What is he doing there? — You see, he is an anthropologist. Sit down beside me. I'll read the letter to you.

Exercise No. 138. Lesestück 1

FRAU CLARKS GEBURTSTAG

Es war der 22. März, der Geburtstag der Frau Clark. An diesem Tag wurde sie fünfunddreißig Jahre alt. Um den Geburtstag zu feiern,[1] ging die Familie Clark zum Essen in ein deutsches Restaurant in der Stadt London.

Als sie in das Restaurant eintraten, sahen sie auf dem Tische, der für Herrn und Frau Clark gedeckt[2] war, einen schönen Korb[3] voll weißer Rosen. Natürlich war Frau Clark überrascht. Sie dankte ihrem lieben Mann, und dann setzte sich die Familie zum Tisch. Eine hübsche, junge Kellnerin[4] reichte ihnen die Speisekarte.[5] Alle bestellten[6] ihre Lieblingsgerichte.[7] Am Ende der Mahlzeit sagte das ältere Mädchen Marie mit gedämpfter[8] Stimme: ,,Jetzt!'' und jedes der vier Kinder nahm von unter dem Tische eine kleine Schachtel[9] hervor. In den Schachteln waren Geschenke[10] für die Mutter. Alle riefen ,,Alles Gute zum Geburtstag,''[11] und jedes Kind reichte der Mutter ein Geschenk. Marie gab ihr ein seidenes Taschentuch, Karl ein Paar Handschuhe, Wilhelm ein wollenes Halstuch, die kleine Anna ein kindisches Porträt der Mutter.

Was für ein schöner Tag, nicht nur für die Mutter sondern auch[12] für Papa und die Kinder.

Zur Übung in Mathematik berechnete Karl die Spesen[13] für diesen Tag.

Das Essen	£6.	0.	0.
Trinkgeld	1.	0.	0.
Blumen	1.	15.	0.
Summa	£8.	15.	0.

,,Der reinste Zufall,''[14] sagte Herr Clark. ,,Acht Pfund fünfzehn, das sind hundertfünfundsiebzig Schilling; das ist fünfmal so viel wie fünfunddreißig Jahre.''

NOTES: 1 to celebrate. 2 Tisch decken, to set a table. 3 der Korb, basket. 4 die Kellnerin, waitress. 5 die Speisekarte, menu. 6 ordered. 7 favourite dishes. 8 in an undertone. 9 die Schachtel, box. 10 das Geschenk, gift. 11 Happy Birthday. 12 nicht nur . . . sondern auch, not only . . . but also. 13 die Spesen (*pl.*), expenses. 14 the purest coincidence. 15 fünfmal so viel wie, five times as much as.

Exercise No. 139. Lesestück 2

EINE AUSSERGEWÖHNLICHE[1] VORSTELLUNG IM KINO

Eines Abends gingen Herr und Frau Clark ins Kino. Die Filme aus Hollywood gefielen ihnen meistens nicht, denn diese bieten viel Schund und Kitsch.[2]

Aber an diesem Abend gab es eine außergewöhnliche Vorstellung in einem Lichtspieltheater[3] ganz in der Nähe ihrer Wohnung. Der Film war ein Dokumentarbericht[4] über Deutschland und zwar in deutscher Sprache.

Herr und Frau Clark kamen um 8.30 Uhr (halb neun Uhr) im Kino an. Fast alle Plätze waren schon besetzt. Also mußten sie in der dritten Reihe sitzen. Das gefiel der Frau Clark nicht, denn die Bewegungen[5] auf der Leinwand[6] taten ihren Augen weh.[7] Glücklicherweise gelang es ihnen, nach einer Viertelstunde ihre Plätze zu tauschen,[8] und danach saßen sie in der dreizehnten Reihe.

Der Familie Clark gefiel dieser Film außerordentlich.[9] Herr Clark hatte den größten Genuß[10] daran.

Als sie das Theater verließen, sagte Herr Clark zu seiner Frau: „Weißt du, Helene, ich glaube, ich werde in Deutschland gut durchkommen[11] können. Ich habe beinahe alles verstanden, was die Schauspieler und Schauspielerinnen auf Deutsch sagten."

Notes: 1 unusual. 2 **Schund und Kitsch**, rubbish. 3 **Lichtspieltheater, Kino**, cinema. 4 documentary. 5 movements. 6 screen. 7 **weh-tun**, to hurt. 8 **tauschen**, to change. 9 extremely. 10 **der Genuß**, enjoyment. 11 **durch-kommen**, get along.

CHAPTER 30

HERR CLARK ERHÄLT EINE ANTWORT AUF SEINEN BRIEF
MR. CLARK RECEIVES AN ANSWER TO HIS LETTER

Im Kapitel 28 las Herr Clark seinem Lehrer einen Brief vor, welchen er an seinen Vertreter in München geschrieben hatte. Gestern hat er die Antwort auf seinen Brief bekommen.

Herr Clark und Herr Müller sitzen wieder im Arbeitszimmer. Der Kaufmann liest eben die Antwort auf seinen Brief vor. Der Lehrer hört aufmerksam zu.

München, den 9. Mai 1967

Sehr geehrter Herr Clark!

Mit großem Vergnügen habe ich Ihren Brief vom 4ten Mai gelesen, in dem Sie mich benachrichtigen, daß Sie in der nächsten Zeit eine Reise nach Deutschland unternehmen werden.

Glücklicherweise werde ich während der Monate Juni und Juli in München sein. Daher werde ich Ihnen ganz zur Verfügung stehen. Auch werde ich das Vergnügen haben, Sie um 10.10 Uhr morgens am 31. Mai am Flugplatz zu erwarten. Ich werde mich bemühen, Ihren Aufenthalt in München möglichst angenehm in Bezug auf das Vergnügen und zugleich auch vorteilhaft für das Geschäft zu machen.

Es wird mir viel Freude machen, mich mit Ihnen in deutscher Sprache zu unterhalten, und ich glaube sicherlich, daß es Ihnen möglich sein wird, das Gespräch vollkommen richtig durchzuführen. Tatsächlich schreiben Sie sehr gut Deutsch.

Da muß ich Ihnen und Ihrem Lehrer wirklich gratulieren.

In Erwartung, Sie baldigst kennen zu lernen, schließe ich,

Ihr ergebener
Heinrich Schiller

In Chapter 28 Mr. Clark read a letter to his teacher, which he had written to his agent in Munich. Yesterday he received the answer to his letter.

Mr. Clark and Mr. Müller are again sitting in the study. The businessman is just reading aloud the answer to his letter. The teacher is listening attentively.

Munich, 9th May, 1967

Dear Mr. Clark,

I have read with great pleasure your letter of May 4th in which you inform me that you will soon travel to Germany.

Luckily I shall be in Munich during the months of June and July. Therefore I shall be entirely at your service. I shall also have the pleasure of awaiting you at the airport at 10.10 a.m. on May 31st. I shall try to make your stay in

Munich as pleasant as possible with respect to recreation, and at the same time advantageous for business.

It will give me great pleasure to converse with you in the German language, and I am sure that it will be possible for you to carry on the conversation with entire correctness. As a matter of fact, you write German very well.

In this respect I must really congratulate you and your teacher.

I look forward to making your acquaintance soon and close,

Sincerely yours,
Henry Schiller

1 Das ist wirklich ein sehr netter Brief, Herr Clark. Bisher haben Sie Herrn Schiller nur als einen ernsten und tüchtigen Vertreter gekannt. Sie werden zweifellos erkennen, daß er auch sehr liebenswürdig ist.

2 Ich glaube sicherlich, daß ich mich unter den Deutschen sehr gut zurecht-finden werde, und das Beste ist daran, daß ich die Möglichkeit haben werde, mit ihnen in ihrer eigenen Sprache zu reden.

3 Da haben Sie ganz recht, und ich bin gewiß, Sie werden jede Gelegenheit ergreifen, Deutsch zu sprechen. Nun, Herr Clark, nächsten Donnerstag kann ich leider nicht vor halb neun kommen.

4 Das macht nichts, Herr Müller. Besser spät, als niemals.

1 That is really a very nice letter, Mr. Clark. Up to now you have known Mr. Schiller only as an earnest and capable agent. You will doubtlessly find out that he is also very likeable.

2 I am certain that I shall get along very well among the Germans, and the best thing about it is that I shall have the opportunity of speaking to them in their own language.

3 In this you are quite right and I am certain that you will take every opportunity to speak German. Well, Mr. Clark, next Thursday unfortunately I cannot come before half past eight.

4 That's all right with me (that doesn't matter), Mr. Müller. Better late than never.

Wortschatz

sich bemühen, to try, to endeavour
durch-führen, to carry on, accomplish
gratulíeren (+ *dat. object*), to
   congratulate
aufmerksam, attentive, attentively
ernst, earnest; **liebenswürdig,** likeable
eigen, own; **in ihrer eigenen Sprache,**
   in their own language
bisher, until now

möglichst, as much as is possible
möglichst angenehm, as pleasant as
   possible
tatsächlich, as a matter of fact,
   actually
zugléich, at the same time
zweifellos, doubtlessly, without doubt
daher, therefore

Strong Verbs. Principal Parts

ergreifen	to seize, to take	**er ergreift**	**ergriff**	**hat ergriffen**
schliessen	to close	**er schliesst**	**schloss**	**hat geschlossen**
unternéhmen	to undertake	**er unternímmt**	**unternáhm**	**hat unternommen**
sich zurecht-finden	to get along	**er findet sich zurecht**	**fand sich zurecht**	**hat sich zurecht gefunden**

Related Words

begegnen, to meet	**unternéhmen**, to undertake
die Begegnung, the meeting	**die Unternéhmung**, the undertaking
hoffen, to hope	**überráschen**, to surprise
die Hoffnung, the hope	**die Überráschung**, the surprise
üben, to practise	**leisten**, to accomplish
die Übung, the exercise, practice	**die Leistung**, the accomplishment
prüfen, to test	**sich unterhálten**, to converse
die Prüfung, the test, examination	**die Unterháltung**, the conversation

Note that all nouns ending in **-ung** are feminine.

Deutsche Ausdrücke

in der nächsten Zeit = bald, soon

zur Verfügung stehen, to be at the service of. **Ich stehe Ihnen zur Verfügung.** I am at your service.

in Bezug auf, in respect to, in the matter of. **Er war uns in Bezug auf das Geschäft behilflich.** He was helpful to us in the matter of business.

das macht nichts ... that doesn't matter.

sich zurechtfinden, to get along. **Ich werde mich dort zurechtfinden.** I shall get along there.

die Gelengenheit ergreifen, to seize (take) the opportunity. **Ich werde jede Gelegenheit ergreifen, Deutsch zu sprechen.** I shall take every opportunity to speak German.

Sprichwort: Besser spät als niemals. Better late than never.

Grammar Notes and Practical Exercises

1 Mixed Verbs

A small number of verbs form their past tense and past participle by adding **-te** and **-t** respectively, like weak (regular) verbs, and also by vowel change, like strong (irregular) verbs. Here are the principal parts of mixed verbs you have already met.

kennen	to know[1]	**er kennt**	**kannte**	**hat gekannt**
erkennen	to find out, recognize	**er erkennt**	**erkannte**	**hat erkannt**
nennen	to name	**er nennt**	**nannte**	**hat genannt**
senden	to send	**er sendet**	**sandte**	**hat gesandt**
denken	to think	**er denkt**	**dachte**	**hat gedacht**
bringen	to bring	**er bringt**	**brachte**	**hat gebracht**
verbringen	to spend	**er verbringt**	**verbrachte**	**hat verbracht**
wissen	to know[1]	**er weiß**	**wußte**	**hat gewußt**

NOTE 1. **kennen**, to know, be acquainted with (persons or things); **wissen**, to know facts (see Chapter 10, Grammar Note 1, p. 52).

Exercise No. 140. Change these sentences to the past and present perfect.

Beispiel: 1. Ich kannte ihn gut. Ich habe ihn gut gekannt.

1 **Ich kenne ihn gut.** 2 **Wir nennen die Dinge auf deutsch.** 3 **Senden Sie ihm einen Brief?** 4 **Er denkt an seine Freundin.** 5 **Was bringst du mir?** 6 **Wie**

verbringen Sie den Sonntag? 7 Ich weiß seinen Namen nicht. 8 Ihr kennt seinen Bruder. 9 Ich erkenne ihn nicht wieder. 10 Wir denken oft an dich.

Grammar Notes and Practical Exercises

2 Infinitive with *zu*

Ich hoffe, Ihnen dort zu begegnen.	I hope to meet you there.
Es ist schwer, eine Sprache zu lernen.	It is difficult to learn a language.
Er arbeitet, um Geld zu verdienen.	He works in order to earn money.
Es ist schon Zeit wegzugehen.	It is already time to go away.
Er wünschte mitzugehen.	He wanted to go along.

(*a*) The use of **zu** with German infinitives usually corresponds to the use of *to* with English infinitives.

(*b*) If the infinitive is a separable verb, **zu** stands between the prefix and the verb (**wegzugehen, mitzugehen**).

(*c*) Note that the infinitive stands last. Objects and modifiers of an infinitive must precede it.

3 Infinitive without *zu*

Ich werde den Arzt rufen.	I shall call the doctor.
Ich muß Ihnen gratulieren.	I must congratulate you.
Wir konnten gar nicht schlafen.	We could not sleep at all.
Sie wollten ins Kino gehen.	They wanted to go to the pictures.
Darf ich Fragen an Sie stellen?	May I ask you questions?
Er ließ mich nicht arbeiten.	He didn't let me work.
Sahen Sie das Flugzeug landen?	Did you see the plane land?
Was hörtest du ihn sagen?	What did you hear him say?

(*a*) **zu** is not used with the infinitive in the future tense.

(*b*) **zu** is not used with the infinitives after the modal auxiliaries: **dürfen, können, mögen, müssen, sollen, wollen**; and after **lassen, sehen,** and **hören**.

Exercise No. 141. Complete the sentences on the right with the correct infinitive.

Beispiel: Sie werden Gelegenheit haben, Deutsch zu sprechen.

1 You will have a chance to speak German.	Sie werden Gelegenheit haben, Deutsch ——.
2 I hope to get a good job.	Ich hoffe, eine gute Stellung ——.
3 Where will you await me?	Wo werden Sie mich ——?
4 All had to get up early.	Alle mußten früh ——.
5 It is now time to get up.	Es ist jetzt Zeit ——.
6 May I visit you tomorrow?	Darf ich Sie morgen ——?
7 We tried to find his home.	Wir versuchten seine Wohnung ——.
8 He let the children play there.	Er ließ die Kinder dort ——.
9 I intend to go to the pictures.	Ich beabsichtige, ins Kino ——.
10 What do you wish to say about it?	Was wünschen Sie darüber ——?
11 One needs money in order to travel.	Man braucht Geld, um ——.
12 I heard him say: 'Good-bye'.	Ich hörte ihn: ,,Auf Wiedersehen!" ——.

Exercise No. 142. Fragen

Lesen Sie noch einmal den Text: **Herr Clark erhält eine Antwort auf seinen Brief,** und dann beantworten Sie diese Fragen!

1 An wen hatte Herr Clark einen Brief geschrieben? **2** Wem hatte er im letzten Kapitel diesen Brief vorgelesen? **3** Wann hat Herr Clark die Antwort auf seinen Brief bekommen? **4** Was tat der Lehrer während der Kaufmann die Antwort vorlas? **5** Wie fängt Herrn Schillers Antwort an? **6** Wo wird der Vertreter während der Monate Juni und Juli sein? **7** Wo wird er Herrn Clark erwarten? **8** Wird er sich mit Herrn Clark in deutscher oder englischer Sprache unterhalten? **9** Wem muß Herr Schiller gratulieren? **10** In welcher Beziehung (in what relation) hat Herr Clark seinen Vertreter bis jetzt gekannt? **11** Was wird er zweifellos erkennen? **12** Wird Herr Clark jede Gelegenheit ergreifen, Englisch zu sprechen?

CHAPTER 31

EINIGE FRAGEN ÜBER DEUTSCHE GEOGRAPHIE
SOME QUESTIONS ABOUT GERMAN GEOGRAPHY

1 Herr Clark, Sie haben die deutsche Geschichte gut gelernt. Nun wollen wir sehen, ob Sie die Geographie Deutschlands ebenso gut kennen wie seine Geschichte. Erlauben Sie, daß ich Ihnen ein paar Fragen stelle.

2 Gewiß. Sagen Sie mir aber, bekomme ich einen Preis, wenn meine Antworten richtig sind?

3 Nein, Herr Clark. Sie bekommen keinen Preis, denn das ist kein Radioprogramm. Fangen wir[1] zuerst mit einer leichten Frage an. In welchem Teile Europas liegt Deutschland?

4 Das ist ja zu leicht. Deutschland liegt in Mitteleuropa.

5 Welcher Fluß trennt Westdeutschland und Ostdeutschland?

6 Die Elbe trennt Westdeutschland und Ostdeutschland.

7 Welcher Fluß ist länger, der Rhein oder die Elbe?

8 Der Rhein ist etwas länger als die Elbe.

9 Richtig. Der Rhein ist der längste und breiteste Fluß Deutschlands.

10 Er ist auch der schönste, nicht wahr?

11 Das ist wahr. Mit Recht nennt man den Rhein den schönsten deutschen Fluß. An seinen Ufern sind Berge, Felsen und malerische Schlösser aus den ältesten Zeiten. Und nun laßt uns über die Gebirge sprechen. Welche Gebirge können Sie nennen?

12 Nun, im Süden befinden sich die Bayerischen Alpen; im Südwesten der Schwarzwald; in Mitteldeutschland der Harz und der Thüringer Wald.

13 Ausgezeichnet! Wie heißt der höchste Gipfel der Bayerischen Alpen?

14 Das ist die Zugspitze. Ich glaube, daß dieser Berg beinahe 10,000 Fuß hoch ist.

15 Richtig. Ist die Zugspitze höher als der Mont Blanc?

16 Nein, die Zugspitze ist niedriger als der Mont Blanc.

17 Nun, die Häfen. Wie heißt der größte Hafen an der Nordsee?

18 Hamburg, an der Mündung der Elbe, ist der größte und beste deutsche Hafen. Ein großer Teil der Waren, die ich aus Deutschland importiere, kommt per Dampfer von Hamburg.

19 Welch anderer großer Hafen ist an der Nordsee?

20 Bremerhafen an der Mündung der Weser.

21 Nennen Sie jetzt die Hauptstädte von Westdeutschland und Ostdeutschland.

22 Die Haupstadt von Westdeutschland ist Bonn; von Ostdeutschland, Ost-Berlin.

23 Hat Westdeutschland mehr oder weniger Einwohner als Ostdeutschland?

24 Westdeutschland hat viel mehr Einwohner als Ostdeutschland.

25 Welches ist die schönste Stadt Deutschlands?

26 Diese Frage möchte ich an Sie stellen, Herr Müller. Was ist Ihre Meinung?

27 Nun, die Deutschen selbst sind sich über diese Frage nicht einig. Die

Münchener sagen, daß ihre Stadt ohne Zweifel die schönste Stadt Deutschlands ist. Die Kölner meinen aber, daß Köln die schönste Stadt von allen ist. Meiner Meinung nach ist die kleine, alte Stadt Rothenburg an der Tauber am allerschönsten. Nun, Herr Clark, die Prüfung ist zu Ende. Ich gratuliere Ihnen.

28 Ich danke vielmals. Ich erwarte nächste Woche mein Diplom.

29 Ach nein, lieber Herr. Noch nicht. Jetzt können wir den zweiten Teil des Kurses beginnen.

NOTE 1. **Fangen wir an!** Let's begin. **Gehen wir!** Let's go. **Essen wir!** Let's eat. The imperative in the first person plural, translated *Let's* or *Let us . . .*, is the inverted **wir** form of the present tense.

1 Mr. Clark, you have learned German history well. Now we want to see whether you know the geography of Germany just as well as its history. Permit me to ask you a few questions.

2 Certainly. But tell me, do I get a prize if I answer correctly?

3 No, Mr. Clark. You will get no prize for this is not a radio programme. Let's begin first with an easy question. In what part of Europe does Germany lie?

4 That is indeed too easy. Germany lies in Central Europe.

5 What river separates West Germany from East Germany?

6 The Elbe separates West Germany from East Germany.

7 Which river is longer, the Rhine or the Elbe?

8 The Rhine is somewhat longer than the Elbe.

9 Correct. The Rhine is Germany's longest and broadest river.

10 It is also the most beautiful, isn't it?

11 That is true. One rightly calls the Rhine the most beautiful German river. On its shores are mountains, rocks, and picturesque castles from the oldest times. And now let us talk about the mountain ranges. Which mountain ranges can you name?

12 Well, in the south are the Bavarian Alps; in the south-west the Black Forest; in central Germany the Harz Mountains and the Thuringian Forest.

13 Splendid. What is the highest peak of the Bavarian Alps?

14 That is the Zugspitze. I believe that this mountain is almost 10,000 feet high.

15 Correct. Is the Zugspitze higher than Mount Blanc?

16 No, the Zugspitze is lower than Mount Blanc.

17 Now the ports. What is the name of the largest port on the North Sea?

18 Hamburg, at the mouth of the Elbe, is the largest and best German port. A large part of the goods which I import from Germany comes by steamer from Hamburg.

19 Which other large port is on the North Sea?

20 Bremerhafen at the mouth of the Weser.

21 Now name the capitals of West Germany and East Germany.

22 The capital of West Germany is Bonn; of East Germany, East Berlin.

23 Has West Germany more or fewer inhabitants than East Germany?

24 West Germany has many more inhabitants than East Germany.

25 Which is the most beautiful city of Germany?

26 I would like to ask you this question, Mr. Müller. What is your opinion?

27 Well, the Germans themselves are not agreed on this question. The inhabitants of Munich say that their city is without doubt the most beautiful

city of Germany. The inhabitants of Cologne, however, think that Cologne is the most beautiful city of all. In my opinion the little old city of Rothenburg on the Tauber is the most beautiful of all. Now, Mr. Clark, the examination is ended. I congratulate you.

28 Many thanks. I'll expect my diploma next week.

29 Oh no, dear sir. Not yet. Now we can begin the second part of the course.

Wortschatz

die Geographíe (geː-oː-gra-fiː), geography
der Berg, *pl.* -e, mountain
der Felsen, *pl.* -, rock, cliff
der Fluß, *pl.* ̈e, river
das Gebírge, *pl.* -, mountain range
der Gipfel, *pl.* -, peak
der Hafen, *pl.* ̈, harbour
das Ufer, *pl.* -, shore
die See, *pl.* -n, sea, ocean

der See, *pl.* -n, lake
der Norden, north; der Süden, south
der Osten, east; der Westen, west
das Diplom, *pl.* -e, diploma
der Kursus, course
die Meinung, *pl.* -en, opinion
der Einwohner, *pl.* -, inhabitant
einig, united, agreed
vielmals, many times; nie, niemals, never

Ausdrücke

mit Recht, rightly, justly
Erlauben Sie! Permit me.
   Erlauben Sie, daß ich einige Fragen an Sie stelle! Permit me to ask you a few questions.
meiner Meinung nach, according to (in) my opinion
deiner (Ihrer, eurer) Meinung nach, according to your opinion
   unsrer (ihrer) Meinung nach, according to our (her, their) opinion
In the sense of *according to*, nach usually follows the noun.

1 Comparison of adjectives

	Positive	Comparative	Superlative
klein	small	kleiner	der, die, das kleinste
breit	wide	breiter	der, die, das breiteste
interessant	interesting	interessanter	der, die, das interessanteste
niedrig	low	niedriger	der, die, das niedrigste
schön	beautiful	schöner	der, die, das schönste
lang	long	länger	der, die das längste
kurz	short	kürzer	der, die, das kürzeste
wenig	little	weniger	der, die, das wenigste

Die Elbe ist lang. Der Rhein ist länger als die Elbe, aber nicht so lang wie die Volga. Die Volga ist der längste Fluß Europas.

The Elbe is *long*. The Rhine is *longer* than the Elbe, but not as long as the Volga. The Volga is *the longest* river of Europe.

Unser Haus ist alt. Euer Haus ist älter als unser Haus. Sein Haus ist das älteste in dieser Straße.

Our house is *old*. Your house is *older* than our house. His house is *the oldest* in this street.

(a) The comparative of adjectives is formed by adding -er to the positive.

(b) The superlative is formed by adding -st or -est to the positive. -est is added for ease in pronunciation when the adjective ends in -t, -d, -s, -ss, -z, -ch.

(c) Most one-syllable adjectives add an **Umlaut** to **a, o, u** in the comparative and superlative. You have met the following: **kurz, lang, alt, jung, warm, kalt, rot, schwarz.**

(d) In comparisons so ... wie = *as ... as;* als = *than.*
Er ist so groß wie ich. He is *as tall as* I am. Er ist größer als ich. He is *taller than* I am.

2 Some Adjectives Irregular in Comparison

groß	big	größer	bigger	der, die, das größte	the biggest
gut	good	besser	better	der, die, das beste	the best
hoch	high	höher	higher	der, die, das höchste	the highest
nah (e)	near	näher	nearer	der, die, das nächste	the nearest
viel	much	mehr	more	der, die, das meiste	the most

Die Zugspitze ist **hoch.** Der Mont Blanc ist **höher** als die Zugspitze. Der Berg Everest ist **der höchste** Berge in der ganzen Welt.

The Zugspitze is *high.* Mount Blanc is *higher* than the Zugspitze. Mount Everest is *the highest* mountain in the whole world.

NOTE: **hoch** drops the **c** whenever the ending begins with **-e** (**der hohe Berg**).

Exercise No. 143. Complete each sentence with the comparative of the adjective in parentheses.

Beispiel: 1. Der Rhein und die Elbe sind **kürzer** als die Volga.

1 Der Rhein und die Elbe sind (kurz) als die Volga. 2 Ist Köln (schön) als Nürnberg? 3 Der Winter in Kanada ist (kalt) als in den Vereinigten Staaten. 4 Karl ist (alt) als Wilhelm. 5 Ist Frankfurt (groß) als Hamburg? 6 Mein Bruder ist (jung) als ich. 7 Was finden Sie (interessant), das Theater oder das Kino? 8 Im Sommer sind die Tage (lang) als im Winter. 9 Er ißt (viel) Fleisch als ich. 10 Das Essen ist zu Hause (gut) als im Restaurant.

3 Case Endings in the Comparative and Superlative

(a) **Das kleine Kind** ist mein Bruder.
Das kleinere Kind ist mein Bruder.
Das kleinste Kind ist mein Bruder.

(b) **Mein alter Freund** kommt heute.
Mein älterer Freund kommt heute.
Mein ältester Freund kommt heute.

(c) Ich trage **den schweren Koffer.**
Sie tragen **den schwereren Koffer.**
Er trägt **den schwersten Koffer.**

(d) Er arbeitete in **dem großen Zimmer.**
Sie arbeitete in **dem größeren Zimmer.**
Wir arbeiteten in **dem größten Zimmer.**

The comparative and superlative of adjectives take the same case endings as the positive (see Chapter 15, Grammar Note 2, p. 80).

Exercise No. 144. In each sentence substitute the comparative of the adjective in place of the positive.

Beispiel: 1. Er kauft sich ein besseres Auto

1 Er kauft sich ein **gutes** Auto. 2 Der **große** Tisch gehört mir. 3 Ich schreibe mit dem **langen** Bleistift. 4 Ich konnte keine **gute** Wohnung finden. 5 Ich habe einen **jungen** Bruder. 6 Sie hat eine **junge** Schwester. 7 Marie hat eine **alte**

Bluse. 8 Die hohen Berge befinden sich in Süddeutschland. 9 Ich gab meinem Freund den guten Platz. 10 Wie heißt Ihr junger Bruder?

Exercise No. 145. In each sentence substitute the superlative of the adjective for the positive.

Beispiel: 1 Am Rhein sieht man die ältesten Schlösser.

1 Am Rhein sieht man die alten Schlösser. 2 Ich lese jetzt das interessante Buch. 3 Ich habe den guten Platz gekauft. 4 Die langen Tage sind im Sommer. 5 Die kurzen Tage sind im Winter. 6 Hier ist das warme Zimmer. 7 Sie macht Einkäufe in den großen Läden. 8 Er sprach von seinem alten Freund. 9 Die guten Plätze sind alle besetzt. 10 Die hohen Berge sind in der Schweiz.

Exercise No. 146. Lesen Sie diesen Text! Dann beantworten Sie die Fragen!

Herr Braun ist fünfundvierzig Jahre alt. Herr Engel ist fünfzig Jahre alt. Herr Schumann ist sechzig Jahre alt.

Herr Braun besitzt 500,000 (fünfhunderttausend) DM. Herr Engel besitzt 400,000 DM. Herr Schumann besitzt 300,000 DM.

Herr Braun ist fünf Fuß sieben Zoll[1] groß. Herr Engel ist fünf Fuß acht Zoll groß. Herr Schumann ist sechs Fuß ein Zoll groß.

1 Wie heißt der älteste Herr? 2 Wie heißt der reichste Herr? 3 Wie heißt der größte (Herr)? 4 Ist Herr Engel älter oder jünger als Herr Braun? 5 Ist Herr Braun größer oder kleiner als Herr Engel? 6 Ist Herr Schumann reicher oder weniger reich als Herr Engel? 7 Wer hat das meiste Geld? 8 Wer hat das wenigste?

NOTE: 1 **der Fuß,** foot; **der Zoll,** inch. Observe the use of the singular in German to indicate quantities or amounts: **fünf Fuß,** five feet; **sieben Zoll,** seven inches; **drei Mark,** three marks; **zehn Pfund,** ten pounds.

Exercise No. 147. Fragen

Lesen Sie noch einmal den Text: **Einige Fragen über deutsche Geographie,** und dann beantworten Sie diese Fragen!

1 Was hat Herr Clark gut gelernt? 2 Was für Fragen will Herr Müller ihm jetzt stellen? 3 Beginnt Herr Müller mit einer leichten oder mit einer schweren Frage? 4 Nennen Sie die zwei längsten Flüsse Deutschlands! 5 Welcher Fluß ist länger und breiter, der Rhein oder die Elbe? 6 Welchen Fluß nennt man den schönsten deutschen Fluß? 7 Wo findet man malerische Schlösser aus den ältesten Zeiten? 8 Nennen Sie den höchsten Berg Deutschlands! 9 Ist die Zugspitze höher oder niedriger als der Mont Blanc in Frankreich? 10 An welcher See befinden sich die zwei größten Seehäfen Deutschlands?

CHAPTER 32

DIE GUTE DEUTSCHE KÜCHE
GOOD GERMAN COOKING

1 Wie Sie wohl wissen, Herr Clark, bietet die gute deutsche Küche dem Touristen eines der größten Vergnügen.

2 Ja, das weiß ich sehr wohl.

3 Sind Sie mit der deutschen Küche ein wenig bekannt?

4 Ja, ich weiß darüber schon ein wenig Bescheid. Wenn mich ein wichtiger Kunde besucht, lade ich ihn ein, mit mir in einem der besten deutschen Restaurants in London zu speisen. Das geschieht oft und macht mir viel Vergnügen.

5 Nun in Deutschland findet man die Kost nie einförmig, und da gibt es für den Reisenden immer eine neue Überraschung.

6 Schön. Wenn ich in Deutschland bin, mache ich eine Liste der Gerichte, die mir am besten schmecken. Dann schicke ich meiner Frau ein gutes deutsches Kochbuch, natürlich in englischer Sprache.

7 Eine vorzügliche Idee!

8 Sagen Sie mir, bitte, Herr Müller, ist die deutsche Küche sehr kompliziert?

9 Eigentlich nicht. Es gibt nur drei Geheimnisse der guten deutschen Küche. Diese drei sind auch die Geheimnisse jeder guten nationalen Küche, ob der deutschen, der französischen, der italienischen, oder irgendeiner anderen.

10 Was sind diese drei Geheimnisse?

11 Erstens muß alles, was man zum Kochen kauft, von der besten Qualität sein: Fleisch, Fisch, Gemüse, Butter, Eier usw. Zweitens muß man richtig kochen, um den Naturgeschmack der Nahrungsmittel zu behalten. Drittens muß man aber vor allem die Kochkunst lieben.

12 Bitte, beschreiben Sie mir die Hauptmahlzeit der Deutschen.

13 Gerne. Das ist das Mittagessen. Es beginnt gewöhnlich mit einer nahrhaften Suppe. Dann kommt Fleisch, Gemüse und Salat. Statt Fleisch gibt es manchmal (besonders Freitags) Fisch.

14 Und wie steht es mit dem Dessert?

15 Zum Dessert oder Nachtisch gibt es entweder Obst oder Obstkuchen, zum Beispiel Apfelkuchen oder Pflaumenkuchen.

16 Und keinen Strudel? Ich esse Strudel am allerliebsten.

17 Ach ja! In Süddeutschland ist der Strudel besonders beliebt.

18 Und was trinkt man am Ende der Mahlzeit?

19 Gewöhnlich trinkt man zum Mittagessen keinen Kaffee oder Tee, aber während des Essens trinkt man fast immer Bier oder Wein.

20 Der Mund wässert mir schon.[1] Herr Müller, wollen Sie mit mir vor meiner Abreise in einem deutschen Restaurant speisen?

21 Mit Vergnügen. Vielen, vielen Dank!

NOTE 1. *Lit.* The mouth is already watering to me.

169

1 As you no doubt know, Mr. Clark, good German cooking offers the tourist one of the greatest pleasures.

2 Yes, I know that very well.

3 Are you at all acquainted with German cooking?

4 Yes, I already know a little about it. When an important customer visits me, I invite him to dine with me in one of the best German restaurants in London. That happens often and gives me great pleasure.

5 Well, in Germany one never finds the food monotonous, and there is always a new surprise for the traveller.

6 Good. When I am in Germany I shall make a list of the dishes which taste best to me. Then I shall send my wife a good German cookery book, naturally in the English language.

7 An excellent idea!

8 Tell me please, Mr. Müller, is German cooking very complicated?

9 Not really. There are only three secrets of good German cooking. These three are also the secrets of every good national cuisine, whether the German, the French, the Italian, or any other.

10 What are these three secrets?

11 First, everything that one buys for cooking must be of the finest quality: meat, fish, vegetables, butter, eggs, etc. Second, one must cook correctly in order to retain the natural flavour of the foods. Third, one must, above all, love the art of cooking.

12 Please describe to me the main meal of the Germans.

13 Gladly. That is the midday meal. It usually begins with a nutritious soup. Then comes meat, vegetables, and salad. Instead of meat there is sometimes fish (especially on Friday).

14 And what about the dessert?

15 For dessert there is either fruit or fruit cake, for example apple cake or plum cake.

16 And no 'strudel'? I like to eat 'strudel' most of all.

17 Oh, yes. In South Germany 'strudel' is especially popular.

18 And what does one drink at the end of the meal?

19 At the midday meal one usually does not drink coffee or tea, but during the meal one almost always drinks beer or wine.

10 My mouth is already watering. Mr. Müller, will you dine with me in a German restaurant before my departure?

21 With pleasure. Many thanks.

Wortschatz

das Dessért = der Nachtisch, dessert
das Gehéimnis, *pl.* -se, secret
das Gemüse, vegetables
der Geschmáck, taste
das Gerícht, *pl.* -e, dish, course
die Küche, *pl.* -n, kitchen, cuisine, cooking
die Nahrungsmittel, foodstuffs
das Obst, fruit; der Salat, salad
kochen, to cook
schicken = senden, to send

speisen, to dine
bekannt, known
kompliziért, complicated
nahrhaft, nourishing
erstens, first, firstly
zweitens, second, secondly
drittens, third, thirdly
irgendein, any
entweder ... oder, either ... of

NOTE 1. der Strudel, very thin pastry (filled with apples).

Strong Verbs. Principal Parts

behálten	to retain, receive	er behält	behielt	hat behalten
beschréiben	to describe	er beschreibt	beschrieb	hat beschrieben
bieten	to offer	er bietet	bot	hat geboten
ein-laden	to invite	er lädt ... ein	lud ... ein	hat eingeladen

Deutsche Ausdrücke

Bescheid wissen, to have knowledge of a thing, to know about, to know one's way. **Über die deutsche Küche wissen wir ein wenig Bescheid.** We know a little about the German cuisine. **In dieser Stadt weiß er Bescheid.** He knows his way around this town.

beliebt, popular; **beliebt bei,** a favourite with. **Der Strudel ist bei uns sehr beliebt.** Strudel is a great favourite with us.

vor allem, above all, first of all. **Wir müssen vor allem fleißig arbeiten.** We must above all work diligently. **Ich dachte vor allem an die Geschäftssachen.** I thought first of all of the business matters.

ob ... oder, whether ... or. **Ob heute oder morgen, wir werden gewiß gehen.** Whether today or tomorrow, we shall surely go.

Sprichwort: Der Mensch ist, was er ißt. Proverb: Man is what he eats.

Grammar Notes and Practical Exercises

1 The *am -sten* form of the superlative of adjectives

Das Wetter ist **am schönsten.**	The weather is *most beautiful.*
Wir haben das schönste Wetter.	We have the most beautiful weather.
In Asien sind die Berge **am höchsten.**	In Asia the mountains are *highest.*
Die höchsten Berge sind in Asien.	The highest mountains are in Asia.

The am -sten form is used mostly in cases where the corresponding English superlative omits *the.* This form is never used before a noun. Some familiar adjectives in the am -sten superlative are: **am kleinsten, am größten, am interessantesten, am schönsten, am längsten, am kürzesten, am kältesten, am wärmsten, am heißesten, am jüngsten, am ältesten, am höchsten, am besten.**

Exercise No. 148. Translate the superlative of the adjective with the **am -sten** form.

1 **Die Berge sind hier** (highest). 2 **Der Herbst ist hier** (most beautiful). 3 **Im Winter sind die Tage** (coldest). 4 **In Afrika ist das Klima** (hottest). 5 **Im Sommer sind die Tage** (shortest). 6 **Diese Zimmer sind** (largest). 7 **In diesem Dorf sind die Häuser** (oldest). 8 **Die Ferientage** (vacation days) **sind** (best).

2 Comparison of adverbs

schnell	quickly	schneller	more quickly
langsam	slowly	langsamer	more slowly
klar	clearly	klarer	more clearly
spät	late	später	later
	am schnellsten	most quickly	
	am langsamsten	most slowly	
	am klarsten	most clearly	
	am spätesten	latest	

früh	early	früher	earlier
gut	good	besser	better
schlecht	bad	schlechter	worse
schön	beautiful	schöner	more beautiful
gern	gladly	lieber	more gladly

am frühesten	earliest
am besten	best
am schlechtesten	worst
am schönsten	most beautiful
am liebsten	most gladly

Ein Auto geht **schnell**. Ein Flugzeug geht **schneller** als ein Auto. Eine Rakete geht **am schnellsten (am allerschnellsten)**.

A car goes *fast*. A plane goes *faster* than a car. A rocket goes *fastest (of all)*.

(*a*) Adverbs are compared like adjectives. The superlative of an adverb, however, always has the **am -sten** form. Many adjectives can be used also as adverbs.

> Er ist **gut**. Er schreibt **gut**.   He is *good* (*adj.*). He writes *well* (*adv.*).

(*b*) As you have already learned, a verb + gern(e) means *to like to*; a verb + **lieber** means *to prefer to*; a verb + **am liebsten** means *to like most* or *best of all*.

Ich esse Apfelkuchen **gern**. Ich esse Pflaumenkuchen **lieber**. Ich esse Strudel **am liebsten**.

I like to eat apple cake. I prefer to eat plum cake. I like to eat 'strudel' most of all.

Exercise No. 149. Ein Gespräch

DEUTSCHE ODER FRANZÖSISCHE KÜCHE

— Ich habe die deutsche Kost sehr gern. Sie auch?

— Ich habe die deutsche Kost lieber als die italienische. Aber die französische Kost habe ich am liebsten.

— Kennen Sie etwas, was den Appetit besser anregt als ein Bismarckhering?

— Gewiß. Das tun die französischen hors d'œuvres (Vorspeisen) am allerbesten.

— Wer tüchtig speisen will, findet ein Wiener Schnitzel mit Rotkohl und dazu ein Seidel dunkles Bier am befriedigendsten.

— Aber nein, man speist nicht weniger gut, wenn man in einem der besseren Pariser Restaurants coq au vin mit haricots verts (Huhn in Wein gekocht mit grünen Bohnen) bestellt.

— Trinken Sie lieber Bier oder Wein zum Mittagessen?

— Ich trinke lieber den französischen Rotwein.

— Wie ist es mit dem Nachtisch? Von allen deutschen Nachspeisen schmeckt mir ein frischer Apfelstrudel am besten.

— Ich nehme öfter Obst als Kuchen. Aber unter den Mehlspeisen bestelle ich am häufigsten die wunderbaren französischen crêpes suzettes. Die sind auch viel besser als die deutschen Pfannkuchen.

— Nun, gibt es denn keine deutschen Gerichte, die Sie am liebsten haben?

— Ich habe nichts gegen die deutsche Kost, aber die französische mag ich eben lieber.

— Und ich erfreue mich am meisten an der deutschen Kost. Es ist doch klar, über den Geschmack läßt sich nicht streiten!

— I like German food very much. Do you?

— I like German food better than the Italian. But I like French food best.

— Do you know of anything that stimulates the appetite better than a pickled herring?

— Certainly. The French hors d'œuvres do that best of all.

— Anyone who wants to dine heartily will find a Vienna veal cutlet with red cabbage and a mug of dark beer with it most satisfying.

— Oh, no, one dines no less well if in one of the better Parisian restaurants one orders coq au vin (capon in wine) with French beans.

— Do you prefer to drink beer or wine with your dinner?

— I prefer to drink French red wine.

— How about dessert? Of all the German desserts I like a fresh apple strudel best.

— I take fruit more often than cake. But in the line of cooked sweets I most often order the wonderful French crêpes suzettes. These are even better than the German pancakes.

— Well, aren't there any German dishes which you like best?

— I have nothing against German food, but I just like French food better.

— And I enjoy German cooking most. Well, it's obvious, there's no disputing about taste!

Exercise No. 150. Fragen

Lesen Sie noch einmal den Text: **Die gute deutsche Küche,** und dann beantworten Sie diese Fragen!

1 Wem bietet die deutsche Küche eines der größten Vergnügen? 2 Wo speist Herr Clark oft mit einem wichtigen Kunden? 3 Wo findet man die Kost nie einförmig? 4 Wem wird Herr Clark ein gutes deutsches Kochbuch senden? 5 Was ist das erste Geheimnis der guten deutschen Küche? 6 Was ist das dritte? 7 Welches ist die Hauptmahlzeit der Deutschen? 8 Womit beginnt gewöhnlich die Mahlzeit? 9 Was kommt dann? 10 Was gibt es zum Dessert? 11 Welches Dessert hat Herr Clark am liebsten? 12 Wo ist der Strudel besonders beliebt? 13 Was trinkt man am Ende der Mahlzeit? 14 Was trinkt man während der Mahlzeit?

CHAPTER 33

WELCHE STÄDTE WERDEN SIE BESUCHEN, HERR CLARK?

WHAT PLACES WILL YOU VISIT, MR. CLARK?

1 Nächste Woche werden Sie nach Deutschland abreisen. Wie lange werden Sie in diesem Lande bleiben?

2 Mir stehen nur sechs Wochen zur Verfügung. Aber ich versichere Ihnen, ich werde versuchen, diese Zeit aufs beste auszunützen.

3 Wissen Sie schon, welche Städte Deutschlands Sie besuchen werden?

4 Ich denke immer daran und lese fleißig in meiner Sammlung von Reisebüchern. Wie Sie schon wissen, führen mich meine Geschäftsangelegenheiten nach München, wo mein Vertreter, Herr Schiller, wohnt.

5 Und wie lange werden Sie in München bleiben?

6 Zwei oder drei Wochen, vielleicht länger.

7 Und welche Sehenswürdigkeiten wollen Sie dort besuchen?

8 Sie wissen, man nennt München das moderne Athen, mit berühmten Kunstmuseen, die ich besuchen will. Das ,,Deutsche Museum'' soll das größte technische Museum Europas sein.

Natürlich muß ich auch die weltberühmte Liebfrauenkirche und das Rathaus mit dem Glockenspiel[1] besuchen. Außerdem gibt es Theater und Oper, auch altbekannte Weinstuben und Bierhallen, u.a.m. und anderes mehr. Ich muß auch einen langen Spaziergang im berühmten Englischen Garten[2] machen.

9 Denken Sie auch Ausflüge aufs Land zu machen?

10 Ja, gewiß. München ist die Pforte zu den Bayerischen Alpen und zur Seegegend. Ich werde den Tegernsee und die anderen malerischen Seen besuchen. Ich möchte auch einen Ausflug zum interessanten Dorf Oberammergau und zum nahegelegenen Garmisch-Partenkirchen machen. Das soll eine der schönsten Berggegenden der Welt sein.

11 Werden Sie noch andere Städte in der Nähe von München besuchen?

12 Jawohl. Ich denke vor allem an Nürnberg, die Stadt der Meistersinger, und an Bayreuth, die Stadt, in der Richard Wagner lebte und komponierte.

Ich glaube mein Vertreter, Herr Schiller, wird mir in meinen Wanderungen behilflich sein, soweit es seine Zeit erlauben wird.

13 Wird Ihre Reise auch andere Teile Deutschlands einschließen?

14 Ach, ja. Ich werde in Frankfurt einige Geschäfte erledigen. Dann will ich eine Rheinreise machen, und dabei werde ich Bonn, die Haupstadt Westdeutschlands, und die Rheinstädte, Köln und Düsseldorf, den Geburtsort von Heinrich Heine,[3] besuchen können. Von dort wird's nach Hamburg gehen, von wo aus ich per Flugzeug die Heimreise unternehmen werde. Was denken Sie darüber, Herr Müller?

15 Was ich darüber denke? Ich beneide Sie, Herr Clark, und ich möchte Sie begleiten. Das ist aber leider unmöglich. Ich werde zu Hause bleiben müssen.

16 Wie schade, Herr Müller. Es tut mir aufrichtig leid.

NOTES: 1 **Das Glockenspiel,** a remarkable clock with chimes on the **Rathaus** (Town Hall) in Munich. Every day at 11 a.m. wooden figures come out and dance to the music of the bells. 2 **Der Englische Garten,** a large beautiful park in Munich. 3 **Heinrich Heine, 1797–1856.** Great German lyric poet. Among his most famous poems are **Die Lorelei, Du bist wie eine Blume** and **Die Zwei Grenadiere.**

1 Next week you will be setting out for Germany. How long will you stay in that country?

2 There are only six weeks at my disposal. But I assure you, I shall try to make use of this time to the best advantage.

3 Do you already know which cities of Germany you will visit?

4 I'm thinking about this matter all the time, and reading diligently in my collection of guide books. As you know, business matters are taking me to Munich, where my agent, Mr. Schiller, lives.

5 And how long will you stay in Munich?

6 Two or three weeks, perhaps longer.

7 And what places of interest do you expect to visit there?

8 You know they call Munich the modern Athens, with famous art museums which I want to visit. The German Museum is said to be the largest technical museum in Europe.

Of course I must also visit the world-famous Church of Our Lady and the Town Hall with the 'Chimes'. Besides these there are theatres and opera, also well-known taverns and beer halls among other things. I must also take a long walk in the famous English Garden.

9 Are you also thinking of making excursions out into the country?

10 Yes, certainly. Munich is the gateway to the Bavarian Alps and the lake region. I shall visit the Tegernsee and the other picturesque lakes. I should also like to take a trip to the interesting village of Oberammergau and to Garmisch-Partenkirchen near by. That is said to be one of the most beautiful mountain regions in the world.

11 Will you visit other cities near Munich?

12 Yes, indeed. I think first of all of Nurnberg, city of the Mastersingers, and of Bayreuth, the city in which Richard Wagner lived and composed.

I believe my agent, Mr. Schiller, will be helpful to me in my travels, as far as his time will permit.

13 Will your trip include other parts of Germany too?

14 Oh, yes. I shall deal with some business matters in Frankfurt. Then I will take a Rhine trip and at the same time I shall be able to visit Bonn, the capital of West Germany, and the Rhine cities of Cologne and Düsseldorf, the birthplace of Heinrich Heine. From there the next stop will be Hamburg, from which place I shall make the home journey by plane. What do you think of this, Mr. Müller?

15 What do I think of it? I envy you, Mr. Clark, and I should like to accompany you. However, that is unfortunately impossible. I shall have to stay at home.

16 That's too bad, Mr. Müller. I'm really very sorry.

Wortschatz

das Dorf, *pl.* ¨er, village	beneíden, to envy
der Gebúrtsort, *pl.* -e, birthplace	besórgen, to take care of, attend to

die Gegend, *pl.* -en, region
die Kirche, *pl.* -n, church
die Pforte, *pl.* -n, gate
die Sammlung, *pl.* -en, collection
die Sehenswürdigkeit, *pl.* -en, place of interest
ab-reisen, to set out
aus-nützen, to make full use of

komponíéren, to compose
versíchern, to assure
bekánnt, known; altbekannt, well known
nahegelegen, near by
technisch, technical
soweit, as far as
dabeí, at the same time; in connexion with that

Strong Verbs. Principal Parts

ein-schließen	to include	er schließt . . . ein	schloß . . . ein	hat eingeschlossen
bleiben	to remain	er bleibt	blieb	ist geblieben
tun	to do	er tut	tat	hat getan

Deutsche Ausdrücke

schade! wie schade! what a pity
Es ist sehr schade. It's a great pity.
ja, gewiß, yes, certainly
u.a.m. (und anderes mehr), and other things
einen Spaziergang machen, to go for a walk
Jeden Tag hat er einen Spaziergang im Park gemacht. Every day he went for a walk in the park.

Grammar Notes and Practical Exercises

1 The Future Tense of Modal Auxiliaries

I shall have to go, you will have to go, etc.

Ich werde heute gehen müssen.   Wir werden heute gehen müssen.
Du wirst heute gehen müssen.   Ihr werdet heute gehen müssen.
Er (sie, es) wird heute gehen müssen.   Sie (Sie) werden heute gehen müssen.

(*a*) In the future tense the infinitive of the modal auxiliary stands last.

(*b*) The present tense of modal auxiliaries is often used to express future time.

Ich muß morgen gehen = Ich werde morgen gehen müssen.

Er kann mich morgen nicht begleiten = Er wird mich morgen nicht begleiten können.

Exercise No. 151. Above is the future of müssen. Practise the future of the other modals by substituting dürfen, können, mögen, sollen, wollen, for müssen.

Exercise No. 152. Ein Gespräch. Practise aloud.

— Wohin werden Sie im nächsten Sommer gehen? — Ich werde nach Deutschland reisen.
— Wann werden Sie London verlassen? — Ich werde am 31. Mai abfahren.
— Wie lange werden Sie in Deutschland bleiben? — Ich werde drei Monate

dort verbringen. — Werden Sie mit einem Dampfer reisen oder per Flugzeug?
— Ich werde per Flugzeug reisen.
— Werden Sie Ihren Vertreter in München sehen? — Jawohl, er wird mich
am Flugplatz erwarten. — Wie lange werden Sie in München bleiben? — Ich
werde drei oder vier Wochen lang dort bleiben.
— Wollen Sie eine Reise nach Berlin machen? — Ja, ich will nach Berlin
reisen, wenn ich Zeit habe. — Kann Herr Müller Sie begleiten? — Ach,
schade! Es wird ihm nicht möglich sein, mich zu begleiten; *or* Er kann mich
nicht begleiten; *or* Er wird mich nicht begleiten können.

Exercise No. 153. Complete the translation of each English sentence.

Beispiel: 1 Er wird drei Wochen in Berlin bleiben müssen.

1 He will have to stay in Berlin three weeks.	1 Er wird drei Wochen in Berlin bleiben ——.
2 Which cities will he visit?	2 —— wird er besuchen?
3 I do not know which cities he will visit.	3 Ich weiß nicht, welche Städte er ——.
4 This lake is said to be beautiful.	4 Dieser See —— schön sein.
5 We shall visit all places of interest.	5 Wir werden —— besuchen.
6 In Cologne we shall be able to visit the Cathedral.	6 In Köln werden wir den Dom besuchen ——.
7 The tourists will want to see the German Museum.	7 Die Touristen werden das „Deutsche Museum" sehen ——.
8 We will make many excursions to the country.	8 Wir werden —— aufs Land machen.
9 Will you be able to accompany me?	9 Werden Sie mich begleiten ——?
10 Will Mr. Schiller await you at the airport?	10 Wird Herr Schiller Sie am Flugplatz ——.

2 The Future Perfect Tense

I shall have learned German, etc.	I shall have gone home, etc.
Ich werde Deutsch gelernt haben.	Ich werde nach Hause gegangen sein.
Du wirst Deutsch gelernt haben.	Du wirst nach Hause gegangen sein,
Er wird Deutsch gelernt haben.	Er wird nach Hause gegangen sein.
Wir werden Deutsch gelernt haben.	Wir werden nach Hause gegangen sein.
Ihr werdet Deutsch gelernt haben.	Ihr werdet nach Hause gegangen sein.
Sie werden Deutsch gelernt haben	Sie werden nach Hause gegangen sein.

The future perfect tense in German, like this tense in English, is rarely used.

Exercise No. 154. Fragen

Lesen Sie noch einmal den Text: **Welche Städte werden Sie besuchen, Herr
Clark?** und dann beantworten Sie diese Fragen!

1 **Wie lange wird Herr Clark in Deutschland bleiben?** 2 **In welchen Büchern
liest er fleißig?** 3 **Wie lange wird er in München bleiben?** 4 **Wie nennt man
München?** 5 **Welches Museum soll das größte technische Museum Europas sein?**
6 **In welchem berühmten Park muß Herr Clark einen Spaziergang machen?**
7 **Nach welchem interessanten Dorf möchte er einen Ausflug machen?** 8 **Welche**

Stadt ist die Stadt der Meistersinger? 9 In welcher Stadt lebte und komponierte Richard Wagner? 10 Welche Städte am Rhein wird Herr Clark besuchen? 11 Wo wurde Heinrich Heine geboren? 12 Von wo aus wird Herr Clark die Heimreise unternehmen? 13 Wer möchte Herrn Clark auf seiner Reise begleiten? 14 Wird er ihn begleiten können?

CHAPTER 34

HERR CLARK REIST NACH DEUTSCHLAND AB
MR. CLARK SETS OUT FOR GERMANY

1 Herr Clark hat nun sechs Monate Deutsch studiert. Er hat viel Zeit im Gespräch mit seinem Lehrer, Herrn Müller, verbracht. Er hat auch die wichtigsten Regeln der Grammatik gelernt und einige Bücher über Deutschland gelesen. Er hat ernst und fleißig gelernt. Jetzt kann er Deutsch sprechen, und erwartet, jede Gelegenheit zu ergreifen, seine Kenntnisse in Deutschland zu benützen.

2 Herr Clark hat seinen Reisepaß besorgt und seine Flugkarte gekauft. Er hat nun alles, was er braucht.

3 Natürlich hat Herr Clark seinem Vertreter in München einen Brief geschrieben, um ihm die Zeit seiner Ankunft mitzuteilen. Herr Schiller, der Vertreter, hat versprochen, ihn am Münchener Flughafen abzuholen.

4 Endlich kommt der 31. Mai, der Tag der Abreise. Das Flugzeug, in dem Herr Clark reisen wird, verläßt den Londoner-Flughafen punkt 8.00 (acht Uhr morgens). Er muß eine Stunde früher am Flugplatz sein, um seine Karte vorzuzeigen, und sein Gepäck abwiegen zu lassen.

5 Die Familie begleitet ihn nicht nach Deutschland, denn die Kinder müssen ja das Schuljahr beenden, und seine Frau muß zu Hause bleiben, um für die Kinder zu sorgen. Außerdem ist das Reisen mit vier Kindern vom fünften bis zum zwölften Lebensjahr nicht nur schwierig sondern auch kostspielig.

6 Natürlich ist die Familie sehr aufgeregt. Die Kinder haben nicht viel geschlafen, und um sechs Uhr früh sind sie alle wach, gewaschen und angezogen.

7 Um ein Viertel nach sechs morgens ist die ganze Familie bereit, zum Flughafen zu fahren. Herr Clark ist reisefertig. Er hat zwei Handkoffer gepackt und bereits in das Auto gebracht. Sie steigen alle ein. Herr Clark bringt das Auto in Gang und sie kommen um ein Viertel vor sieben am Flughafen an.

8 Herr Clark läßt seine Karte und seinen Reisepaß nachprüfen und läßt sein Gepäck wiegen. Und nun ist es Zeit, das Flugzeug zu besteigen.

9 Jetzt umarmt und küßt Herr Clark seine Frau und Kinder, die ihm „Glückliche Reise" wünschen. Während er das Flugzeug besteigt, winkt er seiner Familie, die ihm bewegt nachschaut. Punkt 8.00 Uhr (acht Uhr) startet das Flugzeug.

10 Herr Clark ist auf dem Wege!

1 Mr. Clark has now studied German for six months. He has spent a lot of time in conversation with his teacher, Mr. Müller. He has also learned the most important rules of German grammar and has read some books about Germany. He has studied earnestly and industriously. Now he can speak German and is expecting to take every opportunity to make use of his knowledge in Germany.

179

2 Mr. Clark has obtained his passport and has bought his plane ticket. He now has everything that he needs.

3 Naturally, Mr. Clark has written a letter to his agent in Munich to inform him of the time of his arrival. Mr. Schiller, the agent, has promised to meet him at the Munich airport.

4 Finally the 31st of May arrives, the day of departure. The plane on which Mr. Clark will travel leaves the London Airport at exactly eight o'clock in the morning. He must be at the airport one hour earlier in order to present his ticket and have his luggage weighed.

5 His family is not accompanying him to Germany, for the children must finish the school year, and his wife must remain at home in order to look after the children. Besides, travelling with four children from five to twelve years of age is not only difficult but costly.

6 Naturally the family is very excited. The children have not slept much and at six in the morning they are all awake, washed and dressed.

7 At 6.15 the whole family is ready to go to the airport. Mr. Clark is ready to start. He has packed two suitcases and has put them in the car. They all get in. Mr. Clark starts the car and they arrive at the airport at a quarter to seven.

8 Mr. Clark has his ticket and passport checked and has his luggage weighed. And now it is time to get on the plane.

9 Now Mr. Clark embraces and kisses his wife and children, who wish him 'Happy Journey'. While he is getting on the plane, he waves to his family, who are watching him excitedly. At 8.00 o'clock sharp the plane takes off.

10 Mr. Clark is on his way.

Wortschatz

die **Abreise**, *pl.* **-n**, departure
die **Kenntnis**, *pl.* **-se**, knowledge
das **Lebensjahr**, year of age
das **Reisen**, travelling
die **Regel**, *pl.* **-n**, rule
wiegen, to weigh
ab-holen, to call for; go to get, meet
küssen, to kiss
mit-teilen, to inform
nach-prüfen, to check
nach-schauen, to watch, look after

packen, to pack
sorgen für, to take care of, look after
umármen, to embrace
vor-zeigen, to present
winken, to beckon, wave
aufgeregt, excited
bewégt, moved (*with emotion*)
kostspielig = teuer, costly
reisefertig, ready to start
schwierig, difficult; **wach**, awake
nicht nur . . . sondern auch, not only . . . but also

Strong Verbs. Principal Parts

auf-steigen	to arise, get on	er steigt . . . auf	stieg . . . auf	ist aufgestiegen
besteigen	to get on, mount	er besteigt	bestieg	hat bestiegen
schlafen	to sleep	er schläft	schlief	hat geschlafen
versprechen	to promise	er verspricht	versprach	hat versprochen
bringen	to bring	er bringt	brachte	hat gebracht
verbringen	to spend (time)	er verbringt	verbrachte	hat verbracht
wiegen	to weigh	er wiegt	wog	hat gewogen

Two Word Families

reisen, to travel
das Reisen,[1] travelling
die Reise, trip
ab-reisen, to depart
die Abreise, departure
der Reisende, traveller
reisefertig, ready to depart, ready for travel
das Reisebuch, guide
die Reisetasche, suitcase

sprechen, to speak
das Sprechen,[1] speaking
versprechen, to promise
aus-sprechen, to pronounce
die Sprache, speech, language
die Aussprache, pronunciation
das Gespräch, conversation
sprachlos, speechless
der Sprecher, speaker, orator, announcer

NOTE 1. Infinitives may be used as neuter nouns. The translation is usually a noun ending in -ing: das Schreiben, writing; das Lesen, reading.

Deutsche Ausdrücke

das Auto in Gang bringen, to start the car (*lit.* to bring the car into motion).
Herr Clark hat das Auto in Gang gebracht. Mr. Clark started the car.
Das Flugzeug steigt auf. The plane takes off.
etwas tun lassen, to have something done.
Er läßt sein Gepäck wiegen. He has his luggage weighed. Ich ließ meinen Reisepaß nachprüfen. I had my passport checked.

Grammar Notes and Practical Exercises

1 About the verbs *lassen* (*er läßt, ließ, hat gelassen*) and *verlassen*.
(a) lassen + an infinitive without zu = to let, to allow, to have something done.

Sie läßt uns hier spielen. She lets us play here.
Laßt uns fertig werden! Let's get finished!
Er läßt das Gepäck wiegen. He has the luggage weighed.
Ich lasse mir einen Anzug machen. I'm having a suit made (for myself).

(b) lassen + a direct object = to leave, to let.
Er ließ seinen Hut auf dem Tisch. He left his hat on the table.
Ich ließ ihn gestern fortgehen. I let him go yesterday.
(c) verlassen, to leave (go away from, abandon)
Am Mittwoch hat er die Stadt verlassen. On Wednesday he left the city.

NOTE 2. Adjectives formed from names of towns end in -er in all cases. Example: der Münchener Flughafen; am Münchener Flughafen.

Exercise No. 155. Change these sentences to the present.

Beispiel: 1 Herr Clark lernt die Regeln der Grammatik.

1 Herr Clark hat die Regeln der Grammatik gelernt. 2 Er hat einige Bücher über Deutschland gelesen. 3 Er hat seinen Reisepaß besorgt. 4 Er hat seine Fahrkarte gekauft. 5 Er hat seinem Vertreter einen Brief geschrieben. 6 Er hat eine Antwort bekommen. 7 Der Vertreter hat versprochen, ihn abzuholen. 8 Die Kinder haben dort viel geschlafen. 9 Sie haben sich gewaschen. 10 Sie haben sich angezogen. 11 Die Familie ist zum Flughafen gefahren. 12 Das Flugzeug ist aufgestiegen. 13 Herr Clark hat das Flugzeug bestiegen. 14 Er ist abgereist.

15 Er hat seine Frau und Kinder zu Hause gelassen. 16 Die Familie hat um sieben Uhr den Flughafen verlassen.

Exercise No. 156. Complete these sentences by choosing the infinitive with or without **zu** as each sentence requires.

Beispiel: 1 Der Vertreter hat versprochen, ihn **abzuholen.**

1 Der Vertreter hat versprochen, ihn (abholen, abzuholen). 2 Ich hoffe, Ihnen in München (begegnen, zu begegnen). 3 Wir müssen alle unsere Kenntnisse (ausnützen, auszunützen). 4 Die Passagiere kommen früh, um ihre Reisepässe (vorzeigen, vorzuzeigen). 5 Der Beamte will unsere Koffer (wiegen, zu wiegen). 6 Wir ließen unsere Reisepässe (nachprüfen, nachzuprüfen). 7 Ich werde Ihnen schreiben, um die Zeit meiner Ankunft (mitteilen, mitzuteilen). 8 Ich beabsichtige, Sie am Flugplatz (abholen, abzuholen). 9 Ich werde die Gelegenheit haben, meine Kenntnisse (ausnützen, auszunützen). 10 Herrn Clarks Frau und Kinder können nicht (mitgehen, mitzugehen). 11 Alle sind bereit, zum Flughafen (fahren, zu fahren). 12 Es ist jetzt Zeit, das Flugzeug (besteigen, zu besteigen).

Exercise No. 157. Fragen

Lesen Sie noch einmal den Text: **Herr Clark reist nach Deutschland ab,** und dann beantworten Sie diese Fragen!

1 Wie lange hat Herr Clark Deutsch studiert? 2 Mit wem hat er viel Zeit im Gespräch verbracht? 3 Was hat er gelesen? 4 Kann er jetzt Deutsch sprechen? 5 An wen hat er einen Brief geschrieben? 6 Was hat sein Vertreter ihm versprochen? 7 Welcher Tag kommt endlich? 8 Um wieviel Uhr verläßt das Flugzeug den Londoner Flughafen? 9 Begleiten ihn Frau und Kinder auf der Reise? 10 Warum müssen die Kinder zu Hause bleiben? 11 Warum muß Frau Clark zu Hause bleiben? 12 Um wieviel Uhr ist die ganze Familie bereit, zum Flughafen zu fahren? 13 Wann kommen sie am Flughafen an? 14 Was tut Herr Herr Clark, bevor er das Flugzeug besteigt? 15 Wie sehen ihm Frau und Kinder nach, während er das Flugzeug besteigt?

CHAPTER 35

REVISION OF CHAPTERS 30-34

Weak (Regular) Verbs. No Vowel Changes

1 führen	10 versuchen	1 to lead, carry on	10 to try, taste + *obj.*
2 schicken	11 begegnen	2 to send	11 to meet
3 schmecken	12 gratulieren	3 to taste (*no obj.*)	12 to congratulate
4 speisen	13 ab-reisen	4 to dine	13 to set out
5 sorgen für	14 aus-nützen	5 to look after	14 to make full use of
6 packen	15 mit-teilen	6 to pack	15 to inform
7 küssen	16 ab-holen	7 to kiss	16 to go to meet, to fetch
8 schauen	17 zu-hören	8 to look	17 to listen
9 leben	18 sich bemühen	9 to live	18 to try

Strong (Irregular) Verbs. Vowel Changes

bieten	to offer	er bietet	bot	hat geboten
essen	to eat	er ißt	aß	hat gegessen
trinken	to drink	er trinkt	trank	hat getrunken
bitten (um)	to ask (for)	er bittet	bat	hat gebeten
schließen	to close	er schließt	schloß	hat geschlossen
schlafen	to sleep	er schläft	schlief	hat geschlafen
beschreiben	to describe	er beschreibt	beschrieb	hat beschrieben
besteigen	to mount	er besteigt	bestieg	hat bestiegen
ein-steigen	to get in	er steigt ein	stieg ein	ist eingestiegen
ein-laden	to invite	er lädt ein	lud ein	hat eingeladen
ergreifen	to seize	er ergreift	ergriff	hat ergriffen
unternehmen	to undertake	er unternimmt	unternahm	hat unternommen

Deutsche Ausdrücke

1 mit Recht, rightly; vor allem, above all
2 reisefertig, ready to start
3 ja, gewiß, yes, indeed
4 auf dem Land, in the country (opposite of city); aufs Land, to the country. Wir machen einen Auflug aufs Land. We are taking a trip to the country. Er wohnt auf dem Lande. He lives in the country.
5 zu Tische (oder zum Essen) einladen, to invite to dinner. Ich habe sie zum Essen eingeladen. I have invited her (them) to dinner.
6 meiner (seiner, ihrer, Ihrer, usw.) Meinung nach, according to my (his, her, your, etc.) opinion. nach, in the sense of according to, follows its noun.

7 einen Spaziergang machen, to take a walk
8 die Gelegenheit ergreifen, to take the opportunity
9 Das ist mir angenehm. That's agreeable to me.
10 das Auto in Gang bringen, to start the car
11 Der Mensch ist, was er ißt. (Sprichwort) Man is what he eats.
12 Besser spät als niemals. (Sprichwort) Better late than never.

Exercise No. 158. Ergänzen Sie diese Sätze auf deutsch! Complete these sentences in German.

1 **Wann gehen Sie** (to the country)? 2 **Sie nennen** (rightly) **München das moderne Athen.** 3 **Sie lebten das ganze Jahr** (in the country). 4 **Warum** (don't you take the opportunity) **auf die Universität zu gehen?** 5 (Do you like) **die deutsche Küche?** 6 **Herr Clark** (started the car). 7 **Jeden Tag** (he went for a walk) **im ,,Englischen Garten".** 8 **Wir waren schon** (ready for travel), **als das Auto ankam.** 9 (Take every opportunity), **Deutsch zu reden!** 10 (According to his opinion) **ist München die schönste Stadt Deutschlands.** 11 (According to her opinion) **ist Köln schöner als München.** 12 (We have invited him) **uns zu besuchen.**

Exercise No. 159. Review the principal parts of the strong and weak verbs at the beginning of this chapter. Then complete these sentences with the given tense of the verbs in parentheses.

Beispiel: 1 Der Lehrer hörte aufmerksam zu, als er den Brief vorlas.

1 (zu-hören *past*) **Der Lehrer** —— **aufmerksam** ——, **als er den Brief vorlas.** 2 (essen *pres. perf.*) **Zum Mittagessen** —— **wir Fleisch mit Gemüse** ——. 3 (schmecken, *past*) **Alles** —— **sehr gut.** 4 (ein-laden *pres. perf.*) **Ich** —— **meinen besten Kunden zum Mittagessen** ——. 5 (trinken *past*) **Beim Abendessen** ——**jeder von uns zwei Glas Bier.** 6 (sich zurecht-finden *fut.*) **Ich** —— **mich gewiß in Deutschland** ——. 7 (ergreifen *imperative*) —— **Sie jede Gelegenheit Deutsch zu sprechen!** 8 (beschreiben *fut.*) **Wir** —— **alle Sehenswürdigkeiten** ——. 9 (speisen *pres. perf.*) **Wo** —— **Sie gestern abend** ——? 10 (sich bemühen *past perf.*) **Er** —— **sich** ——, **behilflich zu sein.** 11 (auf-stehen *pres. perf.*) **Die Kinder** —— **um sieben Uhr dreißig** ——. 12 (bieten *pres.*) —— **man etwas Gutes heute?** 13 (müssen *past*) **Die Mütter** —— **für die Kinder sorgen.** 14 (Besteigen *past perf.*) **Nachdem er das Flugzeug** ——, **winkte er mit der Hand.** 15 (ein-steigen *pres. perf.*) **Um drei Uhr nachmittags** —— **alle in den Zug** ——. 16 (bitten um *present*) **Dort ist ein Reisender, der um Auskunft** ——.

Dialog 1

DEUTSCHE ODER ENGLISCHE FILME?

— Sind die deutschen Filme, Ihrer Meinung nach, besser als die englischen?
— Nun, manche[1] sind besser und manche sind schlechter. In beiden Ländern gibt es gute, ernsthafte Filme und auch viele schlechte, minderwertige. In beiden Ländern findet man die besten und auch die schlechtesten Filme.
— Wie gefallen Ihnen die Hollywood-Filme?
— Die gefallen mir meistens nicht. Sie bieten viel Schund und Kitsch, aber ich muß gestehen, dann und wann kommen auch hervorragende Filme aus Hollywood. Am besten gefallen mir (Ich habe am liebsten) Kultur- und Dokumentarfilme.
— Ich nehme an, daß Sie die Westerns nicht mögen.
— Da haben Sie recht! Die Darstellung von Laster und Verbrechen ist nicht nach meinem Geschmack.
— Solche Bilder scheinen jedoch einem großen Teil des Publikums zu gefallen.

— Nun, über den Geschmack läßt sich nicht streiten.

NOTE 1. **mancher,** many a, *pl.* many, some. **Mancher** is a **der-**word; **mancher Mann, manche Frau, manches Kind; manche Männer.**

— In your opinion, are the German films better than the English ones?

— Well, some are better and some are worse. In both countries there are good, serious films and also many bad, inferior ones. In both countries one finds the best as well as the worst films.

— How do you like the Hollywood films?

— Generally I do not like these. They offer a great deal of trash and junk, but I must admit that now and then some outstanding films do come out of Hollywood. I like cultural and documentary films best.

— I assume that you don't care for Westerns.

— That's right! The portrayal of vice and crime is not to my taste.

— Yet such pictures seem to please a large part of the public.

— Well, there's no disputing about taste.

Dialog 2

IM RESTAURANT

— Guten Tag, mein Herr. Hier ist die Speisekarte.

— Danke. Was empfehlen Sie heute?

— Es gibt Beefsteak mit Kartoffeln, Wiener Schnitzel, Rührei mit Schinken, oder Spiegeleier, auch kalten Aufschnitt, Bismarckhering oder eine Gemüseplatte.

— Sehr gut. Ich möchte Wiener Schnitzel. Aber bringen Sie mir zuerst einen Bismarckhering.

— Bitte. Wünschen Sie zu dem Wiener Schnitzel Gemüse? Die übliche Beilage ist Rotkohl.

— Nein, ich danke. Ich nehme nur grünen Salat dazu. Sonst nichts.

— Schön. Wünschen Sie etwas Obst?

— Ach ja. Wie sind die Birnen?

— Sehr gut.

— Schön. Und dazu bringen Sie mir eine Tasse Kaffee.

— Und was trinken Sie zum Essen? Vielleicht eine Flasche Wein?

— Nein, lieber ein Seidel Bier.

— Schön. Ich komme gleich zurück.

Am Ende der Mahlzeit sagt Herr Clark: ,,Bitte, zahlen, Herr Ober!"

— Hier ist die Rechnung.

— Ist der Bedienungszuschlag schon darin enthalten?

— Jawohl, zehn Prozent Bedienung.

Herr Clark bezahlt die Rechnung und verläßt das Restaurant.

— Good morning, sir. Here's the menu.

— Thanks. What do you recommend today?

— There's beefsteak with potatoes, veal cutlet, scrambled egg with ham, or fried eggs, besides cold cuts, pickled herring, or a vegetable dish.

— Fine. I should like veal cutlet. But bring me a pickled herring to start with.

— Certainly. Would you like some vegetable with the veal cutlet? The usual side dish is red cabbage.

— No, thanks. I'll just take lettuce with it. That will be all.

— Very well. Do you care for some fruit?

— Yes indeed. What are the pears like?

— Very good.

— All right. And with it bring me a cup of coffee.

— And what will you have to drink with your meal? How about a bottle of wine?

— No, I'd prefer a mug of beer.

— Good. I'll bring it straight away.

At the end of the meal Mr. Clark says, 'The bill please, waiter.'

— Here is your bill.

— Is the service charge included?

— Yes sir, ten per cent for service.

Mr. Clark pays the bill and leaves the restaurant.

The German Alphabet in Roman and German Type

As pointed out in Chapter 1, paragraph 4, German uses two styles of printing, the Roman type and the German or Gothic type. The latter is seldom used today.

Here is the German alphabet in Roman and German type, followed by a reading selection in both styles of printing. You will find little difficulty in reading the passage in German type.

ROMAN		GERMAN		ROMAN		GERMAN	
A	a	𝔄	a	S	s	𝔖	ſ s
B	b	𝔅	b	T	t	𝔗	t
C	c	ℭ	c	U	u	𝔘	u
D	d	𝔇	d	V	v	𝔙	v
E	e	𝔈	e	W	w	𝔚	w
F	f	𝔉	f	X	x	𝔛	x
G	g	𝔊	g	Y	y	𝔜	η
H	h	ℌ	h	Z	z	𝔷	z
I	i	ℑ	i	Ä	ä	*𝔄e	ä
J	j	ℑ	j	Ö	ö	*𝔒e	ö
K	k	𝔎	k	Ü	ü	*𝔘e	ü
L	l	𝔏	l				
M	m	𝔐	m	DOUBLE LETTERS			
N	n	𝔑	n	ch			ch
O	o	𝔒	o	ck			ck
P	p	𝔓	p	ss ß			ſſ
Q	q	𝔔	q	sz ß			ß
R	r	𝔑	r	tz			tz

Roman s in the German print is s at the end of a word or syllable. Otherwise it is ſ.

Thus: bis, Häuschen, Gras; but ſagen, ſprechen, geſehen. DO NOT confuse f (s) with ſ (f).

* Note that ae, oe, and ue may be substituted for ä, ö, and ü.

Exercise No. 160. Lesestück

FRAU CLARK KAUFT IM „SUPERMARKET" EIN

Es gibt in der Stadt London viele große und schöne Lebensmittelläden[1] mit Selbstbedienung,[2] die man „Supermarkets" nennt. Aber in der Vorstadt, wo die Familie Clark wohnt, gibt es nur einen solchen[3] Markt.

Eines Tages ging Frau Clark mit ihren beiden Jungen zum Einkaufen nach dem „Supermarket". Sie betraten den Laden durch jene wunderbare Tür, die sich von selbst öffnet, wenn man sich ihr nähert.[4] In der Nähe des Eingangs standen in einer Reihe viele Wägelchen.[5] Sie nahmen eines von diesen. Wilhelm, der jüngere Knabe, wollte in dem Wägelchen fahren, aber das erlaubte seine Mutter nicht. Sie sagte: „Mein Junge, diese Wagen sind kein Spielzeug."[6]

Frau Clark und ihre zwei Jungen gingen zuerst nach der Abteilung[7] für Obst und Gemüse. Hier kaufte sie 5 Pfund Kartoffel, eine Tüte[8] Äpfel, ein Dutzend Bananen und andere Gemüse. Von hier gingen sie nach der Abteilung, in der sich die Molkereiprodukte[9] befinden. Frau Clark nahm ein Dutzend Eier, drei Flaschen Milch, ein Pfund Butter und einige Pakete Käse.[10] In anderen Abteilungen des Ladens nahm sie Fleisch, Büchsenwaren,[11] Brot, Kaffee, Zucker und Tee.

Nun war alles in dem Wägelchen, und Frau Clark war bereit, zur Kasse zu treten, um für ihre Einkäufe zu bezahlen. Die Rechnung betrug £3. 8s. (drei Pfund und acht Schilling). Frau Clark gab dem Kassierer £5. – und bekam £1 12s. (ein Pfund zwölf) zurück. Der Kassierer tat all die Einkäufe in drei Tüten. Die Mutter nahm eine, und jeder Knabe nahm eine. Mit ihren Einkäufen in den Händen gingen sie zu dem Ausgang. Draußen fanden sie ihr Auto, stiegen ein und fuhren nach Hause.

NOTES: 1 provision stores, food markets. 2 self-service. 3 **solch,** such. 4 **sich nähern,** to approach. 5 little wagons (baskets on wheels). 6 **das Spielzeug,** toy. 7 section, department. 8 bag. 9 dairy products. 10 cheese. 11 tinned goods.

Frau Clark kauft im „Supermarket" ein

Es gibt in der Stadt London viele große und schöne Lebensmittelläden mit Selbstbedienung, die man „Supermarkets" nennt. Aber in der Vorstadt, wo die Familie Clark wohnt, gibt es nur einen solchen Markt.

Eines Tages ging Frau Clark mit ihren beiden Jungen zum Einkaufen nach dem „Supermarket". Sie betraten den Laden durch jene wunderbare Tür, die sich von selbst öffnet, wenn man sich ihr nähert. In der Nähe des Eingangs standen in einer Reihe viele Wägelchen. Sie nahmen eines von diesen. Wilhelm, der jüngere Knabe, wollte in dem Wägelchen fahren, aber das erlaubte seine Mutter nicht. Sie sagte „Mein Junge, diese Wagen sind kein Spielzeug".

Frau Clark und ihre zwei Jungen gingen zuerst nach der Abteilung für Obst und Gemüse. Hier kaufte sie 5 Pfund Kartoffel, eine Tüte Äpfel, ein Dutzend Bananen und andere Gemüse. Von hier gingen sie nach der Abteilung, in der sich die Molkereiprodukte befinden. Frau Clark nahm ein Dutzend Eier, drei Flaschen Milch, ein Pfund Butter und einige Pakete Käse. In anderen Abteilungen des Ladens nahm sie Fleisch, Büchsenwaren, Brot, Kaffee, Zucker und Tee.

Nun war alles in dem Wägelchen, und Frau Clark war bereit, zur Kasse zu treten, um für ihre Einkäufe zu bezahlen.

Die Rechnung betrug £3. 8s. (drei Pfund und acht Schilling). Frau Clark gab dem Kassierer £5. — und bekam £1. 12s. (ein Pfund zwölf) zurück. Der Kassierer tat all die Einkäufe in drei Tüten. Die Mutter nahm eine, und jeder Knabe nahm eine. Mit ihren Einkäufen in den Händen gingen sie zu dem Ausgang. Draußen fanden sie ihr Auto, stiegen ein und fuhren nach Hause.

CHAPTER 36

ANKUNFT IN MÜNCHEN
ARRIVAL IN MUNICH

Der erste Brief aus München

München, den 4. Juni 1967

Lieber Freund!

1 Als das Flugzeug in München landete, wurde ich mit der Zolluntersuchung bald fertig und ging in den Wartesaal.

2 Sofort kam mir ein fein aussehender Herr entgegen und fragte: ,,Ich bitte um Verzeihung, sind Sie Herr Clark?"

3 Ich antwortete: ,,Ja, ich bin's. Und Sie sind Herr Schiller, nicht wahr? Es freut mich sehr, Sie kennenzulernen." Wir gaben uns die Hand.

4 ,,Das Vergnügen ist ganz meinerseits," erwiderte Herr Schiller.

5 Sie erinnern sich wohl, Herr Müller, daß Herr Schiller der Vertreter unserer Firma in München ist.

6 Dann gingen wir zusammen hinaus und fuhren mit einem Taxi nach dem Hotel Königshof.

7 Das Taxi nahm den Weg nach der Stadt mit höchster Geschwindigkeit. Ich dachte mir: Die Taxifahrer sind überall gleich.

8 Als ich mich umschaute, sah ich, daß alles — Kraftwagen, Lastwagen, Autobusse, Taxis — mit rasender Geschwindigkeit eilte.

9 Schließlich schrie ich dem Taxifahrer zu: ,,Nicht so schnell fahren, bitte! Ich habe gar keine Eile!"

10 ,,Ich auch nicht, mein Herr!" antwortete er mir, indem er um die Ecke raste.

11 Endlich sind wir glücklich am Hotel angekommen und sind ausgestiegen. Herr Schiller ging mit mir hinein.

12 Ich ging zum Empfangschef und sagte zu ihm: ,,Guten Tag. Haben Sie ein Zimmer für Clark reserviert?"

13 ,,Willkommen in München, Herr Clark. Gewiß haben wir für Sie ein feines Zimmer reserviert. Es ist vorne im fünften Stock, Nummer 55."

14 ,,Sehr nett, schönen Dank. Was ist der Zimmerpreis, bitte?"

15 ,,Zwölf DM (Deutsche Mark) täglich, einschließlich der Bedienung."

16 ,,Schön. Wollen Sie bitte mein Gepäck hinauftragen lassen?"

17 ,,Sofort, Herr Clark. Hausdiener! — Aber Sie sprechen sehr gut Deutsch. Wie lange sind Sie schon in Deutschland?"

18 ,,Ich bin soeben angekommen," sagte ich, und war auf mich selbst recht stolz.

19 ,,Sind Sie zum Vergnügen hergereist?"

20 ,,Es ist eine Vergnügungsreise und auch eine Geschäftsreise."

21 Ich plauderte noch ein wenig mit Herrn Schiller, und dann sagten wir adieu.

Als er mich verließ, versprach Herr Schiller, mich anzurufen, um eine Verab-redung festzusetzen.

22 Ich ging im Fahrstuhl zu meinem Zimmer, Nummer 55, hinauf. Es ist ein sehr bequemes Zimmer. Mir fehlt nichts. Ich glaube, Herr Müller, daß es mir in Deutschland sehr gut gefallen wird.

Mit herzlichem Gruß,
Ihr Freund *R. Clark.*

Munich, 4th June, 1967

Dear Friend,

1 When the plane landed in Munich I soon finished with the customs inspection and went into the waiting room.

2 Immediately an elegant man came towards me and asked: 'I beg your pardon, are you Mr. Clark?'

3 I answered: 'Yes, I am. And you are Mr. Schiller, aren't you? I am delighted to meet you.' We shook hands.

4 'The pleasure is all mine,' answered Mr. Schiller.

5 You undoubtedly remember, Mr. Müller, that Mr. Schiller is the repre-sentative of our firm in Munich.

6 Then we went out together and rode in a taxi to the Königshof Hotel.

7 The taxi took the road towards the city at the highest speed. I thought to myself: taxi-drivers are the same everywhere.

8 When I looked around I saw that everything—cars, vans, buses, taxis—was hurrying in mad haste.

9 Finally, I cried out to the taxi-driver: 'Don't drive so fast, please! I am not at all in a hurry!'

10 'Neither am I, sir!' he answered, rushing around the corner.

11 Finally we arrived safely at the hotel and got out. Mr. Schiller went in with me.

12 I went to the manager and said to him: 'Good day. Have you reserved a room for Clark?'

13 'Welcome to Munich, Mr. Clark. Of course we have reserved a fine room for you. It is on the fifth floor front, No. 55.'

14 'Very nice, thank you. And what is the cost of the room, please?'

15 'Twelve marks per day, including service.'

16 'Good. Will you please have my luggage taken up?'

17 'Immediately, Mr. Clark. Porter! But you speak German very well. How long have you been in Germany?'

18 'I have just arrived,' said I, and was very proud of myself.

19 'Have you come here for a pleasure trip?'

20 'It is a pleasure trip and also a business trip.'

21 I chatted with Mr. Schiller a little longer and then we said good-bye. When he left me, Mr. Schiller promised to telephone me in order to arrange an appointment.

22 I went up in the lift to my room, No. 55. It is a very comfortable room. I lack nothing. I believe, Mr. Müller, that I shall like Germany very well.

With best wishes,
Your friend *R. Clark*

Wortschatz

die Eile, hurry
der Fahrstuhl = der Lift, elevator
der Empfángschef, hotel manager
die Geschwíndigkeit, speed
der Hausdiener, *pl.* -, hotel porter
die Verábredung, appointment
die Zolluntersuchung, customs inspection
sich erínnern, to remember

fest-setzen, to set, fix, arrange
um-schauen, to look around
fein aussehend, good-looking, elegant
stolz (auf + *acc.*), proud (of)
schließlich, finally
soében, just now
meinerseits, on my part

Strong Verbs

an-rufen	to call up	er ruft an	rief an	hat angerufen
an-schreien	to cry out to	er schreit an	schrie an	hat angeschrieen
hinauf-tragen	to carry up	er trägt hinauf	trug hinauf	hat hinaufgetragen
gefallen + *dat.*	to please	er gefällt	gefiel	hat gefallen

Deutsche Ausdrücke

kennenlernen, to become (get) acquainted, to get to know. **Es freut mich, Sie kennenzulernen.** I'm pleased to meet you. **Wann hast du sie kennengelernt?** When did you make her acquaintance? **Ich habe sie nie kennengelernt.** I have never met her.

Ich möchte sie kennenlernen. I should like to meet her. **Nun, morgen wirst du sie kennenlernen.** Well, tomorrow, you will meet her.

Nichts fehlt mir. I lack nothing (*lit.* nothing is lacking to me). **Ihm (ihr, Ihnen, etc.) fehlt nichts.** He (she, you, etc.) lacks nothing.

Exercise No. 161

Der Erste Dialog

AM FLUGHAFEN

1 Guten Tag. Herr Schiller. Erwarten Sie jemanden?

2 Jawohl, ich warte auf Herrn Clark, den Chef der Firma, die ich in München vertrete.

3 Kennen Sie ihn?

4 Ich kenne ihn nur durch die Korrespondenz. Aber ich habe seine Photographie, und ich glaube, ich werde ihn erkennen. Er ist ein Mann von ungefähr vierzig.

5 Um wieviel Uhr kommt er an?

6 Das Flugzeug ist um 10.10 Uhr fällig.

7 Hat es Verspätung?

8 Nein, es kommt zur rechten Zeit. Aha, da ist es schön! Es kommt an! Es landet!

9 Entschuldigen Sie, bitte, ich gehe hinüber, um Herrn Clark zu begrüßen.

1 Good morning, Mr. Schiller. Are you expecting someone?

2 Yes, sir, I am waiting for Mr. Clark, the head of the firm I represent in Munich.

3 Do you know him?

4 I know him only by correspondence. But I have his photo and I think I'll be able to recognize him. He is a man of about forty.

5 At what time is he due?

6 The plane is scheduled to arrive at 10.10.

7 Is it late?

8 No, it's on time. Ah, there it is! It's arriving! It is landing!

9 Excuse me, sir, I'm going over to greet Mr. Clark.

Exercise No. 162

Der Zweite Dialog
WILLKOMMEN IN DEUTSCHLAND

1 Sind Sie Herr Clark?

2 Ja, ich bin's. Und Sie sind Herr Schiller, nicht wahr?

3 Jawohl. Willkommen in Deutschland, Herr Clark. Wie ist es auf der Reise gegangen?

4 Außerordentlich gut! Ich freue mich, in Deutschland zu sein.

5 Ich bin sicher, daß es Ihnen hier sehr gut gefallen wird.

1 Are you Mr. Clark?

2 Yes, I'm he. And you are Mr. Schiller, aren't you?

3 Right. Welcome to Germany, Mr. Clark. How did the trip go?

4 Marvellously! I am very happy to be in Germany.

5 I am sure that you will like it here very much.

Grammar Notes and Practical Exercises

1 The Present Participle Used as an Adjective

The present participle is formed by adding **-d** to the infinitive. Thus:

redend	speaking	**folgend**	following	**aussehend**	looking
lachend	laughing	**plaudernd**	chatting	**kommend**	coming

Used as an adjective, the present participle takes adjective case endings:

Ein fein aussehender Mann kam mir entgegen. — A good-looking man came towards me.

Ich freue mich auf die kommenden Ferien. — I am looking forward to the coming holiday.

2 More *sein*-verbs (intransive Verbs Denoting a Change of Place or Condition)

Note the sein-verbs in the text, some familiar, some new.

landen	to land	er landet	landete	ist gelandet
eilen	to hurry	er eilt	eilte	ist geeilt
rasen	to rush (madly)	er rast	raste	ist gerast
her-reisen	to travel here	er reist her	reiste her	ist hergereist
werden	to become, to get	er wird	wurde	ist geworden
fahren	to ride, go	er fährt	fuhr	ist gefahren
hinauf-gehen	to go up	er geht hinauf	ging hinauf	ist hinaufgegangen
hinein-gehen	to go in	er geht hinein	ging hinein	ist hineingegangen
aus-steigen	to get out	er steigt aus	stieg aus	ist ausgestiegen
an-kommen	to arrive	er kommt an	kam an	ist angekommen

Exercise No. 163. Change these sentences to the present perfect. All the verbs are haben-verbs.

Beispiel: 1 Der Kaufmann hat Deutsch studiert.

1 Der Kaufmann studierte Deutsch. 2 Das Taxi nahm den Weg nach der Stadt. 3 Ich hatte gar keine Eile. 4 Sie plauderten noch ein wenig. 5 Mir fehlte nichts. 6 Es gefiel ihm in Deutschland sehr gut. 7 Er verbrachte viel Zeit in München. 8 Sein Freund versprach ihn zu treffen. 9 Er kaufte sich eine Fahrkarte. 10 Wann verließen Sie die Stadt?

Exercise No. 164. Change these sentences to the present perfect. All the verbs are sein-verbs.

Beispiel: 1 Das Flugzeug ist in München gelandet.

1 Das Flugzeug landete in München. 2 Er wurde mit der Zolluntersuchung bald fertig. 3 Dann gingen sie zusammen hinaus. 4 Ein fein aussehender Herr kam ihm entgegen. 5 Sie fuhren mit dem Taxi nach dem Hotel, 6 Das Taxi raste um die Ecke. 7 Es fuhr mit rasender Geschwindigkeit. 8 Endlich kam der Kaufmann glücklich im Hotel an. 9 Die zwei Herren gingen hinein. 10 Um wieviel Uhr stiegst du aus dem Taxi?

Exercise No. 165. Fragen

Lesen Sie noch einmal den Text: **Ankunft in München,** und dann beantworten Sie diese Fragen!

1 Wohin ging Herr Clark, als er mit der Zolluntersuchung fertig wurde? 2 Wer kam ihm im Wartesaal entgegen? 3 Was fragte dieser Herr? 4 Was erwiderte Herr Clark? 5 Wohin fuhren die zwei Herren in einem Taxi? 6 Fuhr das Taxi langsam oder mit größter Geschwindigkeit? 7 Was schrie Herr Clark dem Taxifahrer zu? 8 Was antwortete der Taxifahrer? 9 Wo sind sie endlich angekommen? 10 Wer ging mit Herrn Clark hinein? 11 Was für ein Zimmer hatte man für Herrn Clark reserviert? 12 In welchem Stock befand sich dieses Zimmer? 13 Was war der Zimmerpreis? 14 Was versprach Herr Schiller, als er Herrn Clark verließ?

CHAPTER 37

HERR CLARK BESUCHT DIE FAMILIE SCHILLER
MR. CLARK VISITS THE SCHILLER FAMILY

Zweiter Brief aus München

Lieber Freund!

1 Letzten Montag hat Herr Schiller mich angerufen, um mich für den folgenden Tag zum Essen einzuladen. Natürlich habe ich die Einladung sofort angenommen, denn die Gelegenheit, eine deutsche Familie zu besuchen, war mir sehr angenehm.

2 Ich mietete ein Taxi, und um sieben Uhr machten wir halt vor einem modernen Miethaus in der Thomasstraße.

3 Ich fuhr im Lift zur vierten Etage und klingelte. Da hörte ich sofort rasche Schritte. Ein junges Dienstmädchen öffnete die Tür und lud mich ein hereinzukommen.

4 Herr Schiller kam mir entgegen und begrüßte mich herzlich „Guten Abend, Herr Clark," sagte er, „es macht mir große Freude, Sie bei mir im Hause zu sehen."

5 Damit betraten wir das Wohnzimmer, welches in modernem Stil und geschmackvoll möbliert war. Ich sagte zu ihm: „Diese Wohnung ist sehr hübsch." Herr Schiller stellte mich seiner Frau und seinen Kindern, zwei ernsten und intelligenten Jungen, vor.

6 Die Jungen studieren auf dem Gymnasium. Der ältere möchte Arzt werden, und der jüngere will Anwalt werden.

7 Wir setzten uns zu Tisch, und Frau Schiller wartete mit einem ausgezeichneten deutschen Essen auf. Dieses begann mit einer Vorspeise, danach gab es Suppe, Fleisch mit zwei Sorten Gemüse, Salat, Obst, mehrere Weinsorten, einen Apfelstrudel und Kaffee.

8 Bei Tisch unterhielten wir uns über das Leben in Deutschland, über Kunst und Musik.

9 Nach dem Essen zogen sich die Jungen auf ihre eigenen Zimmer zurück, um ihre Hausaufgaben zu machen.

10 Dann setzte Frau Schiller sich ans Klavier, spielte verschiedene Musikstücke und sang einige deutsche Lieder.

11 Nachdem ich einen so gemütlichen Abend verbracht hatte, verließ ich das Haus, entzückt von meinen neuen Freunden.

12 Dann bin ich nach Hause, das heißt, nach dem Hotel, zurückgefahren.

Die herzlichsten Grüße von
Ihrem Freund

Robert Clark

Dear Friend,

1 Last Monday Mr. Schiller telephoned me to invite me for dinner on the following day. Naturally I accepted the invitation at once, for the opportunity of visiting a German family was very appealing to me.

2 I hired a taxi, and at seven o'clock we stopped in front of a modern block of flats in Thomas Street.

3 I went up to the fourth floor in the lift, and rang. There I immediately heard quick steps. A young housemaid opened the door and invited me to come in.

4 Mr. Schiller came towards me and greeted me cordially. 'Good evening, Mr. Clark,' said he, 'it gives me great pleasure to see you here in my house.'

5 With that we entered the living room, which was furnished tastefully in modern style. I said to him, 'This flat is very nice.' Mr. Schiller introduced me to his wife and to his children, two nice, intelligent boys.

6 The boys are studying at a Grammar School. The older would like to become a doctor, and the younger wants to become a lawyer.

7 We sat down at the table and Mrs. Schiller served an excellent German meal. This began with an hors d'œuvre, then there was soup, meat with two kinds of vegetables, a salad, fruit, several kinds of wine, apple 'strudel', and coffee.

8 At table we talked about life in Germany, about art and music.

9 After the meal the boys retired to their own rooms in order to do their homework.

10 Then Mrs. Schiller sat down at the piano, played various pieces of music, and sang some German songs.

11 After spending such a pleasant evening I left the house, charmed with my new friends.

12 Then I went home, that is to say, to the hotel.

Heartiest greetings from
Your friend
Robert Clark

Wortschatz

der Anwalt, *pl.* ⸚e, lawyer
das Dienstmädchen, *pl.* -, maidservant
die Etáge = der Stock, storey (of house)
die Hausaufgabe, *pl.* -n, homework
das Miethaus, *pl.* ⸚er, block of flats
die Vorspeise, *pl.* -n, hors d'œuvres
die Sorte, *pl.* -n, kind

klingeln, to ring (bell)
an-klingeln, to telephone
auf-warten, to serve, wait on
begrüßen, to greet
halt-machen, to stop
mieten, to rent
hübsch, pretty

Strong Verbs. Principal Parts

an-nehmen	to accept	er nimmt an	nahm an	hat angenommen
an-halten	to stop	er hält an	hielt an	hat angehalten
an-rufen	to ring (telephone)	er ruft an	rief an	hat angerufen
betreten	to step into, enter	er betritt	betrat	hat betreten
sich zurück-ziehen	to withdraw	er zieht sich zurück	zog sich zurück	hat sich zurückgezogen

Deutsche Ausdrücke

entzückt von, delighted with
   Er war von seinen Freunden entzückt. He was delighted with his friends.
anrufen, to ring
   Sie haben mich angerufen. They rang me.
jemanden einladen, to invite someone.
   Wir haben ihn zum Essen eingeladen. We invited him to dinner.
eine Einladung annehmen, to accept an invitation
   Er hat unsere Einladung angenommen. He accepted our invitation.
jemanden vorstellen, to introduce somebody
   Er stellte mich seiner Frau vor. He introduced me to his wife.
das heißt, that is to say
   Er will Arzt (Anwalt) werden. He wants to become a doctor (a lawyer).

Exercise No. 166

EIN TELEPHONGESPRÄCH

Herr Schiller ruft Herrn Clark an. Das folgende Gespräch findet statt.

Schiller: Bitte, ich möchte mit Herrn Clark sprechen.
Clark: Hier Clark. Wer da?
Schiller: Hier Schiller. Nun, Herr Clark, wie befinden Sie sich?
Clark: Ich danke, recht gut.
Schiller: Herr Clark, können Sie morgen Abend zu uns zum Essen kommen? Meine Frau und ich würden uns sehr freuen, wenn wir den Abend mit Ihnen verbringen könnten.
Clarke: Danke vielmals, Herr Schiller. Ich nehme Ihre freundliche Einladung mit Vergnügen an.
Schiller: Schön. Wir erwarten Sie also um sieben Uhr. Adieu, bis morgen Abend.

A TELEPHONE CONVERSATION

Mr. Schiller telephones Mr. Clark. The following conversation takes place.

Schiller: I'd like to speak to Mr. Clark, please.
Clark: This is Clark. Who is speaking?
Schiller: Schiller speaking. Well, Mr. Clark, how are you?
Clark: Quite well, thank you.
Schiller: Mr. Clark, can you come to dinner at our house tomorrow evening? My wife and I would be very happy if we could spend the evening with you.
Clark: Thank you very much, Mr. Schiller. I accept your kind invitation with pleasure.
Schiller: Good. Then we'll expect you at seven o'clock. Good-bye, until tomorrow night.

Exercise No. 167

EINE VORSTELLUNG

Herr Clark, Herr Schiller, Frau Schiller und die Kinder.

Clark: Guten Abend, Herr Schiller.
Schiller: Guten Abend, Herr Clark. Darf ich Ihnen meine Frau Marie vorstellen?

Clark: Es freut mich, Sie kennenzulernen.

Frau Schiller (lächelnd): Das Vergnügen ist ganz meinerseits. (Sie geben sich die Hand.)

Schiller: Und hier sind meine Jungen, Hans und Paul.

Clark: Es freut mich, Sie kennenzulernen.

Hans }
Paul } :Gleichfalls, Herr Clark.

(Sie geben sich die Hand.)

AN INTRODUCTION

Mr. Clark, Mr. Schiller, Mrs. Schiller and the children.

Clark: Good evening, Mr. Schiller.

Schiller: Good evening, Mr. Clark. May I introduce my wife Mary to you?

Clark: How do you do? (*lit.* I'm happy to make your acquaintance.)

Mrs. Schiller (smiling): How do you do? (*lit.* The pleasure is all mine.) (They shake hands.)

Schiller: And here are my boys, John and Paul.

Clark: How nice to meet you.

John }
Paul } :You, too, Mr. Clark (*lit.* same here).

(They shake hands.)

Grammar Notes and Practical Exercises

1 Prepositions with Special Meanings after Certain Verbs

You know the usual meanings of nearly all prepositions. After certain verbs some prepositions have special meanings. You are familiar with the following:

denken an + *acc.* to think of (to have in mind). **Der Kaufmann denkt immer an das Geschäft.** The businessman always thinks of business.

denken über + *acc.* to think about (have an opinion about). **Was denken Sie über meine kommende Reise?** What do you think about my coming trip?

warten auf + *acc.* to wait for. **Er wartete auf seinen Freund im Arbeitszimmer.** He was waiting for his friend in the study.

sich interessieren für + *acc.* to be interested in. **Er hat sich gar nicht für den Sport interessiert.** He was not at all interested in sports.

sich unterhalten über + *acc.* to converse about. **Sie unterhielten sich über das Klima in Deutschland.** They were discussing the climate of Germany.

sich freuen über + *acc.* to be happy about. **Sie freut sich über ihr neues Kostüm.** She is happy about her new suit.

sich freuen auf + *acc.* to look forward to. **Wir freuen uns auf die kommenden Ferien.** We are looking forward to the coming holidays.

sich vorbereiten auf + *acc.* to prepare for. **Er mußte sich auf die Prüfung vorbereiten.** He had to prepare for the examination.

bitten um + *acc.* to ask for. **Er bat um die Speisekarte.** He asked for the menu.

Note carefully the case which follows prepositions with special meanings. The *place where, place to which* rule does not apply to doubtful prepositions with special meanings.

Exercise No. 168. Complete these sentences in German.

Beispiel: 1 Bei Tisch haben wir uns über Kunst und Musik unterhalten.

1 **Bei Tisch haben wir uns** (about art and music) **unterhalten.** 2 **Ich freute mich** (about the invitation) **zum Abendessen und nahm sie sofort an.** 3 (I am looking forward to) **einen gemütlichen Abend.** 4 **Die Jungen des Kaufmanns** (are interested in) **Sport.** 5 (What do you think) **darüber?** 6 **Der Reisende** (is asking for) **eine Fahrkarte.** 7 **Herr Clark wartete gewöhnlich** (for his teacher) **im Arbeitszimmer.** 8 **Haben Sie sich** (for the trip) **vorbereitet?** 9 **Wir denken immer** (of the coming examinations). 10 (I am not thinking) **daran.**

Exercise No. 169. Fragen

Lesen Sie noch einmal den Text: **Herr Clark besucht die Familie Schiller, und dann beantworten Sie diese Fragen!**

1 **Wer hat Herrn Clark zum Abendessen eingeladen?** 2 **Wie kam Herr Clark zu der Wohnung des Herrn Schiller?** 3 **Wo machte das Taxi halt?** 4 **In welcher Etage befand sich die Wohnung der Familie Schiller?** 5 **Wer lud den Kaufmann ein hereinzukommen?** 6 **Wie begrüßte ihn Herr Schiller?** 7 **Wie war das Wohnzimmer möbliert?** 8 **Wem stellte Herr Schiller ihn vor?** 9 **Wo studieren die zwei Jungen?** 10 **Mit was für einem Essen wartete Frau Schiller auf?** 11 **Was gab es zum Dessert?** 12 **Worüber unterhielten sie sich bei Tisch?** 13 **Was taten die zwei Jungen nach dem Essen?** 14 **Wer spielte Klavier und sang einige Lieder?** 15 **Was für einen Abend hatte Herr Clark verbracht?**

CHAPTER 38

EIN AUSFLUG AN DEN AMMERSEE
AN EXCURSION TO AMMERSEE

Dritter Brief aus München

Lieber Freund!

1 Gestern rief ich die zwei Söhne des Herrn Schiller an und fragte sie: „Wollen Sie mit mir einen Ausflug im Auto nach dem Ammersee machen?" Sie nahmen mit Vergnügen an.

2 Heute früh holten mich meine jungen Freunde um 8.30 in meinem Hotel ab.

3 Die Jungen trugen einen Korb, in dem sich ein guter Imbiss befand, den Frau Schiller für uns zubereitet hatte.

4 Das Auto, welches ich gemietet hatte, wartete vor dem Hotel auf uns. Wir stiegen redend und lachend ein, und sieh da! wir waren unterwegs.

5 Wir waren schon an den Vororten der Stadt vorbeigefahren. Ich saß am Lenkrad und fuhr gemütlich entlang, als ich plötzlich einen Lärm hörte, den ich sofort erkannte.

6 „Was ist das? Was ist geschehen?" fragten die Jungen.

7 Ich hielt das Auto an, und wir stiegen aus. „Wir haben eine Reifenpanne," antwortete ich.

8 Ich wollte den Reifen wechseln, und die Jungen wollten mir helfen. Mit Vergnügen fingen sie an, den Wagenheber zu suchen. Aber leider befand sich kein Wagenheber in dem Werkzeugkasten. Was tun?

9 Von Zeit zu Zeit fuhr ein Auto mit großer Geschwindigkeit an uns vorbei. Trotz unsrer verzweifelten Signale hielt niemand an.

10 Es war sehr heiß, und die Sonne brannte auf unsere Köpfe nieder.

11 Endlich kam ein Lastwagen rasch herangefahren und hielt dann plötzlich vor uns an. Der Fahrer stieg herunter.

12 „Habt ihr eine Panne? Wünscht ihr Hilfe?"

13 „Jawohl. Aber wir haben keinen Wagenheber," sagte ich zu ihm. „Aber glücklicherweise haben wir ein Ersatzrad."

14 Der Lastwagenfahrer lieh uns seinen Wagenheber, und wir gingen alle an die Arbeit. In fünf Minuten war alles fertig.

15 Wir dankten ihm tausendmal, und ich versuchte, ihn für seine Hilfe zu bezahlen, aber er wollte nichts annehmen.

16 Dann gaben wir einander die Hand und sagten adieu. Der große Lastwagen machte sich wieder auf den Weg nach München, und wir fuhren auf der Landstraße nach dem Ammersee weiter.

17 Ohne weitere Unfälle erreichten wir unser Ziel. Wir ließen das Auto am Parkplatz und vertraten uns die Beine, indem wir eine kurze Strecke am See spazierten.

18 Dann mieteten wir ein Segelboot, und bald strichen wir über die Wellen.

Wir öffneten unseren Eßkorb und aßen mit tüchtigem Appetit. Bei Singen, Scherzen und Lachen verging die Zeit angenehm und schnell.

19 Es war schon spät am Nachmittag, als wir glücklich wieder zu Hause, das heißt an meinem Hotel, ankamen. Die beiden Jungen dankten mir herzlich für den vergnüglichen und abenteuerlichen Ausflug.

20 Nun muß ich aber schließen, denn heute abend gehe ich ins Konzert, und jetzt muß ich mich umkleiden. So verbleibe ich mit den herzlichsten Grüßen Ihr Freund,

Robert Clark

Dear Friend,

1 Yesterday I telephoned the two sons of Mr. Schiller and asked them: 'Would you like to make an excursion with me by car to Ammersee?' They accepted with pleasure.

2 This morning my young friends called for me at 8.30 at my hotel.

3 The boys were carrying a basket in which there was a good lunch that Mrs. Schiller had prepared for us.

4 The car that I had hired was waiting for us in front of the hotel. We got in, talking and laughing, and behold we were on our way.

5 We had already passed the suburbs of the city. I was at the wheel driving calmly along when all of a sudden I heard a noise that I recognized at once.

6 'What is it? What has happened?' the boys asked.

7 I stopped the car and we got out. 'We have a puncture,' I answered.

8 I wanted to change the tyre and the boys wanted to help me. Very pleased, they began to look for the jack. But unfortunately there was no jack in the tool box. What to do?

9 From time to time a car passed us at great speed. In spite of our desperate signals nobody stopped.

10 It was very hot and the sun was burning down upon our heads.

11 Finally, a lorry approached rapidly and then stopped suddenly in front of us. The lorry driver got down.

12 'Have you a puncture? Do you want help?'

13 'Yes, indeed. But we haven't a jack,' I said to him. 'Fortunately we have a spare wheel.'

14 The truck driver lent us his jack and we all set to work. In five minutes everything was ready.

15 We thanked him a thousand times, and I offered to pay him for his help, but he would not accept anything.

16 Then we shook hands and said good-bye. The big lorry again took to the road towards Munich and we continued on the road towards Ammersee.

17 Without further mishaps we reached our goal. We left the car in the parking area and stretched our legs by walking a short distance along the lake.

18 Then we hired a sailing boat, and soon we were sweeping over the waves. We opened our lunch basket and ate with hearty appetites. With singing, joking and laughing, the time passed pleasantly and quickly.

19 It was already late in the afternoon when we arrived safely again at home, that is, at my hotel. The two boys thanked me heartily for the pleasurable and adventurous excursion.

20 But now I must close, for I am going to a concert tonight and now I must change clothes. And so I remain with the most cordial greetings your friend,

Robert Clark

Wortschatz

das Bein, *pl.* **-e,** leg	**scherzen,** to joke, jest
die Hilfe, help	**strecken,** to stretch
der Imbiß, snack, lunch	**spaziéren,** to walk
der Kopf, *pl.* **¨e,** head	**zu-bereiten,** to prepare
die Landstraße, *pl.* **-n,** road, highway	**sich um-kleiden,** to change clothes
das Segelboot, *pl.* **-e,** sailboat	**unterwegs,** on the way
das Signál, *pl.* **-e,** signal	**vergnüglich,** pleasurable
der Unfall, *pl.* **¨e,** mishap	**trotz** (*prep.* + *gen.*), in spite of
die Welle, *pl.* **-n,** wave; **das Ziel,** *pl.* **-e,** goal	**einánder,** each other
lachen, to laugh	**nieder,** down; **nieder-brennen,** to burn down

Some Car Terms

das Auto, das Automobil, der Wagen, der Kraftwagen, car	**der Reifen,** tyre
VW (fau-ve:), short for **Volkswagen**	**die Panne,** puncture
der Fahrer, der Wagenfahrer, driver	**das Lenkrad,** steering wheel
der Lastwagen, lorry	**der Wagenheber,** jack
der Koffer, trunk	**der Parkplatz,** parking place
der Tank (Benzintank), tank, petrol tank	**das Ersatzrad,** spare wheel
	lenken, to steer

Deutsche Ausdrücke

an die Arbeit gehen, to set to work.
  Sie gingen alle an die Arbeit. They all set to work.
Wir gaben einander die Hand. We shook hands (*lit.* We gave to each other the hand).
sich auf den Weg machen, to set out
  Sie machten sich wieder auf den Weg. They set out (took to the road) again.
Das Auto hält an. The car stops.
  Er hielt das Auto an. He stopped the car.
sich die Beine vertreten, to stretch one's legs

Informal Letters

Terms of address: **Lieber Freund! Liebe Freundin! Lieber Karl! Liebe Anna! Liebes Fräulein Helene!** etc.
Dear Friend: Dear Charles: Dear Anna: Dear Miss Helen: etc.
Endings: **Mit herzlichem Gruß**   With a hearty greeting
  Mit den herzlichsten Grüssen   With the heartiest greetings
  Deine Freundin   ⎫
  Ihr Freund, Ihre Freundin, Dein Freund, ⎬ Your friend
                                                 ⎭
  Ihr Hans, Ihre Marie, Dein Hans, Deine Marie Your Hans, Your Marie
Forms of **du, dein, ihr, euer** are given a capital initial when used in a letter. Thus:
  Lieber Fritz! Ich habe heute Deinen Brief erhalten. Es freut mich zu hören, daß Du Deine Prüfungen gut bestanden hast. Ich gratuliere Dir. Dear Fritz, Today I received your letter. I am glad to hear that you passed the examinations well. I congratulate you.

Grammar Notes and Practical Exercises

1 More Strong (Irregular) Verbs. Principal Parts

helfen + dat. obj.	to help	er hilft	half	hat geholfen
heran-fahren	to ride up	er fährt heran	fuhr heran	ist herangefahren
hinweg-fahren	to ride along	er fährt hinweg	fuhr hinweg	ist hinweggefahren
vorbei-fahren	to ride past	er fährt vorbei	fuhr vorbei	ist vorbeigefahren
leihen	to lend	er leiht	lieh	hat geliehen
vergehen	to pass, to elapse	er vergeht	verging	ist vergangen
sich befinden	to be (located)	er befindet sich	befand sich	hat sich befunden

Exercise No. 170. Change these sentences to the past perfect. Remember! Haben-verbs have in the past perfect the auxiliary verb **ich hatte, du hattest,** etc.; sein-verbs have the auxiliary **ich war, du warst,** etc.

Beispiel: 1 Er hatte die zwei Söhne seines Vertreters angerufen.

1 Er rief die zwei Söhne seines Vertreters an. 2 Die Jungen holten ihn im Hotel ab. 3 Was trugen Sie im Korb? 4 Im Korb befand sich ein guter Imbiß. 5 Wer bereitete diesen guten Imbiß zu? 6 Wartete er lange auf sie? 7 Sie fuhren an den Vororten vorbei. 8 Erkanntest du bald den Lärm? 9 Plötzlich hielt der Lastwagen vor ihnen an. 10 Was ist geschehen? 11 Der Fahrer half ihnen, den Reifen zu wechseln. 12 Er lieh ihnen seinen Wagenheber.

2 The Principal Parts of the Modal Auxiliaries

Infinitive	*Present*	*Past*	*Present Perfect*
dürfen	er darf	durfte	hat gedurft (dürfen)
können	er kann	konnte	hat gekonnt (können)
mögen	er mag	mochte	hat gemocht (mögen)
müssen	er muß	mußte	hat gemußt (müssen)
sollen	er soll	sollte	hat gesollt (sollen)
wollen	er will	wollte	hat gewollt (wollen)

The principal parts of modals follow the pattern of weak verbs, except that the present tense is irregular and the **Umlaut** is dropped in the participle. Note, however, that each modal has a substitute for the past participle, which is identical in form with the infinitive. The past participle is used when the modal has no complementary infinitive. The infinitive substitute is used when the modal has a complementary infinitive. Thus:

Der Mann hat kein Geld **gewollt.**	The man did not want any money.
Der Mann hat kein Geld **annehmen wollen.**	The man did not want to accept any money.

Compare a modal in five tenses with and without a complementary infinitive.

	without a complementary infinitive	*with a complementary infinitive*
Present	**Wir mögen** ihn nicht.	**Wir mögen** ihn nicht sehen.
Past	**Wir mochten** ihn nicht.	**Wir mochten** ihn nicht sehen.

without a complimentary infinitive	*with a complimentary infinitive*
Pres. Perf. **Wir haben** ihn nicht **gemocht.**	Wir haben ihn nicht **sehen mögen.**
Past Perf. **Wir hatten** ihn nicht **gemocht.**	Wir hatten ihn nicht **sehen mögen.**
Future **Wir werden** ihn nicht **mögen.**	**Wir werden** ihn nicht **sehen mögen.**

In general, use the past tense of the modal rather than the present perfect to express past time.

3 The Double Infinitive with *lassen, sehen,* and *hören*

The double infinitive construction (see above with the modals) is also generally used with **lassen, sehen,** and **hören** when these verbs have a complementary infinitive.

Ich habe es dort gelassen.	I have left it there.
Ich habe es dort liegen lassen.	I have left it lying there.
Wir haben ihn gesehen.	We have seen him.
Wir haben ihn tanzen sehen.	We have seen him dance.

Exercise No. 171. Change these sentences to the present perfect and past perfect tenses.

Beispiel: 1 Herr Clark hat (hatte) eine Reise machen müssen.

1 Herr Clark mußte eine Reise machen. 2 Die Jungen wollten helfen. 3 Du durftest das Zimmer verlassen. 4 Ich konnte leider nicht mitgehen. 5 Wir mochten nicht spielen. 6 Ich mußte einen Brief schreiben. 7 Der Mann wollte nichts annehmen. 8 Während des Sommers konnten wir nicht aufs Land gehen. 9 Trotz der Hitze mußten sie in der Stadt bleiben. 10 Trotz des Regens wollten sie Fußball spielen.

Exercise No. 172. Fragen

Lesen Sie noch einmal den Text: **Ein Ausflug an den Ammersee,** und dann beantworten Sie diese Fragen!

1 Wen rief Herr Clark an? 2 Wohin wollte Herr Clark einen Ausflug im Auto machen? 3 Wen lud er ein, mit ihm zu fahren? 4 Wo holten die Jungen Herrn Clark ab? 5 Was war in dem Korb, den die Jungen trugen? 6 Wer hatte den guten Imbiß für sie zubereitet? 7 Was hörte Herr Clark plötzlich, als er gemütlich entlangfuhr? 8 Was war geschehen? 9 Warum konnten sie den Reifen nicht wechseln? 10 Was für ein Wagen hielt plötzlich vor ihnen an? 11 Was lieh ihnen der Wagenfahrer? 12 In wievielen Minuten war alles fertig?

CHAPTER 39

HERR CLARK VERLÄSST DEUTSCHLAND
MR. CLARK LEAVES GERMANY

Brief aus Hamburg

Lieber Freund!

1 Als ich London verließ, hatte ich, wie Sie wissen, bereits vieles über Deutschland gelernt. Ich hatte einige interessante Bücher über die Geschichte und die Sitten des Landes gelesen. Ich konnte schon ziemlich gut Deutsch sprechen. Nun, da ich im Begriff bin, Deutschland zu verlassen, scheint es mir, daß ich viel fließender Deutsch spreche.

2 Ich habe viele Plätze besucht, von denen wir in unseren Gesprächen geredet haben. Wie Sie sich wohl vorstellen können, gefielen mir die Sehenswürdigkeiten Deutschlands, seine schönen Landschaften, seine alten Städte, seine Musik, seine gute Küche sehr gut. Es machte mir viel Freude, mit den Deutschen in ihrer eigenen Sprache zu reden, wodurch ich vieles über sie lernte, was ich nicht aus den Büchern erlernen konnte.

3 Das Leben in den Städten Deutschlands scheint mir nicht ruhiger zu sein als in unseren Städten, und die Taxifahrer rasen ebenso wild einer wie in anderen Ländern. Sie werden sich wohl erinnern, ich habe Ihnen geschrieben, wie der Taxifahrer mich mit solch rasender Geschwindigkeit von dem Flugplatz zu meinem Hotel brachte.

4 Wie Sie wissen, war meine Reise nach Deutschland nicht nur eine Geschäftsreise sondern auch eine Vergnügungsreise. Glücklicherweise konnte ich die Geschäftsangelegenheiten rasch erledigen und danach konnte ich mich ganz dem Vergnügen hingeben. Ich habe kaum Zeit gefunden, Ihnen auch nur ein paar Briefe aus Deutschland zu senden. Ich werde Ihnen aber viel zu erzählen haben über die Leute, die ich kennengelernt, die Plätze, die ich besucht, und über Alles, was ich von dem Leben, den Sitten, und den Künsten Deutschlands gelernt habe.

5 Ich werde sicherlich Deutschland bald wieder besuchen. Ich möchte sogar schon im kommenden Jahr wieder dahin. Aber nächstes Mal nehme ich meine Familie mit. Ich muß Ihnen gestehen, ich habe meine Frau und Kinder auf meiner Reise sehr vermißt und hatte oft Heimweh.

Dies ist der letzte Brief, den ich Ihnen schreibe, ehe ich nach London abreise. Es wird mir ein Vergnügen sein, Sie bei meiner Ankunft anzurufen, um Sie einzuladen, möglichst bald bei uns zu Abend zu speisen.

6 Zweifellos werden wir viele Stunden im Gespräch über Deutschland verbringen, besonders über München und Umgebung, denn diese Stadt lernte ich wirklich lieben.

Mit herzlichen Grüßen
Ihr Freund
R. Clark

Dear Friend

1 As you know, when I left London, I had already learned a great deal about Germany. I had read some interesting books on the history and customs of that country. I already knew how to speak German fairly well. Now that I am about to leave Germany, it seems to me that I am speaking German much more fluently.

2 I have visited many places of which we have spoken in our conversations. As you may well imagine, I liked immensely the places of interest in Germany, its beautiful landscapes, its old cities, its music, its good food. I enjoyed talking to Germans in their own language, thus learning many things about them which I could not acquire from books.

3 Life in the cities of Germany does not seem more tranquil to me than in our cities, and taxi-drivers rush about as madly as in other countries. You will probably remember I wrote to you about how the taxi-driver brought me at breakneck speed from the airport to my hotel.

4 As you know, my trip to Germany was not only a business trip but also a pleasure trip. Luckily I was able to settle my business matters quickly, and after that I was able to devote myself entirely to recreation. I have hardly found time to send you even a few letters from Germany. I shall, however, have much to tell you about the people I have met, the places I have visited and all I have learned about the life, customs, and arts of Germany.

5 I am sure I shall visit Germany again soon. I should even like to go back next year. But the next time I go I shall take my family with me. I must confess to you I missed my wife and children very much on my trip and was often homesick.

This is the last letter which I am writing to you before I leave for London. It will give me great pleasure to ring you on my arrival and to invite you to have dinner with us as soon as possible.

6 Without doubt we shall spend many hours speaking of Germany and especially of Munich and its surroundings, for I have really learned to love this city.

With heartiest greetings
Your Friend

R. Clark

Wortschatz

das Heimweh, homesickness	**sich hin-geben,** to devote oneself
die Sitte, *pl.* **-n,** custom	**scheinen,** to seem, shine (*past* **schien**)
einhér-rasen, to rush madly about	**speisen,** to dine
erlérnen, to learn, acquire	**vermíssen,** to miss
erlédigen, to settle, finish	**kaum,** scarcely, hardly
handeln von, to deal with	**sogar,** even

Deutsche Ausdrücke

Heimweh haben, to be homesick

Er hatte Heimweh, als er in Deutschland war. He was homesick when he was in Germany.

sich erinnern an + *acc.*, to remember, to recall (*lit.* to remind oneself of)

Erinnern Sie sich an Ihre Ankunft in Deutschland? Do you remember your arrival in Germany? **Ja, ich erinnere mich daran.** Yes, I remember it (*lit.* I remind myself of it). **Wir erinnern uns alle daran.** We all remember it.

Grammar Notes and Practical Exercises

1 Summary of German word order in simple sentences and main clauses

(*a*) Normal word order
  Der Kaufmann schrieb gestern an seinen Vertreter.
  In normal word order the verb follows the subject.
(*b*) Inverted word order.
  Gestern schrieb der Kaufmann einen Brief an seinen Vertreter.
  Schrieb der Kaufmann gestern einen Brief an seinen Vertreter?
In inverted order the verb precedes the subject. Inverted word order is used in questions and when the sentence or noun clause begins with words other than the subject (adverbs, phrases, objects).
(*c*) Position of the separable prefix
  Die Kinder stehen gewöhnlich früh **auf.**
  Am Tage der Abfahrt **standen die Kinder** früh **auf.**
In the present and past tenses the separable prefix stands at the end of the simple sentence or main clause.
(*d*) Position of the past participle
  Er hat vieles über Deutschland **gelernt.**
  Ich hatte einige interessante Bücher **gelesen.**
  Die ganze Familie ist heute früh **aufgestanden.**
In the present perfect and past perfect tenses the past participle stands at the end of a simple sentence or main clause. The **ge-** of the past participle of a separable verb stands between the prefix and the verb.
(*e*) Position of the infinitive
  1 **Ich werde** Deutschland bald wieder **besuchen.**
  2 **Ich konnte** die Geschäftsangelegenheiten rasch **erledigen.**
  3 **Ich bin** jetzt im Begriff, **Deutschland zu verlassen.**
  4 **Die Passagiere begannen, in den Zug einzusteigen.**
In the future the infinitive stands last in the sentence or main clause (Sentence 1). Complementary infinitives stand last (Sentences 2, 3, 4). If the infinitive has **zu,** it is set off by commas, after the rest of the sentence or clause (Sentences 3, 4).

2 Summary of word order in subordinate clauses

(*a*) Es scheint mir, **daß ich** schon fließender Deutsch **spreche.**
  Er las einige Bücher, **die** von der Geschichte Deutschlands **handelten.**
In subordinate clauses, whether introduced by a subordinate conjunction or by a relative pronoun, the verb stands last.
(*b*) Ich bin sicher, **daß ich** Deutschland wieder **besuchen werde.**
  Ich habe die Städte besucht, **von denen** wir heute **geredet haben.**
If the verb in the subordinate clause has an auxiliary, the auxiliary part of the verb stands last.
(*c*) **Als Herr Clark** nach Deutschland **abreiste, sprach er** schon ziemlich gut Deutsch.
The separable prefix does not separate from the verb in subordinate word order.
If the subordinate clause comes first, the main clause has inverted word order.

Exercise No. 173. Ergänzen Sie diese Sätze auf deutsch! (Complete these sentences in German.)

Beispiel: 1 Ehe er London verließ, hatte er vieles über Deutschland gelernt.

1 (Before he left London), **hatte er vieles über Deutschland gelernt. 2 Hatte er**

(some interesting books) **gelesen?** 3 **Kannst du** (speak German quite well)?
4 **Es scheint mir,** (that he is speaking German much more fluently). 5 **Er
besuchte alle Plätze,** (about which we have spoken). 6 (Did you like) **die
Sehenswürdigkeiten Deutschlands?** 7 **Mir gefielen** (its music and good cuisine).
8 **Er lernte vieles, was** (he could not acquire out of books). 9 **Das Leben in den
deutschen Städten** (is not more tranquil than in our cities). 10 (I remember)
die rasende Fahrt im Taxi. 11 **Meine Reise war** (not only) **eine Geschäftsreise,**
(but also) **eine Vergnügungsreise.** 12 **Konnten Sie die Geschäftsangelegenheiten**
(to finish quickly)? 13 (Yes, and after that I was able) **mich ganz dem Vergnügen hingeben.** 14 **Er hat vieles** (about the life and customs) **Deutschlands
gelernt.** 15 **Sobald ich zu Hause bin,** (I shall telephone you). 16 (He was homesick), **weil er seine Frau und Kinder vermißte.** 17 **Nächstes Mal** (he will take the
family). 18 **Werden Sie** (have supper with us)? 19 **Dies ist der letzte Brief**
(which I shall write). 20 **Später** (I shall tell you everything).

Exercise No. 174. Lesen Sie noch einmal den Text: **Herr Clark verläßt
Deutschland,** und dann beantworten Sie diese Fragen!

1 **Wer ist im Begriff, Deutschland zu verlassen?** 2 **Was hat ihm in Deutschland
sehr gefallen?** 3 **War Herrn Clarks Reise nur eine Geschäftsreise?** 4 **Was konnte
er rasch erledigen?** 5 **Hat er Zeit gefunden, viele Briefe zu schreiben?** 6 **Wann
möchte Herr Clark wieder nach Deutschland reisen?** 7 **Beabsichtigt er, allein zu
gehen?** 8 **Wen hatte er vermißt?** 9 **Wen wird er bei seiner Ankunft in London
anrufen?** 10 **Wie wird er viele Stunden mit Herrn Müller verbringen?**

CHAPTER 40

REVISION OF CHAPTERS 36-39

Weak (Regular) Verbs. No Vowel Changes

1 eilen	10 erlernen	1 to hurry	10 to acquire (learn)
2 handeln (von)	11 auf-warten	2 to deal (with)	11 to serve, to wait on
3 lachen	12 ab-holen	3 to laugh	12 to go to meet
4 landen	13 halt-machen	4 to land	13 to stop
5 scherzen	14 her-reisen	5 to joke	14 to travel here
6 spazieren	15 vor-stellen	6 to walk	15 to introduce
7 begrüßen	16 zu-bereiten	7 to greet	16 to prepare
8 erwidern	17 sich um-kleiden	8 to answer	17 to change clothes
9 erledigen	18 sich um-schauen	9 to settle, finish	18 to look around

Strong (Irregular) Verbs. Vowel Changes

helfen	to help	er hilft	half	hat geholfen
leihen	to lend	er leiht	lieh	hat geliehen
scheinen	to shine, to seem	er scheint	schien	hat geschienen
betreten	to enter, step into	er betritt	betrat	hat betreten
vergehen	to pass, elapse	er vergeht	verging	ist vergangen
an-nehmen	to accept	er nimmt an	nahm an	hat angenommen
an-rufen	to call to	er ruft an	rief an	hat angerufen
an-schreien	to cry out to	er schreit an	schrie an	hat angeschrieen
an-halten	to stop	er hält an	hielt an	hat angehalten
fliegen	to fly	er fliegt	flog	ist geflogen

Deutsche Ausdrücke

1 **kennenlernen,** to get to know, to become acquainted with
Ich habe ihn eben kennengelernt.

2 **anrufen,** to telephone
Ich habe ihn angerufen.

3 **jemanden vorstellen,** to introduce somebody
Herr Schiller hat ihn seiner Frau vorgestellt.

4 **an die Arbeit gehen,** to set to work
Sie gingen sofort an die Arbeit.

5 **Heimweh haben,** to be homesick
Herr Clark hatte Heimweh.

6 **sich erinnern an,** to remember
Ich konnte mich nicht an ihn erinnern.
I could not remember him.

Exercise No. 175. Complete the translation of each English sentence.

1 I have helped him with the letter.

2 The lorry driver lent them a jack.

3 On the way they were joking and laughing.

1 **Ich —— ihm mit dem Brief ——.**

2 **Der Wagenfahrer —— ihnen einen Wagenheber.**

3 **Auf dem Wege —— und —— sie.**

4 The time passed quickly and merrily.	4 Die Zeit —— schnell und fröhlich.
5 He has invited us to dinner.	5 Er —— uns zum Essen ——.
6 We have accepted the invitation.	6 Wir —— die Einladung ——.
7 'Stop!' he cried out to the driver.	7 „Halt!" —— er den Fahrer an.
8 The taxi driver did not stop.	8 Der Taxifahrer —— nicht an.
9 We entered a nicely furnished living-room.	9 Wir —— ein schön möbliertes Wohnzimmer.
10 Mr. Schiller greeted us most warmly.	10 Herr Schiller —— uns aufs herzlichste.
11 May I introduce my wife Mary to you?	11 Darf ich Ihnen meine Frau Marie ——?
12 After dinner we shall go for a walk to the English Garden.	12 Nach dem Essen —— wir einen Spaziergang im „Englischen Garten" ——.

Exercise No. 176. Ergänzen (Complete) Sie die Sätze auf deutsch!

1 **Herr Clark** (is a businessman in London).
2 **Er machte eine Reise nach München,** (in order to visit the representative of his firm).
3 (He wanted) **ihn persönlich kennenlernen.**
4 **Bevor er London verließ,** (he had learned German).
5 (He had) **einen sehr guten Lehrer.**
6 **Er konnte** (speak, read and write German).
7 **Er las einige Bücher** (about Germany).
8 (He wrote) **einen Brief an seinen Vertreter.**
9 **Nach einigen Tagen** (he received an answer).
10 ('I shall call for you at the airport,') **schrieb ihm sein Vertreter.**
11 **Herr Schiller** (called for him there).
12 **Sie nahmen ein Taxi,** (and rode to the hotel).
13 (Luckily) **erledigte er bald seine Geschäftsangelegenheiten.**
14 **Während seines Aufenthalts in München** (he took a trip to the Ammersee).
15 **Die Söhne des Herrn Schiller** (went with him).
16 (He visited the places) **in der Nähe von München.**
17 **Nach zwei Wochen,** (he left Munich and went for a trip up the Rhine).
18 **Der Rhein ist** (the longest, the broadest and the most beautiful) **Fluß Deutschlands.**
19 (Finally he rode) **mit dem Zug nach Hamburg.**
20 **Von Hamburg** (he flew back to London).
21 **Nächstes Jahr** (Mr. Clark will again make a journey to Germany).
22 **Aber diesmal** (he will take his family with him).

Dialog

AN DER TANKSTELLE

Herr Clark geht zur Tankstelle, um den Tank des Autos anfüllen zu lassen, denn das Benzin ist beinahe alle. Sofort nähert sich ein junger Tankwart, um ihn zu bedienen.

T: Guten Tag, mein Herr, womit kann ich dienen?

C: Guten Tag. Sie dürfen volltanken.

T: Gewöhnliches Benzin oder Super?

C: Was kostet das Benzin?

T: Gewöhnliches kostet 58 Pfennig, Super 64 Pfennig.

C: Für diesen Wagen genügt das einfache Benzin. Wollen Sie so gut sein, auch Öl, Luft und Kühlwasser nachzusehen?

T: Ist gern geschehen.

Der junge Mann füllt den Tank, prüft das Öl, Kühlwasser und die Reifen.

T: Alles in Ordnung.

C: Schönen Dank. Wieviel bin ich schuldig?

T: Im ganzen siebzehn Mark vierzig.

Herr Clark gibt ihm zwei Zehnmarkscheine, und der junge Mann gibt ihm zwei Mark und sechzig Pfennig zurück.

AT THE PETROL STATION

Mr. Clark goes to the petrol station to have the tank of the car filled up, for the petrol is almost all used up. At once a young attendant approaches to serve him.

A: Good day, sir, what can I do for you?

C: Good day. You may fill up the tank.

A: Ordinary petrol or super?

C: What is the price of petrol?

A: Ordinary costs 58 pfennigs, super costs 64 pfennigs.

C: For this car the plain petrol is good enough. And will you please check the oil, air, and water?

A: With pleasure.

The young man fills up the tank, checks the oil, water, and the tyres.

A: Everything is in order.

C: Thank you very much. How much do I owe you?

A: Altogether seventeen marks and forty pfennigs.

Mr. Clark gives him two ten-mark notes and the young man gives him two marks and sixty pfennigs change.

Exercise No. 177. Lesestück 1

DAS DEUTSCHE FERNSEHEN[1]

In England besitzen 80% oder mehr der Einwohner einen Fernsehapparat. In Deutschland ist das nicht der Fall. Fernsehapparate befinden sich bei einer Minderheit[2] der Einwohner, aber die Zahl jener Familien, die Fernsehapparate besitzen, nimmt[3] fortwährend[4] zu, daher auch die Zahl der Personen, die zu Hause fernsehen[5] können.

Es gibt einen wichtigen Unterschied zwischen dem Fernsehen in England und in Deutschland. Jedermann kennt die Reklamebilder,[6] die fast jede Fernsehung begleiten, sei es ein Fernsehspiel, eine Oper, ein Dokumentarbericht,[7] aktuelle Reportage[8] oder Direktübertragung.[9] Das ist beim Fernsehen höchst störend,[10] besonders weil die Reklame oft mitten in dem interessantesten und aufregendsten[11] Teil des Programms vorkommt.[12] Und man ist gezwungen,[13] sich das anzuhören.

Bei dem deutschen Fernsehen ist es anders. Da gibt es keine Reklame, also kann der deutsche Fernsehteilnehmer[11] die interessantesten Fernsehprogramme ohne störende Unterbrechungen[15] genießen. Jeder Besitzer eines Fernsehapparats muß eine monatliche Fernsehgebühr[16] von 5 DM zahlen. Das ist der Beitrag[17] jedes Fernsehapparatbesitzers[18] zu den Kosten des Fernsehbetriebs.[19] Wenn das nur bei uns möglich wäre![20]

NOTES: 1 television. 2 minority. 3 zu-nehmen, to increase. 4 continually. 5 to watch TV. 6 Rekláme, advertisement, advertising. 7 documentary. 8 on-the-spot reporting. 9 live transmission. 10 disturbing. 11 most exciting. 12 to occur. 13 forced. 14 participant in television (viewer). 15 interruptions. 16 television fee. 17 contribution. 18 owner of television set. 19 TV industry. 20 wäre (were), is a subjunctive form. You will learn about the subjunctive in Chapter 41.

Das deutſche Fernſehen

In England beſitzen 80% oder mehr der Einwohner einen Fernſehapparat. In Deutſchland iſt das nicht der Fall. Fernſehapparate befinden ſich bei einer Minderheit der Einwohner, aber die Zahl jener Familien, die Fernſehapparate beſitzen, nimmt fortwährend zu, daher auch die Zahl der Perſonen, die zu Hauſe fernſehen können.

Es gibt einen wichtigen Unterſchied zwiſchen dem Fernſehen in England und in Deutſchland. Jedermann kennt die Reklamebilder, die faſt jede Fernſehung begleiten, ſei es ein Fernſehſpiel, eine Oper, ein Dokumentarbericht, aktuelle Reportage oder Direktübertragung. Das iſt beim Fernſehen höchſt ſtörend, beſonders weil die Reklame oft mitten in dem intereſſanteſten und aufregendſten Teil des Programms vorkommt. Und man iſt gezwungen, ſich das anzuhören.

Bei dem deutſchen Fernſehen iſt es anders. Da gibt es keine Reklame, alſo kann der deutſche Fernſehteilnehmer die intereſſanteſten Fernſehprogramme ohne ſtörende Unterbrechungen genießen. Jeder Beſitzer eines Fernſehapparats muß eine monatliche Fernſehgebühr von 5 DM zahlen. Das iſt der Beitrag jedes Fernſehapparatbeſitzers zu den Koſten des Fernſehbetriebs. Wenn das nur bei uns möglich wäre!

Exercise No. 178. Lesestück 2

HERRN CLARKS RHEINREISE

Nachdem er seine Geschäfte in München erledigt hatte, machte Herr Clark eine Vergnügungsreise durch das Rheinland, zum Teil per Dampfer und zum Teil mit der Eisenbahn.

Man behauptet[1] mit Recht, daß der Rhein einer der schönsten Flüsse Europas ist. Auf der Strecke von Mainz bis Köln bewunderte Herr Clark die dunklen Wälder, die terrassenförmigen Weinberge,[2] die kleinen Dörfer mit ihren altertümlichen[3] Kirchen und Häusern, und die Ruinen alter Schlösser.

Jetzt fuhr der Dampfer an dem Loreleifelsen vorbei. Jedermann kennt die Legende von der Zauberin,[4] die mit ihrem Singen die armen Schiffer in den Tod lockte.[5] Diese Legende hat Heinrich Heine in dem berühmten Liede: „Ich weiß nicht, was soll es bedeuten, daß ich so traurig bin", verewigt.[6]

Bald danach erschien[7] der Drachenfels,[8] wo (der Legende nach) der Held Siegfried einen Drachen erschlug.[9] Die Legende erzählt, daß er sich im Blut des

Drachen badete, um unverwundbar[10] zu werden. In solchen Legenden aus dieser Gegend fand Richard Wagner den Stoff für manche seiner bekannten Opern, wie z.B. Das Rheingold, Siegfried usw.

In einigen der berühmten Rheinstädte hielt das Schiff an. Also konnte Herr Clark die Stadt Mainz, den Geburtsort von Johann Gutenberg, der die Buchdruckerkunst[11] erfunden hat[12], besuchen.

Dann kam Bonn, die Stätte einer alten Universität und seit dem zweiten Weltkrieg die Hauptstadt Westdeutschlands. In dieser Stadt wurde Ludwig van Beethoven geboren.

Der nächste Haltepunkt war Köln. Bewundernswert[13] vor allem ist hier der weltberühmte Kölner Dom, dessen Türme mehr als 500 Fuß in die Höhe ragen.[14]

Die letzte Rheinstadt, die Herr Clark besuchte, war Düsseldorf, die Geburtsstadt des großen deutschen Lyrikers[15] Heinrich Heine.

Von Düsseldorf gings nach Hamburg, wo Herr Clark einige Geschäfte zu erledigen hatte, und von wo aus er die Heimreise per Flugzeug unternahm.

Als Herr Clark wieder zu Hause war, sprach er oft von seiner interessanten und vergnügungsvollen[16] Rheinreise.

NOTES: 1 asserts. 2 terraced vineyards. 3 quaint. 4 sorceress. 5 enticed. 6 immortalized. 7 **erscheinen (erschien, ist erschienen)**, to appear. 8 Dragon Rock. 9 **erschlagen (erschlug, hat erschlagen)**, to kill. 10 invulnerable. 11 art of printing. 12 **erfinden (erfand, hat erfunden)**, to invent. 13 worthy of admiration, remarkable. 14 **in die Höhe ragen**, tower on high. 15 lyric poet. 16 pleasurable.

Herrn Clarks Rheinreise

Nachdem er seine Geschäfte in München erledigt hatte, machte Herr Clark eine Vergnügungsreise durch das Rheinland, zum Teil per Dampfer und zum Teil mit der Eisenbahn.

Man behauptet mit Recht, daß der Rhein einer der schönsten Flüsse Europas ist. Auf der Strecke von Mainz bis Köln bewunderte Herr Clark die dunklen Wälder, die terrassenförmigen Weinberge, die kleinen Dörfer mit ihren altertümlichen Kirchen und Häusern, und die Ruinen alter Schlösser.

Jetzt fuhr der Dampfer an dem Loreleifelsen vorbei. Jedermann kennt die Legende von der Zauberin, die mit ihrem Singen die armen Schiffer in den Tod lockte. Diese Legende hat Heinrich Heine in dem berühmten Liede „Ich weiß nicht, was soll es bedeuten, daß ich so traurig bin," verewigt.

Bald danach erschien der Drachenfels, wo (der Legende nach) der Held Siegfried einen Drachen erschlug. Die Legende erzählt, daß er sich im Blut des Drachen badete, um unverwundbar zu werden. In solchen Legenden aus dieser Gegend fand Richard Wagner den Stoff für manche seiner bekannten Opern, wie z.B. Das Rheingold, Siegfried usw.

In einigen der berühmten Rheinstädte hielt das Schiff an. Also konnte Herr Clark die Stadt Mainz, den Geburtsort von Johann Gutenberg, der die Buchdruckerkunst erfunden hat, besuchen.

Dann kam Bonn, die Stätte einer alten Universität und seit dem zweiten Weltkrieg die Hauptstadt Westdeutschlands. In dieser Stadt wurde Ludwig van Beethoven geboren.

Der nächste Haltepunkt war Köln. Bewundernswert vor allem ist hier der weltberühmte Kölner Dom, dessen Türme mehr als 500 Fuß in die Höhe ragen.

Die letzte Rheinstadt, die Herr Clark besuchte, war Düsseldorf, die Geburts= stadt des großen deutschen Lyrikers Heinrich Heine.

Von Düsseldorf gings nach Hamburg, wo Herr Clark einige Geschäfte zu erledigen hatte, und von wo aus er die Heimreise per Flugzeug unternahm.

Als Herr Clark wieder zu Hause war, sprach er oft von seiner interessanten und vergnügungsvollen Rheinreise.

CHAPTER 41

BRIEF AN EINEN FREUND IN MANCHESTER
LETTER TO A FRIEND IN MANCHESTER

Lieber Freund!

Ich bekam Deinen lieben Brief gerade als ich im Begriff war, meine Rückreise nach der Heimat zu beginnen. Du batest mich, Deine Verwandten in Hamburg aufzusuchen. Das würde ich gern getan haben, wenn ich Zeit gehabt hätte. Wenn Dein Brief nur ein paar Tage früher angekommen wäre, so würde ich sicher Deinen Onkel besucht haben.

Ich dachte, daß es sehr nett sein würde, wenn ich den Onkel wenigstens telephonisch sprechen könnte. Als ich anrief, bekam ich aber leider keine Antwort.

Ich freue mich Dir mitzuteilen, daß meine Reise sehr erfolgreich gewesen ist. Wenn ich aber nicht einen eingeborenen Vertreter in München hätte, der sehr tüchtig und zuvorkommend ist, so wäre es mir nicht möglich gewesen, meine Geschäfte so schnell und leicht zu erledigen. Dank seiner Hilfe habe ich auch die Gelegenheit gehabt, viele Sehenswürdigkeiten und viele nette Leute kennenzulernen.

Wenn Du in der nächsten Zeit nach London kommen solltest, so würde es mich sehr freuen, einige Zeit mit Dir zu verbringen.

Mit herzlichsten Grüßen
Dein Freund *Robert*

Dear Friend,

I received your letter just as I was about to start my journey home.

You asked me to look up your relatives in Hamburg. This I would gladly have done if I had had time. If only your letter had come a few days sooner I would surely have visited your uncle.

I thought it would be very nice if I could at least talk to your uncle on the telephone. But when I rang, unfortunately I received no answer.

I am glad to inform you that my trip has been very successful. But if I did not have a native representative in Munich who is very efficient and very obliging it would not have been possible for me to dispose of my business so quickly and easily. Thanks to his help I had the opportunity to get to know many places of interest and many nice people.

If you should come to London in the near future, I would be very happy to spend some time with you.

With kindest greetings,
Your friend *Robert*

Wortschatz

die Heimat, home, home country	**eingeboren** (*adj.*), native
der Verwándte, *pl.* **-n,** relative	**erfólgreich,** successful
mit-teilen, to inform	**zuvórkommend,** obliging, gracious

214

Grammar Notes and Practical Exercises

1 About the Subjunctive

Subjunctive verb forms have almost disappeared in modern English. About the only survivor is 'were' instead of 'was' in such expressions as: If he were here, he would be happy. She acts as if she were sick. If this were only true!

In the foregoing chapters of this book all the verb forms you have learned have been in what is called the 'indicative' mood. But modern German also has verb forms in what is called the 'subjunctive' mood. In this chapter you will learn the verb forms of the subjunctive and their use in certain types of conditional sentences.

2 The Present Subjunctive

lernen	gehen	sehen	fahren	haben	sein	werden	können
ich lerne	gehe	sehe	fahre	habe	sei	werde	könne
du lernest	gehest	sehest	fahrest	habest	seiest	werdest	könnest
er lerne	gehe	sehe	fahre	habe	sei	werde	könne
wir lernen	gehen	sehen	fahren	haben	seien	werden	können
ihr lernet	gehet	sehet	fahret	habet	seiet	werdet	könnet
sie lernen	gehen	sehen	fahren	haben	seien	werden	können

To form the present subjunctive of any verb, drop the infinitive ending (**-en** or **-n**) and add the personal endings **-e, -est, -e; -en, -et, -en**. The verb **sein** is the only exception to this rule. It lacks the ending **-e** in the first and third person singular (**ich sei, er sei**).

There are no contractions or vowel changes in the present subjunctive. Thus:

Indicative	du hast	du siehst	du fährst	du wirst	du kannst
Subjunctive	du habest	du sehest	du fahrest	du werdest	du könnest

3 The Past Subjunctive

Past Indicative

ich lernte	ging	sah	fuhr	hatte	war	wurde	konnte

Past Subjunctive

ich lernte	ginge	sähe	führe	hätte	wäre	würde	könnte
du lerntest	gingest	sähest	führest	hättest	wärest	würdest	könntest
er lernte	ginge	sähe	führe	hätte	wäre	würde	könnte
wir lernten	gingen	sähen	führen	hätten	wären	würden	könnten
ihr lerntet	ginget	sähet	führet	hättet	wäret	würdet	könntet
sie lernten	gingen	sähen	führen	hätten	wären	würden	könnten

(*a*) The endings of the past subjunctive are the same as those for the present: **-e, -est, -e; -en, -et, -en**.

(*b*) The verbs **haben, sein**, and **werden** have an Umlaut in the past subjunctive (**hätte, wäre, würde**).

(*c*) All strong verbs add an Umlaut to the stem vowel **a, o**, or **u** in the past subjunctive (**sah > sähe, bot > böte, fuhr > führe**).

(*d*) The modals **dürfen, können, mögen, müssen** and the mixed verbs **bringen,**

denken, wissen have an **Umlaut** in the past subjunctive; **sollen** and **wollen** do not add an **Umlaut** (**sollte, wollte**).

Indicative	**durfte**	**konnte**	**mußte**	**mochte**	**brachte dachte**	**wußte**
Subjunctive	**dürfte**	**könnte**	**müßte**	**möchte**	**brächte dächte**	**wüßte**

4 The Compound Tenses of the Subjunctive

Present Perfect		*Past Perfect*	
ich **habe** gelernt	ich **sei** gegangen	ich **hätte** gelernt	ich **wäre** gegangen
du **habest** gelernt	du **seist** gegangen	du **hättest** gelernt	du **wärest** gegangen
er **habe** gelernt	er **sei** gegangen	er **hätte** gelernt	er **wäre** gegangen
wir **haben** gelernt	wir **seien** gegangen	wir **hätten** gelernt	wir **wären** gegangen
ihr **habet** gelernt	ihr **seiet** gegangen	ihr **hättet** gelernt	ihr **wäret** gegangen
sie **haben** gelernt	sie **seien** gegangen	sie **hätten** gelernt	sie **wären** gegangen

Future		*Future Perfect*	
ich **werde** lernen	(gehen)	ich **werde** gelernt haben	(gegangen sein)
du **werdest** lernen	(gehen)	du **werdest** gelernt haben	(gegangen sein)
er **werde** lernen	(gehen)	er **werde** gelernt haben	(gegangen sein)
wir **werden** lernen	(gehen)	wir **werden** gelernt haben	(gegangen sein)
ihr **werdet** lernen	(gehen)	ihr **werdet** gelernt haben	(gegangen sein)
sie **werden** lernen	(gehen)	sie **werden** gelernt haben	(gegangen sein)

The compound tenses in the subjunctive are formed in the same way as in the indicative, except that the subjunctive forms of the auxiliary verbs **haben, sein, werden** are used.

Exercise No. 179. Change the following indicative verb forms to the subjunctive.

Beispiel: 1 ich wäre. 2 sie wären.

1 ich war	9 er lernt	17 er fährt	25 er hat gehabt
2 sie waren	10 du lernst	18 er fuhr	26 sie hat studiert
3 er hatte	11 du siehst	19 ich kann	27 ich bin gewesen
4 wir hatten	12 du sahst	20 er konnte	28 ich war gewesen
5 er schreibt	13 er kommt	21 wir müssen	29 wir sind gekommen
6 er schrieb	14 wir kamen	22 wir mußten	30 wir waren gekommen
7 ich las	15 sie geht	23 ich weiß	31 du hast gelebt
8 sie lasen	16 sie ging	24 er wußte	32 du hattest gelebt

5 The Conditional—Present and Past

Present Conditional		*Past Conditional*	
I should learn (go,) you would learn (go,)		*I should have learned (gone), you would*	
he would learn (go), etc.		*have learned (gone), etc.*	
ich **würde** lernen	(gehen)	ich **würde** gelernt haben	(gegangen sein)
du **würdest** lernen	(gehen)	du **würdest** gelernt haben	(gegangen sein)
er **würde** lernen	(gehen)	er **würde** gelernt haben	(gegangen sein)
wir **würden** lernen	(gehen)	wir **würden** gelernt haben	(gegangen sein)
ihr **würdet** lernen	(gehen)	ihr **würdet** gelernt haben	(gegangen sein)
sie **würden** lernen	(gehen)	sie **würden** gelernt haben	(gegangen sein)

The conditional present and past is formed like the future and future perfect, except that the auxiliary verb is **würden** (should, would) instead of **werden** (shall, will).

6 Use of the Subjunctive in Conditional Sentences

A conditional sentence consists of a subordinate clause with the conjunction **wenn** (if), called the conditional clause, and of a main clause, called the conclusion. There are two types of conditions, *simple* and *contrary-to-fact*.

Simple Conditions

Wenn er das Geld bekommt, wird er das Auto kaufen.
If *he receives* the money, *he will buy* the car.
Wenn er seine Fahrkarte verloren hat, muß er zu Fuß gehen.
If *he has lost* his ticket, *he must walk.*

The **wenn** (if) clause of a simple condition assumes something which may or may not be true. In both clauses German and English use the same tenses of the verbs. The verbs in both clauses of simple conditions are in the indicative mood.

Contrary-to-fact Conditions

(*a*) *Denoting present or future time*

Wenn ich Zeit hätte, (so) würde ich gehen, *or* (so) **ginge ich.** If *I had* time *I would go.*

(*b*) *Denoting past time*

Wenn ich Zeit gehabt hätte, (so) würde ich gegangen sein *or* (so) **wäre ich gegangen.** If *I had had* time *I would have gone.*

In contrary-to-fact conditions the **wenn** (if) clause assumes something which is not true (present contrary-to-fact) or was not true (past contrary-to-fact).

Pattern of Contrary-to-fact Conditions

Denoting present or future time

Wenn-clause: past subjunctive   *Conclusion* { present conditional *or* past subjunctive

Denoting past time

Wenn-clause: past perfect subjunctive   *Conclusion* { past conditional *or* past perfect subjunctive

In the conclusion of contrary-to-fact conditions denoting present or future time, German prefers the present conditional. In the conclusion of contrary-to-fact conditions denoting past time, German prefers the past perfect subjunctive.

7 Word Order in Conditional Sentences

Wenn er nicht krank wäre, (so) würde er spielen.	If he were not sick, (then) he would play.
Er würde spielen, wenn er nicht krank wäre.	He would play, if he were not sick.

A conditional sentence may begin with the **wenn**-clause or with the main clause. If the sentence begins with the **wenn**-clause, the main clause has inverted word order and may be preceded by **so** (then).

8 Omission of *wenn*

Hätte ich Hunger, (so) würde ich essen.   If I were hungry, I would eat.
Hätte es nicht geregnet, (so) wären wir   Had it not rained, we would have
gegangen.   gone.

The conjunction **wenn** may be omitted. The conditional clause must then have inverted word order.

Exercise No. 180. Read each sentence aloud three times. This will help you to get the 'feel' of conditional contrary-to-fact sentences. Translate each sentence.

1 Wenn ich genug Geld hätte, so würde ich eine Reise machen. 2 Wenn das Haus größer wäre, so würde ich es kaufen. 3 Wenn ich jetzt Ferien hätte, so würde ich nach Europa reisen. 4 Wenn das Wetter schön wäre, so würde ich einen Spaziergang machen. 5 Wenn sie Zeit hätte, so würde sie uns öfter schreiben. 6 Wenn er heute käme, so würden wir uns freuen. 7 Wenn wir Tennis spielen könnten, so würden wir euch begleiten. 8 Wir würden uns auf den Weg machen, wenn unsere Freunde schon hier wären. 9 Das Kind würde nicht fallen, wenn es nicht so schnell liefe. 10 Sie könnten es tun, wenn sie es tun wollten. 11 Wenn er Zeit gehabt hätte, so hätte er das ,,Deutsche Museum" besucht. 12 Wenn wir einen Wagenheber gehabt hätten, so würden wir gleich an die Arbeit gegangen sein. 13 Ich würde es nicht geglaubt haben, wenn ich es nicht selber gesehen hätte. 14 Wir wären zu Hause geblieben, wenn wir das gewußt hätten. 15 Hätte Herr Clark keinen Vertreter in München gehabt, so hätte er seine Geschäfte nicht so schnell erledigt.

CHAPTER 42

BERICHT EINES GESPRÄCHS ZWISCHEN HERRN CLARK UND HERRN MÜLLER

REPORT OF A CONVERSATION BETWEEN MR. CLARK AND MR. MÜLLER

Re-read the conversation between Mr. Clark and Mr. Müller in Chapter 27, p. 144. Here is a report of that conversation. It tells what Mr. Müller said, related, or answered and what Mr. Clark said or asked, but not in the exact words of the two speakers. You will note that subjunctive forms appear in this reported conversation. The use of the subjunctive and conditional in reported statements and reported questions will be treated in the 'Grammar Notes and Practical Exercises' of this chapter.

Herr Müller begann das Gespräch

1 Er sagte, daß er etwas von sich selbst erzählen werde; daß er selber das Gesprächsthema sein werde.

2 Herr Clark bemerkte, daß das sicherlich interessant sein würde, und fragte, ob er Fragen an ihn stellen dürfe.

3 Herr Müller erwiderte, daß es ihn immer freue, Fragen zu beantworten. Dann fügte er hinzu, er sei in Deutschland geboren. Er sei jetzt Bürger von Großbritannien. Er sei verheiratet und habe zwei Kinder.

4 Herr Clark fragte, was sein Beruf sei.

5 Herr Müller antwortete ausführlich. Er sagte, er sei Lehrer. Er unterrichte an einer Sekundarschule. Er lehre Deutsch und Französisch.

Dann fügte er hinzu, daß er Französisch und Englisch spreche, lese und schreibe. Er habe auf dem Gymnasium und auf der Universität Französisch und Englisch studiert. Er habe vier Jahre lang in Paris gelebt.

6 Herr Clark fragte, wann er in Paris gewesen sei.

7 Herr Müller antwortete, er sei vom Jahre 1934 bis zum Jahre 1938 dort gewesen. Er habe dort als Zeitungskorrespondent gearbeitet.

8 Herr Clark fragte, wann er nach England gekommen sei.

9 Herr Müller antwortete, daß er im Jahre 1938 hergekommen sei.

10 Herr Clark fragte, ob er sich hier verheiratet habe.

11 Herr Müller antwortete, daß er hier ein englisches Mädchen geheiratet habe.

12 Zuletzt dankte Herr Clark Herrn Müller, und fragte ob die Fragen ihn belästigt hätten.

13 Herr Müller antwortete, daß es ihm ein Vergnügen gewesen sei.

Mr. Müller began the conversation.

1 He said that he would relate something about himself; that he himself would be the topic of conversation.

219

2 Mr. Clark remarked that this would surely be interesting and asked whether he might ask him questions.

3 Mr. Müller answered that he was always glad to answer questions. Then he added he had been born in Germany. He was now a citizen of Great Britain. He was married and had two children.

4 Mr. Clark asked what his profession was.

5 Mr. Müller answered in detail. He said he was a teacher. He was teaching in a secondary school. He was teaching German and French.

Then he added that he spoke, read, and wrote French and English. He had studied French and English at grammar school, and the university. He had lived four years in Paris.

6 Mr. Clark asked when he had been in Paris.

7 Mr. Müller answered he had been there from the year 1934 until the year 1938. He had worked there as a newspaper correspondent.

8 Mr. Clark asked when he had come to England.

9 Mr. Müller answered that he had come here in the year 1938.

10 Mr. Clark asked whether he had married here.

11 Mr. Müller answered that he had married an English girl here.

12 Finally Mr. Clark thanked Mr. Müller and asked whether the questions had annoyed him.

13 Mr. Müller answered that it had been a pleasure.

1 The subjunctive and conditional in indirect speech

A statement or question is said to be in *direct speech* when the exact words or thoughts of a person are reported directly, that is, quoted after verbs of saying, telling, relating, thinking, asking, and the like. A statement or question is said to be in *indirect speech* when the statement or question is reported, but not in the exact words of the speaker or thinker.

Direct statements are put in quotation marks.

Compare the direct statements with the indirect statements in the following English sentences.

Direct Speech		*Indirect Speech*
He said,		He said,
Present	'I speak well.'	that he spoke well.
Past	'I spoke well.'	
Present Perfect	'I have spoken well.'	that he had spoken well.
Past Perfect	'I had spoken well.'	
Future	'I shall speak well.'	that he would speak well.

Now compare the direct speech with the indirect speech in the corresponding German sentences.

Direct Speech		*Indirect Speech*
Er sagte:		**Er sagte,**
Present	,,Ich spreche gut."	**daß er gut spreche** *or* **spräche**
Past	,,Ich sprach gut."	
Present Perfect	,,Ich habe gut gesprochen."	**daß er gut gesprochen habe** *or* **gesprochen hätte.**
Past Perfect	,,Ich hatte gut gesprochen."	
Future	,,Ich werde gut sprechen."	**daß er gut sprechen werde** *or* **würde.**

Pattern of Tenses in Direct and Indirect Speech in German

Direct Speech   *Indirect Speech*

Present   > I. Present Subjunctive   *or* II. Past Subjunctive

⎰ *Past*
⎨ *Present Perfect* > I. Present Perfect Subjunctive *or* II. Past Perfect
⎱ *Past Perfect*   Subjunctive

Future   I. Future Subjunctive   *or* II. Present Conditional
Future Perfect > I. Future Perfect Subjunctive *or* II. Past Conditional

(*a*) Note that the tenses in Type II correspond exactly to those used in English indirect speech. In German either Type I or Type II may be used. If, however, the verb form in Type I is identical in the indicative and subjunctive, Type II is used.

Sie sagte: „Wir **haben** Geld."   Sie sagte, daß sie Geld **hätten** (not **haben**).

(*b*) The same tense pattern is used for indirect questions as for indirect statements.

Wir fragten ihn: „**Haben Sie Geld?**"   Wir fragten ihn, **ob er Geld habe** (*or* **hätte**).

(*c*) **daß** like *that* in English may be omitted in indirect speech.
If **daß** is used, subordinate word order is required.

Er sagte, **daß er in München geboren sei.**   Er sagte, **er sei in München geboren.**

(*d*) An indirect command is expressed by the present or past subjunctive of **sollen** plus an infinitive.

Er sagte zu mir: „**Tue es sofort!**"   Er sagte mir, ich soll (sollte) es sofort tun.
He said to me, 'Do it at once!'   He said to me I should do it at once.

(*e*) The indicative is used in indirect speech if the introductory verb is in the present tense.

Er sagt: „Sie **ist** hier."   Er sagt, daß sie hier **ist.**
Sie fragt: „**War** er gestern hier?"   Sie fragt, ob er gestern hier **war.**

Exercise No. 181. Read each sentence aloud in the direct and indirect speech. Translate the indirect statements and questions and note how the German tenses in Type II correspond exactly to the English tenses.

1 Er sagte: „Ich habe einen Vertreter in München." Er sagte, daß er einen Vertreter in München habe (hätte).

2 Jemand fragte ihn: „Spricht Ihr Vertreter kein Englisch?" Jemand fragte ihn, ob sein Vertreter kein Englisch spreche (spräche).

3 Er sagte: „Ich will mit meinem Vertreter Deutsch reden." Er sagte, daß er mit seinem Vertreter Deutsch reden wolle (wollte).

4 Jemand fragte ihn: „Haben Sie die Stadt nicht gern?" Jemand fragte ihn, ob er die Stadt nicht gern habe (hätte).

5 Er antwortete: „Ich habe die Stadt nicht gern. Es gibt dort zu viel Lärm." Er antwortete, er habe (hätte) die Stadt nicht gern. Es gebe (gäbe) dort zu viel Lärm.

6 Der Reisende fragte: „Wann geht der Zug nach Bonn ab?" Er fragte, wann der Zug nach Bonn abgehe (abginge).

7 Er sagte: „Man kann auf einer Reise ohne viel Geld nicht auskommen." Er sagte, man könne (könnte) auf einer Reise ohne viel Geld nicht auskommen.

8 Die Mutter sagte: ,,Die kleine Anna war gestern krank." Sie sagte, die kleine Anna sei (wäre) gestern krank gewesen.

9 Sie sagte: ,,Der Doktor ist gestern abend hier gewesen." Sie sagte, der Doktor sei (wäre) gestern abend hier gewesen.

10 Die Kinder sagten: ,,Wir sind heute früh aufgestanden. Wir haben uns schnell angezogen." Sie sagten, sie seien (wären) heute früh aufgestanden. Sie hätten sich schnell angezogen.

11 Die Eltern fragten: ,,Sind die Kinder noch nicht zu Bett gegangen?" Sie fragten, ob die Kinder noch nicht zu Bett gegangen seien (wären).

12 Er sagte: ,,Wir haben nach dem Essen einen Spaziergang gemacht." Er sagte, daß sie nach dem Essen einen Spaziergang gemacht hätten.

13 Sie sagte: ,,Ich werde am 1. Mai abreisen." Sie sagte, daß sie am 1. Mai abreisen werde (würde).

14 Ich fragte die Kinder: ,,Werdet ihr heute abend ins Kino gehen?" Ich fragte sie, ob sie heute abend ins Kino gehen würden.

15 Der Junge sagte zu mir: ,,Kommen Sie herein!" Er sagte mir, daß ich hereinkommen solle.

16 Sie sagte zu uns: ,,Setzen Sie sich!" Sie sagte zu uns, daß wir uns setzen sollten.

CHAPTER 43

WAS GESCHIEHT IM HOTEL?
WHAT HAPPENS IN THE HOTEL?

Das Handgepäck wird von dem Hausdiener hineingetragen. Der Gast, Herr Clark, wird von dem Geschäftsführer des Hotels begrüßt. Das Fremdenbuch wird ihm zur Unterschrift vorgelegt. Indessen wird sein Zimmer vorbereitet. Die Fenster werden von dem Zimmermädchen geöffnet. Die Vase auf dem Blumenschemel wird mit frischen Blumen versehen. Ein Thermosbehälter und Wassergläser werden von dem Zimmerkellner auf die Kommode gestellt. Herr Clark wird von dem Hotelboy im Fahrstuhl auf sein Zimmer gebracht. Er ist mit allem zufrieden.

The hand luggage is carried in by the porter. The guest, Mr. Clark, is greeted by the manager of the hotel. The register is placed before him for his signature. In the meantime his room is being prepared. The windows are opened by the chambermaid. The vase on the flower stand is provided with fresh flowers. A thermos jug and water tumblers are placed on the chest of drawers by the room waiter. Mr. Clark is taken in the lift to his room by the page. He is pleased with everything.

Wortschatz

die Blume, *pl*. -n, flower	die Kommode, *pl*. -n, chest of drawers
der Blumenschemel, *pl*. -, flower stand	die Unterschrift, *pl*. -en, signature
der Behälter, *pl*. -, container	der Zimmerkellner, *pl*. -, room waiter
das Fremdenbuch, *pl*. ̈er, register	das Zimmermädchen, *pl*. -, chambermaid
der Gast, *pl*. ̈e, guest	indéssen, in the meantime
die Gastfreundlichkeit, hospitality	vor-legen, to place before

WAS GESCHAH AUF DEM AUSFLUG?

Als Herr Clark mit den Söhnen des Herrn Schiller nach Hause kam, fragte dieser: „Nun, was geschah auf dem Ausflug?" Herr Clark antwortete:

„Anfangs ging alles glatt. Die Strecke durch Stadt und Vorstadt wurde schnell zurückgelegt. Unterwegs wurden von mir und den Jungen allerlei Anekdoten erzählt. Es wurde viel gelacht und gesungen. Plötzlich wurden wir durch einen lauten Knall erschreckt. Es war eine Reifenpanne. Und der Autokoffer war nicht mit einem Wagenheber versehen worden. Während wir auf Hilfe warteten, brannte die Sonne auf uns nieder. Endlich wurde unsere Lage von einem vorbeifahrenden Lastwagenfahrer erkannt. Mit seiner Hilfe wurde der Reifen gewechselt."

WHAT HAPPENED ON THE EXCURSION?

When Mr. Clark got home with the sons of Mr. Schiller, the latter asked him: 'Well, what happened on the picnic?' Mr. Clark answered:

'At first everything went smoothly. The stretch through town and suburbs was covered rapidly. On the way, all sorts of stories were related by me and the boys. There was a great deal of laughter and singing. Suddenly we were frightened by a loud report. It was a puncture. And the toolbox had not been provided with a jack. While we waited for help the sun burned down upon us. Finally our situation was recognized by a passing lorry driver. With his help the tyre was changed.'

Wortschatz

die Anekdóte, *pl.* -n, anecdote
die Lage, *pl.* -n, situation, place
die Rückfahrt, *pl.* -en, return journey
die Ruhepause, *pl.* -n, rest period
aus-packen, to unpack
erschrécken, to frighten

verséhen, to provide (**er versieht, versah, hat versehen**)
zurück-legen, to put behind, to cover
anfangs, at first
glatt, smoothly
sogléich = sofort, at once

1 Uses of the verb *werden* already learned

(*a*) As a main verb meaning *to get, to become*, **werden** is, as you know, used in all tenses.

Principal parts: **werden   er wurde   ist geworden.**

Das Wetter ist schön geworden.   The weather has become nice.

(*b*) As an auxiliary meaning *shall* or *will*, **werden** plus the infinitive of a verb is used to form the future.

Er *wird* uns morgen *besuchen*.   *He will visit* us tomorrow.

You will now learn how **werden** is used as an auxiliary verb to form all tenses of the passive voice.

2 The passive voice

In the active voice the subject performs some act. In the passive voice the subject is acted upon.

Active: The teacher tests the pupil.   *Passive:* The pupil is tested by the teacher.

The person *by whom* or the thing *by which* an act is performed is called the *agent*. Now study the formation of the passive in German.

Present

Ich werde von dem Lehrer **geprüft.**	*I am* (*being*) *tested* by the teacher.
Du wirst von dem Lehrer **geprüft.**	*You are* (*being*) *tested* by the teacher.
Er wird von dem Lehrer **geprüft.**	*He is* (*being*) *tested* by the teacher.
Wir werden von dem Lehrer **geprüft.**	*We are* (*being*) *tested* by the teacher.
Ihr werdet von dem Lehrer **geprüft.**	*You are* (*being*) *tested* by the teacher.
Sie werden von dem Lehrer **geprüft.**	*They are* (*being*) *tested* by the teacher.
Der Schüler wird von ihm **geprüft.**	*The pupil is* (*being*) *tested* by him.
Die Schüler werden von ihm **geprüft.**	*The pupils are* (*being*) *tested* by him.

Past

Ich wurde von ihm **geprüft**, usw.	*I was tested* by him, etc.
Die Schüler wurden von ihm **geprüft**.	*The pupils were tested* by him.

Present Perfect

Ich bin von ihm **geprüft worden**, usw.	*I have been tested* by him, etc.
Die Schüler sind von ihm **geprüft worden**.	*The pupils have been tested* by him.

Past Perfect

Ich war von ihm **geprüft worden**, usw.	*I had been tested* by him, etc.
Die Schüler waren von ihm **geprüft worden**.	*The pupils had been tested* by him.

Future

Ich werde von ihm **geprüft werden**, usw.	*I shall be tested* by him, etc.
Die Schüler werden von ihm **geprüft werden**.	*The pupils will be tested* by him.

Future Perfect (*Very rarely used*)

Ich werde von ihm **geprüft worden sein**, usw.	*I shall have been tested* by him, etc.
Die Schüler werden von ihm **geprüft worden sein**.	*The pupils will have been tested* by him.

The passive in English is formed by tenses of the auxiliary verb *to be* plus the past participle of the main verb; the passive in German is formed by tenses of the auxiliary verb **werden** plus the past participle of the main verb. Note, however, that the past participle of **werden** used in the passive construction is **worden**, not **geworden**.

The agent in the passive is preceded by **von** if the agent is a person, by **durch** or **von** if it is a thing.

Wir wurden *von ihm* gelobt.	We were praised *by him*.
Das Fenster wurde *durch den Wind* gebrochen.	The window was broken *by the wind*.

3 The passive introduced by *es*

The passive is often introduced by **es** when no particular subject is stated; or when some indefinite word like **etwas, nichts, alles** is the subject.

Es wird viel gelacht und gesungen.	There is much laughter and singing.
Es wurde nichts gesagt.	Nothing was said.

4 Substitutes for the passive

(*a*) In general it is preferable and easier to use the active.

(*active*)	**Wagner hat viele Opern geschrieben.**	(*active*)	Wagner has written many operas.
(*passive*)	**Viele Opern sind von Wagner geschrieben worden.**	(*passive*)	Many operas have been written by Wagner.

(*b*) An active sentence with the subject **man** is often used instead of a corresponding passive. Such sentences are often rendered in English by the passive.

man sagt (*passive:* **es wird gesagt**)	one says; they, people, etc. say (*passive:* it is said)
Hier spricht man Deutsch (*passive:* **Hier wird Deutsch gesprochen**).	Here one speaks German (*passive:* Here German is spoken).
Man sah viele Schüler dort (*passive:* **Viele Schüler wurden dort gesehen**).	One saw many pupils there. (*passive:* Many pupils were seen there).

Exercise No. 182. Fragen

Lesen Sie noch einmal die Texte: **Was geschieht im Hotel** und **Was geschah auf dem Ausflug,** und dann beantworten Sie diese Fragen!

1 Was wird von dem Hausdiener hineingetragen? 2 Von wem wird der Gast begrüßt? 3 Was wird ihm vorgelegt? 4 Was wird indessen vorbereitet? 5 Von wem werden die Fenster geöffnet? 6 Was wird mit Blumen versehen? 7 Von wem werden die Wassergläser auf die Kommode gestellt? 8 Von wem wird der Gast auf sein Zimmer gebracht? 9 Wodurch wurden Herr Clark und die Jungen plötzlich erschreckt? 10 Womit war der Autokoffer nicht versehen? 11 Was wurde mit Hilfe des Wagenfahrers gewechselt?

ANSWERS

Exercise No. 1

1 Here is the glass. It is full of water. The water is fresh and clear. Here is the child. The child drinks water.

2 The child plays ball. The ball is red. The ball rolls under the bed.

3 Here is the tea. There is the coffee. The tea is warm. The coffee is cold. The father drinks coffee. The mother drinks tea. The child drinks the soup.

4 The month of June is warm. The winter is cold in Canada. The summer is warm here.

5 Is the coffee cold? Is the tea warm? Is the beer fresh? Is the soup warm? Who drinks tea? Who drinks coffee? Who drinks the soup?

6 Karl is four years old. Mary is seven years old. How old is Jack? How old is the father? How old is the mother? How old is the child?

Exercise No. 2

1 sie 2 er 3 sie 4 er 5 es 6 es 7 sie 8 sie 9 er 10 er

Exercise No. 3

1 der Vater; die Schwester; der Lehrer; der Doktor; der Onkel; die Mutter; der Bruder; der Mann; das Kind; die Tante.

2 die Schule; der Ball; der Hut; die Butter; das Glas; das Wasser; der Tee; der Kaffee; die Klasse; das Brot; der Schuh; der Hut.

Exercise No. 4

1 Ein (kein) Plan 2 Ein (kein) Bett 3 Ein (kein) Auto 4 Eine (keine) Tochter 5 Eine (keine) Frau 6 Ein (kein) Bruder 7 Eine (keine) Schwester 8 Eine (keine) Tür 9 Ein (kein) Glas 10 Eine (keine) Schule 11 Ein (kein) Haus 12 Eine (keine) Tochter

Exercise No. 5

2 Wir lernen 3 Sie kauft 4 Der Stuhl steht 5 Ich spiele 6 Das Kind hat 7 Der Doktor kommt 8 Wer trinkt 9 Er trinkt 10 Der Schüler lernt 11 Wir spielen 12 Es steht 13 Marie singt 14 Sie singt 15 Wir haben 16 Er zählt 17 Wer spielt 18 Was steht

Exercise No. 6

2 Nein, der Schüler geht nicht nach Hause. 3 Der Bruder ist nicht zwölf Jahre alt. 4 Das Wetter ist nicht kühl. 5 Der Mann kauft das Auto nicht. 6 Er ist nicht älter als die Schwester. 7 Das Haus ist nicht sehr alt. 8 Marie singt nicht schön. 9 Der Doktor kommt heute nicht. 10 Sie kommt nicht spät nach Hause.

Exercise No. 8

2 die Knaben 3 die Bücher 4 die Mädchen 5 die Lehrer 6 die Federn und die Bücher 7 die Fräulein 8 die Herren 9 die Hüte 10 die Söhne 11 die Brüder 12 die Männer

Exercise No. 9

1 kaufen Sie; ich kaufe 2 kauft Herr; er kauft 3 kommen die Mädchen; sie kommen 4 singen die Mädchen; sie singen 5 Spielt ihr; wir spielen 6 lernst du; ich lerne 7 wohnt der Kaufmann; er wohnt 8 ich höre, wer spielt 9 stehen die Stühle; sie stehen 10 trinkst du; ich trinke

Exercise No. 10

2 geht 3 spielt 4 trinke 5 singen Sie 6 kommen Sie 7 steht 8 kaufe 9 zähle 10 kaufen Sie

Exercise No. 11

1 Herr Clark ist Kaufmann. 2 Nein, er ist kein Deutscher. 3 Sein Büro ist in London. 4 Er wohnt nicht in London 5 Der Vorort, wo die Familie Clark wohnt, ist nicht weit von London. 6 Er ist vierzig Jahre alt. 7 Sie heißt Helene. 8 Sie ist sechsunddreißig Jahre alt. 9 Sie haben vier Kinder. 10 Die Knaben heißen Karl und Wilhelm. 11 Sie sind zwölf und zehn Jahre alt. 12 Die Mädchen heißen Marie und Anna.

Exercise No. 12

1 Dies ist eine Vorstadt. Sie ist nicht weit von London. 2 Herr C. und seine Familie wohnen hier. 3 Herr C. ist Kaufmann. Er ist nicht Arzt. 4 Der Kaufmann hat eine Frau und vier Kinder, zwei Knaben und zwei Mädchen. 5 Seine Frau heißt Helene. 6 Die Knaben sind älter als die Mädchen. 7 Anna ist fünf Jahre alt. Sie geht nicht in die Schule. 8 Wie heißen Sie und wo wohnen Sie? 9 Spielen die Kinder Ball? Sie spielen nicht Ball. 10 Gehe nach Hause, Kind! Geht nach Hause, Kinder! 11 Gehen Sie nicht, Herr Schmidt! 12 Stehen Sie hier, meine Damen und Herren!

Exercise No. 13

1 Die Tische sind rund. 2 Die Fenster sind offen. 3 Die Türen sind nicht offen. 4 Die Bilder sind schön. 5 Die Fräulein spielen nicht Tennis. 6 Die Herren lernen Englisch. 7 Die Frauen singen schön. 8 Die Schüler spielen Ball. 9 Die Stühle stehen dort. 10 Die Schulen sind nicht weit von hier.

Exercise No. 15

A Er sieht den Tisch, das Tischlein, das Zimmer, den Stuhl, keinen Ball, keine Schule, keinen Schuh, keinen Garten. B Ich sehe die Frau, den Lehrer, das Mädchen, den Bruder, die Tante, die Schwester, den Kaufmann, den Sohn, eine Tochter, keinen Schüler, einen Lehrer, ein Kind, keine Frau, kein Mädchen.

Exercise No. 16

Do you know the businessman Robert Clark? I know him very well.
Do you know Mrs. Clark?—Yes, I know her.
Do you know the children of Robert Clark?—No, I don't know them.
Do you know the house where he lives?—I know it. It is a one-family house.

Exercise No. 17

2 es 3 ihn 4 sie 5 sie 6 sie 7 es 8 ihn 9 sie 10 sie

Exercise No. 18

1 Er hat ein Einfamilienhaus. 2 Es ist nicht groß. 3 Es ist bequem. 4 Es hat sieben Zimmer. 5 Es ist für Herrn Clark. 6 Es hat zwei Badezimmer. 7 Es ist hell. 8 Man sieht einen Garten. 9 Man sieht einen Tisch, ein Büffet und sechs Stühle.

10 Er ist rund. 11 Sie stehen um den Tisch. 12 Es ist für die Eltern. 13 Wir sehen zwei Bettchen, zwei Tischlein, zwei Stühle, einen Kleiderschrank und einige Bilder. 14 Sie haben ein Zimmer.

Exercise No. 19

1 Das Haus von Herrn C. ist nicht groß. Es hat einen Garten. 2 Sehen Sie den Garten? 3 Wir sehen den Tisch. Sechs Stühle stehen um den Tisch. 4 Ein Schlafzimmer ist für die Knaben. Ein Tisch ist für die Mädchen. 5 Sie haben einen Kleiderschrank und eine Kommode. 6 Die Zimmer sind nicht gross, aber sie sind bequem. 7 Das Zimmer hat einen Tisch und einen Stuhl, aber es hat keine Kommode. 8 Hast du einen Bruder und eine Schwester? Ich habe zwei Brüder, aber ich habe keine Schwestern.

Exercise No. 21

2 Deswegen lernt er Deutsch. 3 Jeden Dienstag hat Herr Clark eine Deutschstunde. 4 Nicht weit von hier wohnt der Lehrer. 5 Hier spricht man Deutsch. 6 Durch die Fenster sehen wir einen Garten. 7 Um den Tisch stehen sechs Stühle. 8 Heute gehen die Kinder nicht zur Schule.

Exercise No. 22

2 besuchen 3 antworten 4 sprechen 5 reden 6 einen Hut 7 Kunstgegenstände 8 weit von hier 9 den Kaufmann 10 fleißig

Exercise No. 23

1 Herr Clark ist Kaufmann. 2 Er importiert Kunstgegenstände. 3 Er hat einen Vertreter in München. 4 München ist in Deutschland. 5 Herr Clark will seinen Vertreter besuchen. 6 Er will mit ihm über Geschäftssachen reden. 7 Der Vertreter spricht kein Englisch. 8 Herr Clark hat einen Deutschlehrer. 9 Sein Lehrer heißt Müller. 10 Der Lehrer ist fünfzig Jahre alt. 11 Er wohnt nicht weit von Herrn Clark. 12 Herr Clark hat jeden Dienstag und jeden Donnerstag eine Deutschstunde. 13 Die Deutschstunde ist fast immer bei Herrn Clark. 14 Herr Clark ist intelligent und fleißig. 15 Er lernt schnell.

Exercise No. 24

1 Wer spricht Deutsch? Herr M. spricht Deutsch. 2 Sprechen Sie Deutsch? Nein, ich spreche nicht Deutsch. 3 Wer fragt: Was ist dies? Was ist das? 4 Antwortet Herr C. gut? Ist er intelligent und fleißig? 5 Wen will Herr C. besuchen? Er will seinen Vertreter in München besuchen. 6 Ich will eine Reise nach Deutschland machen. Deshalb lerne ich Deutsch. 7 Herr C. ist weder Lehrer noch Arzt. Er ist Kaufmann. 8 Die Knaben sind nicht faul sondern fleißig.

Exercise No. 25

2 dem Kind 3 dem Freund 4 der Tochter 5 der Mutter 6 den Kindern 7 den Schülern 8 den Mädchen

Exercise No. 26

2 ihnen 3 ihr 4 ihm 5 ihnen 6 ihm 7 ihr 8 ihr

Exercise No. 27

1 The teacher is again at the home of the businessman. 2 Every Tuesday he goes to the businessman. 3 Mr. Clark's house has seven rooms. 4 The gentlemen go out of the room. 5 Mr. C. goes with him to the door. 6 He says to the teacher,

'Good-bye.' 7 Two of the children are boys. 8 Two of them are girls. 9 All except Anna go to school. 10 In the summer Mr. C. is going to Munich. 11 What are you giving Mother for Christmas? 12 We are giving her a scarf. 13 Why don't you go to the doctor? 14 We are just coming from the doctor.

Exercise No. 28

1 aus dem Hause 2 bei dem Lehrer 3 mit einem Buch 4 von der Schule 5 nach einer Stunde 6 mit einer Feder 7 zu dem Kaufmann 8 von der Mutter 9 bei dem Arzt 10 mit den Schülern 11 von den Bildern 12 zu den Kindern 13 von den Herren 14 seit zwei Jahren 15 seit zwei Monaten

Exercise No. 29

1 Nein, es ist nicht groß. 2 Wir sehen eine Landkarte von Deutschland. 3 Er steht vor dem Pult. 4 Der Lehrer ist heute abend wieder beim Kaufmann. 5 Der Lehrer sitzt auf dem Sofa. 6 Der Kaufmann sitzt im Lehnstuhl. 7 Man sieht überall viele Dinge. 8 In England spricht man Englisch. 9 In Deutschland muß man Deutsch sprechen. 10 Ein Bleistift, eine Füllfeder, einige Briefe und Papiere liegen auf dem Pult. 11 Man schreibt mit Bleistift und Feder. 12 Er reicht ihm ein Buch. 13 Am Donnerstag haben sie wieder eine Deutschstunde. 14 Herr Clark geht mit Herrn Müller zur Tür. 15 „Wörterbuch" heißt auf englisch „dictionary".

Exercise No. 30

1 Heute abend ist der Lehrer wieder beim (bei dem) Kaufmann. 2 Herr C. sitzt im Lehnstuhl. 3 Der Lehrer reicht ihm einen Bleistift und fragt auf deutsch: „Was macht man mit einem Bleistift?" 4 „Man schreibt damit," antwortet Herr C. 5 Endlich sagt Herr M. zum Kaufmann: „Das ist genug für heute abend." 6 Er geht mit ihm zur Tür. 7 Wem senden Sie die Bilder? 8 Sie kommen aus dem Arbeitszimmer.

Exercise No. 32

2 in dem Arbeitszimmer 3 an die Wand 4 In der Stadt 5 in die Stadt 6 neben den Lehrer 7 auf der Straße 8 unter den Büchern 9 auf den Tisch 10 hinter der Tür 11 hinter die Tür 12 zwischen den Fenstern

Exercise No. 33

1 Sie gehen in das Arbeitszimmer. 2 Er setzt sich auf das Sofa. 3 Er setzt sich in den Lehnstuhl. 4 Er stellt ihn vor das Sofa. 5 Ein Aschenbecher steht darauf. 6 Neben dem Aschenbecher sind Zigaretten und ein Feuerzeug. 7 Er legt sie auf den Aschenbecher. 8 Er wohnt in der Vorstadt. 9 Er fährt in die Stadt. 10 Sein Büro ist in der Stadt. 11 Er wohnt lieber in der Vorstadt. 12 Frau Clark geht dann und wann in die Stadt. 13 Es ist still und gemütlich. 14 Sie sind in der Vorstadt besser. 15 Herr Clark macht große Fortschritte im Deutschen.

Exercise No. 34

1 Wir gehen in das Arbeitszimmer. 2 Ein Sofa und ein Lehnstuhl sind im Arbeitszimmer. 3 Vor dem Sofa ist ein Tisch. 4 An der Wand sind Bilder. 5 Sie haben recht, eine Landkarte hängt zwischen den zwei Fenstern. 6 Herr M. sitzt im Lehnstuhl. 7 Herr C. setzt sich auf das Sofa. 8 Legen Sie Ihre Zigarette auf den Aschenbecher. 9 Wir wohnen nicht in der Stadt. 10 Ich fahre jeden Wochentag in die Stadt.

Exercise No. 37

1 des Kaufmanns 2 des Klaviers 3 des Automobils 4 der Kleider 5 der Tinte

6 der Bleistifte 7 einer Frau 8 eines Mannes 9 der Landkarte 10 des Arztes-
11 des Tages, der Nacht 12 des Lärmes

Exercise No. 38

1 Die Wohnung des Kaufmanns ist nicht groß. 2 Wir kennen schon das Arbeitszimmer. 3 Es steht in einer Ecke neben einem Fenster. 4 Eine Photographie
steht darauf. 5 Auf dem Klavier steht eine Photographie der Kinder von Herrn
Clark. 6 Über dem Klavier hängt das Porträt seiner Frau. 7 Sie sitzen im Wohnzimmer. 8 Die Frau des Herrn Clark spielt sehr gut Klavier. 9 Sie gehen oft ins
Konzert. 10 Es ist außerordentlich interessant. 11 Er ist der Chef der Firma.

Exercise No. 39

1 Kennen Sie die Firma des Kaufmanns? 2 Herr C. ist der Chef der Firma.
3 Wir wissen, wo der Kaufmann wohnt. 4 Sein Haus ist in der Vorstadt. 5 Die
Zimmer des Hauses sind nicht groß. 6 Ein Klavier ist in einer Ecke des Wohn-
zimmers. 7 Eine Photographie der Kinder steht auf dem Klavier. 8 Die Farbe des
Klaviers ist schwarz. 9 An der Wand hängt das Porträt von Frau C. 10 Das
Zimmer der Knaben ist größer als das Zimmer der Mädchen.

Exercise No. 40

1 (*d*) 2 (*g*) 3 (*f*) 4 (*b*) 5 (*j*) 6 (*c*) 7 (*a*) 8 (*e*) 9 (*h*) 10 (*i*)

Exercise No. 41

1 **die Haustür,** front door 2 **die Wanduhr,** wall clock 3 **das Schlafzimmer,** bedroom
4 **das Bilderbuch,** picture book 5 **das Gartenhaus,** summer house 6 **der Deutschlehrer,**
teacher of German 7 **das Wörterbuch,** dictionary 8 **die Geschäftsreise,** business trip
9 **das Musikinstrument,** musical instrument 10 **das Vaterland,** fatherland

Exercise No. 43

2 eine Wohnung in der Vorstadt 3 die Zimmer der Wohnung 4 die Freunde der
Kinder 5 die Wände des Zimmers 6 Bilder . . . den Wänden 7 dem Eßzimmer . . .
einen Tisch 8 der Tisch 9 den Tisch 10 der Lehrer . . . einem Stuhl 11 der Kaufmann . . . das Sofa 12 dem Klavier . . . einer Frau 13 einen Vertreter 14 den
Vertreter 15 eine Stadt

Exercise No. 44

2 Die Kinder des Kaufmanns spielen im Garten. 3 Ich bringe der Schwester den
Hut. 4 Die Kinder lieben die Lehrerinnen. 5 Die Knaben suchen den Ball. 6 Der
Lehrer spricht zu den Schülern. 7 Das Porträt der Frau hängt im Wohnzimmer.
8 Der Knabe schreibt mit dem Bleistift. 9 Das Mädchen schreibt mit der Feder.
10 Der Vater fragt die Kinder. 11 Ich gebe der Mutter die Briefe.

Exercise No. 45

MR. CLARK IS LEARNING GERMAN

Mr. Clark is a businessman. He imports art objects from Germany. His office is in
an office block in the city of London. His house, however, is not in the city but in a
suburb not far from it. Every weekday Mr. Clark goes into the city by train and carries
on his business there.

The firm of Mr. Clark has a representative in Germany. His name is Henry Schiller
and he lives in the city of Munich. In the spring of this year Mr. Clark is taking a trip
to Germany in order to visit Mr. Schiller. He wants to talk with his agent about
important business matters. Unfortunately Mr. Schiller speaks no English and Mr.
Clark speaks no German. Therefore Mr. Clark is beginning to learn German.

Mr. Clark has a good teacher. The latter is a German by birth and his name is Karl Müller. Every Tuesday and Thursday the teacher comes to the home of his pupil in order to give him a German lesson. Mr. Clark is industrious and intelligent and learns quickly. During the first lesson he learns these German expressions by heart: Good day; How are you?; Many thanks; Please; Good-bye, etc. (and so forth). He already knows the German names for many things in his living-room and can answer these questions correctly: What is this? What is that? Where is that? Why is that? etc.

Mr. Müller is very satisfied with the progress of his pupil and says: 'Very good. That is enough for today. I'll come again Thursday. Good-bye.'

Exercise No. 46
GERMANY

Germany lies in Central Europe. Since the end of the Second World War Germany is divided into two parts, West Germany and East Germany. The Elbe separates the two parts of Germany.

West Germany is the Federal Republic of Germany. East Germany is the German Democratic Republic.

The capital of West Germany is Bonn. The capital of East Germany is East Berlin.

Among the large cities in West Germany are Cologne, Munich, Stuttgart, Frankfurt, Düsseldorf, and the large port cities Hamburg and Bremen. Among the large cities in East Germany are Leipzig, Dresden and Chemnitz.

Exercise No. 48

1 Where does the representative of your firm live?—The representative of our firm lives in Munich.—How long has he lived there?—He has been living there for a year.

2 Whose portrait is that?—It is the portrait of my wife.—Is this the photograph of your children?—Yes, this is the photograph of our four children.

3 Is your residence in the city?—No, my residence is in the suburbs.—And where is your office?—My office is in the city.

4 Where is your school, children?—Our school is on Charles Street.—Do you walk there?—No, we go by bus.

Exercise No. 49

1 deines 2 eu(e)re Eltern 3 Ihr 4 ihrer 5 seines 6 ihres 7 uns(e)ren 8 Ihrer 9 mein 10 ihre 11 uns(e)rem 12 Ihren

Exercise No. 50

1 Er ist ein Freund von Herrn Clark. 2 Es ist im selben Gebäude wie das Büro des Herrn Clark. 3 Er spricht Deutsch. 4 Er will erfahren, was für Fortschritte Herr Clark macht. 5 Er sitzt an seinem Pult. 6 Er liest Briefe. 7 Plötzlich tritt sein Freund, Herr Engel, ins Büro. 8 Er beginnt sofort, auf deutsch zu sprechen. 9 Herr Clark antwortet seinem Freund auf deutsch. 10 Er studiert schon seit einigen Monaten Deutsch. 11 Er beabsichtigt, im Sommer eine Reise nach Deutschland zu machen 12 Er fliegt. 13 Morgen geht er zur Fluglinie. 14 Die Herren geben sich die Hand.

Exercise No. 51

1 Herr Engel, ein Freund von Herrn C. tritt in sein Büro ein. 2 Er fragt auf deutsch: „Wie lange studierst du schon Deutsch?" 3 Ich will eine Reise nach Deutschland machen. 4 Warum willst du nach Deutschland reisen? 5 Unsere Firma hat einen Vertreter in München. 6 Spricht der Vetreter deiner Firma nicht Englisch? 7 Der Vertreter unserer Firma spricht nicht Englisch. 8 Herr Clark, wohnen Sie in der Stadt? Nein, mein Haus ist in der Vorstadt.

Exercise No. 52

(*a*) dreißig (*b*) zehn (*c*) fünfzig (*d*) zwölf (*e*) sieben (*f*) sechzig (*g*) siebzig (*h*) neunzehn (*i*) vierzehn (*j*) einunddreißig (*k*) fünfundzwanzig (*l*) dreiundvierzig (*m*) neunundachtzig (*n*) neunzig (*o*) hundert (*p*) neununddreißig (*q*) achtundzwanzig (*r*) sechsunddreißig (*s*) fünfzehn (*t*) zwölf

Exercise No. 53

2 Das Jahr hat zwölf Monate. 3 Der Tag hat vierundzwanzig Stunden. 4 Die Stunde hat sechzig Minuten. 5 Die Minute hat sechzig Sekunden. 6 Der Monat September hat dreißig Tage. 7 Der Monat Juli hat einunddreißig Tage. 8 In den Vereinigten Staaten sind fünfzig Staaten. 9 Der Vater ist vierzig Jahre alt. 10 Die Mutter ist sechsunddreißig Jahr alt. 11 Ein Dutzend ist zwölf. 12 Die Hand hat fünf Finger.

Exercise No. 56

2 dieses (jenes) Kaufmanns 3 in diesem (jenem) Hochhaus 4 diese (jene) Land-karte 5 diesem (jenem) Hause 6 diese (jene) Wörter 7 diesen (jenen) Mädchen 8 dieses (jenes) Wort 9 dieser (jener) Kinder 10 dieser (jener) Frau

Exercise No. 57

2 Welcher Mann 3 Welcher Lehrer 4 Welches Schlafzimmer 5 Mit welchem Bleistift muß er schreiben? 6 Welche Bücher können alle Schüler lesen? 7 Welche Wörter kennt der Schüler? 8 Welche Herren kennen wir nicht? 9 Welche Wörter muß sie schreiben? 10 Mit welchen Kindern will sie sprechen?

Exercise No. 58

1 Dieses Kapitel heißt „Zahlen, Zahlen und wieder Zahlen." 2 Die Zahlen sind ebenso wichtig wie die Hauptwörter und Zeitwörter. 3 Im modernen Leben kann man ohne Zahlen nicht auskommen. 4 Es gibt viele Fälle, wo man Zahlen gebraucht. 5 Der Kaufmann denkt zuerst an Kaufen und Verkaufen. 6 Ohne Geld kann man nicht kaufen und verkaufen. 7 Man gebraucht Zahlen beim Angeben des Datums und der Temperatur, auch zum Telephonieren.

Exercise No. 59

1 Wieviel kostet dieser Hut? Fünfundzwanzig Mark. 2 Wie viele Studenten hat diese Klasse? Fünfzehn Studenten. 3 Wie alt ist jenes Haus? Hundert Jahre. 4 Eine Woche hat sieben Tage und ein Jahr hat zwölf Monate. 5 Der Monat Juli hat einunddreißig Tage. 6 Kannst du (können Sie) von eins bis hundert zählen? 7 Welches Auto kaufen Sie? Ich kaufe jenes Auto. 8 Ich kann diese Wörter nicht lesen.

Exercise No. 60

(*a*) fünfhundert (*b*) sechshundertfünfundzwanzig. (*c*) siebenhundertsechsundvierzig (*d*) zweihundertsiebenundvierzig (*e*) hundertsechsunddreißig (*f*) neunhundertneun-undneunzig (*g*) tausendsechshundertvierzig (*h*) fünftausenddreihundertzwanzig (*i*) im Jahre sechzehnhundertzwanzig (*j*) im Jahre neunzehnhundertsiebzig

Exercise No. 62

2 ... zur Schule, wenn das Wetter schön ist. 3 Wir wissen, daß dieser Kaufmann einen Vertreter in München hat. 4 ... schnell, denn er ist ... 5 Wenn ich in München bin, will ich mit diesem Mann reden. 6 Ich weiß, daß Sie im Sommer eine Reise nach Deutschland machen. 7 ... kaufen, aber es ist viel zu teuer. 8 ... nennen, wenn man in Deutschland ist. 9 ... gehen, denn ich habe viel zu tun. 10 ... Kino, und wir müssen zu Hause bleiben.

Exercise No. 63

1 Eine Mark hat hundert Pfennig. 2 Das Pfund ist ungefähr zehn Mark wert. 3 Ich bekomme 350 (dreihundertfünfzig) DM zurück. 4 Ich bekomme 210 (zweihundertzehn) DM zurück. 5 Ich habe im ganzen 2803.50 DM (zweitausendachthundertdrei Mark fünfzig Pfennig.) 6 Ich bekomme 90 (neunzig) DM zurück. 7 Eine Million geteilt durch zehn ist hunderttausend.

Exercise No. 64

1 Jeder Reisende braucht Geld. 2 Er muß Mathematik gebrauchen, wenn er Geld wechselt. 3 Können Sie diesen Fünfhundertmarkschein wechseln? Nein, ich habe nur vierhundertfünfzig Mark. 4 Ein Pfund ist ungefähr zwölf Mark wert, und eine Mark hat hundert Pfennig. 5 Ich brauche etwas Geld. Kannst du mir tausend Mark leihen? 6 Das Geldsystem Deutschlands ist leicht zu erlernen. 7 Dieses Auto kostet sechstausendsiebenhundertdreiundsechzig Mark. 8 Ich weiß, daß das Geldsystem Deutschlands leicht ist.

Exercise No. 65

2 des schweren Koffers 3 diesem schweren Koffer 4 die schweren Koffer . . . im großen Wartesaal 5 der runde Tisch 6 diesen runden Tisch 7 dem roten Bleistift 8 die neuen Hefte 9 jene deutschen Bücher 10 dieser deutschen Landkarte 11 welche englischen Bücher

Exercise No. 66

1 ein englischer Kaufmann 2 in einem kleinen Vorort 3 in einem schönen Einfamilienhaus 4 ein kleiner Garten 5 in ihrem kleinen Garten 6 in der großen Stadt . . . einen tüchtigen Vertreter 7 eine kurze Reise 8 seinen deutschen Vertreter 9 eine große Bestellung 10 ein schwerer Koffer

Exercise No. 67

1 Sie wollen heute über den Gebrauch der Mathematik reden. 2 Vier Personen speisen in Restaurant. 3 Die Rechnung beträgt 40 Mark. 4 Wir lassen dem Kellner 4 Mark. 5 Er trägt einen schweren Handkoffer. 6 Dieser schwere Handkoffer wiegt 30 Kilo oder 66 Pfund. 7 Man rechnet die Entfernung in Kilometern. 8 Er geht in einen Laden. 9 Der Betrag von allen Einkäufen ist 64 Mark. 10 Das Thema für Donnerstag ist die Tageszeit. 11 Das ist ein wichtiges Thema. 12 Er erwartet ein interessantes Gespräch.

Exercise No. 68

1 Dieser Handkoffer ist schwer. Es ist ein schwerer Handkoffer. Er trägt einen schweren Handkoffer. 2 Dieser Laden ist groß. Sie kaufen immer in diesem großen Laden. 3 Dieses Gespräch ist interessant. Ich erwarte ein interessantes Gespräch. 4 Diese Handschuhe sind sehr schön. Ich kaufe diese schönen Handschuhe. 3 Sie kauft ein seidenes Taschentuch. 6 Dieses Problem ist schwer. Das ist ein schweres Problem. 7 Es gibt große Läden in dieser Stadt. 8 Der Hut ist neu. Sie kauft einen neuen Hut.

Exercise No. 69

(*a*) ein Viertel nach eins (*b*) zehn Minuten nach fünf (*c*) ein Viertel nach acht (*d*) ein Viertel vor drei (*e*) zwanzig Minuten nach drei (*f*) fünf Minuten vor vier (*g*) elf Uhr (*h*) zwanzig Minuten nach vier (*i*) halb eins (*j*) halb acht (*k*) ein Viertel vor zehn (*i*) dreiundzwanzig Minuten nach zehn

Exercise No. 70

2 siebzehn Uhr fünfundzwanzig 3 fünfzehn Uhr vierzehn 4 acht Uhr fünfundzwanzig 5 sechs Uhr fünfundzwanzig—achtzehn Uhr fünfzig 6 neunzehn Uhr—zwanzig Uhr zehn 7 neunzehn Uhr dreißig 8 vierzehn Uhr dreißig 9 zweiundzwanzig Uhr dreißig

Exercise No. 71

2 gibt . . . zurück 3 fährt . . . ab 4 stehen . . . auf 5 kommst . . . zurück 6 fangen . . . an 7 kommt . . . an 8 fangen . . . an 9 steht . . . auf 10 komme . . . zurück

Exercise No. 72

1 mich 2 mir 3 Sie 4 uns 5 Ihnen 6 euch 7 dir 8 dich 9 mich 10 Sie 11 mir

Exercise No. 73

1 Jedermann will wissen, wieviel Uhr es ist. 2 Herr Clark spielt die Rolle des Reisenden. 3 Er will eine Fahrkarte kaufen. 4 Die Fahrkarte kostet 12 Mark. 5 Er kauft eine Fahrkarte zweiter Klasse. 6 Es gibt einige Züge nach Köln. 7 Er spielt die Rolle des Touristen. 8 Er wünscht Auskunft über die Vorstellung. 9 Es gibt drei Vorstellungen. 10 Die letzte fängt um 7.10 (sieben Uhr zehn) abends an. 11 Der Film heißt Wochenschau. 12 Er kauft zwei Karten.

Exercise No. 74

1 Wie spät ist es? Es ist ein Viertel nach neun. 2 Danke schön. Bitte sehr. 3 Um wieviel Uhr beginnt die letzte Vorstellung? 4 Die letzte Vorstellung beginnt um halb acht. 5 Wieviel kostet die Karte? 6 Der Tourist bezahlt für zwei Eintrittskarten. 7 Reisen Sie mit dem Flugzeug oder mit der Eisenbahn? 8 Ich reise weder mit dem Flugzeug noch mit der Eisenbahn, ich reise im Auto. 9 Um wieviel Uhr geht das Flugzeug nach Hamburg ab? Es geht um 18 Uhr 20 ab. 10 Der Autobus aus Düsseldorf kommt um 14 Uhr 10 an.

Exercise No. 75

1 Mark gegen Pfund wechseln. 2 glückliche Reise 3 macht große Fortschritte 4 Auskunft 5 zu Fuß 6 Ich denke an 7 Eines Abends 8 Seit wann 9 Ich studiere 10 Ich gebe ihm die Hand 11 Es freut mich 12 Fangen wir an

Exercise No. 76

1 —What are you reading?—I am reading the German newspaper.—What is he reading?—He is reading an English newspaper.

2 —What are you giving Mother for her birthday?—I am giving her a silk handkerchief.—What is Karl giving her?—He is giving her a pretty scarf.

3 —Does Herr Kurz speak English and French?—He speaks neither English nor French. He speaks only German.

4 —Which suit is he wearing today?—He is wearing his new brown suit.

5 —At what time does he leave the house every day?—He leaves the house at seven o'clock sharp.

6 —How long are you remaining here in this city?—I am remaining here a whole year.

7 —Have you a large suitcase?—I have a large one and a small one.—Please lend me the large.—Gladly.

8 —What a pretty dress!—What a lovely garden!—What a beautiful lady!

Exercise No. 77

1 (e) 2 (f) 3 (a) 4 (h) 5 (b) 6 (j) 7 (i) 8 (c) 9 (g) 10 (d)

Exercise No. 78

2 dem roten Bleistift 3 einen schweren Handkoffer 4 den schweren Handkoffer 5 einer schönen Frau 6 dieses englischen Kaufmanns 7 jenem kleinen Tisch 8 den runden Tisch 9 ein schönes Mädchen! 10 dem europäischen Kontinent 11 dieser großen Firma 12 dem gemütlichen Zimmer 13 kein altes Auto 14 uns(e)res schweren Koffers 15 seinen deutschen Vertreter

Exercise No. 79

2 diese schönen Bilder kosten 3 unseren deutschen Lehrern 4 diese kleinen Mädchen 5 Wo sind die Wohnungen deiner neuen Freundinnen? 6 Die deutschen Übungen sind . . . 7 Wo sind die neuen Hefte? 8 keine deutschen Bücher 9 jener hübschen Kinder 10 den deutschen Zeitungen 11 Liebe Freunde! 12 Liebe Freundinnen!

Exercise No. 80

1 uns 2 ihn 3 Sie 4 uns 5 ihm 6 ihr 7 Sie 8 dir 9 sie 10 Er 11 Sie 12 Es

Exercise No. 81

CHARLES DOES NOT LIKE STUDYING MATHEMATICS

One day Charles comes from school and says to his mother: 'I don't like learning mathematics. It is too difficult. Why must we do so many exercises and examples. We have calculating machines, haven't we?'

The mother looks at her son and says: 'You are wrong my child. One can do nothing without mathematics. We use mathematics not only in daily life but also in all fields of science.' The mother stops talking, for she sees her son is not paying attention to what she is saying.

'Just tell me, my dear boy, doesn't football interests you?'

'Go on, Mother! You're joking.'

'Well then, if Hotspurs win eight games and lose three, do you know what percentage of games they win?'

Charles answers: 'For the percentage of games I don't need any mathematics. I find all that worked out in the newspaper. But you're right, Mother. I must study more. I hope to go to a university some day and therefore I must pass the school examinations well, not only in mathematics but also in the other subjects.'

Exercise No. 82

1 May I ask you how old you are? 2 May I ask you for your name? 3 May I leave the room? 4 May I pass you the bread? 5 May I ask you for a light? 6 May I introduce my friend to you? 7 May we come in? 8 At half past two they may leave the school. 9 The children are not permitted to play in the street. 10 Nobody is permitted to enter this room. 11 May I offer you a cigarette? 12 Nobody may come in.

Exercise No. 83

1 At what time do you get up?—I get up at seven o'clock. 2 Do you dress (yourself) quickly?—Yes, I dress (myself) quickly. 3 Do the children have a good time in the park?—They have a very good time. 4 What do the parents talk about at breakfast?—They talk about the children. 5 At what time do you sit down to breakfast?—We sit down to breakfast at half past seven. 6 Do you shave every morning?—Yes, I shave almost every morning.

Exercise No. 84

2 sich 3 mich 4 sich 5 sich 6 sich 7 uns 8 uns 9 sich 10 dich—dich 11 sich 12 uns

Exercise No. 85

1 Mr. Clark gets up early every working day. 2 He washes and shaves very quickly. 3 He dresses quickly. 4 Mr. Clark and his wife have breakfast together. 5 He goes to the station in his car. 6 The train arrives soon. 7 Mr. Clark boards the train with many other people. 8 The train leaves in a few minutes. 9 The train arrives in London in half an hour. 10 All the passengers get off. 11 Mr. Clark walks to his office. 12 He works hard all day.

Exercise No. 86

3 —daß er sich schnell anzieht. 4 —daß Herr C. und seine Frau zusammen frühstücken. 5 —daß er mit dem Auto nach der Station fährt. 6 —daß der Zug bald ankommt. 7 —daß Herr C. mit . . . einsteigt. 8 —daß der Zug in einigen Minuten abfährt. 9 —daß der Zug in einer halben . . . ankommt. 10 —daß alle Passagiere aussteigen. 11 —daß Herr C. zu Fuß ins Büro geht. 12 —daß er den ganzen Tag tüchtig arbeitet.

Exercise No. 87

1 Er muß um sechs Uhr aufstehen. 2 Er braucht eine halbe Stunde dazu. 3 Gegen sieben Uhr setzt er sich zum Frühstück. 4 Er frühstückt mit seiner Frau. 5 Sie unterhalten sich über die Kinder. 6 Gewöhnlich hat er Orangensaft, Semmeln, Speck mit Ei und Kaffee. 7 Die Kinder stehen manchmal auf, bevor er weggeht. 8 Er fährt im Auto nach der Station. 9 Er liest die Post. 10 Er telephoniert mit verschiedenen Kunden. 11 Zum Mittagessen braucht er nur zwanzig Minuten. 12 Um fünf Uhr verläßt er sein Büro. 13 Um ein Viertel nach sechs kommt er nach Hause. 14 Am Ende des Tages fühlt er sich müde. 15 Er freut sich, zu Hause zu sein.

Exercise No. 88

1 Die Kinder stehen früh auf und ziehen sich schnell an. 2 Vor dem Frühstück dürfen sie nicht spielen. 3 Um sieben Uhr morgens setzen wir uns zum Frühstück. 4 Sie setzen sich um sechs Uhr abends zum Abendessen. 5 Wann setzt ihr euch zum Mittagessen? 6 Ich arbeite sehr schwer und bin am Ende des Tages müde. 7 Nach dem Abendessen unterhalten sie sich über die Kinder. 8 Es freut uns, Sie zu sehen.

Exercise No. 90

2 Was sagte der Junge? 3 Was antwortete . . . 4 Sein Vater wartete . . . 5 Sie redeten . . . 6 Ich machte . . . 7 Ich lernte . . . 8 Wir setzten uns . . . 9 Sie kaufte . . . 10 Wohntest du . . . 11 Ich wohnte . . . 12 Hattet ihr . . . 13 Wir hatten . . . 14 Was fragte . . . 15 Diese Leute arbeiteten . . .

Exercise No. 91

2 Die Kinder standen . . . auf. 3 Wann aßen Sie . . . 4 Wir fuhren . . . 5 Es gab . . . 6 Um wieviel Uhr kam . . . an? 7 Um wieviel Uhr ging . . . ab? 8 Er trug . . . 9 Viele Leute standen . . . 10 Die Herren saßen . . . 11 In der deutschen Klasse sprachen wir . . . 12 Schriebst du . . .

Exercise No. 92

1 Der Titel dieses Kapitels ist „Die kleine Anna war krank." 2 Es war im Monat Februar. 3 Das Wetter war sehr kalt. 4 Herr Müller kam zur Wohnung des Herrn Clark. 5 Karl öffnete ihm die Tür. 6 Er gab dem Jungen Hut und Überzieher 7 Herr Clark wartete im Arbeitszimmer. 8 Die kleine Anna war krank. 9 Sie hatte Halsschmerzen. 10 Sie hatte die Grippe. 11 Sie sollte Fruchtsaft trinken. 12 Am Abend ging es ihr besser. 13 Sie redeten über Herrn Clarks Familie. 14 Herr Clark ging mit Herrn Müller zur Tür. 15 Sie sagten: „Auf Wiedersehen!"

Exercise No. 93

1 Es war im Monat März. 2 Ich kam zum Haus des Herrn C., und sein älterer Sohn öffnete die Tür. 3 Er sagte: „Guten Abend, kommen Sie herein." 4 Ich gab ihm meinen Hut und meinen Regenmantel. 5 Herr C. erwartete mich in seinem Arbeitszimmer. 6 Wir setzten uns und begannen zu reden. 7 Die kleine Anna war krank. 8 Was fehlte ihr? 9 Anna hatte die Grippe. 10 Sie hatte Fieber und Kopfschmerzen.

Exercise No. 94

2 Standen 3 kam 4 fuhr 5 fing 6 stiegen aus 7 stiegen ein 8 zogen 9 gab . . . zurück 10 nahm 11 trat . . . ein 12 gingen . . . hinein

Exercise No. 95

2 . . . Abendessen, sobald Herr Clark nach Hause kam. 3 . . . müde, weil er den ganzen Tag fleißig arbeitet. 4 Wissen Sie, ob der Zug pünktlich ankommt? 5 . . . Zimmer, als Herr Clark seiner Stenographin Briefe diktierte. 6 Als Herr Müller Herrn Clarks Wohnung erreichte, goß es in Strömen. 7 . . . kaufen, weil es zu viel kostet. 8 . . . aus, wenn der Zug in Hamburg ankommt. 9 Wenn Papa nach Hause kommt, freuen sich die Kinder. 10 Während du spielst, muß ich arbeiten.

Exercise No. 96

1 Der Titel ist „Welch schreckliches Wetter." 2 Es goß in Strömen. 3 Wilhelm öffnete ihm die Tür. 4 Der Lehrer gab dem Jungen Hut und Regenmantel. 5 Herr Clark erschien. 6 Herr Müller sollte Tee trinken. 7 Das Wetter war ein passendes Thema für diesen Abend. 8 Sie gingen in das Eßzimmer. 9 Frau Clark brachte ihnen den Tee. 10 Sie nahm eine Flasche Whisky vom Büfett herunter. 11 Sie stellte den Whisky neben die Teekanne. 12 Sie verließ das Eßzimmer. 13 Als sie tranken, sprachen die Herren über das Wetter.

Exercise No. 97

1 Es regnete aber Herr M. ging doch aus. 2 Als er das Haus erreichte, war er durch und durch naß. 3 Der jüngere Sohn des Herrn C. öffnete die Tür und sagte: „Kommen Sie schnell herein." 4 Herr M. trat schnell hinein. 5 Jetzt kam Herr C. in den Hausflur. 6 Er sagte zu seinem Lehrer: „Kommen Sie ins Eßzimmer und trinken Sie eine Tasse Tee. Wir können über das Wetter reden, während wir Tee trinken." 8 Die beiden traten ins Eßzimmer.

Exercise No. 99

2 Er erwartete mich . . . 3 Wir begannen . . . 4 Er verstand mich und ich verstand ihn. 5 Wir besprachen . . . 6 Ich erfuhr, daß . . . 7 Um zwölf Uhr gingen wir . . . 8 Die Rechnung . . . betrug . . . 9 Während wir die Rechnung bezahlten, entstand . . . 10 Wir gingen . . . was los war.

Exercise No. 100

1 ihr 2 deinem Vater 3 gehört 4 ihnen 5 Verzeihen Sie mir 6 Ihnen 7 glauben ihm nicht 8 Wem 9 uns 10 meiner Schwester 11 Unser neues Zimmer gefällt uns. 12 ihnen

Exercise No. 101

1 Sie redeten weiter. 2 Er fühlte sich wohl. 3 Es war ihm nicht mehr kalt. 4 Der Winter in London ist kalt. 5 Von Zeit zu Zeit bekommt man Schnee. 6 Im Frühling wird das Wetter schön, 7 Ein warmer Regen fällt. 8 Ihm gefällt der Herbst am besten. 9 Er mag im Herbst die kühle, frische Luft. 10 Herr C. hat den Frühling am liebsten. 11 In Deutschland ist der Frühling am schönsten. 12 Sie gehen am liebsten

spazieren. 13 Die Kinder singen, wenn sie den Kuckuck hören. 14 Die vier Jahreszeiten sind der Frühling, der Sommer, der Herbst und der Winter.

Exercise No. 102

1 Die vier Jahreszeiten sind der Frühling, der Sommer, der Herbst und der Winter. 2 Ich habe den Frühling gern. Sie hat den Sommer lieber. Er hat den Herbst am liebsten. 3 Im Frühling gehe ich gern spazieren. 4 Im Sommer spielt er gern Tennis. 5. Im Herbst spielen sie gern Fußball. 6 Im Winter gehen sie gern Schilaufen. 7 Es ist nun Frühling, und die Tage werden länger. 8 Sie sprechen über das Klima Deutschlands.

Exercise No. 103

1 The children admired all the things (that, which) they saw in the office. 2 The office, which Mr. Clark has occupied for two years, is in a large office block, 3 The cars which were running past on the street below seemed to be very small. 4 Today Mr. Clark had a pleasant surprise, about which he wants to tell his teacher. 5 Do you know the gentleman who came into the office yesterday? 6 Yes, he is the German friend about whom Mr. C. told us. 7 This friend lives in a suburb, most of the inhabitants of which work in the city. 8 The pictures of which we spoke yesterday are very expensive. 9 Do you like the coat (which) I bought yesterday? 10 Mrs. Clark whose daughter is ill, sends for the doctor. 11 The pupils whose books and copy books are lying here should take them away immediately. 12 Little Anna, who is only five years old, had 'flu.

Exercise No. 104

2 die 3 den (welchen) 4 denen 5 der (welcher) 6 das (welches) 7 die (welche) 8 die 9 dem 10 den

Exercise No. 105

2 wovon 3 woran 4 womit 5 worauf 6 wovon 7 worin 8 wodurch

Exercise No. 106

1 Er erzählte ihm von einer angenehmen Überraschung. 2 Er war im Begriff, einen Brief zu diktieren. 3 Er stand auf und sagte: „Was für eine Überraschung!" 4 Auf einem Tisch lagen illustrierte Zeitschriften. 5 Die Kinder bewunderten die farbigen Plakate. 6 Die kleine Anna war besonders neugierig. 7 Er arbeitet dort schon zwei Jahre (seit zwei Jahren). 8 Es befindet sich auf dem zehnten Stock. 9 Die Kinder sahen die Autos. 10 Sie gingen alle in ein Restaurant. 11 Es befindet sich nicht weit vom Büro. 12 Alle aßen mit gutem Appetit. 13 Karl hat immer riesigen Appetit. 14 Er freute sich über den Besuch seiner Familie. 15 Das Sprichwort bedeutet: „Appetite comes with eating."

Exercise No. 107

1 Eines Tages besuchte die Familie des Herrn C. ihn in seinem Büro. Das war eine Überraschung! 2 Die Kinder bewunderten alles, was sie in seinem Büro sahen. 3 Sie bewunderten die farbigen Plakate an den Wänden und die Zeitschriften, die auf dem Tische lagen. 4 Es war beinahe 1 Uhr und die Kinder hatten Hunger. 5 Herr C. sagte: „Ich kenne ein gutes Restaurant, das nicht weit von hier ist." 6 Karl, der immer einen riesigen Appetit hat, sagte: „Gehen wir!"

Exercise No. 108

1 Es tut mir leid, zu hören . . . 2 Was fehlt ihm? 3 Kopfschmerzen und Fieber 4 —aber jetzt fühlt sie sich besser. 5 Vor fünf Jahren . . . 6 —aber ich habe Kaffee

lieber. 7 befindet sich. 8 Es machte mir viel Freude ... 9 den Doktor kommen lassen. 10 zum Abendessen. 11 Es tut uns leid ...

Exercise No. 109

1 (*i*) 2 (*c*) 3 (*a*) 4 (*g*) 5 (*f*) 6 (*l*) 7 (*j*) 8 (*d*) 9 (*e*) 10 (*b*) 11 (*k*) 12 (*h*)

Exercise No. 110

1 (*c*) 2 (*e*) 3 (*h*) 4 (*f*) 5 (*g*) 6 (*a*) 7 (*i*) 8 (*d*) 9 (*k*) 10 (*b*) 11 (*j*)

Exercise No. 111

1 Herr C. muß 2 Ich will 3 Kann er 4 Wir müssen 5 Der Zug soll 6 Ich mag 7 Darf ich 8 Er will 9 Können Sie 10 soll ich 11 Darf er 12 Ich muß 13 Wir wollen 14 Kannst du 15 soll ich 16 Willst du 17 Kann ich 18 Er mag

Exercise No. 112

1 Ich wollte 2 Wir sollten 3 Ich konnte 4 mochten nicht 5 konnten nicht 6 durfte 7 durften nicht 8 Ich mochte 9 wollten 10 sollten

Exercise No. 113

2 ... machen, wenn die Kinder so viel Lärm machen. 3 ... reden, als wir das Examen machten. 4 ... warten, bis der Doktor nach Hause kommt. 5 ... gehen, weil es in Strömen regnete. 6 ... spielen, weil sie müde ist. 7 ... gehen, sobald du mit der Arbeit fertig bist. 8 ... waschen, bevor sie sich an den Tisch setzen. 9 ... arbeiten, während alle sich amüsierten. 10 ... aufstehen, als der Lehrer ins Zimmer hereintrat. 11 Ich weiß nicht, ob der Autobus um sieben Uhr abfährt. 12 Weißt du, ob wir für morgen eine Aufgabe haben?

Exercise No. 114

2 wusch und rasierte 3 zog 4 frühstückten 5 fuhr 6 warteten 7 kam 8 stieg ... ein 9 fuhr ... ab 10 versuchten 11 lasen 12 kam, stiegen aus

Exercise No. 115
MR. CLARK WAS ILL

On Thursday, 20 April, at eight o'clock in the evening, Mr. Müller arrived at the house of his pupil. The older son, a boy of twelve years, opened the door and greeted the teacher politely. They went into the living-room, where Mr. Clark usually awaited his teacher.

But this evening he wasn't there. Mrs. Clark wasn't there either. Mr. Müller was very surprised and asked the boy: 'Where is your dad?' The boy answered sadly: 'Father is ill. He is in bed, for he has a cold and a temperature. Mother tried to telephone you in order to tell you that you should not come this evening. The telephone operator said, however, that your telephone is out of order.'

The teacher said: 'I am very sorry that Mr. Clark is ill. I wish him a quick recovery. If he is well and cheerful next week we can study two consecutive hours. Well, until next Tuesday. Good-bye, young man.' The boy answered, 'Good-bye Mr. Müller.'

Exercise No. 117

2 am siebenundzwanzigsten August 3 am neunzehnten Juni 4 am zwanzigsten Januar 5 am neunten Juli 6 am zehnten Mai 7 am zweiundzwanzigsten März 8 am einundzwanzigsten März 9 Der erste Januar 10 das vierundzwanzigste Kapitel

Exercise No. 118

1 Herr Clark was eines Abends allein zu Hause. 2 Herr Müller trat bei ihm ein.
3 Frau Clark war im Kino mit den Kindern. 4 Dann und wann sieht er gern einen
guten Film. 5 Das Kino ist eigentlich nicht nach seinem Geschmack. 6 Er geht
lieber ins Theater. 7 Sie genießen ein gutes Lustspiel usw. 8 Das Parkett ist meistens
zu teuer für sie. 9 Sie sitzen gewöhnlich in der ersten, zweiten oder dritten Reihe.
10 Sie ziehen das Kino vor. 11 Es befindet sich in der Nähe. 12 Sie gehen zu Fuß.
13 Sie sitzen gerne in der zwölften, dreizehnten, vierzehnten oder fünfzehnten Reihe.
14 Herrn Clarks Fortschritt ist erstaunlich.

Exercise No. 119

2 gesehen 3 geantwortet 4 gearbeitet 5 geschrieben 6 angesehen 7 gestanden
8 gerechnet 9 geredet 10 gesprochen 11 verkauft 12 gekauft

Exercise No. 120

2 Wir haben . . . gegeben. 3 Ich habe . . . getrunken. 4 Ich habe . . . gelesen.
5 Die Kinder haben . . . gesessen. 6 Sie hat . . . geantwortet. 7 Was hat . . . ge-
fragt? 8 Haben Sie . . . gearbeitet? 9 haben wir . . . gehört 10 Was haben . . .
gesehen? 11 Ich habe . . . beantwortet.

Exercise No. 122

1 Herr Clark hat die deutschen Zahlen gut gelernt. 2 Sie üben Zahlen in Form
von Daten. 3 Er zitiert wichtige Daten der deutschen Geschichte. 4 Er muß für
jedes Datum ein wichtiges Ereignis angeben. 5 Hermann hat die Römor geschlagen.
6 Sie haben ein Reich gebildet. 7 Er hieß Otto von Bismarck. 8 Die Alliierten haben
sie besiegt. 9 Die Diktatur hat im Jahre 1933 angefangen. 10 Das Jahr 1945 bezeichnet seinen Tod und Niedergang. 11 Herr Clark hat alle Fragen richtig beantwortet.

Exercise No. 123

2 Er hatte sich . . . gewaschen und angezogen. 3 Unsere Familie hatte . . . gefrühstückt. 4 Der Vater hatte . . . gelesen. 5 Um sieben Uhr hatten wir uns . . . gesetzt. 6 Die Mutter hatte . . . bereitet. 7 Der Kaufmann hatte . . . gelesen. 8 Die
Kinder hatten sich . . . amüsiert. 9 Wir aber hatten uns . . . gelangweilt. 10 Was
hatten . . . getan?

Exercise No. 125

3 sind 4 Haben 5 haben 6 ist 7 Ist 8 hat 9 sind 10 Haben

Exercise No. 126

3 waren 4 Hatten 5 hatten 6 war 7 War 8 hatte 9 waren 10 Hatten

Exercise No. 127

1 Er ist um halb zehn aufgestanden. 2 Sie waren vor ihm aufgestanden. 3 Nein,
sie hatten noch nicht gefrühstückt. 4 Um zehn Uhr haben alle sich zum Frühstück
gesetzt. 5 Er hat die Sonntagszeitung gelesen. 6 Sie spielten. 7 Die älteren
besuchten Freunde. 8 Die Mutter hatte eine schmackhafte Mahlzeit bereitet. 9 Sie
wollten ins Kino. 10 Sie mußten also mit ihnen ins Kino. 11 Sie haben sich
gelangweilt. 12 Sie sind nach Hause gegangen. 13 Er hat an einen Freund
geschrieben. 14 Er hat einige deutsche Kurzgeschichten gelesen. 15 Er ist um elf
Uhr zu Bett gegangen.

Exercise No. 129

2 , warum Sie . . . verlassen haben? 3 , daß Sie . . . gewesen sind? 4 , wie Sie den Sonntag verbringen. 5 , daß Sie . . . machen. 6 , weil die Kinder gehen wollten. 7 , weil der Film . . . hatte. 8 , während die Mutter . . . bereitete? 9 , nachdem er . . . gelesen hatte? 10 , daß ich . . . gemacht habe.

Exercise No. 130

1 Herr Clark hat es erzählt. 2 Herr Müller möchte heute etwas von sich selbst sagen. 3 Er ist in Deutschland geboren. 4 Er ist verheiratet. 5 Er unterrichtet in einer Sekundarschule. 6 Er lehrt Deutsch und Französisch. 7 Er hat diese Sprachen auf dem Gymnasium und an der Universität studiert. 8 Er hat vier Jahre lang dort gelebt. 9 Er hat an einer französischen Zeitung gearbeitet. 10 Im Jahre 1938 wanderte er hier ein. 11 Er hat eine Stellung an einer Sekundarschule bekommen. 12 Er hat ein englisches Mädchen geheiratet.

Exercise No. 131

2 Ich werde 3 werden Sie 4 Wir werden 5 Werden Sie 6 wird er 7 Wirst du 8 Ich werde 9 Wer wird 10 wird diese

Exercise No. 132

2 Ich werde . . . bleiben. 3 Er wird . . . besuchen. 4 Du wirst . . . mitgehen. 5 Wir werden . . . sein 6 Ich werde . . . sein. 7 Werden Sie . . . schreiben? 8 Ich werde . . . ankommen. 9 Sie wird . . . sein. 10 Er wird . . . heiraten.

Exercise No. 133

2 , ob ich . . . vorlesen werde. 3 , daß sie . . . besuchen werden. 4 , ob das Wetter . . . sein wird. 5 , daß unsere Freunde . . . kommen werden. 6 , wo Sie unterrichten werden. 7 , daß niemand . . . kommen wird. 8 , daß du . . . bereiten wirst.

Exercise No. 134

1 Er hat einen Brief an seinen Vertreter geschrieben. 2 Er wird seinem Lehrer eine Kopie dieses Briefes vorlesen. 3 Herr C. beabsichtigt, eine Reise nach Deutschland zu machen. 4 Am 31. Mai wird er London verlassen. 5. Er wird fliegen. 6 Er wird am 31. Mai ankommen. 7 Dort wird er zwei oder drei Wochen bleiben. 8 Er wird vielleicht die Schweiz und Österreich besuchen. 9 Er wird Herrn Schiller kennenlernen. 10 Herr Schiller reist viel umher. 11 Er weiß es. 12 Er wird ihm in München begegnen.

Exercise No. 135

1 kennenlernen 2 stellen 3 antworten 4 beantwortet 5 kann 6 einen Ausflug 7 belästigt 8 Im Gegenteil . . . gefallen 9 fertig . . . keine Fehler 10 mit Vergnügen

Exercise No. 136

2 Dort hat sie . . . gemacht. 3 Sie hat . . . bezahlt. 4 Sie hat . . . gebracht. 5 Da hat sie . . . vermißt. 6 Sie ist . . . gelaufen. 7 Gott sei dank, sie hat . . . gefunden. 8 Der Kassierer hat . . . gereicht. 9 Frau C. hat . . . gedankt. 10 Sie ist . . . eingestiegen.

Exercise No. 137

1 While the gentlemen were talking about the weather, it was raining in torrents. 2 After he had drunk the tea and a glass of whisky Mr. Müller felt very well. 3 As his wife and children entered the office the businessman was dictating a letter to his

stenographer. 4 When we go to the theatre we prefer to sit in the stalls rather than in the balcony. 5 Since I have been in England I have been teaching in this school. 6 We shall wait on the platform until the train from Bremen arrives. 7 We know that you have been of great service to our firm. 8 Mr. Müller knows English, since he studied this language at the gymnasium (German secondary grammar school). 9 Although the parents did not like the cinema, they nevertheless went with the children to see the new picture. 10 You will succeed in getting a good position as soon as you come to London.

Exercise No. 138
MRS. CLARK'S BIRTHDAY

It was 22 March, the birthday of Mrs. Clark. On this day she was thirty-five years old. To celebrate her birthday, the Clark family went out to dinner in a German restaurant in the West End of London.

As they entered the restaurant they saw on the table, which was set for Mr. and Mrs. Clark, a beautiful basket full of white roses. Naturally, Mrs. Clark was surprised. She thanked her dear husband, and then the family sat down at the table. A pretty young waitress handed them the menu. All of them ordered their favourite dishes. At the conclusion of the meal the eldest girl, Mary, said in a subdued voice, 'Now!' and each of the four children drew out from underneath the table a pretty little box. In the boxes were presents for Mother. They all cried, 'Happy Birthday,' and each child handed Mother a present. Mary gave her a silk handkerchief, Charles a pair of gloves, William a woollen scarf, little Ann a childish portrait of Mother.

What a beautiful day, not only for Mother but also for Dad and the children.

As practice in arithmetic, Charles worked out the expenses for this day.

	£	s.	d.
The meal	6	0	0
Tip	1	0	0
Flowers	1	15	0
Total	£8	15	0

'The purest coincidence,' said Mr. Clark. 'Eight pounds fifteen is one hundred and seventy-five shillings; that is five times as much as thirty-five years.'

Exercise No. 139
AN EXTRAORDINARY PERFORMANCE AT THE CINEMA

One evening Mr. and Mrs. Clark went to the cinema. The films from Hollywood generally did not please them, for they offer a great deal of trash and junk.

But on this evening there was an extraordinary performance in a cinema right in the vicinity of their home. The film was a documentary about Germany and actually in the German language.

Mr. and Mrs. Clark arrived at the cinema at 8.30. Almost all the seats were already occupied. So they had to sit in the third row. Mrs. Clark didn't like that, for the movements on the screen hurt her eyes. Fortunately they were able, after a quarter of an hour, to change their seats, and after that they sat in the thirteenth row.

The Clark family liked this film extremely. Mr. Clark found a great deal of enjoyment in it.

As they were leaving the cinema Mr. Clark said to his wife, 'Do you know, Helen I think I shall be able to get along well in Germany. I understood almost everything the actors and actresses were saying in German.'

Exercise No. 140

2 Wir nannten; wir haben ... genannt. 3 Sandten Sie; haben Sie ... gesandt? 4 Er dachte; Er hat ... gedacht. 5 brachtest du; hast du ... gebracht? 6 verbrachten Sie; haben Sie ... verbracht? 7 Ich wußte; Ich habe ... gewußt. 8 Ihr kanntet; Ihr habt ... gekannt. 9 Ich erkannte; Ich habe ... erkannt. 10 Wir dachten; wir haben ... gedacht.

Exercise No. 141

2 zu bekommen 3 erwarten 4 aufstehen 5 aufzustehen 6 besuchen 7 zu finden 8 spielen 9 zu gehen 10 zu sagen 11 zu reisen 12 sagen

Exercise No. 142

1 Herr C. hatte einen Brief an seinen Vertreter geschrieben. 2 Er hatte ihn seinem Lehrer vorgelesen. 3 Gestern hat er die Antwort bekommen. 4 Der Lehrer hörte aufmerksam zu. 5 Sie fängt an: ,,Sehr geehrter Herr Clark!" 6 Er wird in München sein. 7 Er wird ihn am Flugplatz erwarten 8 Er wird sich mit Herrn Clark in deutscher Sprache unterhalten. 9 Er muß Herrn Clark und seinem Lehrer gratulieren. 10 Er hat ihn bis jetzt nur als Geschäftsvertreter gekannt. 11 Er wird erkennen, daß Herr S. auch sehr liebenswürdig ist. 12 Nein, er wird jede Gelegenheit ergreifen, Deutsch zu sprechen.

Exercise No. 143

2 schöner 3 kälter 4 älter 5 größer 6 jünger 7 interessanter 8 länger 9 mehr 10 besser

Exercise No. 144

2 der größere Tisch 3 dem längeren Bleistift 4 keine bessere Wohnung 5 einen jüngeren Bruder 6 eine jüngere Schwester 7 eine ältere Bluse 8 die höheren Berge 9 den besseren Platz 10 Ihr jüngerer Bruder

Exercise No. 145

2 das interessanteste Buch 3 den besten Platz 4 die längsten Tage 5 die kürzesten Tage 6 das wärmste Zimmer 7 den größten Läden 8 seinem ältesten Freund 9 die besten Plätze 10 die höchsten Berge

Exercise No. 146

1 Der älteste heißt Herr S. 2 Der reichste heißt Herr B. 3 Der größte heißt Herr S. 4 Herr E. ist älter. 5 Herr B. ist kleiner. 6 Herr S. ist weniger reich. 7 Herr B. hat das meiste Geld. 8 Herr S. hat das wenigste.

Exercise No. 147

1 Herr C. hat die deutsche Geschichte gut gelernt. 2 Herr M. will ihm jetzt Fragen über die deutsche Geographie stellen. 3 Er beginnt mit einer leichten Frage. 4 Die zwei längsten Flüsse sind die Elbe und der Rhein. 5 Der Rhein ist länger und breiter. 6 Man nennt den Rhein den schönsten deutschen Fluß. 7 An seinen Ufern findet man malerische Schlösser aus den ältesten Zeiten. 8 Die Zugspitze ist der höchste Berg Deutschlands. 9 Die Zugspitze ist niedriger als der Mont Blanc in Frankreich. 10 Die zwei größten Seehäfen befinden sich an der Nordsee.

Exercise No. 148

1 am höchsten 2 am schönsten 3 am kältesten 4 am heißesten 5 am kürzesten 6 am größten 7 am ältesten 8 am besten

Exercise No. 150

1 Die deutsche Küche bietet dem Touristen eines der größten Vergnügen. 2 Herr C. speist oft mit einem wichtigen Kunden in einem der besten deutschen Restaurants. 3 In Deutschland findet man die Kost nie einförmig. 4 Er wird seiner Frau ein gutes deutsches Kochbuch senden. 5 Das erste Geheimnis der guten deutschen Küche ist, daß man zum Kochen alles von der besten Qualität kaufen muß. 6 Das dritte ist, daß man die Kunst der Küche lieben muß. 7 Die Hauptmahlzeit der Deutschen ist das Mittagessen. 8 Sie beginnt mit einer guten Suppe. 9 Dann kommt Fleisch mit Gemüse und Salat. 10 Zum Dessert gibt es Obst oder Obstkuchen. 11 Herr C. hat Strudel am liebsten. 12 Der Strudel ist besonders in Süddeutschland beliebt. 13 Am Ende der Mahlzeit trinkt man nichts. 14 Während der Mahlzeit trinkt man Bier oder Wein.

Exercise No. 153

2 Welche Städte 3 besuchen wird 4 soll 5 alle Sehenswürdigkeiten 6 können 7 wollen 8 viele Ausflüge 9 können 10 erwarten

Exercise No. 154

1 Herr C. wird sechs Wochen in Deutschland bleiben. 2 Er liest fleißig in Reisebüchern. 3 Er wird zwei oder drei Wochen in München bleiben. 4 Man nennt München das deutsche Athen. 5 Das „Deutsche Museum" soll das größte sein. 6 Er muß im „Englischen Garten" einen Spaziergang machen. 7 Er möchte einen Ausflug nach Oberammergau machen. 8 Diese Stadt ist Nürnberg. 9 Wagner lebte und komponierte in Bayreuth. 10 Er wird Bonn, Köln und Düsseldorf besuchen. 11 Er wurde in Düsseldorf geboren. 12 Herr C. wird die Heimreise von Hamburg aus unternehmen. 13 Herr Müller möchte ihn begleiten. 14 Nein, er wird ihn nicht begleiten können.

Exercise No. 155

1 Er liest . . . Deutschland. 3 Er besorgt . . . Reisepaß. 4 Er kauft . . . Fahrkarte. 5 Er schreibt . . . Brief. 6 Er bekommt . . . Antwort. 7 Der Vertreter verspricht, ihn abzuholen. 8 Die Kinder schlafen dort viel. 9 Sie waschen sich. 10 Sie ziehen sich an. 11 Die Familie fährt zum Flughafen. 12 Das Flugzeug steigt auf. 13 Herr C. besteigt das Flugzeug. 14 Er reist ab. 15 Er läßt . . . zu Hause. 16 Die Familie verläßt . . . Flughafen.

Exercise No. 156

2 zu begegnen 3 ausnützen 4 vorzuzeigen 5 wiegen 6 nachprüfen 7 mitzuteilen 8 abzuholen 9 auszunützen 10 mitgehen 11 zu fahren 12 zu besteigen

Exercise No. 157

1 Herr C. studiert nun seit sechs Monaten Deutsch. 2 Er hat viel Zeit im Gespräch mit seinem Lehrer verbracht. 3 Er hat einige Bücher über Deutschland gelesen. 4 Er kann jetzt Deutsch sprechen. 5 Er hat einen Brief an seinen Vertreter geschrieben. 6 Dieser hat ihm versprochen, ihn am Flughafen abzuholen. 7 Endlich kommt der Tag der Abreise. 8 Das Flugzeug verläßt den Flughafen Punkt 8.00 Uhr. 9 Nein, Frau und Kinder begleiten ihn nicht auf der Reise. 10 Die Kinder müssen das Schuljahr beenden. 11 Sie muß für die Kinder sorgen. 12 Um ein Viertel nach sechs morgens ist die ganze Familie bereit. 13 Um ein Viertel vor sieben kommen sie am Flughafen an. 14 Herr C. läßt seine Karte und seinen Reisepaß nachprüfen und sein Gepäck wiegen. 15 Frau und Kinder sehen ihm bewegt nach.

Exercise No. 158

1 aufs Land 2 mit Recht 3 auf dem Lande 4 ergreifen Sie nicht die Gelegenheit 5 Mögen Sie . . . *or* Haben Sie . . . gern? 6 brachte das Auto in Gang 7 machte er einen Spaziergang 8 reisefertig 9 Ergreifen Sie jede Gelegenheit 10 Seiner Meinung nach 11 Ihrer Meinung nach 12 Wir haben ihn eingeladen

Exercise No. 159

2 haben wir . . . gegessen 3 schmeckte 4 ich habe . . . eingeladen 5 trank 6 Ich werde . . . zurechtfinden 7 Ergreifen Sie 8 Wir werden . . . beschreiben 9 haben . . . gespeist 10 Er hatte sich bemüht 11 sind . . . aufgestanden 12 Bietet 13 mußten 14 bestiegen hatte 15 sind . . . eingestiegen 16 bittet

Exercise No. 160

There are in London many large and nice provision stores with self-service which are called 'supermarkets'. But in the suburb in which the Clark family resides there is only one such market.

One day Mrs. Clark went with her two boys to shop at the supermarket. They entered the store through that marvellous door which opens by itself as you approach it. Near the entrance many little wagons stood in a row. They took one of these. William, the younger boy, wanted to ride in the little wagon, but his mother wouldn't permit it. She said, 'My boy, these wagons are not toys.'

Mrs. Clark and her two boys went first to the department for fruits and vegetables. Here she took 5 lb. of potatoes, a bag of apples, a dozen bananas, and some more vegetables. From here they went to the department in which the dairy products are. Mrs. Clark took a dozen eggs, three bottles of milk, a pound of butter, and several packages of cheese. In other departments of the store she took meat, tinned goods, bread, coffee, sugar, and tea.

Now everything was in the little wagon and Mrs. Clark was ready to go to the cash counter to pay for her purchases.

The bill amounted to £3 8*s*. Mrs. Clark gave the cashier £5 and received £1 12*s*. change. The cashier put all the purchases into three bags. Mother took one, and each of the boys took one. With their purchases in their hands they went to the exit. Outside they found their car, got in, and went home.

Exercise No. 163

2 Das Taxi hat . . . genommen. 3 Ich habe . . . gehabt. 4 Sie haben . . . geplaudert. 5 Mir hat nichts gefehlt. 6 Es hat . . . gefallen. 7 Er hat . . . verbracht. 8 Sein Freund hat versprochen, ihn zu treffen. 9 Er hat . . . gekauft. 10 Haben Sie . . . verlassen?

Exercise No. 164

2 Er ist . . . geworden. 3 Dann sind sie . . . hinausgegangen. 4 Herr ist . . . entgegengekommen. 5 Sie sind . . . gefahren. 6 Das Taxi ist . . . gerast. 7 Es ist . . . gefahren. 8 Endlich ist der Kaufmann . . . angekommen. 9 Herren sind hineingegangen. 10 bist du . . . gestiegen?

Exercise No. 165

1 Er ging in den Wartesaal. 2 Ein feinaussehender Herr kam ihm entgegen. 3 Er fragte: „Sind Sie Herr Clark?" 4 Herr Clark erwiderte: „Ja, ich bin's." 5 Sie fuhren nach dem Hotel Königshof. 6 Es fuhr mit größter Geschwindigkeit. 7 Er schrie: „Nicht so schnell fahren, bitte! Ich habe keine Eile!" 8 Der Taxifahrer antwortete: „Ich auch nicht." 9 Endlich sind sie beim Hotel angekommen. 10 Herr S. ging mit ihm hinein. 11 Man hatte ein feines Zimmer für ihn reserviert. 12 Es befand sich im fünften Stock. 13 Der Preis war zwölf DM täglich. 14 Er versprach, ihn anzurufen.

Exercise No. 168

2 über die Einladung 3 Ich freue mich auf 4 interessieren sich für 5 Was denken Sie 6 bittet um 7 auf seinen Lehrer 8 auf die Reise 9 an die kommenden Prüfungen 10 Ich denke nicht daran

Exercise No. 169

1 Herr S. hat ihn eingeladen. 2 Er fuhr mit einem Taxi. 3 Es machte vor einem modernen Mietshaus halt. 4 Die Wohnung befand sich in der vierten Etage. 5 Ein Dienstmächen lud ihn ein hereinzukommen. 6 Herr S. begrüßte ihn herzlich. 7 Es war im modernen Stil möbliert. 8 Herr S. stellte ihn seiner Frau vor. 9 Sie studieren auf dem Gymnasium. 10 Sie wartete mit einem ausgezeichneten deutschen Essen auf. 11 Zum Dessert gab es Apfelstrudel und Kaffee. 12 Sie unterhielten sich über das Leben in Deutschland, usw. 13 Sie zogen sich auf ihre eigenen Zimmer zurück. 14 Frau S. spielte Klavier und sang einige Lieder. 15 Er hatte einen gemütlichen Abend verbracht.

Exercise No. 170

2 Die Jungen hatten . . . abgeholt. 3 Was hatten Sie . . . getragen? 4 Im Korb hatte sich . . . befunden. 5 Wer hatte . . . zubereitet? 6 Hatte er . . . gewartet? 7 Sie waren . . . vorbeigefahren. 8 Hattest du . . . erkannt? 9 Plötzlich hatte der Lastwagen . . . angehalten. 10 Was war geschehen? 11 Der Fahrer hatte . . . geholfen, den Reifen zu wechseln. 12 Er hatte . . . geliehen.

Exercise No. 171

2 Die Jungen haben (hatten) helfen wollen. 3 Du hast (hattest) das Zimmer verlassen dürfen. 4 Ich habe (hatte) leider nicht mitgehen können. 5 Wir haben (hatten) nicht spielen mögen. 6 Ich habe (hatte) einen Brief schreiben müssen. 7 Der Mann hat (hatte) nichts annehmen wollen. 8 . . . haben (hatten) wir nicht aufs Land gehen können. 9 . . . haben (hatten) sie in der Stadt bleiben müssen. 10 . . . haben (hatten) sie Fußball spielen wollen.

Exercise No. 172

1 Er rief die zwei Söhne des Herrn S. an. 2 Er wollte einen Ausflug nach dem Ammersee machen. 3 Er lud die Söhne des Herrn Schiller ein. 4 Sie holten ihn an seinem Hotel ab. 5 Ein guter Imbiß war im Korb. 6 Die Mutter hatte ihn zubereitet. 7 Er hörte einen Lärm. 8 Sie hatten eine Reifenpanne. 9 Sie hatten keinen Wagenheber. 10 Ein Lastwagen hielt endlich vor ihnen an. 11 Er lieh ihnen einen Wagenheber. 12 In fünf Minuten war alles fertig.

Exercise No. 173

2 einige interessante Bücher 3 ganz gut Deutsch sprechen? 4 daß er viel fliessender Deutsch spricht. 5 von denen wir gesprochen haben. 6 Gefielen Ihnen 7 seine Musik und seine Küche. 8 was er nicht aus Büchern erlernen konnte. 9 ist nicht ruhiger als in unseren Städten. 10 Ich erinnere mich an 11 nicht nur . . . sondern auch 12 rasch erledigen? 13 Ja, und dannach konnte ich 14 über das Leben und die Sitten 15 werde ich Sie antelephonieren (or anrufen). 16 Er hatte Heimweh. 17 wird er die Familie mitnehmen. 18 bei uns zu Abend speisen? 19 den ich schreiben werde. 20 werde ich Ihnen alles erzählen.

Exercise No. 174

1 Herr C. ist im Begriff, Deutschland zu verlassen. 2 Die Sehenswürdigkeiten, die schönen Landschaften, die alten Städte, usw. haben ihm sehr gefallen. 3 Sie war nicht nur eine Geschäftsreise, sondern auch eine Vergnügungsreise. 4 Er konnte seine

Geschäfte rasch erledigen. 5 Er hatte Zeit gefunden, nur ein paar Briefe zu schreiben.
6 Im kommenden Jahr möchte er wieder nach Deutschland reisen. 7 Nein, er
beabsichtigt, die Familie mitzunehmen. 8 Er hatte seine Frau und Kinder vermißt.
9 Er wird Herrn Müller anrufen. 10 Er wird viele Stunden im Gespräch über
Deutschland verbringen.

Exercise No. 175

1 habe ... geholfen 2 lieh 3 scherzten und lachten 4 verging 5 hat ...
eingeladen 6 haben ... angenommen 7 rief 8 hielt 9 betraten 10 begrüßte
11 vorstellen 12 werden ... machen

Exercise No. 176

1 ist ein Geschäftsmann in London. 2 um den Vertreter seiner Firma zu besuchen.
3 Er wollte 4 hatte er Deutsch gelernt. 5 Er hatte 6 Deutsch sprechen, lesen und
schreiben. 7 über Deutschland. 8 Er schrieb 9 bekam er eine Antwort. 10 „Ich
werde Sie am Flughafen abholen," 11 holte ihn dort ab. 12 fuhren zu dem Hotel
13 Glücklicherweise 14 machte er einen Ausflug zum Ammersee. 15 gingen mit ihm.
16 Er besuchte die Plätze 17 verließ er München und machte eine Rheinreise.
18 der längste, der breiteste und der schönste 19 Schließlich fuhr er 20 flog er nach
London zurück. 21 wird Herr C. wieder eine Reise nach Deutschland machen
22 wird er seine Familie mitnehmen.

Exercise No. 177
GERMAN TELEVISION

In England 80% or more of the inhabitants own a television set. In Germany this
is not the case. Television sets are found only in a minority of the population, but the
number of families who possess TV sets is constantly increasing, hence also the number
of persons who can watch TV at home.

There is an important difference between television in England and in Germany.
Everyone knows the advertisements which accompany almost every TV broadcast,
whether it be a TV play, an opera, a documentary, on-the-spot reporting, or live
transmission. This is most disturbing when one watches television, particularly since
the advertising often occurs in the middle of the most interesting and exciting part of
the programme. And one is compelled to listen to this.

In German television it is different. Here there is no advertising, so that the German
TV viewer can enjoy the most interesting television programmes without annoying
interruptions. Every owner of a television set has to make a monthly payment as a
television fee. This amounts to 5 marks and this is the contribution of every TV-set
owner to the expenses of the TV industry.

If this were only possible in our country!

Exercise No. 178
MR. CLARK'S RHINE JOURNEY

After he had settled his business in Munich, Mr. Clark took a pleasure trip through
the Rhineland, partly by steamer and partly by train.

People assert quite rightly that the Rhine is one of the most beautiful rivers of
Europe. On the stretch from Mainz to Cologne, Mr. Clark admired the dark forests,
the terraced vineyards, the small villages with their quaint churches and houses, and
the ruins of old castles.

Now the steamer sailed past the Lorelei Rock. Everybody knows the legend of the
sorceress who enticed the boatmen to their death with her singing. Heinrich Heine has

immortalized this legend in the famous song: 'I do not know the meaning of my sadness.' (Lit. 'what it signifies that I am so sad.')

Soon after, the Dragon Rock appeared, where according to the legend the hero Siegfried killed a dragon. The legend relates that he bathed in the blood of the dragon in order to become invulnerable. In such legends from this region Richard Wagner found the material for some of his well-known operas, as for example *Das Rheingold*, *Siegfried*, etc.

The ship stopped at several of the famous Rhine cities. Thus Mr. Clark was able to visit the city of Mainz, the birthplace of Johann Gutenberg, who invented the art of printing.

Then came Bonn, the site of an old university, and since the Second World War the capital of West Germany. Ludwig van Beethoven was born in this city.

The next stop was Cologne. Here the most remarkable thing is the world-famous Cologne cathedral, whose towers reach more than 500 feet high.

The last Rhine city which Mr. Clark visited was Düsseldorf, the birthplace of the great German lyric poet Heinrich Heine.

From Düsseldorf the journey continued to Hamburg, where Mr. Clark had some business to settle and from which place he undertook the home journey by plane.

When Mr. Clark was at home again he often spoke of his interesting and pleasurable Rhine trip.

Exercise No. 179

3 er hätte 4 wir hätten 5 er schreibe 6 er schriebe 7 ich läse 8 sie läsen 9 er lerne 10 du lernest 11 du sehest 12 du sähest 13 er komme 14 wir kämen 15 sie gehe 16 sie ginge 17 er fahre 18 er führe 19 ich könne 20 er könnte 21 wir müssen 22 wir mußten 23 ich wisse 24 er wüßte 25 er habe gehabt 26 sie habe studiert 27 ich sei gewesen 28 ich wäre gewesen 29 wir seien gekommen 30 wir wären gekommen 31 du hebest gelebt 32 du hättest gelebt

Exercise No. 180

1 If I had enough money I would take a trip. 2 If the house were larger I would buy it. 3 If I had a vacation now I would travel to Europe. 4 If the weather were nice I would take a walk. 5 If she had time she would write us more often. 6 If he came today we would be happy. 7 If we could play tennis we would accompany you. 8 We would set out if our friends were already there. 9 The child would not fall if he did not run so fast. 10 They could do it if they wanted to do it. 11 If he had had time he would have visited the German Museum. 12 If we had had a jack we would have set to work at once. 13 I would not have believed it if I had not seen it myself. 14 We would have stayed at home if we had known that. 15 If Mr. Clark had not had a representative in Munich, he would not have settled his business matters so quickly.

Exercise No. 181

1 He said that he had a representative in Munich. 2 Somebody asked him whether his representative spoke no English. 3 He said that he wanted to talk German with his representative. 4 Somebody asked him whether he did not like the city. 5 He answered that he did not like the city. There was too much noise there. 6 He asked when the train left for Bonn. 7 He said one could not get along on a trip without much money. 8 She said little Anna had been ill yesterday. 9 She said the doctor had been here last evening. 10 They said they had got up early today. They had dressed quickly. 11 They asked whether the children had not yet gone to bed. 12 He said that they had taken a walk after the meal. 13 She said that she would leave on 1 May. 14 I asked them whether they would go to the cinema this evening. 15 The boy said to me that I should come in. 16 She said to us that we should sit down.

Exercise No. 182

1 Das Gepäck wird von dem Hausdiener hineingetragen. 2 Der Gast wird von dem Geschäftsführer begrüßt. 3 Das Fremdenbuch wird ihm vorgelegt. 4 Indessen wird sein Zimmer vorbereitet. 5 Sie werden von dem Zimmermädchen geöffnet. 6 Eine Vase wird mit Blumen versehen. 7 Sie werden von dem Zimmerkellner auf die Kommode gestellt. 8 Er wird von dem Hotelboy auf sein Zimmer gebracht. 9 Die Jungen wurden plötzlich durch einen lauten Knall erschreckt. 10 Der Autokoffer war nicht mit einem Wagenheber versehen. 11 Der Reifen wurde gewechselt.

GERMAN—ENGLISH VOCABULARY

Accent marks are used in the end vocabularies to indicate the stressed syllable of words when the stressed syllable is not the first. The accent mark is simply a pronunciation aid and not part of the spelling.

The cardinal and ordinal numerals are not included in the end vocabularies. The cardinals 1–100 are given in Chapter 13, Grammar Note 1; above 100 in Chapter 14, Grammar Note 1. The ordinals are given in Chapter 24, Grammar Note 1.

A

der **Abend, -s, -e,** evening; **am Abend, abends** in the evening

das **Abendessen, -s, -,** supper

aber, but, however

ab-fahren, er fährt ab, fuhr ab, ist abgefahren, to depart, leave

ab-holen, to call for, fetch

die **Abreise, -n,** departure

ab-reisen, to depart, leave

abwesend, absent

acht-geben (auf) er gibt acht, gab acht hat achtgegeben, to pay attention (to)

alle, all, everyone; **alles,** everything

allerlei, all kinds of

als, *sub. conj.* when, as (*in comparisons* than)

also, so, thus, therefore; well

alt, old; **älter,** older

das **Ame´rika,** America; der **Amerika´ner,** American; **amerika´nisch,** *adj.,* American

sich **amüsie´ren,** to have a good time, enjoy oneself

an, *prep. w. dat. or acc.,* at, on, to, up against

an-bieten, er bietet an, bot an, hat angeboten, to offer

ander, other; der **andere,** the other; die **anderen,** the others; etc. **anders,** different

der **Anfang, -s, ¨e,** beginning; **anfangs,** at first

an-fangen, er fängt an, fing an, hat angefangen, to begin

an-geben, er gibt an, gab an, hat angeben, to indicate

die **Angelegenheit, -en,** matter, affair

angenehm, pleasant, comfortable

an-halten, er hält an, hielt an, hat angehalten, to stop

an-kommen, er kommt an, kam an, ist angekommen, to arrive

an-nehmen, er nimmt an, nahm an, hat angenommen, to take on, accept

an-rufen, er ruft an, rief an, hat angerufen, to call up, telephone

an-schauen, to look at

an-sehen, er sieht an, sah an, hat angesehen, to look at; **etwas ansehen,** to look over, view, inspect

anstatt, *prep. w. gen.,* instead of

an-telephonie´ren, to ring up

die **Antwort, -en,** answer

antworten, *w. dative,* to answer

an-ziehen, er zieht an, zog an, hat angezogen, to put on, clothes; **sich anziehen,** to get dressed

der **Anzug, -s, ¨e,** suit (man's)

der **Apfel, -s, ¨,** apple

der **Apparat´, -s, -e,** apparatus, appliance

der **Appetit´, -s,** appetite

die **Arbeit´, -en,** work

arbeiten, to work

das **Arbeitszimmer, -s, -,** workroom, study

der **Arm, -s, -e,** arm

der **Arzt, -es, ¨e,** doctor, physician

der **Aschenbecher, -s, -,** ashtray

auch, also, too

auf, *prep. w. dat. or acc.,* on, upon

auf-bleiben, er bleibt auf, blieb auf, ist aufgeblieben, to stay awake

der **Aufenthalt,** stay, sojourn

die **Aufgabe, -n,** task, exercise

aufgeregt, excited

sich **auf-halten, er hält sich auf, hielt sich auf, hat sich aufgehalten,** stay, sojourn

auf-hören, to stop

251

auf-machen, to open
aufmerksam, attentive
der Aufsatz, -es, ⁓e, composition
auf-stehen, er steht auf, stand auf, ist aufgestanden, to stand up, get up
auf-warten, to wait on, serve
auf-suchen, to look up, seek out
das Auge, -es, -en, eye
aus., prep. w. dat., out, out of, from
der Ausdruck, -es, ⁓e, expression
der Ausflug, -s, ⁓e, excursion
ausführlich, in detail
der Ausgang, -s, ⁓e, exit
aus-gehen, er geht aus, ging aus, ist ausgegangen, to go out
ausgezeichnet, excellent
aus-kommen, er kommt aus, kam aus, ist ausgekommen, to get along
die Auskunft, ⁓e, information
aus-nützen, to make full use of
aus-packen, to unpack
aus-rufen, er ruft aus, rief aus, hat ausgerufen, to cry out
aus-sehen, er sieht aus, sah aus, hat ausgesehen, to look, appear
außer, prep. w. dat., outside of, except
außerdem, besides, moreover
außergewöhn'lich, unusual
außeror'dentlich, extraordinary
aus-steigen, er steigt aus, stieg aus, ist ausgestiegen, to get out, climb out (of a vehicle)
ausverkauft, sold out
das Auto, -s, -s; das Automobil, -s, -e, car
der Autobus, -usses, -usse, bus

B

baden, to bathe
das Badezimmer, -s, -, bathroom
der Bahnof, -s, ⁓e, railway station
der Bahnsteig, -s, -e, railway platform
bald, soon
der Balkon', -s, -e, balcony
der Ball, -es, ⁓e, ball
beabsichtigen, to intend
der Beamte, -n, -n, official
beantworten, to answer
bedeu'ten, to mean
die Bedeu'tung, meaning
been'den, to finish
sich befin'den, to feel; ich befinde mich wohl, I feel well
sich befin'den, to be located; Wo befindet sich das Hotel? Where is the hotel?

bege'gnen, w. dat., to meet
begin'nen, er beginnt, be-gann, hat begonnen, to begin
beglei'ten, to accompany
begrüßen, to greet
behal'ten, er behält, behielt, hat behalten, to retain
behilf'lich, helpful
bei, prep. w dat., at, with, beside, at the house of; bei uns, at our house
beide, both; die beiden Herren, both gentlemen
das Bein, -es, -e, leg
beina'he, almost
bekannt', known
bekom'men, er bekommt, bekam, hat bekommen, to receive
beläs'tigen, to annoy
beliebt' (bei), popular (among, with)
bemer'ken, to notice
sich bemü'hen, to try, endeavour
benei'den, to envy
bequem', comfortable
bereit', ready; bereits, already
berei'ten, to prepare
der Berg, -es, -e, mountain
berich'ten, to report, inform
der Beruf', -s, -e, occupation, profession
berühmt', famous
beschäf'tigt, busy
beschrei'ben, er beschreibt, beschrieb, hat beschrieben, to describe
besetzt', occupied
besich'tigen, to view
beson'ders, especially
besor'gen, to take care of, to obtain
bespre'chen, er bespricht, besprach, hat besprochen, to discuss
besser, better; best-, am besten, best
beste'hen, er besteht, bestand, hat bestanden, to pass (an examination)
beste'hen (auf), to insist (on)
beste'hen (aus), to consist of
bestei'gen, er besteigt, bestieg, hat bestiegen, to get on, mount
bestel'len, to order (goods)
besu'chen, to visit
betre'ten, er betritt, betrat, hat betreten, to step into (a place)
das Bett, -s, -en, bed
bevor', conj., before
bewoh'nen, to occupy
bewun'dern, to admire
bewun'dernswert, wonderful, admirable
bezah'len, to pay

bezeich'nen, to denote

die **Bibliothek'**, -en, library

das **Bier**, -es, -e, beer

bieten, er bietet, bot, hat geboten, to offer

das **Bild**, -es, -er, picture

bilden, to form, shape

bis, until

bisher, until now

ein **bißchen,** a little

bitte, please; you are welcome

bitten (um,) er bittet, bat, hat gebeten, to ask for, to request

blau, blue

bleiben, er bleibt, blieb, ist geblieben, to remain, stay

der **Bleistift**, -s, -e, pencil

die **Blume**, -, -n, flower

die **Bluse**, -, -n, blouse

das **Blut**, -es, blood

böse, angry

brauchen, to need, use

braun, brown

breit, broad

der **Brief**, -es, -e, letter

bringen, er bringt, brachte, hat gebracht, to bring

das **Brot**, -es, -e, bread

das **Brötchen**, -s, -, roll

der **Bruder**, -s, ∵, brother

das **Buch**, -es, ∵er, book

das **Büfett**, -s, -e, sideboard

das **Büro'**, -s, -s, office

der **Bürger**, -s, -, citizen

C

der **Chef,** head, manager

D

da, *adv.*, there, then; *conj.*, since, because

dabei, at the same time, in connexion with that

daher', therefore

die **Dame,** -n, lady

damit, with it; **damit'**, *sub. conj.*, so that

der **Dampfer**, -s, -, steamer

danach', after that

der **Dank,** gratitude; **vielen Dank!** thanks a lot!

danken, *w. dat.*, to thank; **danke!** thank you! **danke schön!** thank you kindly!

dann, then; **dann und wann,** now and then

die **Darstellung,** -en, performance

das, the, that, that one, who, which

daß, *sub. conj.*, that

dasselbe, the same

das **Datum**, -s, die **Daten**, date

dauern, to last

dein, deine, dein, etc., your

denken, er denkt, dachte, hat gedacht, to think; **denken an,** *w, acc.*, to think of

denn, *conj.*, *for*, because; *adv.*, then

dennoch', nevertheless

der, the, that, that one, who, which

dersel'be, dieselbe, dasselbe, the same

das **Dessert'**, -s, dessert

deshalb, deswegen, therefore

das **Deutsch,** German (language); **auf deutsch,** in German

deutsch, *adj.* German; der **Deutsche,** the German (man)

das **Deutschland,** -s, Germany

der **Dezem'ber**, -s, December

der **Dichter**, -s, -, poet, writer

die, the, that, that one, who, which

der **Dienstag**, -s, -e, Tuesday

das **Dienstmädchen**, -s, -, maid, servant girl

dieser, diese, dieses, this

diktie'ren, to dictate

das **Ding,** -es, e, thing

dividie'ren durch, divide by

doch, nevertheless

der **Doktor**, -s, **Dokot'ren,** doctor

der **Dollar**, -s, -s, dollar

der **Dom**, -es, -e, cathedral

der **Donnerstag**, -es, -e, Thursday

Donnerwetter! the dickens!

das **Dorf,** es, ∵er, village

dort, there

das **Drama**, -s, -en, drama

draußen, outside

dunkel, dark

dünn, thin

durch, *prep. w. acc.*, through

durch-führen, to carry on, carry out, accomplish

durch-kommen, er kommt durch, kam durch, ist durchgekommen, to get along

der **Durst**, -es, thirst; **Ich habe Durst,** I am thirsty

dürfen, er darf, durfte, hat gedurft, to be permitted to, allowed to, may

das **Dutzend**, -s, -e, dozen

duzen, to address with **du; sich duzen,** to say **du** to each other

E

eben, *adv.*, just, just now

ebenso, just as

die **Ecke, -n,** corner
die **Eile,** haste
ehe, *sub. conj.*, before
das **Ei, -es, -er,** egg
eigen, own
eigentlich, really, actually
eilen, to hurry
ein, eine, ein, *indef. art.*, a, an, one
einander, each other, one another
das **Einfamilienhaus, -es, ̈-er,** private house
der **Eingang, -s, ̈-e,** entrance
einige, several, some
der **Einkauf, -s, ̈-e,** purchase
ein-kaufen, to purchase
ein-laden, er lädt ein, lud ein, hat eingeladen, to invite
die **Einladung, -en,** invitation
ein'mal, once; **auf einmal',** all at once
ein-schliessen, er schließt ein, schloß ein, hat eingeschlossen, include, enclose, lock in
die **Eisenbahn, -en,** railway
ein-steigen, er steigt ein, stieg ein, ist eingestiegen, to get on (vehicle)
ein-treten, er tritt ein, trat ein, ist eingetreten, to step into, enter
die **Eintrittskarte,** entrance ticket
ein-wandern, to immigrate
der **Einwohner, -s, -,** inhabitant
einzig, single, sole
das **Eisen, -s,** iron; **eisern,** *adj.*, iron
die **Eltern,** parents
empfeh'len, er empfiehlt, empfahl, hat empfohlen, to recommend
das **Ende, -s, -n,** end; **zu Ende,** at an end; **endlich,** finally, at last
das **Englisch,** English; *adj.*, **englisch,** English; **auf englisch,** in English
die **Entfer'nung, -en,** distance
entfernt', distant
entschul'digen, to excuse, pardon
entste'hen, er entsteht, entstand, ist entstanden, to arise, originate
entweder . . . oder, either . . . or
das **Ereig'nis, -nisses, nisse,** event
erfah'ren, er erfährt, erfuhr, hat erfahren, to find out, come to know
der **Erfolg', -s, -e,** success
ergrei'fen, er ergreift, ergriff, hat ergriffen, to seize, take
erhal'ten, er erhält, erhielt, hat erhalten, to receive
erin'nern an, *w. acc.*, to remind (of); **sich erinnern an,** *w. acc.*, to remember

sich erkäl'ten, to catch cold
erken'nen, er erkennt, erkannte, hat erkannt, to recognize, know, discern
erklä'ren, to syate, declare
erlau'ben, to permit, allow
erle'digen, to settle, finish
erler'nen, to learn, acquire (knowledge), master
ernst, earnest
errei'chen, to reach
erschei'nen, er erscheint, erschien, ist erschienen, to appear
erschre'cken, to frighten
erst, first, only, not until
erwar'ten, to await, expect
erwi'dern, to answer
erzäh'len, to relate
die **Erzäh'lung, -en,** story, tale
essen, er ißt, aß, hat gegessen to eat
das **Essen, -s, -,** meal
das **Eßzimmer, -s, -,** dining-room
euer, -e, euer, your
etwa, approximately, about
etwas, something
das **Europa,** Europe; **europäisch,** European

F

die **Fabrik', -en,** factory
fahren, er fährt, fuhr, ist gefahren, to ride
der **Fahrer, -s, -,** driver
die **Fahrkarte, -n,** ticket (for vehicle)
der **Fahrplan, -s, ̈-e,** time-table
der **Fahrstuhl, -s, ̈-e,** lift
fallen, er fällt, fiel, ist gefallen, to fall
die **Fami'lie, -n,** family
die **Farbe, -n,** colour
fast, almost, nearly
der **Februar, -s,** February
die **Feder, -n,** pen
fehlen, *w. dat.*, to be lacking; **was fehlt dir?** what is the matter with you?
der **Fehler, -s, -,** mistake
das **Feld, -(e)s, -er,** field
der **Felsen, -s, -,** rock, cliff
das **Fenster, -s, -,** window
die **Ferien** (*pl. only*), holidays
das **Fernsehen, -s,** television
fertig, finished, done
fest-setzen, to fix, to arrange
das **Feuer, -s, -,** fire
das **Fieber, -s,** fever
der **Film, -(e)s, -e,** film, motion picture
finden, er findet, fand, hat gefunden, to find
die **Firma, -en,** firm, business

der **Fisch**, **-es**, **-e**, fish
die **Flasche**, **-en**, bottle, flask
das **Fleisch**, **-es**, meat
fleißig, diligent, industrious
fliegen, er **fliegt**, **flog**, ist **geflogen**, to fly
fließend, fluent(ly)
der **Flughafen**, **-s**, **˙:**, airport
das **Flugzeug**, **-s**, **-e**, airplane
der **Fluß**, **Flusses**, **Flüsse**, river
folgen, *w. dat.*, to follow
der **Fortschritt**, **-s**, **-e**, progress
die **Frage**, **-n**, question; **Fragen stellen**, to ask (put) questions
fragen, to ask
das **Franzö′sisch**, French; **auf französisch**, in French
das **Frankreich**, France
die **Frau**, **-en**, woman, wife, Mrs.
das **Fräulein**, **-s**, **-**, young lady, Miss
frei, free, unoccupied
der **Freitag**, **-s**, **-e**, Friday
die **Freude**, **-en**, joy, pleasure; **Es macht mir Freude**, It gives me pleasure
freuen, to please; **sich freuen über**, *w. acc.*, to be happy about; **sich freuen auf**, *w. acc.*, to look forward to
der **Freund**, **-es**, **-e**, friend
frisch, fresh
froh, happy, glad
fröhlich, cheerful, happy, gay
früh, early
der **Früh′ling**, **-s**, **-e**, spring
das **Früh′stück**, **-s**, **-e**, breakfast
früh′stücken, to have breakfast
fühlen, to feel (something)
sich fühlen, to feel (well, sick, etc); **Ich fühle mich wohl**. I feel well.
führen, to lead, to guide
die **Füllfeder**, **-n**, fountain pen
für, *prep. w. acc.*, for
der **Fuß**, **-es**, **˙:e**, foot

G

die **Gabel**, **-n**, fork
ganz, whole, quite, entire
gar nicht, not at all
gar nichts, nothing at all
der **Garten**, **-s**, **˙:n**, garden
der **Gast**, **-es**, **˙:e**, guest
das **Gebäu′de**, **-s**, **-**, building
geben, er **gibt**, **gab**, hat **gegeben**, to give
das **Gebir′ge**, **-s**, **-**, mountain range
gebo′ren, born; **Ich bin geboren**, I was born; **er wurde geboren**, he was born (*now dead*)

der **Gebrauch**, **-s**, **˙:e**, use, custom
gebrauchen, to use, make use of
die **Geburt′**, **-en**, birth
der **Geburts′tag**, **-s**, **-e**, birthday
gedul′dig, patient
gefal′len, *w. dat.*, er **gefällt**, **gefiel**, hat **gefallen**, to please; **es hat mir gefallen**, it pleased me, I liked it
gegen, *prep. w. acc.*, towards, against
die **Gegend**, **-en**, neighbourhood, region
das **Gegenteil**, **-s**, **-e**, opposite
das **Geheim′nis**, **-nisses**, **-nisse**, secret
gehen, er **geht**, **ging**, ist **gegangen**, to go
gehö′ren, *w. dat.*, to belong to
gelb, yellow
das **Geld**, **-es**, **-er**, money
der **Geldbeutel**, **-s**, **-**, purse
gelin′gen, es **gelingt**, **gelang**, ist **gelungen**, to be successful; **es gelang mir**, I succeeded
die **Gele′genheit**, **-en**, opportunity
das **Gemü′se**, **-s**, **-**, vegetable, vegetables
gemüt′lich, sociable, cosy, comfortable
die **Gemüt′lichkeit**, comfort, sociability
genießen er **genießt**, **genoß**, hat **genossen**, to enjoy
genug′, enough
die **Geographie′**, geography
das **Gepäck′**, **-s**, baggage
gera′de, just now; straight
das **Gericht′**, **-s**, **-e**, food, dish
gern, gladly; **er spielt gern**, he likes to play
das **Geschäft′**, **-s**, **-e**, business
der **Geschäfts′mann**, **-s**, businessman; **Geschäftsleute**, businessmen
die **Geschäfts′sache**, **-n**, business matter
gesche′hen, es **geschieht**, **geschah**, ist **geschehen**, to happen
das **Geschenk′**, **-s**, **-e**, gift
die **Geschich′te**, **-n**, history, story
geschmack′voll, tasty
das **Gespräch′**, **-s**, **-e**, conversation
geste′hen, er **gesteht**, **gestand**, hat **gestanden**, to confess
gestern, yesterday
die **Gesund′heit**, health
das **Gewicht′**, **-s**, **-e**, weight
gewin′nen, er **gewinnt**, **gewann**, hat **gewonnen**, to win
gewiß′, certain, certainly
gewöhn′lich, usual, usually
gießen, er **gießt**, **goß**, hat **gegossen**, to spill, pour
der **Gipfel**, **-s**, **-**, peak

das **Glas, -es, ⸚er,** glass
glauben, to believe, think
glücklich, happy, fortunate
glücklicherweise, luckily
der **Gott, -es, ⸚er,** god
das **Gras, -es, ⸚er,** grass
gratulie'ren, *w. dat.,* to congratulate
grau gray
groß (größer, am größten), big, great
großartig, splendid
grün green
gründllich, thorough, thoroughly
der **Gruß, -es, ⸚e** greeting
grüßen, to greet
der **Gummischuh, -s, -e,** rubber overshoe
gut (besser, am besten), good
das **Gymna'sium, -s, -ien,** German secondary grammar school

H

das **Haar, -es, -e,** hair
haben, er hat, hatte, hat gehabt, to have
der **Hafen, -s, -,** harbour
halb half; **halb fünf (Uhr),** half past four
der **Hals, -es, ⸚e,** neck; **Halsschmerzen,** sore throat
das **Halstuch, -s, ⸚er,** scarf, neckerchief
halten, er hält, hielt, hat gehalten, to hold
halt-machen, to stop
die **Hand, ⸚e,** hand; **sie geben sich die Hand,** they shake hands
handeln, to deal
der **Handkoffer, -s, -,** suitcase
der **Handschuh, -s, -e,** glove
die **Handtasche, -n,** handbag
hängen, to hang
das **Haupt, -es, ⸚er,** head, chief
die **Hauptstadt, ⸚e,** capital
das **Haus, -s, ⸚er,** house; **zu Hause,** at home; **nach Hause,** (towards) home
die **Hausaufgabe, -n,** homework
die **Hausfrau, -en,** housewife
das **Heft, -es, -e,** notebook
die **Heimat,** native place or country
heim-kommen, to come home
das **Heimweh, -s,** homesickness; **er hat Heimweh,** he is homesick
heißen, er heißt, hieß, hat geheißen, to be called; **wie heißen Sie?** what is your name?
helfen *w. dat.,* **er hilft, half, hat geholfen,** to help
hell, bright
der **Held, -en, -en,** hero
das **Hemd, -(e)s, -en,** shirt

her, *shows direction* (hither)
herkommen, to come here
der **Herbst, -es, -e,** autumn
herein'-kommen, to come in
der **Herr, -n, -en,** gentleman, Mr., Lord
her-reisen, to travel here (hither)
herrlich, splendid
herun'ter-nehmen, er nimmt herunter, nahm herunter, hat heruntergenommen, to take down
herzlich, sincere, sincerely, hearty, cordial
heute, today; **heute früh,** this morning
hier, here
die **Hilfe,** help
der **Himmel, -s,** heaven, sky
hin, *shows direction away*; **hin und her,** to and fro
hinauf-tragen, er trägt hinauf, trug hinauf, hat hinaufgetragen, to carry up
hinaus-schauen, to look out
sich hingeben, er gibt sich hin, gab sich hin, hat sich hingegeben, to devote oneself
hinten, at the back
hinter, *prep. w. dat. or acc.,* behind, at the back of
hinzu'-fügen, to add, say further
die **Hitze,** heat
hoch (hoh- *before* **-e)** **höher, am höchsten,** high
das **Hochhaus, -es, ⸚er,** high (multi-storey) building
hoffen, to hope
hoffentlich, I hope, it is to be hoped
die **Hoffnung, -en,** hope
hören, to hear
das **Hotel, -s, -s,** hotel
hübsch, pretty
der **Hunger, -s,** hunger; **ich habe Hunger,** I am hungry
der **Hut, -es, ⸚e,** hat

I

ich, I
ihr, *pers. pron. fam. plu.,* you; **ihr,** *poss. adj.,* her, their; **Ihr,** *poss. adj. pol., form* your
illustrie'ren, to illustrate
der **Imbiß, -isses, -isse,** snack
immer, always; **immer wieder,** again and again
importie'ren, to import
der **Importeur', -s, -e,** importer
in, *prep. w. dat. or acc.,* in, into

indem', *subj. conj.*, while
indes'sen, *adv.*, meanwhile
intelligent', intelligent
interessant', interesting
das Interes'se, -s, -en, interest
interessie'ren, to interest; sich interessie'ren für, to be interested in
irgendein, irgendwelcher, any (whatsoever)
das Ita'lien, Italy
das Italie'nisch, Italian (language)
italie'nisch, *adj.*, Italian

J

ja, yes
die Jacke, -n, jacket
das Jahr, -es, -e, year
die Jahreszeit, -en, season
jährlich, yearly, annual
der Januar, -s, January
jawohl', yes indeed
jeder, -e, -es, that, each, every
jedermann, everybody
jedesmal, every time
jemand, somebody
jetzt, now
der Juli, -s, July
jung, young
der Junge, -n, -n, boy, youth
der Juni, -s, June

K

der Kaffee', -s, coffee
der Kaiser, -s, -, emperor
der Kalen'der, -s, -, calendar
kalt, cold
die Kälte, cold
das Kapi'tel, -s, -, chapter
die Karte, -n, ticket
der Kartenschalter, -s, -, ticket office
kaufen, to buy
der Käufer, -s, -, the buyer
der Kaufmann, -s, *pl.* Kaufleute, businessman
kaum, scarcely
kein, keine, kein, no, not a
keiner, nobody
der Kellner, -s, -, waiter
kennen, er kennt, kannte, hat gekannt, to
know, be acquainted with; kennenlernen, to get to know, make the acquaintance of
die Kenntnis, -nisse, knowledge, information

die Kera'mik, ceramics
der Kessel, -s, -, kettle
das Kilo, -s, -s, kilogram
der Kilome'ter, -s, -, kilometer
das Kind, -es, -er, child
das Kino, cinema, ins Kino gehen, to go
to the cinema
die Kirche, -n, church
klar, clear
die Klasse, -n, class
das Klavier', -s, -e, piano
das Kleid, -(e)s, -er, dress; *pl.* clothes
klein, small
das Klima, -s, -s, climate
klingeln, to ring
klug, clever, wise
der Knabe, -n, -n, boy
kochen, to cook
kommen, er kommt, kam, ist gekommen,
to come
die Kommode, -n, dresser
komponie'ren, to compose
der König, -s, -e, king
können, er kann, konnte, hat gekonnt, to
be able, can; er kann Deutsch, he
knows German
das Konzert', -s, -e, concert; ins Konzert
gehen, to go to the concert
der Kopf, -es, ¨e, head
der Korb, -es, ¨e, basket
kostbar, dear, expensive
köstlich, delicious
kräftig, strong, powerful
der Kraftwagen, -s, -, automobile
krank, sick, ill
die Krankheit, -en, illness
die Krawat'te, -n, necktie
der Krieg, -(e)s, -e, war
die Küche, -n, kitchen, cuisine
der Kuchen, -s, -, cake
kühl, cool
die Kultur', -en, culture
der Kunde, -n, -n, customer
die Kunst, ¨e, art
der Kursus, des Kursus, die Kurse, course
kurz, short
küssen, to kiss
der Kuß, Kusses, Küsse, kiss

L

lachen, to laugh
der Laden, -s, ¨, shop, store
die Lage, -n, situation, location, position
die Lampe, -n, lamp

das **Land, -es, -er,** land, country; **auf dem Lande,** in the country; **aufs Land,** to the country
die **Landkarte, -n,** map
die **Landschaft, -en,** landscape
lang, long
langsam, slowly
sich **langweilen,** to be bored
der **Lärm, -(e)s,** noise
lassen, er läßt, ließ, hat gelassen, to let, allow, have something done
der **Lastwagen, -s, -,** van
laut, loud
das **Leben, -s, -,** life
leben, to live, be alive
lebhaft, lively
legen, to put, place
die **Legende, -n,** legend
der **Lehnstuhl, -(e)s, -e,** easy-chair
lehren, to teach
der **Lehrer, -s, -,** teacher
leicht, easy, light
das **Leid,** sorrow; **es tut mir leid,** I am sorry
leider, unfortunately
leihen, er leiht, lieh, hat geliehen, to lend
leisten, to perform, achieve; **Dienste leisten,** to render services
die **Lektion', -en,** lesson
lernen, to learn
lesen, er liest, las, hat gelesen, to read
das **Lesebuch, -(e)s, -er,** reader, reading book
letzt, last
die **Leute,** people
lieb (lieber, am liebsten), dear, agreeable; **ich gehe lieber,** I prefer to go; **ich spiele am liebsten,** I like best of all to play
liebenswürdig, likeable, charming
das **Lied, -es, -er,** song
liegen, er liegt, lag, hat gelegen, to lie, be situated
die **Liste, -n,** list
loben, to praise
der **Löffel, -s, -,** spoon
die **Luft, -e,** air
das **Lustspiel, -s, -e,** comedy
der **Lyriker, -s, -,** lyric poet

M

machen, to make, do
das **Mädchen, -s, -,** girl
die **Mahlzeit, -en,** meal

das **Mal, -es, -e,** time; **einmal, zweimal, usw.,** once, twice, etc.; **manchmal,** sometimes; **das erste Mal,** the first time
der **Mai, -s,** May
malerisch, picturesque
man, *indef. pron.,* one, people, they
mancher, -e, -es, many a; *pl.,* many, some
der **Mann, es, -er,** man, husband
der **Mantel, -s, -,** coat
die **Mark,** mark (unit of German currency, now about 2 shillings)
der **Markt, -es, -e,** market
der **März, -es,** March
die **Masse, -n,** mass
die **Mathematik',** mathematics
die **Medizin',** medicine
mehr, more
mehrere, several
die **Meile, -n,** mile
mein, meine, mein, my
meinen, to mean, to believe
die **Meinung, -en,** opinion, meaning; **meiner Meinung nach,** in my opinion
meist, most; **meistens,** for the most part
der **Meister, -s, -,** master
der **Mensch, -en, -en,** human being, man
das **Messer, -s, -,** knife
mieten, to rent
das **Miethaus, -es, -er,** block of flats
die **Milch,** milk
mild, mild
mildern, to moderate, soften
die **Minute, -n,** minute
mit, *prep. w. dat.,* with
der **Mittag, -s, -e,** noon
das **Mittagessen, -s, -,** noon meal
die **Mitte,** middle
mit-teilen, to inform, impart
der **Mittwoch, -s, -e,** Wednesday
möbliert', furnished
modern', modern
mögen, er mag, mochte, hat gemocht, to like, care to, may
möglich, possible
die **Möglichkeit, -en,** possibility
möglichst bald, as soon as possible
der **Monat, -s, -e,** month
der **Montag, -s, -e,** Monday
der **Morgen, -s, -,** morning; **guten Morgen,** good morning; **morgen,** tomorrow; **morgen früh,** tomorrow morning
müde, tired
multiplizie'ren, to multiply
munter, cheerful

das **Museum**, -s, **Muse′en**, museum
die **Musik′**, music
müssen, er muß, mußte, hat gemußt, to
  have to, must
die **Mutter**, ⁚, mother

N

nach, *prep. w. dat.*, after, to, according to
die **Nachbarschaft**, -en, neighbourhood
nachdem, *sub. conj.*, after
nach-prüfen, to check
die **Nachricht**, -en, report, news
nach-schauen, to look after
die **Nacht**, ⁚e, night
nah (näher, nächst), near
die **Nähe**, vicinity
nahrhaft, nutritious
die **Nahrungsmittel**, *pl.*, foods, groceries
der **Name**, -ns, -n, name
nämlich, namely, that is
naß, wet
die **Natur**, nature
natür′lich, naturally, of course
neben, *prep. w. dat. or acc.*, beside, next
  to
nehmen, er nimmt, nahm, hat genommen,
  to take
nein, no (opposite of **ja**)
nennen, er nennt, nannte, hat gennant, to
  name, call
nett, nice
neu, new
neugierig, curious
die **Neuigkeit**, -en, pieces of news; *pl.*
  news
neulich, recently
nicht, not; **nicht wahr?** isn't that so?
nichts, nothing
nie, never; **niemals**, never
nieder, down
niedrig, low
niemand, nobody
nimmer, never
noch, still, yet; **noch ein**, one more; **noch**
  einmal, once more; **noch nicht**, not yet
der **Norden**, -s, north
das **Notenheft**, -s, -e, music book
die **Nummer**, -n, number
nun, well, now; **nun also**, well then
nur, only; **nicht nur . . . sondern auch**, not
  only . . . but also

O

ob, whether, if

obwohl′, *sub. conj.*, although
das **Obst**, -es, fruit
oder, or; **entweder . . . oder**, either . . . or
offen, open
öffnen, to open
oft, often; **öfter**, oftener
ohne, *prep. w. acc.*, without
der **Onkel**, -s, -, uncle
die **Oper**, -n, opera
die **Operet′te**, -n, musical comedy
die **Oran′ge**, -n, orange; der **Orangen-**
  saft, orange juice
der **Osten**, east

P

das **Paar**, -(e)s, -e, pair; **ein Paar**
  (Schuhe), a pair (of shoes);
ein paar, a couple, a few, some
packen, to pack
das **Papier′**, -s, -e, paper
der **Park**, -es, -e, park
das **Parkett′**, -s, -e, orchestra (part of
  theatre), stalls
der **Passagier′**, -s, -e, passenger
die **Person′**, -en, person
persön′lich, personally
der **Pfennig**, -s, -e, pfennig, penny
das **Pfund**, -es, -e, pound
die **Photographie′**, -n, photograph
plagen, to pester, annoy
das **Plakat′**, -(e)s, -e, placard, poster
die **Platte**, -n, record, disc
der **Platz**, -es, ⁚e, place, seat
plaudern, to chat
plötzlich, sudden(ly)
die **Polizei′wache**, -n, police station
das **Porträt′**, -s, -e, portrait
die **Post**, mail
das **Postamt**, -s, ⁚er, post office
der **Preis**, -es, -e, price, prize
das **Problem′**, -s, -e, problem
der **Profes′sor**, -s, **Professo′ren**,
  professor
das **Programm′**, -s, -e, programme
das **Prozent′**, -s, -e, per cent
der **Prozent′satz**, percentage
prüfen, to test, examine
die **Prüfung**, -en, the test, examination;
  eine Prüfung bestehen, to pass an examination
das **Pult**, -(e)s, -e, desk
der **Punkt**, -es, -e, period; **punkt neun**
  Uhr, nine o'clock sharp
pünktlich, punctual(ly), on time

Q

die **Qualität'**, -en, quality
die **Quantität'**, -en, quantity

R

das **Radio**, -s, radio; **im Radio,** on the radio
der **Rang**, -es, ⸚e, balcony (of theatre)
rasch, quickly
rasen, to rage, rush madly, speed
raten, *w. dat.*, **er rät, riet, hat geraten,** to guess; **ich rate Ihnen,** I advise you
der **Rauch**, -es, smoke
rauchen, to smoke
sich **rasie'ren**, to shave oneself
rechnen, to do sums, reckon
die **Rechnung**, -en, bill, sum
das **Recht**, -es -e, right; **mit Recht,** correctly, rightly; **sie haben recht,** you are right
reden, to talk
die **Regel**, -n, rule
der **Regen**, -s, rain
der **Regenmantel**, -s, ⸚, raincoat
der **Regenschirm**, -s, -e, umbrella
regnen, to rain
reich, rich
reichen, to hand, to pass
die **Reihe**, -en, row
die **Reise**, -n, trip
reisen, to travel
das **Reisebuch**, -(e)s, ⸚er, guide book
reisefertig, finished, ready to travel
der **Reisende**, -n, -n, traveller
der **Reisepaß**, -es, -pässe, passport
das **Restaurant**, -s, -s, restaurant
reservie'ren, to reserve
richtig, correct, right
die **Rolle**, -n, role
rot, red
die **Rückreise**, -n, trip back
die **Rückfahrkarte**, -n, return ticket
die **Rückfahrt**, -en, trip back
rufen, er ruft, rief, hat gerufen, to call
ruhen, to rest
die **Ruhepause**, -n, rest period
ruhig, quiet
rund, round

S

der **Saal**, -es, **Säle,** hall, large room
die **Sache**, -n, thing
sagen, to say, tell

der **Salat'**, -s, -e, salad
die **Sammlung**, -en, collection
der **Samstag**, -s, -e, Saturday
sanft, softly, gently
der **Sänger**, -s, -, singer
der **Satz**, -es, ⸚e, sentence
die **Schachtel**, -n, box
scharf, sharp
schätzen, to estimate
das **Schauspiel**, -s, -e, play
der **Schauspieler**, -s, -, actor
der **Scheck**, -s, -e, check
scheinen, er scheint, schien, hat geschienen, to seem, to shine
schenken, to present
scherzen, to joke
schicken, to send
schlafen, er schläft, schlief, hat geschlafen, to sleep
das **Schlafzimmer**, -s, -, bedroom
schlagen, er schlägt, schlug, hat geschlagen, to hit, defeat
schlecht, bad(ly)
schließen, er schließt, schloß, hat geschlossen, to close
schließlich, finally
schlimm, bad
das **Schloß, Schlosses, Schlösser,** castle
schmecken, to taste
der **Schnee**, -s, snow
schneiden, er schneidet, schnitt, hat geschnitten, to cut
schnell, quick(ly), fast
schneien, to snow
der **Schnellzug**, -(e)s, ⸚e, express
schon, already
schön, beautiful, fine
der **Schrank**, -es, ⸚e, cupboard; der **Kleiderschrank,** wardrobe
schrecklich, terrible
schreiben, er schreibt, schrieb, hat geschrieben, to write
die **Schreibmaschine**, -n, typewriter
der **Schreibtisch**, -es, -e, desk
der **Schuh**, -es, -e, shoe
schulden, to owe
die **Schule**, -n, school
der **Schüler**, -s, -, schoolboy, pupil
der **Schutzmann**, -s, **Schutzleute,** policeman
schwach, weak
schwärmen, to be enthusiastic
schwarz, black
schwer, heavy, difficult
die **Schwester**, -n, sister

schwierig, difficult, hard

der **See, -s, -n,** lake

die **See, -n,** ocean, sea

sehen, er sieht, sah, hat gesehen, to see

die **Sehenswürdigkeit, -en,** sight, object of interest

sehr, very

seiden, *adj.,* silk, silken

die **Seife, -n,** soap

sein, er ist, war, ist gewesen, to be

sein, -e, sein, his

seit, *prep. w. dat.,* since; **seit einer Woche,** for a week

seitdem, *sub. conj.,* since; *adv.,* since then

die **Seite, -n,** page

die **Sekun'de, -n,** second

selber, self; **ich selber,** I myself, etc.

selbst, self; **ich selbst,** I myself, etc.

selbstverständlich, obviously, it goes without saying

die **Semmel, -n,** roll

senden, er sendet, sandte, hat gesandt, to send

der **September, -s,** September

das **Servier'brett, -(e)s, -er,** tray

setzen, to place, put

sich setzen, to sit down, seat oneself

sicher, sure

sicherlich, surely

sie, she, they; **Sie,** you

singen, er singt, sang, hat gesungen, to sing

die **Sitte, -n,** custom

sitzen, er sitzt, saß, hat gesessen, to sit

so, so, thus; **so groß wie,** as large as

sobald, *sub. conj.,* as soon as; *adv.,* immediately

soeben, just, just now

das **Sofa, -s, -s,** sofa

sofort', at once, immediately

sogar', even

sogleich'=sofort', immediately

der **Sohn, -(e)s, ̈e,** son

solcher, -e, -es, such; **solch ein,** such a

sollen, er soll, sollte, hat gesollt, shall, to be supposed to, ought to, should

der **Sommer, -s, -,** summer

sondern, but, but on the contrary; **nicht nur . . . sondern auch,** not only . . . but also

der **Sonntag, -s, -e,** Sunday

sonst, otherwise

sorgen für, to care for, to take care of

die **Sorte, -n,** kind

sowie, as well as

sowohl als, as well as

das **Spanien, -s,** Spain

spanisch, Spanish

spät, late

spazie'ren, to walk, stroll

spazie'ren-gehen, er geht spazieren, ging spazieren, ist spazierengegangen, to go for a walk

der **Spazier'gang, -s, ̈e,** walk

die **Speise, -n,** food

die **Speisekarte, -n,** menu

speisen, to dine

spielen, to play

der **Sport, -(e)s, -e,** sport

die **Sprache, -n,** language speech

sprechen, er spricht, sprach, hat gesprochen, to speak

das **Sprichwort, -(e)s, ̈er,** proverb

der **Staat, -es, -en,** state

der **Staatsmann, -s, ̈er,** statesman

die **Stadt, ̈e,** city

der **Stamm, -es, ̈e,** trunk; tribe

stark, strong

die **Station', -en,** station

statt, *prep. w. gen.,* instead of

statt-finden, er findet statt, fand statt, hat stattgefunden, to take place

stehen, er steht, stand, hat gestanden, to stand

stellen, to place, put; **Fragen stellen,** to ask questions

die **Stellung, -en,** position, job

sterben, er stirbt, starb, ist gestorben, to die

stets, always

still, still, quiet

stimmt! that's correct

der **Stock, -es, ̈e,** stick, storey (of house)

der **Stoff, -es, -e,** stuff, material

stolz, proud

die **Straße, -en,** street

die **Strecke, -n,** stretch, distance

strecken, to stretch

streiten, er streitet, stritt, hat gestritten, to quarrel, fight

der **Strudel, -s,** strudel

das **Stück, -(e)s, -e,** piece

der **Student', -en, -en,** student

studie'ren, to study

das **Studium, -s, Studien,** study

der **Stuhl, -es, ̈e,** chair

die **Stunde, -n,** hour, lesson

stürmisch, stormy

suchen, to look for, seek

der **Süden, -s,** south

die **Summe, -n,** sum
die **Suppe, -n,** soup

T

der **Tag, -es, -e,** day
täglich, daily
tanken, to buy petrol, fill up
die **Tante, -n,** aunt
tanzen, to dance
das **Taschentuch, -(e)s, ∹er,** handkerchief
die **Tasse, -n,** cup; **eine Tasse Kaffee,** a
   cup of coffee
tatsäch'lich, in fact
tauschen, to change
das **Taxi, -s, -s,** taxi
der **Tee, -s,** tea
der **Teil, -(e)s, -e** part; **zum Teil,** in part
teilen, to divide; **geteilt durch,** divided by
das **Telefon, -s, -e,** telephone
telefonie'ren mit, to carry on a telephone
   conversation with a person
telefo'nisch anrufen, to telephone (someone)
der **Teller, -s, -,** plate
die **Temperatur',** temperature
teuer, dear, expensive
das **Thea'ter, -s, -,** theatre; **ins Theater
   gehen,** to go to the theatre
das **Thema, -s, Themen,** theme, topic
die **Tinte, -n,** ink
das **Tier, -(e)s, -e,** animal
der **Titel, -s, -,** title
die **Tochter, ∹,** daughter
der **Tod, -es -e,** death
die **Torte, -n,** tart, cake
die **Toilet'te,** ladies' or men's room
der **Tourist', -en, -en,** tourist
tragen, er trägt, trug, hat getragen, to
   carry
traurig, sad
trennen, to separate
trinken, er trinkt, trank, hat getrunken,
   to drink
das **Trinkgeld, -(e)s, -er,** tip, gratuity
trotz, *prep w. gen.,* in spite of
das **Tuch, -es, ∹er,** cloth
tüchtig, capable
tun, er tut, tat, hat getan, to do
die **Tür, -en,** door

U

üben, to practise
über, *prep. w. dat. or acc.,* over, across,
   about
überall', everywhere

überhaupt', at all
übermorgen, day after tomorrow
überra'schen, to surprise
die **Überra'schung, -en,** surprise
überset'zen, to translate
die **Überset'zung, -en,** translation
der **Überzieher, -s, -,** overcoat
die **Übung, -en,** exercise
das **Ufer, -s, -,** shore
die **Uhr, -en,** watch, clock; **wieviel Uhr ist
   es?** what time is it? **um wieviel Uhr?** at
   what time?
um, *prep. w. acc.,* around; **um . . . zu,** in
   order to
die **Umge'bung, -en,** surroundings
umher-reisen, to travel around
sich umkleiden, to change clothes
um-schauen, to look around
und, and; **und so weiter (usw.),** and so
   forth (etc.)
der **Unfall, -s, ∹e,** mishap
ungefähr', about, approximately
die **Universität', -en,** university
unter, *prep. w. dat. or acc.,* under, among
**unterhal'ten, er unterhält, unterhielt, hat
   unterhalten,** to entertain; **sich unterhalten (über),** to converse (about)
**unterneh'men, er unternimmt, unternahm,
   hat unternommen,** to undertake
der **Unterricht, -s,** instruction
unterrich'ten, to teach, instruct
der **Unterschied, -s, -e,** difference
die **Untersuch'ung, -en,** inspection
die **Untertasse, -n,** saucer
unterwegs', on the way

V

der **Vater, -s, ∹,** father
die **Verab'redung, -en,** appointment
das **Verb, -(e)s, -en,** verb
die **Verän'derung, -en,** change
**verbrin'gen, er verbringt, verbrachte, hat
   verbracht,** to spend (time)
verdie'nen, to earn
die **Verei'nigten Staaten,** United States
**verges'sen, er vergißt, vergaß, hat verges-
   sen,** to forget
das **Vergnü'gen, -s, -,** pleasure
vergnü'gungsvoll, pleasurable
verhei'ratet, married
verkau'fen, to sell
**verlas'sen, er verläßt, verließ, hat verlas-
   sen,** to leave, desert
verlie'ren, er verliert, verlor, hat verloren,
   to lose

der **Vers, -es, e-,** verse
verschie′den, different, varied
verschrei′ben, er verschreibt, verschrieb, hat verschrieben, to prescribe
versich′ern, to assure, to insure
verspre′chen, er verspricht, versprach, hat versprochen, to promise
die **Verspä′tung, -en,** lateness, delay; **der Zug hat Verspätung,** the train is late
verste′hen, er versteht, verstand, hat verstanden, to understand; **das versteht sich,** that goes without saying
versu′chen, to try, taste
der **Vertre′ter, -s, -,** representative, agent
der **Verwand′te, -n, -n,** relative
verzei′hen, er verzeiht, verzieh, hat verziehen, to pardon
die **Verzei′hung,** pardon; **ich bitte um Verzeihung,** I beg your pardon
viel (mehr, meist), much, many
vielleicht, perhaps
vielmals, often, many times
voll, full
vollkom′men, fully, completely
von, *prep. w. dat.,* from of
vor, *prep. w. dat. or acc.,* before, in front of; **vor einer Woche, a** week ago
voraus, ahead; **im voraus,** in advance
vorbei′fahren, er fährt vorbei, fuhr vorbei, ist vorbeigefahren, to ride past
sich vorbereiten (auf), *w. acc.,* to prepare for
vorgestern, day before yesterday
vorig, former, last; **voriges Jahr,** last year
vor-legen, to place before
vorne, in front
der **Vorort, -es, -e,** suburb
vor-stellen, to introduce
die **Vorstellung, -en,** performance, introduction
vorteilhaft, advantageous
vor-ziehen, er zieht vor, zog vor, hat vorgezogen, to prefer
vorzüg′lich, excellent

W

der **Wagen, -s, -,** wagon, car
wählen, to choose
wahr, true; **nicht wahr?** isn't it true
die **Wahrheit, -en,** truth
während, *prep. w. gen.,* during; *sub. conj.* = **indem,** while
wahrschein′lich, probable, probably
der **Wald, -es, ∹er,** forest
die **Wand, ∹e,** wall

die **Wanduhr, -en,** wall clock
wann? when?
die **Ware, -n,** goods, ware
warm, warm
sich wärmen, to warm oneself
warten auf, *w. acc.,* to wait for
der **Wartesaal, -es, -säle,** waiting-room
warum′? why?
was, what; **was für,** what kind of; **was für ein Tag!** what a day!
sich waschen, er wäscht sich, wusch sich, hat sich gewaschen, to wash (oneself); **sie waschen sich die Hände,** they are washing their hands
das **Wasser, -s,** water
wechseln, to change; **er wechselt Pfund gegen Mark,** he changes pounds into marks
weder . . . noch, neither . . . nor
der **Weg, -es, -e,** way; **weg,** away
wegen, *prep. w. gen.,* on account of
weg-gehen, to go away
weh-tun, es tut weh, tat weh, hat wehgetan, to hurt; **es tut mir weh,** it hurts me
die **Weihnachten,** Christmas; **zu Weihnachten,** for Christmas
weil, *sub. conj.,* because
die **Weile,** while
der **Wein, -es, -e,** wine
die **Weise,** manner, way; **auf diese Weise,** in this way
weiss, white
weit, far
weiter, further, farther; **lesen Sie weiter!** read on, continue reading
weiter-fahren, er fährt weiter, fuhr weiter, ist weitergefahren, to ride, drive on
weiter-sprechen, er spricht weiter, sprach weiter, hat weitergesprochen, to go on speaking
welcher, -e, -es, *interrog. adj. & pron.,* which, what; *rel. pron.,* who, which, that
die **Welt, -en,** world
wenig, little, few; **weniger,** less, minus; **ein wenig,** a little
wenigstens, at least
wenn, *sub. conj.,* if, when, whenever
wer? who? he who
werden, er wird, wurde, ist geworden, to become, get; **er wird alt,** he is getting old
wert, worth
wertvoll, useful, worthwhile
der **Westen, -s,** west

das **Wetter, -s,** weather
wichtig, important
wie? how? **so groß wie,** as large as
wieder, again
wiederho'len, to repeat
Wiedersehen; auf Wiedersehen! good-bye,
au revoir
wiegen, er wiegt, wog, hat gewogen, to
weigh
wieviel'? how much? **wie viele?** how
many?
der **Wind, -es, -e,** wind
winken, to beckon
der **Winter, -s, -,** winter
wir, we
wirklich, really
wissen, er weiß, wußte, hat gewußt, to
know (a fact)
die **Wissenschaft, -en,** science
wo? where? (at what place?)
die **Woche, -n,** week
die **Wochenschau, -en,** newsreel
woher? from where?
wohin? where? (to what place?)
wohl, well, indeed (*used for emphasis:* **ich
bin wohl müde,** I am indeed tired)
wohnen, to dwell, live
die **Wohnung, -en,** dwelling, home, flat
das **Wohnzimmer, -s, -,** living-room
die **Wolke, -n,** cloud
der **Wolkenkratzer, -s, -,** skyscraper
wolkenlos, cloudless
wollen, er will, wollte, hat gewollt, to
want to, wish to, intend to
das **Wort, -(e)s,** die **Worte** (*words in
phrases and sentences*), die **Wörter**
(*words not connected in sense*)
das **Wörterbuch, -s, ⁻er,** dictionary
wunderbar, wonderful
sich wundern (über *w. acc.*), to be surprised (at)
wünschen, to wish

Z

die **Zahl, -en,** number

zahlen, to pay
zählen, to count
zeigen, to show
die **Zeit, -en,** time
zeitig, early
die **Zeitschrift, -en,** magazine
die **Zeitung, -en,** newspaper
**zerbrechen, er zerbricht, zerbrach, hat
zerbrochen,** to break to pieces
ziehen, er zieht, zog, hat gezogen, to
pull
das **Ziel, -(e)s, -e,** goal
ziemlich, rather, fairly
die **Zigaret'te, -n,** cigarette
das **Zimmer, -s, -,** room
das **Zimmermädchen, -s, -,** chambermaid
zitieren, to cite
die **Zivilisation',** civilization
zu, *prep. w. dat.,* to, towards; *adv.,* too
zu-bereiten, to prepare
die **Zuckerdose, -n,** sugar bowl
zuerst, first, at first
zufrie'den, satisfied
der **Zug, -(e)s, ⁻e,** train
zugleich, at the same time
zu-hören, to listen to
**sich zurecht'-finden, er findet sich
zurecht, fand sich zurecht, hat sich
zurechtgefunden,** to get along
**sich zurück-ziehen, er zieht sich zurück,
zog sich zurück, hat sich zurückgezogen,**
to withdraw
**zurück-geben, er gibt zurück, gab zurück,
hat zurückgegeben,** to give back, to return
zurück-legen, to put back, to cover a
distance
die **Zuversicht,** confidence, faith
zuvor'kommend, obliging
zusam'men, together
zwar, it is true
der **Zweifel, -s, -,** doubt
zweifel'los, doubtless
zwischen, *prep. w. dat. or acc.,* between

ENGLISH–GERMAN VOCABULARY

Accent marks are used in the end vocabularies to indicate the stressed syllable of words when the stressed syllable is not the first. The accent mark is simply a pronunciation aid and not part of the spelling.

The cardinal and ordinal numerals are not included in the end vocabularies. The cardinals 1–100 are given in Chapter 13, Grammar Note 1; above 100 in Chapter 14, Grammar Note 1, The ordinals are given in Chapter 24, Grammar Note 1.

A

able (to be), können, er kann, konnte, hat gekonnt

actor, der Schauspieler, -s, -

advantageous, vorteilhaft

affair, die Angelegenheit, -en

after, nach, *prep. w. dat.*; nachdem, *sub. conj.*

again, wieder; **again and again,** immer wieder

against, gegen, *prep. w. acc.*

air, die Luft, -, ⸚e

airport, der Flughafen, -s, ⸚

all, aller, -e, -es, **all kinds of,** allerlei; **not at all,** gar nicht

almost, fast, beina'he

already, schon

also, auch; **not only . . . but also,** nicht nur . . . sondern auch

always, immer, stets

although, obgleich' *sub. conj.*

and, und; **and so forth, etc.,** und so weiter, usw.

another (one more), noch ein

answer, die Antwort, -, -en

answer (to) (*a person*), antworten, *w. dat.*; (*a question*), antworten auf, *w. acc.*, or beant'worten, *w. acc.*

apartment house, das Mietshaus, -es, ⸚er

appetite, der Appetit'; **I have an appetite,** ich habe Appetit'

arm, der Arm, -es, -e

arrive (to), ankommen

around, um, *prep. w. acc.*

art, die Kunst, ⸚e

as . . . as, so . . . wie; as soon as, sobald, *sub. conj.*

ashtray, der Aschenbecher, -s, -

ask (to), fragen; **to ask for,** bitten um; **to ask questions,** Fragen stellen

assignment, die Aufgabe, -en

aunt, die Tante, -n

at, an, *prep. w. acc.*

attentive, aufmerksam

automobile, das Automobil', -s, -e; das Auto, -s, -s; der Kraftwagen, -s, -

autumn, der Herbst, -es, -e

await (to), erwar'ten

B

bad, schlecht

balcony, der Rang, -es, ⸚e

basket, der Korb, -es, ⸚e

bathroom, das Badezimmer, -s, -

be (to), sein, er ist, war, ist gewesen; **to be located,** sich befinden

beautiful, schön

because, weil, *sub. conj.;* denn, *co-ord. conj.*

become (to), werden, er wird, wurde, ist geworden

bed, das Bett, -es, -en

bedroom, das Schlafzimmer, -s, -

beer, das Bier, -es, -e

before, vor, *prep. w. dat. or acc.;* ehe (bevor), *sub. conj.*

beginning, der Anfang, -s, ⸚e

begin (to), beginnen, er beginnt, begann, hat begonnen; an-fangen, er fängt an, fing an, hat angefangen

behind, hinter, *prep. w. dat. or acc.*

believe (to), glauben (*w. dat. of persons*)

belong to (to), gehö'ren *w. dat.*

beside, neben *prep. w. dat. or acc.*; bei *prep. w. dat.*

besides, außerdem

better, besser

between, zwischen, *prep. w. dat. or acc.*

big, groß

bill, die Rechnung, -en

birthday, der Geburts'tag, -es, -e

black, schwarz

blue, blau

book, das Buch, -es, ⁻er

bored (to be), sich langweilen

both, beide

bottle, die Flasche, -n

boy, der Knabe, -n, -n; der Junge, -n, -n

bread, das Brot, -es, -e

breakfast, das Frühstück, -(e)s, -e

breakfast (to), frühstücken

bring (to), bringen, er bringt, brachte, hat gebracht

bright, hell

broad, breit

brother, der Bruder, -s, ⁻

brown, braun

building, das Gebäude', -s, -

business, das Geschäft', -es, -e

busy, beschäf'tigt

but, aber; but (on the contrary), sondern; not only . . . but also, nicht nur . . . sondern auch

buy (to), kaufen

buyer, der Käufer, -s, -

C

cake, der Kuchen, -s, -

calendar, der Kalen'der, -s, -

call (to), rufen, er ruft, rief, hat gerufen; to call for, ab-holen; to call up, anrufen

called (to be), heißen, er heißt, hieß, hat geheißen

capable, tüchtig

capital, die Hauptstadt, ⁻e

car, der Wagen, -s, -; das Auto, -s, -s; people's car, der Volkswagen

carry (to), tragen, er trägt, trug, hat getragen; to carry up, hinauftragen

certain(ly), gewiß', sicher

chair, der Stuhl, -es, ⁻

change (to), wechseln

chat (to), plaudern

cheerful, munter, fröhlich

child, das Kind, -es, -er

cigarette, die Zigaret'te, -n

citizen, der Bürger, -s, ·

city, die Stadt, ⁻e

class, die Klasse, -n

clear, klar

clever, klug

climate, das Klima, -s, -s

clock, die Uhr, -en; what time is it? wieviel Uhr ist es?

close (to), schließen, er schließt, schloß, hat geschlossen

clothes, die Kleider *pl.*

coat, der Mantel, -s, ⁻

coffee, der Kaffee', -s

cold, kalt; to catch cold, sich erkälten

colour, die Farbe, -n

come (to), kommen, er kommt, kam, ist gekommen; to come in, herein'-kommen

comfortable, angenehm, bequem

cool, kühl

concert, das Konzert', -s, -e; to go to a concert, ins Konzert gehen

congratulate (to), gratulie'ren, *w. dat.*

conversation, das Gespräch', -s, -e

cook (to), kochen

correct, richtig

cost (to), kosten

count (to), zählen

country, das Land, -es, ⁻er, to the country, aufs Land; in the country, auf dem Lande

cup, die Tasse, -, -n

curious, neugierig

customer, der Kunde, -n, -n

cut (to), schneiden, er schneidet, schnitt, hat geschnitten

D

daily, täglich

dance (to), tanzen

dark, dunkel

date, das Datum, -s, Daten

daughter, die Tochter, ⁻

day, der Tag, -es, -e; day after tomorrow, übermorgen; day before yesterday, vorgestern

dear, teuer (expensive), lieb

depart (to), ab-reisen, abfahren

departure, die Abreise, -n

describe (to), beschrei'ben, er beschreibt, beschrieb, hat beschrieben

desk, der Schreibtisch, -es, -e; das Pult, es, -e

dictionary, das Wörterbuch, es, ⁻er

different, anders, verschie'den

difficult, schwer

diligent, fleißig

dine (to), speisen

dining-room, das Eßzimmer, -s, -

dinner (*midday*), das Mittagessen, -s, -

dish, der Teller, -s, -; die Platte, -n
divide (to), dividi'eren, teilen
do (to), tun, machen
doctor, der Doktor, -s, Dokto'ren; der Arzt (**physician**), -es, ⸚e
door, die Tür, -en
doubt, der Zweifel, -s, -; **doubtless,** zweifellos, ohne Zweifel
dozen, das Dutzend, -s, -e
drama, das Drama, -s, Dramen
dress, das Kleid, -es -er
dress oneself, sich an-ziehen
driver, der Fahrer, -s, -
drink (to), trinken, er trinkt, trank, hat getrunken
during, während, *prep. w. gen.*
dwell (to), wohnen

E

each, jeder, -e, -es
early, früh
earnest, ernst
earn, verdie'nen
easy, leicht
eat (to), essen, er ißt, aß, hat gegessen
egg, das Ei, -es, -er
either . . . or, entweder . . . oder
end, das Ende, -s, -en; **at an end,** zu Ende
English, das Englisch, *noun*; englisch, *adj.*; **in English,** auf englisch
enjoy (to), genießen, er genießt, genoß, hat genossen; **to enjoy oneself,** sich amüsie'ren
enough, genug
enter (to), ein-treten
entrance, der Eingang, -s, ⸚e
even, sogar
evening, der Abend, -s, -e; **in the evening,** am Abend; **evenings,** abends
event, das Ereig'nis, -ses, -se
everybody, jedermann
everywhere, überall
examination, die Prüfung, -en
excellent, vorzüg'lich, ausgezeich'net
except, außer, *prep. w. dat.*
excited, aufgeregt
excursion, der Ausflug, -s, ⸚e
exercise, die Übung, -en
exit, der Ausgang, es, ⸚e
expensive, teuer, kostbar
explain (to), erklären
express (train), der Schnellzug, -s, ⸚e
extraordinary, außeror'-dentlich
eye, das Auge, -s, -n

F

factory, die Fabrik, -en
fall (to), fallen, er fällt, fiel, ist gefallen
family, die Fami'lie, -n
famous, berühmt'
far, weit, fern
fast, schnell, rasch
father, der Vater, -s, ⸚
feel (to), fühlen; **to feel well, sick, etc.,** sich fühlen; **I feel well,** ich fühle mich wohl
fever, das Fieber, -s, -
finally, schließlich, endlich
foot, der Fuß, -es, ⸚e
French, das Franzö'sisch; französisch *adj.;* **in French,** auf französisch
friend, der Freund, -es, -e
from, von, *prep. w. dat.*
fruit, das Obst, -es, -e; die Frucht, ⸚e
full, voll
further, weiter; **read further,** lesen Sie weiter!

G

garden, der Garten, -s, ⸚
German, das Deutsch; deutsch, *adj.*; **in German,** auf deutsch
get (to), bekom'men, erhal'ten; **to get along,** sich zurecht'-finden; **to get on** (*mount*), bestei'gen, einsteigen; **to get out** (*of vehicle*), aus-steigen; **to get up,** auf-stehen
gift, das Geschenk', -s, -e
girl, das Mädchen, -s, -
give (to), er gibt, gab, hat gegeben; **to give back,** zurück-geben
glad, froh
gladly, gern; **he likes to play,** er spielt gern
glass, das Glas, -es, ⸚er
glove, der Handschuh, -s, -e
go (to), gehen, er geht, ging, ist gegangen
goal, das Ziel, -es, -e
good, gut
goods, die Ware, -n
grey, grau
green, grün
greet (to), grüßen
greeting, der Gruß, -es, ⸚e
guest, der Gast, -es, ⸚e

H

hand, die Hand, ⸚e
hand (to), reichen

handbag, die Handtasche, -n
handkerchief, das Taschentuch, -s, ⸗er
hang (to) (*something*), hängen
happen (to), gesche'hen, es geschieht, geschah, ist geschehen
happy, glücklich
hat, der Hut, -es, ⸗e
have (to), haben; **to have to,** müssen, er muß, mußte, hat gemußt
head, der Kopf, -es, ⸗e
hear (to), hören
heavy, schwer
help, die Hilfe
help (to), helfen, *w. dat.*, er hilft, half, hat geholfen
here, hier
high, hoch; **higher,** höher; **highest,** der, die, das höchste
hold (to), halten, er hält, hielt, hat gehalten
home, die Wohnung, -en, das Heim; **home country,** die Heimat; **I am going home,** ich gehe nach Hause; **I am at home,** ich bin zu Hause; **homesickness,** das Heimweh; **he was homesick,** er hatte Heimweh
homework, die Hausaufgabe, -n
hope (to), hoffen
hot, heiß
hotel, das Hotél, -s, -s
hour, die Stunde, -n
house, das Haus, -es, ⸗er
how? wie? how many? wie viele (wieviele); how much? wievel?
human being, der Mensch, -en, -en
hunger, der Hunger; **I am hungry,** ich habe Hunger
hurry, eilen
hurt (to), weh-tun, *w. dat.*; **it hurts me,** es tut mir weh

I

if, wenn, *sub. conj.*
immediately, sofort', sobald', sogleich'
import (to), importie'ren
important, wichtig
in, into, in, *prep. w. dat. or acc.*
industrious, fleißig
information, die Auskunft, ⸗e
inhabitant, der Einwohner, -s, -
ink, die Tinte, -n
intelligent, intelligent'
interested; to be interested in, sich interessie'ren für
interesting, interessant'

introduce, vor-stellen
introduction, die Vorstellung, -en
invitation, die Einladung, -en
invite (to), ein-laden, er lädt ein, lud ein, hat eingeladen

J

job, die Stellung, -en
joke (to), scherzen
joy, die Freude; **it gives me pleasure,** es macht mir Freude
just: just now, soe'ben

K

kind, die Sorte, -n
kilogram, das Kilogramm', -s, -e; das Kilo, -s, -s
kilometre, der Kilome'ter, -s, -
kiss (to), küssen
kitchen, die Küche, -n
knife, das Messer, -s, -
know (to): to know facts, wissen; **to know be acquainted with,** kennen; **to get to know,** kennen-lernen
known, bekannt'

L

lady, die Dame, -n
lake, der See, -s, -n
lamp, die Lampe, -n
land, das Land, -es, ⸗er
language, die Sprache, -, -n
last, letzt
last (to), dauern
late, spät
laugh (to), lachen
lead (to), führen
leave (to) on a trip, abreisen, ab-fahren; **to leave a person or place,** verlassen
lend (to), leihen, er leiht, lieh, hat geliehen
less, weniger
lesson, die Stunde, -, die Lektion', -en **assignment,** die Aufgabe, -n
let (to), lassen, er läßt, ließ, hat gelassen
letter, der Brief, -es, -e
library, die Bibliothek', -en
lie (to), liegen, er liegt, lag, hat gelegen
life, das Leben, -s, -
like (to), mögen, er mag, mochte, hat gemocht; *verb* + gern I **like to read,** ich lese gern
listen (to), zu-hören
little, klein; **a little,** ein wenig, ein bißchen

live (to), leben; (*dwell*), wohnen
living room, das Wohnzimmer, -s, -
long, lang
look, sehen, er sieht, sah, hat gesehen; schauen; **to look at,** an-schauen; **to look for,** suchen
lose (to), verlie´ren, er verliert, verlor, hat verloren
loud, laut
love (to), lieben
luckily, glücklicherweise

M

magazine, die Zeitschrift, -en
maid (**servant**), das Dienstmädchen, -s, -
mail, die Post
make (to), machen
man, der Mann, -es, ⸚er
manager (**head**), der Chef, -s, -s
many, viel, viele
map, die Landkarte, -n
mark (*unit of German currency*), die Mark
married, verhei´ratet
market, der Markt, -es, ⸚e
may (*to be permitted to*), dürfen, er darf, durfte, hat gedurft
meal, die Mahlzeit, -en
mean (to), bedeu´ten, meinen
meat, das Fleisch, -es
medicine, die Medizin´
meet (to), begeg´nen, *w. dat.*; **to get acquainted with,** kennenlernen
menu, die Speisekarte, -n
merchant, der Kaufmann, -s, die Kaufleute
milk, die Milch
minute, die Minu´te, -en
mistake, der Fehler, -s, -
Miss, das Fräulein, -s, -
money, das Geld, -es, -er
month, der Monat, -s, -e
more, mehr
morning, der Morgen, -s, -; **good morning!** guten Morgen; **tomorrow morning,** morgen früh; **this morning,** heute morgen
most, der, die, das meiste; **for the most part,** meistens
mother, die Mutter, ⸚
mount (to) (*a vehicle*), ein-steigen
cinema, das Kino; **I am going to the cinema,** ich gehe ins Kino
Mr., der Herr, -n -en
museum, das Muse´um, -s, die Muse´en
music, die Musik´

must, müssen, er muß mußte, hat gemusst

N

name (to), nennen, er nennt, nannte, hat genannt
named (to be), heißen, hieß, hat geheissen
naturally, natür´lich
near, nah(e); **nearer,** näher
nearly, fast, beina´he
need (to), brauchen
never, nie, niemals, nimmer
neither . . . nor, weder . . . noch
new, neu
news, die Nachricht, -en
newspaper, die Zeitung, -en
next, der, die das nächste
nevertheless, doch
nice, nett
night, die Nacht, ⸚e
no, nein; **no, not a, not any,** kein, keine, kein
nobody, keiner, niemand
not, nicht; **not at all,** gar nicht
notebook, das Heft, -es, -e
nothing, nichts
now, jetzt, nun
number, die Zahl, -en; die Nummer, -n

O

occupation, der Beruf´, -s, -e
occupied, besetzt´
occupy (to), bewoh´nen
of, von, *prep. w. dat.*
offer (to), bieten, er bietet, bot, hat geboten; anbieten
office, das Büro´, -s, -s
often, oft, vielmals
old, alt; **older,** älter
on (on top of), auf, *prep. w. dat. or acc.*, **on** (at, up against), an, *prep. w. dat. or acc.*
one (people, they), man *indef. pron.*; **one says (people say, it is said),** man sagt
once, einmal; **all at once,** auf einmal
only, nur
open, offen
open (to), öffnen, aufmachen
opportunity, die Gele´genheit, -en
or, oder; **either . . . or,** entweder . . . oder
order: in order to, um . . . zu
other, der, die, das andere
otherwise, sonst
ought, sollen, er soll, sollte, hat gesollt

out of, aus, *prep. w. dat.*
outside, draußen
outside of, außer, *prep. w. dat.*
over, über, *prep. w. dat. or acc.*

P

pack (to), packen
page, die Seite, -n
pair, das Paar, -es, -e
paper, das Papier', -s, -e; **newspaper,** die Zeitung, -en
pardon (to), entschul'digen *w. acc.*; verzei'hen, *w. dat.*, er verzeiht, verzieh, hat verziehen
parents, die Eltern
parking lot, der Parkplatz, -es, ⸚e
part, der Teil, -es, -e; **in part,** zum Teil
pass (to) (*an examination*), bestehen
passenger, der Passagier', -s, -e
passport, der Reisepaß, -passes, -pässe
pay (to), (be)zahlen
pay attention (to), achtgeben
pen, die Feder, -n
pencil, der Bleistift, -s, -e
people, die Leute
performance, die Vorstellung, -en
perhaps, vielleicht'
permit (to), erlau'ben
permitted (to be), dürfen, er darf, durfte, hat gedurft
person, die Person', -en
photograph, die Photographie', -n
piano, das Klavier', -s, -e
picture, das Bild, -es, -er
piece, das Stück, -es, -e
place, der Platz, -es, ⸚e
place (to), setzen; **to place before,** vorlegen
plate, der Teller, -s, -e
play, das Schauspiel, -s, -e
play (to), spielen
pleasant, angenehm
please, bitte!
please (to), gefal'len, *w. dat.*, er gefällt, gefiel, hat gefallen
pleasure, das Vergnü'gen, -s, -
popular (with), beliebt' (bei)
portrait, das Porträt', -s, -e
position, die Stellung, -en
possible, möglich
post office, das Postamt, -s, ⸚er
pound, das Pfund, -es, -e
practise, üben
praise, loben

prefer (to), vor-ziehen; lieber + *verb*: I **prefer spring,** ich habe den Frühling lieber
prepare (to), berei'ten
present (to), schenken
present, das Geschenk', -s, -e
pretty, hübsch
price, der Preis, -es, -e
probably, wahrschein'lich
problem, das Problem', -s, -e
profession, der Beruf', -s, -e
professor, der Profes'sor, -s, Professo'ren
programme, das Programm', -s, -e
progress, der Fortschritt, -s, -e
promise (to), verspre'chen
proud (of), stolz auf, *w. acc.*
pupil, der Schüler, -s, -
purchase, der Einkauf, -s, ⸚e
purchase (to), kaufen, einkaufen
put (to), stellen

Q

question, die Frage, -n
quickly, schnell, rasch
quiet, ruhig, still
quite, ganz, recht

R

radio, das Radio, -s; **on the radio,** im Radio
rain, der Regen, -s
rain (to), regnen
raincoat, der Regenmantel, -s, ⸚
rather, zeimlich
reach (to), errei'chen
read (to), lesen, er liest, las, hat gelesen
really, eigentlich, wirklich
recently, neulich
receive (to), bekom'men; erhal'ten
recognize (to), erken'nen
record, die Schallplatte, -n
red, rot
relate (to), erzäh'len
remain (to), bleiben, er bleibt, blieb, ist geblieben
remember (to), sich erin'nern an, *w. acc.*
rent (to), mieten
report (to), berich'ten
representative, der Vertre'ter, -s, -
rest (to), ruhen
restaurant, das Restaurant', -s, -s
rich, reich
ride, fahren, er fährt, fuhr, ist gefahren; **to ride past,** vorbei-fahren

right, das Recht; rightly mit Recht; you are right, Sie haben recht
ring up (to), an-rufen
role, die Rolle, -, -n
room, das Zimmer, -s, -
round, rund
row, die Reihe, -n
run (to), laufen, er läuft, lief, ist gelaufen

S

sad, traurig
say (to), sagen
satisfied, zufrie′den
saucer, die Untertasse, -n
scarcely, kaum
school, die Schule, -n
sea, die See, -n
season, die Jahreszeit, -en
seat, der Platz, -es, ⁀e; der Sitz, -es, -e
see (to), sehen, er sieht, sah, hat gesehen
sell (to), verkau′fen
send (to), senden, schicken
several, einige, mehrere
sharp, scharf; 5 o'clock sharp, punkt 5 Uhr
shirt, das Hemd, -es, -en
shoe, der Schuh, -es -e
shop, der Laden, -s, ⁀
shop (to), ein-kaufen, Einkäufe machen
short, kurz
should, sollen, er soll, sollte, hat gesollt
show (to), zeigen
sick, krank
side, die Seite, -n
since, seit, *prep. w. dat.;* seitdem′, *sub. conj.*
sincerely, herzlich
sing (to), singen, er singt, sang, hat gesungen
single (*sole*), einzig
sister, die Schwester, -n
sit (to), sitzen, er sitzt, saß, hat gesessen; to sit down, sich setzen
sleep, schlafen, er schläft, schlief, hat geschlafen
slow, langsam
small, klein
smoke, (to) rauchen
snow (to), schneien
so, so, also
sofa, das Sofa, -s, -s
some, etwas, einige, mehrere
somebody, jemand
something, etwas
son, der Sohn, -es, ⁀e

soon, bald; as soon as, sobald′ *sub. conj.*
sorry: I am sorry, es tut mir leid
soup, die Suppe, -n
speak (to), sprechen, er spricht, sprach, hat gesprochen
spend (to) (*time*), verbrin′gen; (*money*), ausgeben
spite: in spite of, trotz, *prep. w. gen.*
splendid, herrlich, großartig
spoon, der Löffel, -s, -
spring, der Frühling, -s
stand (to), stehen, er steht, stand, hat gestanden; to stand up, auf-stehen
station, die Station′, -en; der Bahnhof, -s, ⁀e
stay (to), bleiben, er bleibt, blieb, ist geblieben
steamship, der Dampfer, -s, -
still, ruhig, still
stop (to), halt-machen; (cease), auf-hören
store, der Laden, -s, ⁀
story, die Geschich′te, -, -n
street, die Straße, -n
student, der Student′, -en -en
study (*workroom*), das Arbeitszimmer, -s, -
suburb, der Vorort, -s, -e
succeed (to), gelin′gen *w. dat.,* es gelingt, gelang, ist gelungen; I succeed, es gelingt mir
such, solcher, -e, -es; such a, solch ein
suddenly, plötzlich
suit (*man's*), der Anzug, -s, ⁀e, (*woman's*), das Kostüm′, -s, -e
suitcase, der Handkoffer, -s, -
sum, die Summe, -n
summer, der Sommer, -s
supper, das Abendessen, -s, -
supposed: to be supposed to, sollen, er soll, sollte, hat gesollt
surely, sicherlich, gewiß
surprise, die Überra′schung, -en

T

take (to), er nimmt, nahm, hat genommen; to take place, statt-finden
talk (to), reden, sprechen
taste (to), *w. obj.,* versu′chen; it tastes good, es schmeckt gut
taxi, das Taxi, -s, -s
tea, der Tee, -s
teacher, der Lehrer, -s, -
teach (to), lehren, unterrich′ten
telephone, das Telephon′, -s, -e

telephone (to), telepho'nisch an-rufen
television, das Fernsehen; (set), der Fernsehapparat
test (to), prüfen
thank, danken, *w. dat.*, thanks, danke!, danke schön; many thanks, vielen Dank!
that, jener, -e, -es; daß, *sub. conj.*; das (pointing out) that is a book, etc., das ist ein Buch, usw.
theatre, das Thea'ter, -s, -; to the theatre, ins Theater
their, ihr, ihre, ihr
then, dann, denn; now and then, dann und wann
there, dort, da
therefore, deshalb, deswegen, daher
thing, die Sache, -n; das Ding, -es, -e
think (to), denken, er denkt, dachte, hat gedacht; to think of, denken an *w. acc.*
thirst, der Durst; I am thirsty, ich habe Durst
through, durch, *prep. w. acc.*
ticket, die Karte, -n (*of admission*), die Eintrittskarte, das Billet'. -s, -e; (*for vehicle*), die Fahrkarte, -n
time, die Zeit, -en; once, twice, three times, etc., einmal, zweimal, dreimal, usw., at the same time, zugleich'
tip, das Trinkgeld, -s, -er
tired, müde
to, zu, *prep. w. dat.*, up to, bis
today, heute
together, zusam'men
too, zu; (*also*), auch
tourist, der Tourist', -en, -en
train, der Zug, -es, ⁀e
travel (to), reisen
travel, der Reisende, -n, -n
trip, die Reise, -n
true, wahr; isn't it true, nicht wahr?
truth, die Wahrheit, -en
try (to), versu'chen
typewriter, die Schreibmaschine, -n

U

uncle, der Onkel, -s, -
under, unter, *prep, w. dat. or acc.*
understand (to), versteh'en, er versteht, verstand, hat verstanden
unfortunately, leider
university, die Universität', -en
until, bis

use (to), gebrau'chen
usual, gewöhn'lich

V

vacation, die Ferien (*plur.*)
vegetable, das Gemü'se, -s, -
very, sehr
village, das Dorf, -es, ⁀er
visit (to), besu'chen

W

wait (to), warten; to wait for, warten auf, *w. acc.*
waiter, der Kellner, -s, -
waiting room, der Wartesaal, -s, -säle
walk, gehen, er geht, ging, ist gegangen; to take a walk, spazie'rengehen, einen Spazier'gang machen
wall, die Wand, ⁀e
want, wollen, er will, wollte, hat gewollt
warm, warm; warmer, wärmer
wash (to), waschen, er wäscht, wusch, hat gewaschen; to wash oneself, sich waschen
watch, die Uhr, -en
water, das Wasser, -s
weather, das Wetter, -s
week, die Woche, -n
well, gut, wohl; well-known, bekannt
wet, naß
what? was? welcher, -e, -es? what kind of? was für ein?
when, whenever, wenn, *sub. conj.;* wann, *interr.*
where? wo? (*at what place?*); wohin? (*to what place?*)
whether, ob, *sub. conj.*
which, welcher, -e, -es
while, während, *sub. conj.*
white, weiß
who? wer?
whole, ganz
why? warum?
win (to), gewin'nen, er gewinnt, gewann, hat gewonnen
window, das Fenster, -s, -
wine, der Wein, -es, -e
winter, der Winter, -s, -
wish (to), wünschen
with, mit, *prep. w. dat.*
without, ohne, *prep. w. acc.*
woman, die Frau, -en
wonderful, wunderbar

word (*in phrases and sentences*), das Wort,
-es, -e; (*not connected in sense*), das
Wort, -es, ⸚er
work, die Arbeit, -en
work (to), arbeiten
world, die Welt
write, schreiben, er schreibt, schrieb, hat
geschrie′ben

Y

year, das Jahr, -es, -e
yesterday, gestern
yet, noch; **not yet**, noch nicht
you, du, ihr, Sie; **your**, dein, deine, dein;
euer, euere, euer; Ihr, Ihre, Ihr
young, jung